UNIX®
NETWORKING

HAYDEN BOOKS UNIX® System Library

Topics in C Programming
Stephen G. Kochan, Patrick H. Wood

UNIX® Shell Programming, Second Edition *(forthcoming)*
Stephen G. Kochan and Patrick H. Wood

UNIX® System Security
Patrick H. Wood and Stephen G. Kochan

UNIX® Text Processing
Dale Dougherty and Tim O'Reilly

Exploring the UNIX® System, Second Edition
Stephen G. Kochan and Patrick H. Wood

UNIX® System Administration
David Fiedler and Bruce H. Hunter

RELATED TITLES

The Waite Group's UNIX® Communications
Bart Anderson, Bryan Costales, Harry Henderson

The Waite Group's UNIX® Primer Plus
Mitchell Waite, Donald Martin, Stephen Prata

The Waite Group's Tricks of the UNIX® Masters
Russell G. Sage

The Waite Group's UNIX® Papers
The Waite Group

The Waite Group's UNIX® System V Bible
Stephen Prata, Donald Martin

The Waite Group's Advanced UNIX®--A Programmer's Guide
Stephen Prata

C Programmer's Guide to NetBIOS
W. David Schwaderer

C Programmer's Guide to Serial Communications
Joe Campbell

PC LAN Primer
The Waite Group

For the retailer nearest you, or to order directly from the publisher, call 800-428-SAMS. In Indiana, Alaska, and Hawaii call 317-298-5699.

UNIX®
NETWORKING

STEPHEN G. KOCHAN AND PATRICK H. WOOD, eds.

Pipeline Associates, Inc.

HAYDEN BOOKS

A Division of Howard W. Sams & Company
11711 North College, Suite 141, Carmel, IN 46032 USA

FIRST EDITION
THIRD PRINTING—1990

International Standard Book Number: 0-672-48440-4
Library of Congress Catalog Card Number: 89-61050

Acquisitions Editor: *Jennifer Ackley*
Development Editor: *C. Herbert Feltner*
Manuscript Editor: *Sara Bernhardt Black*
Production Coordinator: *Marjorie Jo Hopper*
Cover Illustration: *RTS Color Graphics*
Typesetting: *Pipeline Associates, Inc.*

This entire text was processed under UNIX. The text was formatted using `troff`, with the assistance of `tbl` for the tables and MacDraw and `pic` for the figures. The `troff` output was converted to PostScript using `devps`. The camera ready copy was printed on an Apple LaserWriter Plus, with no pasteup required.

Printed in the United States of America

Trademark Acknowledgements

All terms mentioned in this book that are known to be trademarks or service marks are listed below. Howard W. Sams & Company cannot attest to the accuracy of this information. Use of a term in this book should not be regarded as affecting the validity of any trademark or service mark.

AT&T and UNIX are registered trademarks of American Telephone and Telegraph.
BSD is a trademark of University of California, Berkeley.
DEC, Ultrix, and VAX are registered trademarks of Digital Equipment Corp.
Ethernet is a trademark and Xerox is a registered trademark of Xerox Corp.
IBM is a registered trademark and PC-DOS is a trademark of International Business Machines Corp.
devps is a trademark of Pipeline Associates, Inc.
LaserWriter Plus is a trademark of Apple Computer, Inc.
Lan Manager/X, Microsoft, MS-DOS, and XENIX are registered trademarks of Microsoft Corporation.
Network File System (NFS), NeWS, and Sun Microsystems are trademarks of Sun Microsystems.
PostScript is a registered trademark of Adobe Systems, Inc.

Hayden Books
UNIX
Library

The UNIX System Library is an integrated series of books covering basic
to advanced topics related to the UNIX system. The books are written
under the direction of Stephen G. Kochan and Patrick H. Wood, who
worked for several years teaching introductory and advanced UNIX
courses, and who themselves have written many books on the C programming language and the UNIX system.

The first title in the UNIX series is *Exploring the UNIX System*. The
text introduces the new user to the UNIX system, covering things such as
logging on, working with the file system, editing files with the vi editor, writing simple shell programs, and formatting documents. Also included in this text are descriptions of how to use electronic mail and networks and how to administrate a UNIX system.

UNIX Shell Programming uses a clear, step-by-step approach to
teach all the features of the shell and shows the reader how to write programs using many actual examples. Also covered are tools used by
many shell programmers, such as grep, sed, tr, cut, and sort,
and a detailed discussion on how to write regular expressions. The
newer Korn shell is also covered in detail in the book.

UNIX Text Processing gives a comprehensive treatment of the many
tools that are available for formatting documents under UNIX. The book
shows how troff can be used to format simple documents like letters
and also how to exploit its capabilities to format larger documents like
manuals and books. The text shows how to use the popular mm and ms
macro packages and how to write custom macro packages.

UNIX System Administration is an essential guide to administration
for anyone who owns or operates a UNIX system. The text describes
how to set up file systems, make backups, configure a system, connect
peripheral devices, install and administrate UUCP, work with the line
printer spooler, and write shell programs to help make the administration process more manageable.

UNIX System Security is the only text devoted specifically to this
important topic. Security for users, programmers, and administrators is
covered in detail, as is network security. Source code listings for many
useful security-related programs are given at the end of the book.

UNIX Networking contains practical discussions of several important UNIX networking systems including UUCP, TCP/IP, NFS, RFS,
Streams, and LAN Manager/X. Each chapter is written by a noted expert in the field of UNIX networking.

C O N T E N T S

1

INTRODUCTION

Networks play an important role in today's information age. The need to share information and resources makes networks a necessity in almost any computing environment. In many cases, the network can be thought of as a large, distributed computer, with disks and other resources on big systems being shared by smaller workstations on people's desks. The speed and capabilities of some networks today are so great that a general user may use the network constantly without even knowing it. Terminals, modems, and serial lines of yesterday are being replaced by diskless workstations and high-speed network connections.

Because of its simplicity and its availability in source form to the educational and research community, the UNIX system has been a favorite development bed for networks since the mid 1970s. Today, few UNIX systems exist without some network connection. In fact, almost all UNIX systems shipped by vendors today have some form of networking built in.

This book provides both a historical and technical look at UNIX networks. The book is organized with the earliest UNIX networks appearing first, and each chapter has an overview of the history of the development of that networking system. Each chapter is also written by an expert on that particular network.

Since there are many UNIX networks, and space in this book is limited, only the most popular and widely available networks are described. Also, networking hardware (Ethernet, the telephone system, etc.) is only covered where needed to describe the networking software, which is the focus of this book.

Chapter 2 describes UUCP, the first UNIX network. Originally designed to work over serial lines and the telephone system, UUCP has been modified and extended many times since its inception. Today, UUCP works over a variety of low- and high-speed transmission systems. Although primitive by today's standards of networking, UUCP remains the only UNIX network available on practically all versions of UNIX running on almost any hardware platform. Chapter 2 was written by Brian Redman of Bell Communications Research (BELLCORE). He is one of the three main collaborators on the current incarnation of UUCP distributed by AT&T.

Chapter 3 describes TCP/IP, one of the first high-speed network protocols available on UNIX systems. TCP/IP is the underlying transport mechanism for many UNIX and non-UNIX networking systems. In fact, most of the networking software described in this book can run over TCP/IP. This chapter was written by Douglas Comer, Professor of Computer Sciences at Purdue University and author of the book *Internetworking with TCP/IP*[†], and Thomas Narten, also of Purdue.

Chapter 4 describes NFS, the Network File System from Sun Microsystems. NFS allows a user to access files across a network without even being aware that the files are on another system. After developing NFS, Sun put the protocols in the public domain and licensed the source code to third parties, including their own competitors. Since its introduction, NFS has gained widespread support and is now licensed and implemented to run on over 110 different computer platforms. NFS is the most widely used networking system for sharing files between UNIX systems and is used extensively between non-UNIX systems. Chapter 4 also describes RPC, the Remote Procedure Call, and XDR, the External Data Representation. This chapter was written by Louis Delzompo, Product Line Manager, Networking Products, at Sun.

Chapter 5 describes Streams, a flexible, modular facility for network design. Originally developed by Dennis Ritchie at Bell Labs for the research version of UNIX, Streams is now a standard part of the UNIX system from AT&T and is available in System V, Release 3 and later versions. Streams improves the modularity of device drivers and network protocols. Chapter 5 was written by Doug Harris, Head of the Mathematics, Statistics, and Computer Science Department at Marquette University. He teaches several networking classes and is a long-time advocate of Streams.

Chapter 6 describes the Transport Layer Interface (TLI), a programming interface to any network provider that follows the ISO-OSI Reference Model (see definition that follows). This is also a standard part now of System V, Release 3.

Chapter 7 describes RFS, the Remote File Sharing network from AT&T. RFS is similar to NFS in many ways and includes features (such as sharing devices like tape drives directly across the network) that NFS doesn't provide. Although something of a competitor to NFS, both networks will be available in System V, Release 4. Chapters 6 and 7 were also written by Doug Harris.

Chapter 8 describes LAN Manager/X, a network protocol for OS/2, MS-DOS, and UNIX from Microsoft. Announced in 1988, LAN Manager/X is a new network designed with the idea of using OS/2 and UNIX systems as file servers for a mixed computing environment. It was written by Martin Dunsmuir, Director of Xenix Development at Microsoft.

Chapters 9 and 10 describe the X Window System and Sun NeWS, respectively. These systems are graphics programming environments designed to run over networks. Although they are not networking systems per se, they are, perhaps, the largest sources of network activity after remote file access. These chapters describe X and NeWS from a networking perspective. Chapter 9 was written by Adrian Nye of O'Reilly and Associates, author of the books *Xlib*

[†] Full bibliographic information for the books mentioned here is available in the appropriate chapters.

Programming Manual and *Xlib Reference Manual.* Chapter 10 was written by Owen Densmore, Senior Staff Engineer, at Sun Microsystems, who has taught many introductory classes on NeWS at UNIX trade shows and conferences.

Useful Terms

A quick overview of networking terminology is in order.

A *server* is a system or a program on a system that provides some service to other systems across a network. A typical server is a *file server*, which provides remote file access to users somewhere else on the network. A *client* is the system or program that requests and receives some action from a server. On windowing systems, the usual roles of the workstation as client and the host as server are reversed: the "server" is the graphics display (typically the workstation), and the "client" is a program (potentially running anywhere on the network) that makes requests for graphics operations on the server.

A *diskless workstation* is a system that has no disk drive and uses the network for all disk activity, usually including booting the operating system at startup time.

A *stateless* network is one in which each network request is satisfied without reference to any previous request. In other words, the network doesn't maintain any state information from request to request. A *statefull* network is one in which network requests can change the state of the network and affect subsequent requests.

A *protocol* is simply a method agreed upon by both the server and the client for exchange of data. It typically includes some way for the client to send requests or commands to the server and a way for the server to send replies and data back to the client. A protocol may also have an identification mechanism to determine where a request came from and where a reply is destined to and may have an error correction mechanism so that corrupted requests and replies are detected and retransmitted.

The *International Standards Organization (ISO) Open Systems Interconnect (OSI) Reference Model* defines seven layers of communications activities and the interfaces between them (see Fig. 1-1). When applications (the top layer) talk to each other over a network, they do so by calling routines in the presentation layer. Similarly, each of the successive layers communicates with the adjacent layers above and below it. The lowest layer is responsible for communicating with the actual network hardware. Like layers on different systems communicating with each other coordinate their activity indirectly by passing messages through the intervening layers.

A *provider* is anything that provides a specific network service, e.g., a Transport Layer provider gives service to programs at the OSI Transport Layer.

For a solid introduction to networking in general, the standard text is *Computer Networks*, by Andrew Tanenbaum, Prentice-Hall, 1981.

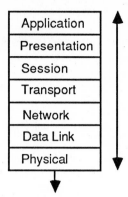

Media (coaxial, twisted-pair, fiber optic, microwave, etc.)

Fig. 1-1. ISO/OSI Reference Model

UUCP UNIX-to-UNIX Copy

Brian Redman
Bell Communications Research

◆ Introduction ◆

UUCP is a `cp` program between UNIX machines; however, it is much more than
a copy program. Its ability to copy files from one machine to another is just one
application for which this general networking program is used. It is a batch-
processing/spooling system. UUCP is a misnomer in that it seems to constrain
the uses. Perhaps UU would be a better name because it more clearly indicates
that UUCP is a system of many programs enabling file transfer, remote execution, maintenance, and administration. All these programs have been tradition-
ally named UU*something* and as such fall under the UUCP umbrella.

A discussion of UUCP holds a prominent place in a UNIX networking text.
The first UNIX network application was designed to run on UNIX systems using
typical UNIX-like command syntax and depending on other UNIX programs for
support and execution. UUCP needs `mail`, `sh`, and `cron` to function. These
dependencies allude to both the strengths and weaknesses of UUCP. Because
`sh` can and is used to implement arbitrarily complicated and convoluted remote
command executions, UUCP is less complicated. But as new semantics may be
added to `sh`, new syntax may stress UUCP's ability to suppress its abuse. Program modules are often assembled to produce synergistic packages. Yet the
package is as likely to break as is its most fragile component.

At this writing, debates about the merits of UUCP continue. UUCP's raison
d'être continues to be questioned by proponents of more "sophisticated" networking systems. Dennis Ritchie said "UNIX is a simple, coherent system that
pushes a few good ideas and models to the limit."[†] He was undoubtedly speaking of the UNIX system that he codesigned and implemented. UUCP fit well

---

† Dennis M. Ritchie, "Reflections on Software Research," *Communications of the ACM*, Vol.
27, No. 8, August 1984, pp. 758–760.

into that system, and although strange and absurd versions have emerged over the years, the most successful and long-lived implementation adheres to the design principles of generality of both function and hardware dependence, modularity of system components, and exploitation of existing and future programs and devices.

UUCP has always been popular because it is cheap. It is efficient in terms of peripheral devices, processing cycles, and administrative expertise. UUCP is a convenient tradeoff of most networking issues; ergo, it is a general networking system. This chapter discusses UUCP for two purposes. Primarily, it is to familiarize you with the first UNIX networking solution. UUCP has been running for a long time. The programs have evolved and new components have been added, but the basic strategies remain the same. The greatest design flaw of UUCP was that it was not designed to accommodate the number of machines and vast amount of data which it would need to handle. This has since been remedied, but details of its realization and the measures taken to deal with the associated problems may serve some educational purposes. In addition, it provides the necessary information to become a UUCP expert. Be warned that being an expert is more than understanding how a system is supposed to work. Expertise is gained by investigating why a system doesn't work. The basic strategies for debugging UUCP are discussed; but you may not appreciate them until you apply them.

Those familiar with UUCP ought to keep in mind the distinction between it and the services it supports. Electronic mail and networked bulletin boards may depend upon UUCP, but they are not a part of UUCP. Whether getting one's mail "dropped on the floor" is a problem with UUCP or the mail system is by no means obvious a priori. These are the principle uses of UUCP, yet with a bit of understanding UUCP can be applied to many more interesting tasks. Due to its low startup cost and generality of function, UUCP allows you to get into the business of networking (not necessarily the networking business) quickly and cheaply.

◆ History/Background ◆

Some time before January 1977, in the Renaissance period of UNIX,[†] Mike Lesk of Bell Laboratories created UUCP. This is deduced from the agenda of the UNIX/MERT Users Meeting held February 24, 1977, printed in the January 1977 issue of the *Mini-System Newsletter*, circulated within Bell Laboratories.

Interestingly enough, item four, "UNIX-to-UNIX Communication," doesn't mention UUCP. It mentions only:

---

† Stuart I. Feldman, "An Architecture History of the UNIX System," in *USENIX Association Summer 1984 Conference Proceedings* (Keynote Address), Salt Lake City, 1984.

- Ken Thompson on MPX driver

- Dale Dejager on UCAT

- Lee McMahon on CU

- PWB Intermachine communication

- Ken Thompson on possible uses of the KMC microprocessor for communication use

But if we read between the lines of item seven, "Automatic Delivery of Software":

- Mike Lesk on scheme for better distribution and local testing

- Discussion

we recognize that scheme as UUCP.

The next issue of the same publication carried the following:

> There is a new command, "uucp" which invokes a system for copying files between UNIX systems. The system was written by Mike Lesk and copies files over 300 baud phone lines between any two UNIX machines with an ACU as host and intermediary. The USG is interested in using this technique to improve code sharing. Anyone with a UNIX and an ACU who is interested should contact Aaron Cohen on MH X6920.

The July 1977 issue announced the availability of the "stockroom" for contributing and obtaining unsupported software. It used UUCP. The work was finally published in February 1978. Lesk's objective was to build a system to automate administration of the growing number of UNIX machines in his center. A prerequisite for such a system was a mechanism to automatically move files among those machines. As nothing existed to suit this purpose, he wrote UUCP. The uucp command spooled the request by creating files in a spool directory. The data to be sent was copied to an f file, and the destination system and file name, the user (a chown was attempted on the destination system), and mode of the file (or'ed with 4096 if it was binary) was copied to an s file. An r file containing similar information was created for requests. uucp then executed tdemon, which processed the spooled files.

tdemon executed files beginning with e while files whose names began with c were conditionally executed. They contained a list of file names followed by a blank line, which was followed by the commands. When all the files referenced were available, the commands were executed. tdemon connected to the remote machine using the various files to indicate the type of connection (hardwired or dialup), the telephone number if applicable, login name, password, and home directory of UUCP's utility programs. The files containing sensitive information such as phone numbers and login names were stored in encrypted form. The programs that accessed these files had the decryption key compiled into them. The key itself was encrypted to prevent easy decoding from the program binary, and the decryption of the key was performed by the program containing the key. The key was then used as an argument to `crypt` to decode the sensitive files. As the care of this information may lead the reader to suspect, this version of UUCP logged into a remote system and got a regular shell. The first thing it did was a `chdir` to the UUCP directory. The `tdemon` program then ran `transmit`. `transmit` is a general utility that takes as arguments a message on the remote machine to be waited for and a response to be typed. Lesk notes in his memo that one user was using `transmit` to call up the ARPANET and copy his mail to UNIX. The programs that copied files also had the ability to convert binary files for transmission through 7-bit interfaces. They computed checksums and retransmission could be requested. However, experience with 300 baud lines is that retransmission is pointless; virtually all checksum errors are program bugs (sometimes in the line drivers).

The next version of UUCP was built by Lesk and Dave Nowitz.[†] This second version was the first to be widely distributed (PWB and V7). It was a total rewrite, but with the same purposes. The most significant change was that UUCP no longer received an interactive shell when it logged in but rather a program (uucico) which was virtually unusable by a human being. `uucico` ran on both ends of the communications line—one being master and the other slave—and exchanged roles until no more work was to be found. Other significant changes were the addition of `uux` and better transmission protocols.

`uux` provided a user interface to the remote command execution. Perhaps the need for a transmission protocol became evident when not all the checksum errors were due to software bugs. Greg Chesson wrote the original and still standard telephone line protocol (g protocol) that packetized, checked, and retransmitted data if necessary. Lesk and Nowitz were farsighted enough to provide for mulitple protocols. Clearly, the overhead of the highly reliable g protocol was not necessary on a hard-wired connection between two machines colocated. These two types of interconnection were all that existed at the time. But selection of arbitrary protocols has been useful in later versions that use all types of connections. Outwardly, the later versions of UUCP look very much like the second version. That version was the standard from 1978 until 1983 before users understood it well enough to rewrite it. Work on UUCP up until then was directed toward bug fixes. UUCP was not so poorly designed or so inadequately coded that it required five years and dozens of people to debug it. The dilemma was that UUCP usage was out of control. No organized effort could generate a version that wasn't already outdated.

It wasn't until UUCP was stressed beyond patching that redesign was expedient. Sending mail to users on other systems was the most significant event for the UNIX community to date. UUCP is probably responsible for UNIX's dramatic growth. UNIX became so popular because it was so easy to understand and, therefore, to change and add things to. This includes the

---

† D. A. Nowitz, "UUCP Implementation Description," in *UNIX Programmers Manual, Seventh Edition*, Vol. 2B, October 1978.

commands and applications as well as the kernel. Source code was readily available and cheerfully distributed. With the advent of UUCP came more timely distribution, fast and frequent (and often furious) communication between users. More software was employed in more places creating more demand for UNIX. More UNIX systems created more software, which created more demand, and the cycle continued. A UUCP designed when 1200-baud asynchronous modems were the state of the art just couldn't hold up to the growth of the UNIX network, divergent UNIX versions, and the compulsion to send more bits (disseminate information) farther and faster. The big problems were security, performance, and device dependence. The Mcgeady bug list was the best source of UUCP information. In an ongoing effort, he compiled all the UUCP bug reports he could find into a lengthy document. Here's a sample entry:

```
12) Sequence number generation is inefficient, slow, ineffective

    References: gename.c
    Solution: install Alan Watt's gename() mods - use base 36 or 64
    Reported-by: ittvax!swatt (7/82)
    Applicability: V7, BSD, S3
```

There are 39 entries followed by discussions of various versions and detailed communications concerning those 39 entries. All in all there are 39 pages of information from more than 22 people compiled between 11/81 and 11/82 alone. This wasn't the final word, but it offered significant enlightenment. By this time, six versions (amazingly enough all compatible) were known to readers of the bug list, and untold versions were available elsewhere. Now an organized effort could fold all these fixes and enhancements into one UUCP.

UUCP was so vital to so many people that it had to be dealt with. Significant projects depended on electronic mail and bulletin boards. System administrators had to keep up with debugging, enhancing, and administrating UUCP or else lose data and block communication paths. For the people that cared, the task had become much too time consuming. The growth in usage continued to outpace development. As is often the case for those who administrate computing systems, particularly the most experimental systems, it wasn't their job. Perhaps their job was hardware design, but if they needed UNIX to be more effective in that task, they became software experts. Or perhaps their job was to write a thesis but they ran a UNIX system because it was more enticing. In any event, the users and not the suppliers (as has often been the case with UNIX) got into the business of support and development.

In April 1983, Martin Levy of Bell Labs sent mail around to some of his fellow employees who had a known interest in UUCP. His message was essentially a plea to come up with a UUCP version that everyone would use and that would eliminate the current multiplication of effort. If a single version was run by all, then presumably less work would be needed to administrate UUCP. Clearly, a significant part of UUCP administration is consulting with others, figuring out why their UUCP doesn't work. You have to do that to prove the fault doesn't lie with your version. So, in mid-April 1983, a dozen or so UUCP heavies from Bell Labs gathered face to face. The most constructive thing to come directly from the meeting was a consensus on which version of UUCP would be best as a staring point. From Peter Honeyman's notes:

> A lively discussion on uucp hacking consumed the major part of the meeting. There are as many versions of uucp as there are sites, with the major contenders being USG 6.0, the new code by Morris, and Tom Truscott's hacks. Cohen grimly cautioned on the difficulty of getting good stuff into 6.0, nonetheless, the company flag was raised, all saluted, and we agreed to use the organizational heavy as a starting point for producing a version that would satisfy all (and ourselves, in particular).

What came indirectly from the meeting was some motivation to do work. Honeyman (login: *honey*), Nowitz (*dan*), and Redman (*ber*) immediately began coding a version of UUCP that is now known as *Honey DanBer*. Steve Bellovin is credited with significant contributions of code that enabled Honey DanBer to run on Berkeley UNIX versions using TCP/IP. The result was a single version that was known to run on AT&T-distributed, Berkeley, and Research versions of UNIX. This satisfied everyone's needs if not their egos. Honey DanBer became AT&T's standard (aliased Basic Networking Utility) and was accepted by the research organization that invented UUCP (as well as UNIX). Although Berkeley distributes a different version the following text from the source README file:

```
@... HoneyDanBer [sic] uucp (aka BNU 1) which is as
close to a standard uucp as there is...
```

makes the point. Regardless of which version you run, the underlying principles (and many of the details) are probably the same as those of the Lesk/Nowitz version. Certainly this is the case of Honey DanBer and the Berkeley version. The following discussions will apply to Honey DanBer unless otherwise noted.

♦ General Description and Overview ♦

Is UUCP a networking utility? What's a network? If we think of a network as a set of machines among which we can transfer files and on which we can execute commands remotely, then UUCP *may* be used to implement a network. A network suggests some sort of cooperation among all the machines of which it's composed. However, because UUCP doesn't impose any administrative controls on the sites that run it, a UUCP network tends to be anarchic. That is to say, although a set of machines may all employ UUCP, there is no assurance that any two machines can communicate with each other. And even if they do, the levels of remote execution (which set of commands) and the ability to transfer files (from which and to which directories) may vary greatly. Being a member of the

UUCP network doesn't necessarily mean that you can communicate with all other members of the network. That's because it is not really a network. The communication mechanism (device, login, etc.) for each machine that may be accessed must be listed in the local machine's database. UUCP is a set of programs that two sites may use to give them the mechanism if not the ability to transfer files and remotely execute commands. The ability is somewhat independent of the mechanism and is realized through mutual agreement. That agreement establishes a communications link. The details of what may transpire over that link are individually established by each site. Two machines can have a relationship whereby one may receive files from another and remotely execute commands while the other may send files only and may not execute any commands remotely. One UUCP site might accept connections from any other that chooses to connect to it while another might only accept connections from a site that is known to it. Most administrators on a well-known UUCP site that permits unknown machines to connect to it have been frustrated by receiving electronic mail directly from a machine that knows how to communicate with them but for which they have no way to respond because they don't know how to access that site.

The radically different policies imposed on individual sites make any presumptions about members of the network highly speculative. About the only thing you can count on regarding a UUCP neighbor is that you'll be able to send files to a public spooling area and that you'll be able to execute the `rmail` command remotely, enabling you to send mail to users on that neighbor. Even these seemingly standard interactions may not be permitted. A UUCP relationship is one between the UUCP administrators of two machines. By default, UUCP is a one-to-one network. When the many system administrators agree concerning access permissions on all the machines concerned, then UUCP represents more of a general network.

`uucp` is a command, but UUCP is a package. There are several commands that put UUCP into action. The basic ones are `uucp`, which requests that a file be sent from one machine to another where either of the machines may be the local site or a remote host. `uux` requests that a command be executed on (usually) a remote machine. Commands may be a single program or a series of programs where each program (and their file arguments) may be prefixed with the machine name on which it is to execute. These commands are not interactive, that is, when the `uux` command completes, the requested action has not necessarily been performed. They spool requests for the UUCP system, which may be acted on immediately or at some unspecified time in the future. This may depend on administrative policy concerning system load, economics concerning the time of connection to another system, or availability of connection resources. The main types of UUCP interconnections are direct dedicated lines, data PBX lines, the Internet, and dial-up telephone lines. A remote site may be accessed by any or all of these connections, or there may be no way to initiate connection at all. The spooled request will not be activated until the remote site establishes a connection. In this case, the local machine is a "passive" site.

When the user issues a UUCP command, files are created in a spool directory (usually `/usr/spool/uucp`) which specifies control and contains data. In the case where a `uucp` command option has specified (or defaulted to) not copying the file to the spool directory, no data file is created. The control file indicates the actual path name of the file to be copied. There is a subdirectory in the spool directory for each remote machine. In older versions, all files were created in the spool directory itself, but the number of files often became so great on heavily used machines that the time required to search the directory for these files exceeded reasonable limits, and UUCP gave up only to make another attempt later and fail repeatedly. The Berkeley version uses Tom Truscott's implementation to store control files in subdirectories. Although this only decreases the number of files in a directory by a small factor unrelated to the number of machines a site communicates with, the problem isn't as bad on Berkeley systems because files are not stored as linear lists in directories. Directory clusters have improved the file access performance considerably.

The UUCP command invokes `uucico` (UNIX-to-UNIX copy in copy out—pronounced by sounding each of the letters) to perform the actual transfer. In the case where `uucico` fails for one of the reasons mentioned (wrong time, no resources, etc.), an attempt will be made later when `cron` invokes `uucico` periodically. `uucico` determines the connection mechanism from the `Systems` file (`L.sys` in some versions, in any event usually located in `/usr/lib/uucp`). Then an appropriate device is selected from the `Devices` file (`L-devices`). It opens the device and uses the information from the `Systems` file to connect to the remote site. In the case of dial-up access, it opens an ACU and dials the number. For a data PBX, it opens a line and supplies the PBX with the remote system name or address. For an Internet connection, it uses TCP/IP to get to the remote site. When a dedicated direct line is used, it is opened, and the the remote site is there. The various `open()` routines are likely to set parameters such as speed, modes such as raw, etc. They may also be specific interactions with the device such as sending a newline to a data PBX to get its attention. These device-specific interactions are indicated in the `Dialers` file. When a connection is established to the remote machine, it and the local machine usually enter into a conversation that results in the remote machine executing `uucico` also. This conversation is typically a login sequence. It's specified in the `Systems` file as a list of *expect/send* tokens, such as

```
login: uucp Password: sipglip
```

where `uucico` will wait for (expect) the remote to send the string `login:` and when it gets it will send `uucp`; then when the remote sends `Password:`, `uucico` sends `sipglip`.

In the case of a login, the shell invoked for UUCP is not an interactive command shell, but `uucico`. Note that when the conversation tokens are sent by the local system, they are implicitly terminated by a carriage return. Special characters can defeat this as well as indicate delays, etc. They are listed in Table 2-1 (see p. 48).

Once the two machines are communicating each with `uucico`, the work begins. `uucico` operates in either master or slave mode depending on the arguments issued when it was invoked. Typically, when a `uucp` or `uux` command initiates `uucico` or when it is invoked from `cron`, the `-r1` flag is used to indicate that it should initially assume the master role. Likewise, when `uucico` is invoked from a `uucp` login sequence, no flag is given, causing it to start out in the slave role. The details of the interaction are chronicaled in the sample session later in this chapter. Briefly, the master connects to the remote machine specified by the argument `-s<machine>`. When the connection is established, the login sequence is performed resulting in the invocation of `uucico` on the remote machine. That `uucico` (the slave) sends an identification message containing that machine's name. The master acknowledges that it has reached the correct machine. It then sends its name, a sequence number, which the remote site may use to verify its identity, and a debugging flag, which may have been an argument to `uucico`. The remote system appends debugging diagnostics to a file named `.Admin/audit` in its UUCP spool directory. The slave then sends a list of available protocols from which the master selects one. The master then tells the slave which protocol will be used, and a main loop is entered. The master scans the spool directory for control files that pertain to the remote machine. If a file is to be sent, the master indicates the destination to the remote. The remote machine checks that this is permissible by looking at its `Permissions` file, which specifies what directories each machine may place files in. Access permissions are determined either by login or machine name, depending on the nature of the machine's connection (caller or callee). The remote indicates whether the transfer is acceptable, and the master either sends the file or doesn't, depending on the indication. When all the control files have been acted upon, the master has no more work to do and indicates this to the slave by issuing a hangup message. At this point, the slave may affirm the hangup and complete the conversation or abort the hangup if the slave has found work on the remote system relevant to the local system. If the hangup is denied both `uucicos` reverse roles, and the local invocation becomes the slave and the remote the master. Then the transfer loop is entered once again in the new master/slave relationship. This flip-flopping of roles will continue until no more relevant work on either machine is found. (It's possible that after the master has handed control over that more work arrives, so the role reversals may continue indeterminately.)

Now it is time to introduce `uuxqt` (named after uuexecute, but pronounced by sounding each letter). `uucp` and `uux` create both control and possibly data files for a remote machine. However, when the data files generated by `uux` are sent to the remote machine, they become execution files upon arrival (prefixed with `X`). Each time `uucico` completes its conversation with another machine, it invokes `uuxqt`, which deals with the execution files. `uuxqt` may be unable to complete its task for a number of reasons. All the files required may not be present at the time. Or it may be configured so as not to execute under certain conditions such as system load, or only a limited number of `uuxqts` may be permitted to run simultaneously (to prevent a system from being bogged down by too many remote executions). Therefore, `uuxqt` may be invoked periodically from `cron`. `uuxqt` looks through the execution files for work. The execution file indicates the command to be run and any requisite files, which may have also been transmitted from a remote machine. It also indicates how to report the status of the execution back to the invoker. There are many options for the reporting of status allowing for notification if the command succeeds or fails and also providing for the return of the command's standard input (so one can maybe see why it failed).

The backbone programs of UUCP have been introduced. They are the user commands `uucp` and `uux` and the underlying programs `uucico` and `uuxqt`. There are several other commands associated with UUCP for users and administrators. They are discussed in the following sections along with more details concerning these four programs. But these four are the key. They comprise the minimum set for a functioning UUCP system.

♦ Hardware Requirements ♦

The hardware requirements for a UUCP installation are minimal. This is one of the most important features of UUCP (along with kernel independence) and clearly that which gained it such widespread use. Actually, there are no hardware requirements for UUCP other than what hardware might be used for normal user access (such as tty ports and possibly modems). A passive site may get along without any means to reach out to another UUCP system, depending instead on other systems to initiate contact. A machine is a full-fledged site if it can initiate access. This is most simply accomplished by dedicated wires connecting two machines back to back. A different connection is usually installed for each direction (i.e., one for logging into another machine and one for it to login on). There are programs that allow UUCP to use a port to reach out while allowing the same port to be used for logging in (hard-wired or modem). These will not be discussed, suffice it to say they generally have a special `getty` that steps aside when UUCP needs to dial out to another machine. As mentioned, UUCP can make use of almost any hardware that will support a full-duplex communication path. This includes twisted pair, dial-up modems, Automatic Calling Units (ACUs)/Modem combinations, Ethernet boards, and Data PBXs.

The `Systems`, `Devices`, and `Dialers` files have been mentioned. Let's examine them more closely. First of all, access to a remote system may be possible via a number of different devices and perhaps a number of different paths using the same device (e.g., multiple telephone numbers). The mechanisms used may depend on a number of factors. Time of day may determine the best rates for telephone or data carrier services. The time may also indicate when not to use a certain method. For example, if the remote system is accessed through the same modems that users dial up, then the remote administrators may ask that they not be called during peak human usage hours so as not to tie up the modems. All of these sorts of constraints are indicated in the `Systems` file. Here is a sample:

```
compunerd Any TCP,e Any compunerd
compunerd SaSu,Wk1700-0900 Develcon 9600 compuner in: uucp
compunerd Any ACU 1200 boston5558827 in: uucp
compunerd SaSu,Wk2300-1800 ACU 1200 boston6666373 in: uucp
```

The first field is the remote system's name. The second is the time to call for this device, the third is the type of device, the fourth indicates the speed, the fifth field is the "telephone number," and the following fields are the login sequence. The time to call is of the general form

<day[s]><hour range>,...[; <retry time>]

The days of the week may be abbreviated to the first two characters. Capitalization of the first letter is always required. There are two special tokens that can be used in place of the day of the week. They are `Wk` meaning `MoTuWeThFr`, and `Any` meaning `SaSuWk`. The time range is in 24-hour format indicating a start time and an end time separated by a hyphen (-). If no time is indicated then `0000-2359` is assumed. There may be several day/time entries each separated by a comma (,). Time ranges may wrap around (e.g., `1700-0800`). Finally a semicolon (;) introduces a subfield that is the minimum time (in minutes) to wait before retrying after a failed communications attempt.

The local system administrator defines the device type (third field). It is a class name used to locate entries in the `Devices` file. There each member of the generic group is listed. For example, we have just seen an entry for the classes `Develcon`, `TCP`, and `ACU`. Assuming there are three tty lines connected to a Develcon data switch and two lines connected to autodial modems, the devices entries might appear as:

```
Develcon tty10 - Any develcon \D
Develcon tty11 - Any develcon \D
Develcon tty12 - Any develcon \D
ACU tty14 - 1200 penril \D
ACU tty13 - 1200 vadic \D
TCP TCP 64 uucp TCP \D
```

The first field is the class name, the second indicates the actual device (in `/dev`) used to access that class, and the third field is an arbitrary string sent to the device function. The `64` in the `TCP` entry is used internally by the `tcpcall()` function, specifying the server number to connect to. (64 is the default for some systems while 540 is used for most Berkeley systems.) The fourth field is also used by the internal function and usually specifies the speed for the line. TCP device indicates the server name, for DN/TTY combinations and specifies the DN device (e.g., `cua0`). The fifth field is a string that maps into the dialers file. That's where any class-specific interactions are specified. The remaining fields are sent to the device and include the "phone number," either exactly as it appears in the fifth field of the `Systems` file using `\D` or translated via the

`Dialcodes` file using `\T`. Note that a hyphen is entered in unused fields. `Dialcodes` is used to expand or translate alphabetic strings that prefix the phone number. For instance:

```
boston 91617
```

will cause the replacement of `boston` in the foregoing phone numbers with `91617`. The administrator should indicate any special dialing sequences (e.g., `9`) in the `Dialcodes` file to get an outside line on a PBX or other codes that may be used to dial certain locations most economically. The `Dialers` entries relevant to our sample are:

```
penril =W-P    ""  \d > s\p9\c )-W\p\r\ds\p9\c-) y\c : \E\TP > 9\c OK
vadic  =K-K    ""  \005\p *-\005\p-*\005\p-* D\p BER? \E\T\e \r\c LINE
develcon ""    ""  \r\c est:\007 \E\D\e \007
```

The first field is the key used to map this line to the entry in the `Devices` file, and the second field is a string of translations to map generic special characters to their specific representations for the device. Due to the historic precedence of the DEC 801 calling unit popular before the advent of autodial modems, the equal sign (=) and the hyphen (-) are commonly embedded in phone numbers to indicate "wait for dial-tone" and "pause," respectively. The penril uses `W` and `P` for these functions, and the dialers entry indicates that to UUCP. The remaining fields are a chat script similar to the login sequence of the `Systems` file (i.e., *expect/send* but the leadoff order is different). Here it starts with *send*. In the `Systems` file, it begins with *expect*. The special characters listed in Table 2-1 for the `Systems` file are valid here too. `\D` and `\T` are as described in the `Devices` file, the "telephone number" either translated using the `Dialcodes` file or not. The others in this example should be evident as the penril sequence is described. Just like the `Systems` file login script, each *send* token is implicitly terminated with a carriage return unless a `\c` is appended. Note that a hyphen in the *expect* sequence means if that which is expected is not received, then the string after the hyphen is sent and the string following the next hyphen is expected. This applies to the `Systems` file login sequence as well. Not all legal characters listed in Table 2-1 are meaningful for both the `Systems` and `Dialers`, but the implementations for both share the same code. The penril example is somewhat complicated but demonstrates the capabilities of the `Dialers` file.

Nothing is expected (`""`) then a delay (~2 seconds) is issued followed by (an implicit) carriage return. A > prompt is then expected. Then an s followed by a pause (~.25–0.5 seconds) followed by a 9 and no carriage return is sent. A) is expected. (The number register 9 is being set. The penril is expected to reply with "`Sure? (Y/N)`".) If the) is not received within the timeout period (site configurable often ~45 seconds), then a W followed by a pause, a carriage return, followed by a delay, an s, followed by a pause, and a 9 (not followed by a carriage return) is sent. Again, a) is expected. Having received the expected) from either the first s9 or the second, a y and no carriage return is sent. A : is expected. (The penril says "No.:"). Then the translated phone number followed by a P and a carriage return is sent. The \E turns on echo checking ensuring that each character sent is echoed before the next character is sent. This is necessary for slow devices that may have their input queues overrun. Next an > is expected after which a 9 sans carriage return is sent. (This dials the contents of number register 9). Finally the string "OK" is expected indicating that the number was dialed and the remote machine answered.

Going back to the sample Systems entry using the ACU, after the number is dialed and the remote (compunerd) answers, the in: (from login:) is expected. Then uucp is sent. That completes the login sequence from the Systems file, and uucico begins its conversation with the remote uucico. Presumably, this system does not require a password for the uucp login. That's okay since uucico is the login shell and difficult (but not impossible) to compromise.

Getting back to the main point of this section, that UUCP is very flexible regarding devices, the sample Systems entry shows that the system compunerd can be accessed four different ways. The order of preference is indicated by the ordering of the entries. Thus, the most desirable way to connect to compunerd is through the Internet as indicated by TCP in the device field. Note that a subfield (in this case e) is optional to indicate the preferred protocol. Protocols are discussed in another section. If the Internet path fails, then the next entry suggests the use of a Develcon data switch. This is the next highest speed connection available in the example (9600 baud). However, the time field only permits use of that connection on weekends or weekdays after 5 p.m. or before 9 a.m. Presumably, compunerd's data switch connections are dear during normal business hours. The next entry is for a dial-up, and there is no time restriction. That's likely to be a telephone number reaching a modem or group of modems dedicated to UUCP's use. But if that number is busy, the last entry provides us with another number that can be used. But only on weekends and weekdays between 11 p.m. and 6 p.m. The data switch users probably dial into that number from home, and the administrators want to keep it free.

The nested file lookup may be confusing at first. This section ends with an overview of connecting to the example system using a sample ACU entry.

The Systems file is first looked at to determine an appropriate entry for the desired remote machine. The ACU entry is chosen because the Internet is down and it is noon on a Monday. The Devices file is gleaned for the ACU entry. That entry indicates that the first choice is the Penril autodialer connected to /dev/tty14. The Dialers file instructs the program how to communicate with the penril to get it to dial the number specified in the Systems file which is first translated using the Dialcodes file to change the string boston to 91617 reflecting the need to first dial 9 to get an outside line, then 1 for the default long distance carrier, and 617 to reach the Boston area.

Since other programs such as cu or tip may make use of the same sorts of information as UUCP, the UUCP internal calling function can be compiled STANDALONE and included as library routines for other commands. This then gives those other commands the same benefits UUCP derives from the files described. It also permits these files to act as a single repository for device and system access information available to applications other than UUCP.

◆   Protocols, Layers, Error Detection, and Recovery   ◆

Two layers of communication protocols are involved in a UUCP connection. The high-level layer is the UUCP protocol that exchanges system identification, sends a sequence number and a debugging flag, negotiates the low-level protocol, sets up file transfers, coordinates master/slave role reversals, and does the disconnect sequence. Before the low-level protocol is agreed upon and after the hangup sequence is initiated, the UUCP protocol uses a simple technique for error detection. Each message is prefixed with a sync character (^P) and appended with a null (^@) or newline (^J). Error detection simply means the absence of the synch character. There is no recovery at this point. Once the low-level protocol has been established, the UUCP protocol uses it for error detection and recovery.

   Selection of a low-level protocol is one of UUCPs shining features. Because it can use many different media for communication, it is important that it use an appropriate protocol for the chosen medium. Greg Chesson, then of Bell Laboratories, wrote the first protocol used by UUCP, the Packet Driver (PK) or g protocol.[†] In this protocol the data is represented by sequence-numbered packets. The transmitter may send packets within a certain defined window of sequence numbers. As the receiver acknowledges the packets after verifying the checksum, the window is moved forward through the data. Negative or missing acknowledgments cause retransmission. The g protocol is quite effective for data transmission over telephone lines at speeds up to 9600 baud. The g protocol or something compatible exists in every UUCP implementation. Other common protocols include the error-free or e protocol. This simply sends a byte count and the data. This protocol is used over paths that incorporate their own error detection and recovery techniques, such as the Internet. There are also protocols for Datakit (d), X.25 (x), and Telnet (f) as well as at least one other for TCP (t). There are probably many other sites whose protocols have been designed for their particular needs. The only practical limit on the number of possible protocols available to a given UUCP installation is an arbitrary number (probably 20) used to dimension an array of protocols.

   Two inputs select a protocol. The first is a recommendation stated in the Systems file as a comma-separated subfield of the device field. Note the entry TCP,e in the sample Systems entries for the machine named compunerd. The e states that that protocol should be used if possible. That will be possible if the remote machine (compunerd in this example) has the e protocol compiled into its version of UUCP. This is determined when uucico starts up. After the calling machine sends its name, the remote site responds with a list of available

---

† G. L. Chesson, "Packet Driver Protocol," in Distributed with UNIX Eighth Edition Documents.

protocols (e.g., `getf`). The local machine then selects from that list on the basis of availability and preference. If no preference is indicated by the `Systems` entry, then the first available protocol is used.

These protocols are compiled into UUCP in much the same way that devices are compiled into the UNIX kernel. There is a table like `cdevsw[]` that lists the protocol name (one character, e.g., `g`), and the entry points (function names) for turn on, read message, write message, read data, write data, and turn off routines. Installing a new protocol involves adding an entry to that table, supplying the indicated functions, and relinking UUCP.

◆ Implementation Specifics (UNIX and non-UNIX) ◆

UUCP, as the name implies, is a UNIX utility; however, it has been adapted to other operating systems. The version currently distributed by Berkeley can be conditionally compiled for VMS/EUNICE. Other people (notably Lauren Weinstein) have developed UUCP-compatible programs from scratch to run on PCs under DOS. The implementation specifics of Honey DanBer ("as close to a standard uucp as there is") are discussed here. Many of these parameters must be considered when installing or debugging UUCP or when writing programs that work with UUCP.

Details of the UUCP system are very difficult to pin down because so many of the parameters are set at installation or even at run time. The most commonly changed items appear as manifest constants in the file `parms.h` (`uucp.h` in the Berkeley version). They are:

The Version of UNIX in Use (AT&T System n, 4.n BSD, nth Edition (Vn), etc.)

There are many subtle (as well as dramatic) differences between the various versions of UNIX. UUCP needs to know what environment it's running on to do the right things. Some of the major incompatibilities that deal with location and naming of system include files and the existence of standard C library routines. Also, the syntax and sometimes the semantics of the C library routines and system calls are different among the three major UNIX version groups if the functions exist in all versions. Although you can determine the OS version during run time and use conditionals to select the correct logic, this isn't efficient in terms of coding, debugging, or processing.

The Uid and Gid for UUCP

Although the UUCP programs are generally owned by the `uucp` login with the setuid bit on, there may be some quirks when setuid programs are invoked by other setuid programs or by the root. The conservative measure is to do a `setuid`(*UUCP_UID*) just in case the effective uid isn't honored under some circumstances.

High-Resolution Sleep

Another feature very much dependent on the UNIX version is the high-resolution timer. Several implementations allow programmers to put together a `sleep()` for a fraction of a second. These include special device drivers, the `nap()` system call, busy loops, or even writing to a tty line at a given baud rate.

Disk Utilization

One of the biggest problems with older versions of UUCP was their behavior when confronted with "out of space" or "out of inode" conditions when attempting to copy a file. The `write()` system calls were rarely checked, thus files that seemed to be copied were, in fact, dropped on the proverbial floor. Current versions not only check the return values from system calls but also determine if there is room on the file system before attempting a copy. Checking first saves time and resources and permits a reasonable diagnostic to be issued, such as "No space available on remote" rather than a somewhat cryptic "Write failed." It is no longer practical, as in the "good old days" when it was standard practice when exchanging UUCP login information for two systems to communicate, to also create reciprocal guest logins for the UUCP administrators so they could access a remote system to see what "Write failed" might have meant. The number of systems and the growth from a small circle of associated administrators makes it necessary to provide meaningful diagnostics.

The most efficient way to check the file system is with a system call if it exists. Otherwise, the UUCP installer can specify a program that behaves like the `ustat()` system call, which takes a major/minor device as arguments and returns the free block and free inode count. Such a program can be written with the shell using `df`.

Semipublic or Restricted `Systems` File

For debugging purposes, the exchanges between two systems may be reported to a user who requests such information. The exchanges (especially in the early conversation during login) may contain sensitive information that is usually not public. Even the telephone number of a system may be considered private, let alone the `uucp` login and password. In fact, the telephone number is probably the most sensitive piece of information stored about a system. One way to ensure privacy is not to output such data even when debugging is turned on, but this is not a good solution for the debugger. Only permitting the root uid to get debugging information may also hide problems that are encountered only by nonroot users. Therefore, a range of group IDs may be defined where users whose group IDs fall within the range may receive full debugging information.

Dynamic Determination of Site Name

Each UNIX version has a unique method to identify itself. The `uname()` and `gethostname()` system calls and `cat /etc/whoami` are all in use. It's amazing how many UNIX sites are named `unix` or `erewhon` or `kilroy`.

Wait Time Before Reattempting to Connect

Honey DanBer uses an exponential back-off algorithm to determine the minimum period between attempts to access a remote site. Each time a try is made, the period doubles until it reaches a maximum (also a manifest constant). This was implemented to minimize tying up exclusive-use devices in attempts to access a system that was down. The longer a system is inaccessible, the more likely it is to continue to be inaccessible.

Environmental `PATH` for Remotely Executed Commands

Setting the `PATH` variable for commands is a simple and effective way to limit remote capabilities when coupled with a mechanism that also limits direct path name specification. The `Permissions` file supports a flexible method for determining remote access privileges to individual or classes of sites. It supplants the original `USERFILE` concept which was also used to restrict file access on the basis of directories and login names. The `Permissions` file allows the use of host names as well and is less cryptic. Another manifest is the set of commands which a remote host may execute by default. Most sites permit `rmail`, which is a restricted mail command used specifically for receiving remote mail.

Unknown Systems to Communicate with This Host

Implemented as a measure to eliminate mail with unreachable return addresses, the definition of `NOSTRANGERS` causes UUCP to reject any access from sites that are not listed in the `Systems` file. The message "You are unknown to me." is sent back to the remote during the initial dialog after the login sequence.

Number of `uuxqt` and `uusched` Processes That Run Simultaneously

Two files may exist to limit dynamically the number of these processes in execution (e.g., during peak hours). `uusched` is used to execute `uucico` for systems for which there is work. It randomly selects the order in which the `uucico` for each system is invoked.

Home for Lock Files and Format

Lock files are used to prevent multiple access to the same remote site and to implement exclusive use of some devices. Device locks are used by other programs (cu, tip), and the files ought to be in a more public location than /usr/spool/uucp. The name of that directory is specified at installation time. Because other programs may use the information written in the lock files (the pid of the locking process), its format is also parameterized.

◆ User Interface (Commands, Calls, and Files) ◆

uucp

Options:

- -C makes a copy of the file to be sent in the spool directory. The default uses the actual file specified.

- -f does not create directories. The default is to create any necessary directories. For example, the command

      uucp *file* remote!~/dir/file

  will, by default, create the directory ~/dir if it doesn't exist. The -f option suppresses that creation. (~ is expanded on the remote system to UUCP's public spool directory, usually /usr/spool/uucppublic, where by default any system can write files.)

- -g<*grade*> is a character that assigns a relative priority to the transfer. The smaller the ASCII value, the greater the priority.

- -j causes a job identifier to be printed on the the standard output. This identifier may be used to inquire into the status of or to delete a request.

- -m causes mail to sent to the user when the request has been completed.

- -n<*user*> causes notification to *user* on the remote system when the request has been completed.

- -r prevents UUCP from invoking uucico after the request has been spooled.

- -s<*file*> writes a report after the request is attempted.

- -x<*N*> sets debugging to level *N*. If *N* is not supplied, then the debugging level is set to 1, minimum debugging output. *N* may be in the range 0–9.

uux

Options:

- `-` uses `uux`'s standard input as the standard input for the command string.
- `-a<name>` uses *name* instead of the actual invoker of `uux` for notification. This is useful when `uux` is invoked by a setuid program, and the true user name should be preserved (e.g., `mail`).
- `-b` exits with a nonzero status and sends the command's input to the user along with any notification.
- `-C` copies any files to the spool directory rather than the default which is to use the actual files.
- `-g<grade>` sets the transfer priority to the single-character grade. A smaller ASCII character sets a greater priority.
- `-j` outputs the request identifier. The identifier may be used to query the status of or remove requests from the queue.
- `-n` does not notify the user if the command fails.
- `-r` prevents `uux` from invoking `uucico` after the request is spooled.
- `-s<file>` writes the status of the transfer attempt into *file*.
- `-x<N>` sets the debugging output level to *N*. If *N* is not supplied, sets the level to 1, the minimum. *N* may be in the range 0–9.
- `-z` notifies the user if the requested command succeeds.

uucico

`uucico` is not usually executed directly except for debugging. It is the main functional component of UUCP invoked by UUCP programs that spool requests for it to complete and `uusched`. The sample session in a later section details the operations of `uucico`.

Options:

- `-d<dir>` uses *dir* as the spool directory rather than the default, which is most likely set to be `/usr/spool/uucp`.

- −r[*role*] causes uucico to start up as master (*role*=1) or slave (*role*=0). If started as master, a remote system must be specified with −s. If started as slave, uucico expects to be connected to a master over standard input and output.

- −s<*system*> is the name of the remote system that uucico should connect to as master. It has no effect if uucico is running as slave.

- −x<*N*> indicates that the −x*N* convention is being used to determine the existence and extent of debugging diagnostics at run time. The higher the number *N*, the more verbose.

uuxqt

uuxqt is also executed by other commands (uux or uucico after it disconnects from the remote) except for debugging. It examines the spool directories searching for execute files and performing the executions as indicated (see the following description of execute files). It depends on the Permissions file and certain defaults as already mentioned to determine what commands may be executed by a remote system.

Options

- −s<*system*> looks only for files to be executed on behalf of the system specified.

- −x<*N*> as usual, provides diagnostic output for debugging.

uulog

UUCP maintains log files that detail each attempt to communicate and subsequent events that transpire as well as information related to locally or remotely executed commands. These log files reside under the UUCP spool directory in the .Log subdirectory. Under there is a directory for each of uux, uucp, uucico, and uuxqt. In these directories, there is a file for each remote system referenced. With no arguments, uulog will output the concatenation of all the uucico log files. The −x option directs uulog to output uuxqt log files instead. The −s option is used to specify a particular system. A number of −s options can be issued. The −f option causes uulog to perform as tail −f on the system log file specified by the single −s<*system*> given.

uuname

uuname outputs all the sites listed in the `Systems` file. This file is normally not readable by users, but `uuname` is setuid to the UUCP administrative login. The `-l` option causes `uuname` to output only the local system name.

uustat

`uustat` is a general utility to monitor UUCP queues, connections, and activity and can be used to cancel pending requests. If no options are used, the status of all pending requests associated with the user invoking `uustat` is printed.

Options

- `-a` lists all pending requests.
- `-m` reports the status of the last access to each site and a summary of pending requests.
- `-p` executes a `ps` for each process ID associated with each lock file in the lock directory.
- `-q` lists the requests queued for each machine indicating the number of control and execute files, their age, a connection status, and the number of failed access attempts.
- `-r<`*jobid*`>` "touches" the files associated with *jobid* so they appear new and are not expired.
- `-k<`*jobid*`>` removes the requests associated with *jobid* from the queue.
- `-s<`*system*`>` reports the status of all requests for *system*.
- `-u<`*user*`>` reports the status of all requests issued by *user*.

uusched

As described previously, `uusched` invokes `uucico` for each system for which there is work. The ordering of the `uucicos` is randomized. The `-x` option takes a single-digit argument to generate debugging output from `uusched`. The `-u` option is used to pass a `-x` to `uucico`.

uucheck

`uucheck` is an administrative tool. It checks for the presence of the necessary UUCP system files and directories. Given the `-v` option, it will also produce a detailed interpretation of the `Permissions` file. The `Permissions` file is described later. It determines the access `Permissions` for remote systems to files and commands. There is also a `-x` option used for debugging `uucheck`.

uucleanup

uucleanup is intended to automate much of the work of a UUCP administrator in cleaning files that may be orphaned due to aborted transfers or that may not be acted upon do to persistent communications failures. The program scans the UUCP spool directory searching for files older than some limit determined by command line options or defaults. The defaults are 7 days for command and data files, 2 days for execute and unknown file types. There is also the provision to send warnings (defaulted to 1 day old files) to users, apprising them that their requests have not been carried out. The options are: −C<*days*>, −D<*days*>, −X<*days*>, and −o<*days*>. These determine how many days after which to delete command, data, execute, and other files, respectively. −W<*days*> determines when to begin sending warning messages to users. The −m<*string*> option includes string in the warning messages mailed to the users. It may be a good idea to use this to include the name of the UUCP administrator. The −s<*system*> option is used to direct uucleanup's activity to a specific system's spool directory.

uucleanup was originally written as a shell command. It was gradually developed by coding the actions of UUCP administrators as they located and dealt with various files in the spool directories. The developers hoped that uucleanup would continue to grow as the need arose. For now it does a commendable job of disposing of these files. It looks into the file to determine the type of data and attempts to identify, for example in a mail message, the originator and recipient, forwarding the mail if possible or returning it to its sender. Since netnews is responsible for a great deal of UUCP activity, code identifies netnews data and posts it when appropriate. uucleanup is somewhat light in its task, sending consolatory mail to users signed Sincerely, uucp. Many find the idea of a sincere program to be somewhat disconcerting.

◆ Periodic Daemons ◆

The following four shell programs are usually invoked periodically by cron.

uudemon.admin

This program sends status reports to the UUCP administrator.

uudemon.cleanu

This program consolidates log files removing those that are older than a given threshold. (The trailing p makes the name too long for some UNIX versions.)

uudemon.hour

As the name implies, this program is intended to be run hourly. It invokes uucico via uusched.

uudemon.poll

UUCP has the ability to contact passive systems to permit work queued there to be acted upon in the same manner as if the passive system had initiated the connection. A regularly scheduled periodic contact of such a system is a *poll*. Infrequent polling of a small number of sites can be carried out effectively by placing uucico commands in crontab. However, when a moderate number of polls several times daily is required uudemon.poll helps manage the task. A single crontab entry invokes this program, which uses the poll file (described later) to make all the necessary calls to passive systems. A special file in the remote systems spool directory, which appears as an empty UUCP data file, is created.

◆ Other Programs ◆

Several other programs have been created independently of, but for use with, UUCP.

uuencode and uudecode

This pair of programs permits the user to encode a binary file into ASCII. This can then be mailed through an arbitrary path to another user who then decodes it back to its original format. This program was required before the uucp command could execute requests that spanned several machine hops. The remote mail command was well known to have that ability and, thus, became a method for remote remote file transfers. uucp now can "forward" data through several machines just as mail is forwarded. For example:

```
uucp myfile   sys1!sys2!sys3!yourfile
```

is acceptable syntactically. It causes the generation of a uux command to execute uucp on the intermediate systems. Thus, forwarding is not a special case but uses the general remote execution facilities. uuencode and uudecode are still useful when sending binary data over communications links that are not transparent.

uuto and uupick

This pair was developed to simplify the task of transmitting entire directory trees using the uucp command. There is no recursing option to uucp. uuto not only sends files (and the contents of directories) but also causes mail to be sent to the recipient instructing them in how to collect the files. The files are sent to a public spool directory. The recipient executes uupick, which lists the files and directories received. The user then indicates where to place them, and uupick moves them from the spool area.

◆ Files ◆

The following files are located in the UUCP library directory (typically, /usr/lib/uucp). The name in parentheses is the name of a similar file in other UUCP versions, if it exists at all.

Systems (L.sys)

Many of the details of the Systems file have been described. This file lists the systems that UUCP can contact and the devices used to contact them. It may also determine the sites that may access this host if NOSTRANGERS is defined at compilation time. It specifies the the times of day and days of the week to use a given device to access a particular system and permits the specification of preferred protocols to use with a given device when connecting to a system. Each line is an entry associated with a system. Multiple entries for a system may specify different devices, phone numbers, etc. An entry cannot be composed of more than one line. Lines beginning with a pound sign (#) are treated as comments. The fields within an entry are separated by spaces or tabs. They are:

system time device class number login

system is simply the name of the remote system. It must agree with the name the remote system uses to identify itself. Some older versions of UUCP truncate system names to seven characters. If a system truncates its full name, then the Systems file entry should use the truncatated name because that is the true name as far as UUCP is concerned.

time indicates the days of the week and hours of day for which this entry may be used. The days of the week may be abbreviated to the first two characters. The first character must be capitalized. The hours are a range in 24-hour format (two 4-digit numbers separated by a hyphen (-)). They are appended to the day string. If no hour range is given, then 0000–2359 is assumed. An arbitrary number of day-of-the-week/hour-range sets may appear in a single entry separated by commas. A final subfield is the minimum number of minutes to wait before a retry to connect to a remote system following a failed attempt. It overrides the default retry time compiled into uucico. This subfield is separated from the others by a semicolon. The special token Wk is the same as MoTuWeThFr. Another token, Any means SaSuWk. Some sample *time* fields are:

```
Any

Sa,Su,Wk1800-0600

Any;30
```

device is the type of connecting device such as TCP, ACU, and Micom. These may be built in (801, 212, TCP, DK, Sytek, Unetserver) or defined in the Devices file. This field may have appended to it a subfield indicating the preferred protocols for this entry. This subfield is separated by a comma. For example, the e protocol is usually used with the TCP device. Some device fields are:

```
TCP,e

ACU

Develcon
```

class is some specifier used with the device. In the case of devices that use tty lines (ACUs, direct connections, data PBXs), it is the line speed to be used. A hyphen (–) can be used when the class is immaterial (e.g., TCP) or the special token Any may be used to indicate any speed.

number is the "address" of the remote machine: a telephone number when used with devices that dial over telephone lines or a name presented to data PBXs or for Internet connection routines. In the case where *number* is a telephone number, it may be prefixed with an alphabetic string that is mapped to a number using the Dialcodes file. For example:

```
arizona5558632
```

login is the remaining fields of the entry used to interact with the remote system to login and connect to uucico. The *login* fields are not always present. For instance, a TCP connection may directly result in a remote uucico without requiring a login. If a login is necessary there may or may not be a password. The login fields may also be used to negotiate with some remote data PBX, supplying it with names of subswitches, for example. The *login* fields are strings with alternating meanings. The first string is what is expected from the connection, the second is sent, the third is an expected sequence, etc. The received string will be matched if the expected string is a substring of it. For example:

```
gin uucp rd sipglip
```

will send uucp when the gin of login: is received and send sipglip when rd of `Password:` is recognized. The send string is terminated with a carriage return unless otherwise specified. Specifying otherwise is accomplished by appending the string with `\c`, one of the many special strings available (see Table 2-1 for a complete list). The expect string may also contain alternate send strings. These alternates are introduced by enclosing them with hyphens within the expect strings. For example:

```
ogin--in
```

will expect `ogin`. If it isn't received within the timeout period (often as long as 45 seconds, depending upon compile-time options), it sends the null string (appended with carriage return) and looks for `in`.

Here's a sample complete `Systems` entry. It negotiates with two Micoms on the remote end.

```
james Any;20 ACU 1200 sanfrancisco5557330 "" ""  ENTER "" ASS
N123\r\d\d LASS-\r-LASS g\d\d GO \r\r\d ogin:-\r-ogin:
ellcor assword: sipglip
```

If it's not clear what this entry is doing, reread this section.

Hints: Look at Table 2-1. The Micom prompts with `ENTER  CLASS`. `N123` and `g` are Micom resource names.

Maxuuscheds and Maxuuxqts

These files, as mentioned previously, control the number of simultaneously executing `uusched` and `uuxqt` process. They should contain a number in ASCII determining the maximum of such processes.

Permissions (USERFILE)

The `Permissions` file is used to control interactions with remote machines with respect to file access, remotely requested command execution, and login permissions. There are also mechanisms for testing. In essence, the `Permissions` file is used to modify defaults on a per system or system group basis. There are two main specifiers indicating options when a remote site calls and when a remote site is called. Each entry in the `Permissions` file contains a number option/value assignments separated by spaces, tabs, or line continuations (`\<newline>`). Blank lines and lines beginning with `#` are ignored. The option keyword is separated from the value by `=`. The values are separated by colons. The options keywords follow:

LOGNAME. This introduces a set of parameters to be used when a remote site accesses the local host using the logins specified. For example:

```
LOGNAME=xuucp:yuucp:zuucp ...
```

Each login that is used to access this system must be mentioned in one and only one `LOGNAME` entry. The UUCP installation procedure gleans the password file for all entries whose login shell is `uucico` and creates a default `Permissions` file with a `LOGNAME` entry for each one.

MACHINE. This keyword introduces a set of parameters to be used when a remote site is called or when `uuxqt` is executing commands on behalf of a remote site. The `LOGNAME` and `MACHINE` keywords may be used in a single entry if they are to share common parameters when being called by or calling a given remote site. For example:

```
LOGNAME=xuucp MACHINE=xunix ...
```

REQUEST. This keyword is used with the `LOGNAME` or `MACHINE` keyword to indicate whether a remote site may request files to be sent to it from the local host. By default:

```
REQUEST=no
```

It may be explicitly set to "yes" for any logins or machines as desired.

READ. The ability to request files may be further restricted by the `READ` keyword. This may be supplied with a list of paths of which any requested file must be prefixed. By default, the value of `READ` is the UUCP public directory, which is usually:

```
READ=/usr/spool/uucppublic
```

NOREAD. This may be used in conjunction with `READ` to provide exceptions. For example:

```
LOGNAME=juucp REQUEST=yes READ=/usr/joe NOREAD=/usr/joe/private
```

allows a machine which logs in as `juucp` to request any files in `/usr/joe` except those in `/usr/joe/private`.

WRITE. This is analogous to `READ`, defaulting to:

```
WRITE=/usr/spool/uucppublic
```

NOWRITE. This modifies a `WRITE` entry in the same way that `NOREAD` modifies a `READ` entry.

SENDFILES. This keyword accepts a "yes" or "no" value to determine whether files queued for a remote system will be sent if that system calls (when `uucico` reverses the master/slave roles, and the called system looks for work). The default is:

    SENDFILES=no

This ensures that files are only sent when the local site initiates the call and is presumably more certain of communicating with the desired machine. `SEND-FILES` doesn't mean anything if it is part of a `MACHINE` entry since such an entry is for outgoing connections anyway.

CALLBACK. This keyword is used with a `LOGNAME` entry. Taking a "yes" or "no" (the default) value, it causes the conversation to be terminated and the remote machine to be called back. Again, this helps ensure machine identities.

COMMANDS. The `COMMANDS` keyword is used with a `MACHINE` entry to specify a list of commands that the machine may invoke on the local host. The default list is determined at compile-time and usually includes `rmail`. Full path names may be included in the list. In this case when a command whose path is not specified is requested, the path in the `COMMANDS` value is used, overriding the default compiled in `PATH`. The special command `ALL` permits the execution of any command in the `PATH`. For example:

    MACHINE=princeton COMMANDS=/usr/local/bin/lp:ALL:/usr/berbell/bin/gm

allows the machine named `princeton` to execute any command in the default path as well as `/usr/local/bin/lp` and `/usr/berbell/bin/gm`. The path names need not be supplied for the `lp` and `gm` commands.

VALIDATE. This keyword is used with a `LOGNAME` entry to tie a machine name to a login name. The entry:

    LOGNAME=vineyards VALIDATE=yquem

requires that `yquem` log in using `vineyard`.

MYNAME. Used principally for debugging (and masquerading), `MYNAME` is associated with the `LOGNAME` or `MACHINE` entry to instruct the local machine to identify itself with a different name. Thus:

    LOGNAME=testuucp MYNAME=testunix

or

    MACHINE=testunix MYNAME=debug

causes the local host to identify itself as `testunix` to machines that login as `testuucp` and `debug` when it calls `testunix`. Using these mechanisms, a machine can call itself and run UUCP.

PUBDIR. This final keyword is used to redefine the UUCP public directory with a `LOGNAME` or `MACHINE` entry. The default might be written:

```
LOGNAME=uucp MACHINE=OTHER PUBDIR=/usr/spool/uucppublic
```

Note the use of `OTHER`. This special token is used to specify all machines not listed in `MACHINE` entries. There is no equivalent for `LOGNAME` since all logins must be listed.

Here is a sample `Permissions` file:

```
# no secret files here
LOGNAME=uucp READ=/ NOREAD=/etc:/usr/ber \
WRITE=/usr/spool/uucppublic:/tmp \
    SENDFILES=yes REQUEST=yes


# these guys need to access the entire directory structure
MACHINE=bellcore:princeton:research \
    READ=/ WRITE=/
# make sure these machines use the highly secret login since they
# have wide permissions
LOGNAME=suucp VALIDATE=vortex:ames

MACHINE=vortex:ames COMMANDS=ALL
```

Poll

The `Poll` file is used by `uudemon.poll` to schedule polling of passive (or budget-minded) systems. The format is an entry for each site beginning with the site name followed by a tab then the hours in which to poll (0–23) separated by spaces. For example:

```
bellcore   0 1 2 3 4 5 6 7 8 9 10 11 12 13 14 15 16 17 18 19 20 21 22 23
borealis   0 13 16 20
blia       5
sdl        8 9 10 11 12 13 14 15 16 17 18 19 20 21
```

Contacts

This file is not standard, but it should be. It contains a list of the UUCP administrators for each site in the `Systems` file. Each entry contains the site name,
administrators name, office telephone number, and login. This has proven to be
invaluable for sorting out problems. The following shell program helps ensure
that the database is up to date:

```
#! /bin/sh

IFS='

while read site name phone login
do
    mail $site!$name <<!
    Just checking to make sure you haven't been fired yet.
    Please confirm your existence.
!
done
```

remote.unknown

In Honey DanBer the `NOSTRANGERS` manifest is set to the name of a program,
which is executed when a remote site connects that is not in the `Systems` file.
The name of the remote site is sent as an argument to the program. By default
the program is `/usr/lib/uucp/remote.unknown`, a shell script that logs the
event in the file `/usr/spool/uucp/.Admin/Foreign`.[†]

The following files are found in the `.Admin` subdirectory of the UUCP
spool directory.

audit

This file is appended to with debug output from `uucico` when a remote system
is connected and its `uucico` is invoked with the `-x` flag. This file is usually
truncated periodically by `uudemon.cleanu` since debuggers running `uucico`
`-x9` can quickly dump a lot of garbage into it. To prevent this, the manifest
`RMTDEBUG` can be set to `/dev/null` instead of `audit`. This is not always
necessary since people soon tire of `-x9`.

errors

This file contains the text logged by UUCP assert statements.

---

† `remote.unknown` was changed to an executable binary program in System V
Release 3.2.

uucleanup

uucleanup logs diagnostics in this file.

xferstats

This file contains an entry for each file transfer indicating the system, user, role (master or slave), time, process ID, number of files transferred by this process, the device, the direction of the transfer, the number of bytes transferred, and the time it took. For example:

```
obt2!root S (10/3-1:42:16) (C,27947,1) [tty00] -> 49360 / 449.380 = 109.8
obt2!root S (10/3-1:42:24) (C,27947,2) [tty00] -> 209 / 1.380 = 151.4
rutgers!daemon M (10/3-1:45:32) (C,29254,1) [TCP] -> 457 / 0.001 = 457000.0
rutgers!daemon M (10/3-1:45:38) (C,29254,2) [TCP] -> 260 / 0.001 = 260000.0
obt2!root S (10/3-1:50:06) (C,27947,3) [tty00] -> 50162 / 456.380 = 109.9
obt2!root S (10/3-1:50:12) (C,27947,4) [tty00] -> 209 / 1.340 = 155.9
attunix!attunix S (10/3-2:08:04) (C,29825,1) [tty02] <- 229 / 13.440 = 17.0
attunix!attunix S (10/3-2:08:20) (C,29825,2) [tty02] <- 152 / 13.080 = 11.6
```

The C before the process ID implicates uucico as the program responsible. A U is used by uucp; X, by uux; and Q, with uuxqt. But these other programs don't write to this file anyway.

The following are subdirectories of UUCP's spool directory.

.Old

The subdirectory .Old contains old copies of logfiles from .Admin and consolidated files from .Log. The cleanup daemon overwrites them each time it executes with fresh old files.

.Status

This subdirectory contains a file for each remote system accessed. The files contain a coded status, number of attempts, the "unix time", the retry time, the status in ASCII, and the machine name. For example, cat /usr/spool/uucp/.Status/* might result in:

```
21 11 591847471 39600 CALLER SCRIPT FAILED alice
0 0 591862384 0 SUCCESSFUL attunix
4 0 591818100 0 CONVERSATION FAILED co
21 8 591832080 38400 CALLER SCRIPT FAILED decvax
2 0 591853847 0 WRONG TIME TO CALL ka9q
6 239 591868050 900 LOGIN FAILED lion
1 60 591868143 39600 NO DEVICES AVAILABLE meritec
0 0 591677650 0 SUCCESSFUL oakley
```

```
6 2 591867664 900 LOGIN FAILED pyuxe
21 49 591861001 14400 CALLER SCRIPT FAILED star
3 0 591869693 0 TALKING tness7
19 2 591867065 600 REMOTE REJECT, UNKNOWN MESSAGE utah-cs
0 0 591869733 0 SUCCESSFUL yquem
```

.Sequence

Each time a control executes or a data file is created, it is composed of a prefix identifying the type of file (C., X., D.), a system name, a grade of service (possibly specified with a -g option), a number, and a site name. The number is possibly the only unique part of the file name. The .Sequence subdirectory stores the last used number for each system in a file. When a number is used, it is incremented. They are ASCII representations of hexadecimal numbers. In the past, a single sequence number was incremented for all systems. Heavy usage caused the number to wrap around (it was base 10) resulting in naming conflicts. One solution to this was Allan Watts' modification, which generated base 64 numbers. This produced wild and amusing file names, and it was difficult to make any sense of them when doing serious debugging. The sequence-number-per-system solution used in Honey DanBer solves the problem in a reasonable manner. These sequence numbers should not be confused with conversation sequence numbers, which are used for site verification. If the file SQFILE exists in the UUCP library directory, it contains entries of the form:

```
name count month/day-hour:minute
```

For example:

```
kremvax 666 4/1-00:00
```

If a system is listed in this file, then conversations are numbered. When a connection is established, the remote and local sites must agree on the conversation sequence count or the connection is aborted. Counts are modulo 10,000. This reduces the possibility of masquerading and raises the odds to almost certainty that a masquerade will be detected. It is, however, rarely used.

.Xqtdir

Remotely requested commands execute in this directory.

.Workspace

Here is where temporary internal system files are created and (we hope) destroyed.

The following three file types are created by UUCP in the remote systems spool directory.

Control File (C.*)

The control file contains the information necessary to perform the transfer. It contains as many lines as there are requests issued in a single uucp command. A uux command generates a control file for each system used in the command string. The file has eight fields for receiving files and nine for sending. For example:

```
S  /usr/ber/.profile ~/ber/.profile ber -dc D.0 644 ber
```

Note that there is a null final field. The first is S for send or R for receive. The next is the source file, followed by the destination. The fourth field is the local user, followed by options indicating whether to create directories as needed and if the file is being transferred from a copy or the true source. The next field is the name of the data file that contains a copy of the destination. This field is not present in entries requesting that files be received from a remote system. In the case where the true source file is used (as in this example), the data file field is a dummy place holder. The next two fields are the mode of the source file and the name of the user to be notified in case of problems (may be specified with the -n option). Finally, the last argument, which may be null, is the file in which to report the transfer status, as supplied with the -s option.

Execute Files (X.)

These files are placed on a machine as the result of a uux command on some remote site. The format is somewhat flexible. Each line of the file begins with a one-character field specifying the meaning of the remainder of the line. The uux program actually generates comment lines that are inserted into the execute files to assist the peruser. The line types are:

- # is a comment.
- F is a file necessary for execution. The X. file won't be processed until this file exists.
- I is standard input.
- O is standard output.
- C is the command to execute.
- U is the user to notify for command execution status.
- B instructs uux to return the standard input to the user if the command fails.

- M is the file name in which to write the execution status report.

- R is the return address for mail (specified to uux with the −a option if not the user).

- Z sends notification if the command fails (exit status is not zero).

- N doesn't send notification even if the command fails.

- n sends notification if the command succeeds (exit status is zero).

Data Files (D.)

These files have no format; they are copies of source data. They may may be created by users of uucp with the −C option or by uux to place an execute file on the remote system.

Sample Session (Connection, Handshake, Transfer, Acknowledgment, and Cleanup)

Lines in italics are annotations added to the actual output.

```
$ uucp -r /usr/ber/.profile gnash!~/ber/.profile
```

Use the −r *option to invoke the* uucico *and examine its output.*

```
$ uucico -r1 -x7 -sgnash
```

−r1 *(act as slave),* −x7 *(set debugging level to 7, one greater than the most useful level),* −sgnash *(call the system named* gnash*).*

```
mchFind called (gnash)
list (rmail) list (rnews) num = 2
name (gnash) not found; return FAIL
list (rmail) list (rnews) num = 2
name (OTHER) not found; return FAIL
_Request (FALSE), _Switch (TRUE), _CallBack (FALSE), _MyName (),
_Commands rmail _Commands rnews/fP
```

The mchFind *diagnostics indicate the search through the* Permissions *file for an entry describing special behavior for* gnash. *No entry exists naming* gnash *or* OTHER *so the* FAIL *messages appear. These are expected and not to be taken as errors (unless a* MACHINE=gnash *or* MACHINE=OTHER *entry is in the* Permissions *file). The lines beginning with* list *show the allowable command array being built. In this case, the defaults are used. Finally, the variables set through the* Permissions *file are printed.*

```
chdir (/usr/spool/uucp/gnash)
```

Change to the spool subdirectory for gnash.

```
conn(gnash)
```

conn() *is an internal UUCP function. It returns a file descriptor open for reading and writing connected to a* uucico *on the remote end.*

```
ProtoStr = e
Device Type TCP wanted
Internal caller type TCP
tcpdial host gnash, port 64
addr: 555.12.34.56
getto ret 5
```

The ProtoStr *string is initialized from the* Systems *file entry. That entry is:* gnash Any TCP, e Any gnash in:--in: uucp rd: sipglip. *The internal dialer type and port number are taken from the* Devices *file whose relevant entry is* TCP TCP 64 uucp TCP D. getto() *returns the file descriptor* (5). *The login must first be negotiated before* conn() *is satisfied.*

```
expect: (in:)
login:got it
```

The expect/send sequences reflect the login fields of the Systems *file entry for* gnash. *The string in parenthesis is literally what's expected. The following text up to* got it *is what was received.*

```
sendthem (uucp^M<CR> written
)
expect: (rd:)
Password:got it
sendthem (sipglip^M<CR> written
)
imsg >^PShere=gnash^@Login Successful: System=gnash
imsg >^PROK^@msg-ROK
```

The imsg *labels indicate incoming messages.* imsg() *is used before the protocol is selected. Here we see the first message from a slave* uucico (Shere=). *Since the remote identified itself as the machine we called, the login is considered* SUCCESSFUL. *The next message sent is not shown here; it's where the local system sends its name, the conversation sequence count, and the debugging flag* (yquem -Q0 -x7). *After the local site sends this information, the remote responds with* R *then a status. In this case,* OK. *Other messages that might be seen include* LCK *if the two systems are already talking,* LOGIN *if the remote* Permissions *file* VALIDATE *and* LOGNAME *entries don't match those used,* CB *if the remote* Permissions *file indicates a callback for this system,* You are unknown to me *if the remote has set* NOSTRANGERS *and this site is not listed in the remote* Systems *file, and* BADSEQ *if conversation sequence counts are in use (according to the remote site) and the number sent does not match the expected sequence number. Anything else is an unknown response.*

```
Rmtname gnash, Role MASTER,   Ifn - 5, Loginuser - ber
```

This line indicates things we already know because of the high debugging level and because user
ber invoked uucico.

```
rmesg - 'P' imsg >^PPge^@got Pge
wmesg 'U'e
Proto started e
```

The next step is for the master to receive the list of protocols available on the remote site. It selects
one from the list. In this case e because it was specified in the Systems file entry. Had it not
been, the g would have been selected because it appeared first in the list. The master then informs
the slave which protocol was selected, the protocol function table is populated from the appropriate
protocol entry, and further communications proceed using those functions.

```
*** TOP ***  -  role=1, gtwvec: dir /usr/spool/uucp/gnash
```

This is the top of the work loop. Role 1 is master.   gtwvec () generates an array of control files
to relevant to the remote system.

```
insert(C.gnashN8306)  insert C.gnashN8306 at 0
        return - 8
```

There are eight arguments in the current line of C.gnashN8306.

```
Wfile - /usr/spool/uucp/gnash/C.gnashN8306,Jobid = gnashN8306
Request: yquem!/usr/ber/.profile --> gnash!~/ber/.profile (ber)
```

This is the requested transfer as it appears in the control file.

```
wrktype - S
 wmesg 'S' /usr/ber/.profile ~/ber/.profile ber -dc D.0 644 ber
```

The local site sends an S command followed by the foregoing arguments.

```
rmesg - 'S' got SY
 PROCESS: msg - SY
```

The remote acknowledges the S and indicates acceptance with Y. Alternatively it might have sent
back SN and a number indicating a rejection such as remote access denied.

```
SNDFILE:
ewrmsg write 514
ewrmsg ret 514
-> 514 / 0.150 secs
```

The e protocol write message routine sends 514 bytes in .15 seconds. At this point the local site
expects to receive notification that the remote has received the file and copied it to the specified
destination.

```
rmesg - 'C' got CY
 PROCESS: msg - CY
RQSTCMPT:
mailopt 0, statfopt 0
```

The copy succeeded. Had it failed, the local site would have received N and a number as above rather than Y.

```
*** TOP ***  -  role=1, gtwvec: dir /usr/spool/uucp/gnash
Finished Processing file: /usr/spool/uucp/gnash/C.gnashN8306
```

The loop continues from the top, and it discovers that the remote system has no more work. The local system asks if the connection should be hung up.

```
wmesg 'H'
rmesg - 'H' got HY
 PROCESS: msg - HY
HUP:
wmesg 'H'Y
cntrl - 0
```

The remote system has no work so it indicates that indeed the connection should be hung up. The local system concurs, the protocol is abandoned and a series of Os is sent (over and outs).

```
send OO 0,imsg >HY^@^POOOOOO^@exit code 0
Conversation Complete: Status SUCCEEDED
```

The following is what the remote system logged in its audit file for this transaction:

```
sys-yquem
logFind called (name: uucp, rmtname: yquem)
validateFind (yquem) FAIL
```

Should the uucp login be validated? Not in this example.

```
list (rmail) list (rnews) list (uusend) num = 3
_Request (TRUE), _Switch (TRUE), _CallBack (FALSE), _MyName (),
return from callcheck: FALSE
chdir(/usr/spool/uucp/yquem)
 Rmtname yquem, Role SLAVE,  Ifn - 0, Loginuser - uucp
wmesg 'P'ge
rmesg - 'U' imsg >^PUe^@got Ue
Proto started e
*** TOP ***  -  role=0, rmesg - '' got S /usr/ber/.profile ~/ber
/.profile ber -dc D.0 644 ber
 PROCESS: msg - S /usr/ber/.profile ~/ber/.profile ber -dc D.0 644
ber
```

```
SNDFILE:
msg - S
Remote Requested: yquem!/usr/ber/.profile --> gnash!~/ber/.profile
(ber)
```

The ~ is a way to specify the UUCP public spool directory, which is usually writable by anyone.

```
SLAVE - filename: /usr/spool/uucppublic/ber/.profile
chkpth ok Rmtname - yquem
TMname(/usr/spool/uucp/yquem/TM.16258.000)
```

All transfers go through a temporary file.

```
wmesg 'S'Y
ask 20 got 20
```

The initial read is a 20-byte message. That message says how many bytes the actual data is.

```
erdblk msglen 514
ask 514 got 514
erdblk ret 514
<- 514 / 0.268 secs
wmesg 'C'Y
*** TOP *** - role=0, rmesg - '' got H
 PROCESS: msg - H
HUP:
SLAVE-switchRole (TRUE)
wmesg 'H'Y
rmesg - 'H' got HY
 PROCESS: msg - HY
HUP:
wmesg 'H'Y
cntrl - 0
send OO 0,imsg >^POOOOOO^@ret restline - -1
exit code 0
Conversation Complete: Status SUCCEEDED
```

Performance and Reliability

UUCP shares the faults and virtues of the systems upon which it is built. It certainly performs no better than the subnetwork it uses to communicate to a remote site, be that the Public Switched Telephone network or the Internet. And because UUCP executes as user programs, it may be severely affected by the loads on the systems on which it is executing. Clearly, it is no more reliable than those mechanisms it uses to communicate and the software that supports it, be it kernel, system library, or command. These are limiting factors independent, to a large extent, of the UUCP software. These factors favor UUCP in general because of its flexibility. UUCP can use the fastest communications media available. It can run on any type of computing hardware that supports UNIX and many that don't. Performance may also be related to constraints. For example, if the callback option is used when connecting to a given system, then two calls are necessary rather then one. Also, perceived reliability problems are often the result of restrictive permissions, which may result in the ability to transfer a file or execute a command. The following test indicates a gross comparison between UUCP using TCP and the rcp command:

```
rcp web2 gnash:/usr/spool/uucppublic/rcpfile & uucp web2 gnash!~/uucpfile
```

An ls on the gnash shows:

```
-rw-rw-rw-  1 bcruucp    2486813 Oct   4 03:52 uucpfile
-r--r--r--  1 ber        2486813 Oct   4 03:52 rcpfile
```

the same time to the nearest second (reversing the execution order produced the same results). If the Ethernet were down, UUCP would have used the Micom. rcp would have timed out after a few seconds and given up.

Another factor when evaluating performance and reliability is the fact that UUCP is batch system. Requests are queued, then acted upon later (instants or days) when resources are available. This cuts both ways. On the one hand, a user gets a sense of satisfaction when the command prompt reappears after executing a UUCP command. On the other, there have been far too many instances when the request was never carried out. The fault can lie anywhere from improperly installed UUCP software on the local site to a buggy kernel on the remote site. Most of the frustrations resulting from failures have been resolved by notification mechanisms. But new frustrations arise when a user receives mail from UUCP first warning them that the transfer is overdue, then that it just isn't going to happen.

The confusion between the file transfer and remote execution facility and the commands that are used to execute remotely further complicates the issues. The two greatest uses of UUCP are electronic mail and networked bulletin boards (not necessarily in that order). The failure rates of various packages implementing these functions has reflected badly on UUCP, as the bearer of bad news.

In general, however, UUCP performance and reliability is proportional to its use. (The more it is relied upon, the more likely it is that things will be properly maintained.) Although this was the opposite case as few as 5 years ago, today the software is basically sound. There are ample administrative tools to maintain it. UUCP has matured into a reliable, maintainable software package and continues to fill the needs of a very wide class of users from PCs to megaframes.

Debugging

Debug UUCP in the same manner as you would any other complex system. The observed problem should be reproduced. If you can't reproduce a problem, you either don't know that there is a problem or you're not going to be able to find it. Even obscure race conditions can be repeated. If necessary, write a program to execute many commands simultaneously. Have it repeat this loop, checking the command status, and run it overnight. Include other programs in the loop that might be related (`cu`, `rcp`). The problem will turn up. If a problem is reported by a user, duplicate that user's environment. Too often an inappropriate PATH variable sends administrators chasing after phantom bugs.

    Inability to connect to a remote system will likely be the biggest headache you encounter with UUCP. Once you establish a connection, the diagnostics are usually useful enough to point to the source of the difficulties. The following messages appear most commonly in the system's status file (`/usr/spool/uucp/.Status/<system>`).

CALLER SCRIPT FAILED. The first step is to run `/usr/lib/uucp/uucico -r1 -x6 -s<the problem system>`. It's likely that the `uucico` will exit prematurely with the diagnostic "RETRY TIME *<some number>* NOT REACHED." If so, remove `/usr/spool/uucp/.Status/<the problem system>` and try again. Observe the interactions. If nothing is obviously wrong, then attempt the connection by hand to see if that turns something up. If `uucico` is attempting to connect by dialing a telephone number, pick up the telephone and dial that number. Is it busy? Is there no answer? Does a human answer? Do you get a message saying:

```
You have dialed a non-working number at Bell Laboratories Murray
Hill, if you need assistance please call 555-3000.
```

Make sure the number makes sense. Does it include any special number such as "9" to get an outside line? Also make sure that extra numbers aren't being inserted by the dialers or dialcodes files. Pick a convention, outside access in one place, `Systems`, `Dialers`, or `Dialcodes`. If the number is correct to the best of your knowledge, then you're stymied. Comment the disappointing line out of your `Systems` file, refer to your list of contacts, and get the right number.

WRONG TIME TO CALL. This isn't necessarily a problem unless it's persistent. Check the time field of the `Systems` file. Does it make sense? Is it syntactically correct? Sometimes people use the token `Never` to prevent calls from being initiated. This works because `Never` doesn't match `Mo`, `Tu`, `We`, `Th`, `Fr`, `Sa`, `Su`, `Wk`, or `Any`. Neither does `Any`, `fr`, or `Week`. If there is deliberately no valid time to call because the system is supposed to poll you, and they aren't, phone up your contact and ask why. Maybe they don't want to call you any longer.

TALKING. Is it really talking? Is there a lock file (for example, `/usr/spool/locks/LCK..<system>`)? What's the pid in the file? Is the process running? Does it run for an unreasonable amount of time? Kill it. If the process doesn't exist, the lock file ought not be honored. If removing the lock file for a nonexistent process fixes the problem, then that's your solution, even if that's not supposed to work.

LOGIN FAILED. Run `uucico -r1 -x6 -s<system>`. It's expecting some string that it's not receiving. Note what that is, then look at the `Systems` file entry. Make the connection by hand. Does the remote end need a carriage return and you're not sending it? Insert `""` `""` in the login sequence (expect nothing, send carriage return). Whatever you do by hand to get the remote's attention, incorporate that into the `Systems` file entry. Keep in mind timing. Perhaps a couple delays are in order. If you get the login and password prompts but `uucico` times out (looking for `Shere=`), there is probably a typo in the login or password listed in `Systems`. Call up the system manually and see what happens when you try to login using the information in your `Systems` file.

REMOTE DOES NOT KNOW ME. Have your contact on the remote site install your system name in the contact's `Systems` file.

NO DEVICES AVAILABLE. Check for a typo in the device entry of the `Systems` file. Also check the `Devices` and `Dialers` files to be sure logical devices have physical devices associated with them. Is the required device in use by some other program? Check the lock directory. Do a `ps`. Is the device accessible by UUCP? Try to `cat` into it. Does the open fail?

BAD SEQUENCE CHECK. The remote has implemented conversation sequence counts for your machine. Is your machine participating? If sequence checking is what you want to do and this error arises, maybe another machine has masqueraded as your site. On the other hand, maybe something's wrong with your sequence file (`/usr/lib/uucp/SQFILE`). In any event, you'll have to either contact the remote and disable the checking or change your sequence file manually, whichever is appropriate. If a masquerade seems like the cause, arrange for a new UUCP password for the remote system.

WRONG MACHINE NAME. You accessed the wrong machine. This is not so rare since many large installations use the same UUCP login and passwords and the telephone numbers may be similar. It's also possible that they booted a new UNIX and neglected to set their machine name properly.

REMOTE HAS A LOCK FILE FOR ME. The remote system thinks it's already talking to your site. Is that the case? It could be a hung process on their end. Contact them and have them kill it and remove the lock file. It might also be a masquerade.

REMOTE REJECT AFTER LOGIN. This is most likely due to a validation error.

Your site logged in using the wrong UUCP account. Contact the site administrator.

CALLBACK REQUIRED. Make sure callback is what is intended. Two systems that each have callback set for each other will make a lot of calls but never converse.

Those are the most straightforward problems to trace. In general, manually dialing a system and logging in as UUCP would will be illuminating. For example, one problem that causes many versions of `uucico` to dump core occurs when a remote site has an exceedingly long banner message. Naive software will happily stuff the received data into an array when it's looking for an *expect* sequence. The banner message may overflow the array limit. The variable MAX-CHARS is used to determine when to give up. This parameter has been growing year after year as users encounter systems greetings of epic length. Some systems even insist that each user read all system messages before they do any work. This can boggle `uucico`.

Check `.Admin/errors` in the UUCP spool directory when you're having problems. A clue might be found there. `assert` errors referencing the Packet protocol (e.g., `PKCGET READ`) are generally due to noisy telephone lines. This is fairly common and acceptable unless it happens consistently. Put a telephone on the line and listen for obvious problems. Attach the ACU to another line and see if that helps. Try another dialer. Be systematic. Change one thing at a time so when you resolve the problem you know what it is you've fixed. Be suspicious of cables as well; they deteriorate after years of being yanked on and tread upon.

Security

Just as performance and reliability depend on the underlying programs and devices, security issues can be sloughed off to other parts of the system. We can make the blanket statement that a system can't be secure if it allows access from remote machines through a public network. The last paragraph of the manual page for `uucp` dated 12/16/76 (in the BUGS section) states:

> As usual, you have a choice of getting more work done or worrying about protecting what you already did; this choice is perhaps more acute if you use UUCP.

That's a very wise and time-enduring statement.

Allowing remote execution and file transfer is opening up a world of security risks. Minimizing the risks is the task of the installers and maintainers of UUCP and the system as a whole. Most of the security holes discovered in UUCP have had to do with embedded escapes from the shell. For instance, it's common to permit any site to execute the `rmail` command. UUCP software would duly check that `rmail` was the requested command. But early version didn't check the arguments. Since `system()` was used to invoke the command, the following would normally net the user a shell on a remote system:

```
uux site-a!"rmail bob `/bin/sh`"
```

These well-known holes have been plugged, but new software with new holes appears constantly. The `Permissions` file can help using CALLBACK and VALIDATE, but in general it is there to permit the relaxation of default restrictions in an organized manner. It can be be abused. Be aware when granting access to files and commands that there is potential danger. Setting COMMAND=ANY is like giving every user on the remote site indicated by that entry a general-purpose login on your system. The most effective method for maintaining a reasonably secure system is vigilance. Check the log files. Have the `cron grep` through them for `/etc/passwd` and send you mail. Be aware of what's happening on your system so that you know when patterns vary. This applies to general system administration. Log files, console messages, and accounting data should all be accessible.

A useful technique (if a site can afford it) is to dedicate a telephone number for use by UUCP. Then a special `getty` on that line can assert that only UUCP logins can access it. Thus, giving out the site's phone number is not so risky. Anyone that calls it will get `uucico` running in slave mode. Define NOSTRANGERS at installation-time if you're not running a general mail server. If any special permissions are given to machines in the `Permissions` file, use VALIDATE and try to ensure that the login/password used by those machines remains private. Honey DanBer UUCP comes as secure as it can be by default. Less security (and more functionality) can be granted by changing default parameters and modifying the system's files. Do not be afraid to change things to suit your needs, simply be sure the effects are what you intend. More easily understood file formats, better installation techniques and documentation, report generators, etc., help UUCP to be used and adapted wisely. It is as secure as such a system can be expected to be, which is reasonably secure. It can be made unreasonably insecure if it's not maintained in a conscientious fashion.

◆ Future Directions ◆

UUCP has continued and probably will continue in the same directions—toward more flexibility, more automated maintenance, better performance, better diagnostics, and more standardization. As long as UUCP can make use of any available network, it will grow with the development of those networks. UUCP has become a fairly solid utility. It's a 12 year old program that's had at least three major rewrites. Yet it has always maintained its original function and purpose. UUCP will likely be put to new uses, but that's always been its direction.

♦ Comparison ♦

Principally, UUCP uses other networks discussed in the book. The main difference, if a comparison is to be made, is that UUCP is a batch-oriented system. Also, logins on remote sites are not required by UUCP users.

TABLE 2-1. System file special characters

Function	
BREAK[†]	Sends a break by the best way
EOT[†]	Sends \004\n\004\n
\T	Sends a translated phone number when used from the Dialers file, sends a null string when used in the Systems file
\D	Sends the untranslated phone number when used from the Dialers file, sends a null string when used in the Systems file
\E	Turns on echo checking, thus the write is as slow as necessary to ensure that each character is echoed before the next is sent
\e	Turns off echo checking
\K	Sends a break by the best way
\N	Sends NULL (\000)
" "	Represents nothing (is ignored, but a carriage return is sent)
\d	Pauses for 2 seconds
\c	Means not to append a carriage return if this is at the end of the string
\s	Sends a space
\p	Pauses for 0.5 second
\\	Sends \
\b	Sends a backspace
\n	Sends a newline
\r	Sends a carriage return
\t	Sends a tab
xxx	Sends the character represented by the octal code *xxx*

† BREAK and EOT cannot be used if they are to be part of a greater string.

TCP/IP

Douglas E. Comer
Thomas Narten
Computer Science Department
Purdue University

◆ Introduction ◆

Networking has been the dominant force in computing during the last decade. It is dissolving the geographic barriers that separate users, making it easy for them to exchange information whether they are located at the same site or at opposite ends of the country. People use networks to exchange such information as programs, data files, and mail. Networking is leading us to the information age, providing people with facilities that allow them to communicate quickly and conveniently with others sharing common interests.

Networks come in various shapes and sizes, and no single network technology satisfies everyone. Typically, sites choose a network technology that meets their specific budget and service needs. The technology known as *internetworking* draws the plethora of diverse network technologies into a common framework that combines networks into *internets*. Internetworking generalizes the facilities provided by networks, creating a virtual network to which all hosts connect. In particular, it allows applications to communicate with applications located on distant networks as easily as with those at the same site.

This chapter focuses on the Department of Defense internetworking protocol suite, popularly known as TCP/IP†. Applications use the TCP/IP protocols to communicate with applications running on remote machines that connect to the internet. The largest operational internet, the Defense Advanced Research Projects Agency (DARPA) Internet, consists of thousands of hosts and hundreds of networks located around the world—all using the TCP/IP protocol suite. The DARPA Internet consists primarily of scientists carrying out government-supported work. For the remainder of this chapter, we will use the term Internet

---

† For more extensive coverage of TCP/IP, see *Internetworking with TCP/IP*, Douglas E. Comer, Prentice-Hall, Englewood Cliffs, NJ, 1988.

(with a capital I) when referring specifically to internets that use the TCP/IP protocols.

The remainder of the chapter is organized as follows: We begin with a history of networking activities that led to the TCP/IP protocol suite. We then survey existing network technologies, focusing on capabilities that they provide. Next, we present the TCP/IP protocol suite in a "bottom up" fashion. Our discussion proceeds bottom up because each layer on the protocol suite is built using the services provided by the layers beneath it. Thus, each layer uses the services of the layers beneath it to create higher-level services. We then describe three important internet services—remote login, electronic file transfer, and electronic mail. Next, we describe the application interface to the TCP/IP protocols provided by the 4.3 edition of Berkeley UNIX, detailing the library routines and system calls that application programs use. Our discussion of the interface includes example programs that illustrate how applications use the interface. The last section outlines future directions.

♦ History ♦

In 1969, DARPA sponsored an experiment in resource sharing called the ARPANET. The ARPANET provided multiply connected, high-bandwidth (56 kilobits per second) communication links between major computing sites at government, academic, and industrial laboratories. The ARPANET provided users the ability to exchange mail and files and allowed users to log into remote hosts. The ARPANET experiment decisively demonstrated the benefits and feasibility of cross-country packet-switched networks.

During the 1970s, DARPA was the primary funding agency for packet-switching network research. In addition to the ARPANET, which used point-to-point leased line interconnections, DARPA sponsored research in alternative technologies. One project used mobile radio transmitters to build a packet-switched network, while another project investigated satellite links.

By the mid 1970s, researchers began searching for a common framework that would tie the various technologies together into a single network. The results of that effort, the TCP/IP protocol suite, began being deployed on the ARPANET by the end of the decade. To spur conversion to the new protocols, DARPA decided to make an implementation available at low cost. At the time, many universities were using a version of the UNIX operating system available as part of the University of California's "Berkeley Standard Distribution." DARPA funded Bolt Beranek and Newman, Inc. (BBN) to develop a TCP/IP implementation for UNIX and Berkeley to integrate the software into its distribution.

The Berkeley distribution of the Internet protocols came at a significant time. Many sites were acquiring local area networks and adding new machines and workstations. Along with the Internet protocols themselves, Berkeley supplied application programs that used the new protocols. In many cases, network services were simple extensions of services previously available in single-machine environments, making them easy to use. By January 1983, all computers connected to the ARPANET were running the new Internet protocols. Moreover, many sites not connected to the ARPANET embraced the new protocols for use on their internal networks.

By 1984, the National Science Foundation (NSF) recognized that networking was crucial to link researchers with supercomputers and to one another. Moreover, ARPANET access was restricted to those sites supported by a small set of government agencies and was not generally available to researchers. Recognizing the presence of a have-have not situation, NSF embarked on a program to build a network that would link researchers with supercomputer sites and provide the framework for a future, general-purpose, academic network.

Based on DARPA's experience, NSF decided to adopt the Internet protocols and build a "network of networks" rather than a single large network. NSF focused its efforts in two areas, creating a backbone network linking existing supercomputer centers and funding development of regional networks that connected to the NSFnet backbone and to networks located at universities, industrial sites, and government labs. By summer 1988, the NSFnet backbone had expanded to 20 nodes connected by T1/3 speed links with plans to upgrade to T1 speeds. "T1 speed" is an acronym for lines with speeds of 1.544 megabits per second.

At present, NSF is the dominant force in computer networking. While NSFnet is expanding and is investigating new technologies, the ARPANET is essentially unchanged from its original design. Although additional nodes have been added to the ARPANET, it still uses 56 kilobits-per-second lines, which are considered slow by today's standards. DARPA, uncomfortable in a role supporting a production rather than experimental network, has announced its intention to terminate the ARPANET and sponsor research in new technologies.

The Internet protocol suite is popular because it offers a high degree of interoperability among applications running on machines that support different architectures and operating systems. In the following sections, we present the Internet protocols in detail. We begin with a discussion of current network technologies upon which the Internet protocols are built.

◆ Physical Layer ◆

Host computers attach to *physical networks* that transport messages among them. The hosts do not know the details of how messages are physically transferred. Networks come in various speeds and topologies, because no one technology satisfies all users. *Local area networks* (LANs) provide high bandwidth and low delay. They cover small geographic areas such as a building. *Long haul networks* span larger geographic areas but usually cost much more to maintain and operate.

Networks carry variable size messages called *frames*. Frames vary in size between some minimum and maximum value, the actual values depend on the particular network. Each frame contains a *header* and *data* portion. The header contains control information that helps the network deliver the frame to its destination and allows the receiving host to determine from where an arriving frame originated. The data portion contains the information being transferred by the communicating applications. When a host wants to send data, it places the data in the data portion of the frame, fills in the header with the appropriate destination, and hands the frame to the network device. The network delivers the frame to the interface at the destination host, which in turn passes it to the receiving host. In the following subsections, we examine three representative network technologies.

Bus Technologies

Based on a simple idea, broadcast bus technologies typified by the Ethernet have become one of the most popular LAN technologies. The Ethernet is a *bus* because all interfaces attach to a common communication channel—a coaxial cable known as the "ether." It is *broadcast* because all interfaces receive every transmission. Technically, Ethernet is called Carrier Sense Multiple Access (CSMA) because multiple access (MA) points sense a carrier wave (CS) to determine when the network is idle. When no transmission is sensed, the host interface may transmit. When an interface begins transmission, however, the signal does not reach all parts of the network simultaneously. Thus, it is possible for two stations to start transmitting at the same time. The resulting *collision* of the transmissions scrambles the two signals, and the sending station detects the condition and aborts the transmission. Technically, the monitoring is called collision detect (CD), and Ethernet is termed a CSMA-CD network. Upon detecting a collision, the sender waits a short while and tries again.

Each interface has a 48-bit Ethernet address. Addresses are associated with the interface rather than hosts. If the interface moves to another machine, its address moves with it. Interfaces can also be configured to recognize other addresses. A *broadcast* address is recognized by all stations, permitting one station to send frames to all others. *Multicast* addresses allow a limited form of broadcasting in which a subset of all stations accepts a frame. Manufacturers assign addresses to interfaces in such a way that no two interfaces have the same address.

Ethernet frames range from 64 to 1536 *octets* in size (see Fig. 3-1). Using network terminology, an octet refers to an 8-bit byte. Each frame header includes the address of the sender and destination, and a 16-bit type field used by higher-layer protocols to identify frame contents and data format. The hardware appends a 32-bit cyclic redundancy code (CRC) to each frame to detect transmission errors. Ethernets have a raw bandwidth of 10 megabits per second, although the actual bandwidth available to applications is slightly lower.

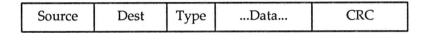

| Source | Dest | Type | ...Data... | CRC |

Fig. 3-1. Format of an Ethernet frame

Ring Technologies

Another popular LAN technology is the token-passing ring typified by the proNET-10. Like the Ethernet, the proNET-10 has a raw carrying capacity of 10 megabits per second, and all nodes on the network see each frame. ProNET-10 frame headers also contain the source and destination interface addresses, but addresses are only 8 bits long. One implication of small addresses is that addresses are not globally unique, and the network administrator must assign addresses in such a way that no two nodes on a network have the same address. ProNET-10 frames carry up to 2044 octets of user data, have a single parity bit for error detection, and include a *refuse bit*, which is described later.

Rather than connecting passively to a common transmission media, ring interfaces are active participants in the network. Interfaces have one send and one receive line that connect to one upstream and one downstream neighbor, respectively. Interfaces connect in the shape of a ring, and frames flow unidirectionally around the ring. As a frame travels around the ring, each interface copies it from the receive to the send line, and the frame eventually returns to the sender on its receive line. The sender, of course, terminates the ring, preventing a frame from looping forever. Frames include a refuse bit that the destination node clears if it accepts the frame. Thus, the sender can detect when the destination node is down.

Ring networks are token-passing networks, because a token continually circulates around the ring. When an interface wants to send a frame, it waits for the token to appear, removes it from the ring, and begins transmission. To prevent any one node from monopolizing the network, senders return the token to the ring after each transmission. Thus, when several nodes have data to send, each one is granted permission in a fair, deterministic manner. Indeed, one of the primary advantages of a ring is its behavior under heavy load. On an Ethernet, the number of collisions rise with increasing load, reducing the amount of usable bandwidth. One disadvantage of the ring becomes apparent when the token is lost. A token might be lost, for instance, if the node holding the token crashes. Token-passing networks use special protocols to regenerate lost tokens.

Point-to-Point Networks

Long haul networks such as the ARPANET and NSFnet span thousands of miles and consist of small computers called *packet-switching nodes* (PSNs) connected by *point-to-point* lines. Nodes perform *store-and-forward* frame switching. When a frame arrives on an incoming line, the node chooses a neighbor node closer to the frame's ultimate destination and enqueues the frame for output on the line leading to the chosen neighbor. The process of selecting a next node is known as *routing*.

One important difference between LAN technologies and store-and-forward networks is that PSNs in store-and-forward networks must route frames. Moreover, each node is an independent machine, and nodes can become confused and disagree as to the best way to route frames. Thus, frames can be drawn into *routing loops*, where the frame travels along a cyclic path indefinitely. One way that store-and-forward networks reduce the problems caused by such loops is to limit the amount of time a frame can remain in the network. Frames can contain a *time-to-live* (TTL) field in their headers that switching nodes decrement when they process the frame. The TTL value is initialized to a large value, and if it ever reaches 0, the frame is discarded.

Although long haul networks differ internally from LANs, the important point for our purposes is that they are functionally similar to LANs. In particular, they carry frames containing arbitrary data from one host to another. To a user, the main difference between long haul networks and LANs is cost and performance. Long haul networks typically use expensive, leased telephone lines or satellite links. Consequently, they usually carry data at significantly lower rates, and frame transmission time is usually orders of magnitude larger than for a LAN.

◆ Internet Protocol ◆

If all hosts connected to a single network, any host would be able to communicate directly with every other host. Unfortunately, there are many individual networks. *Internetworking* refers to any technology that joins independent networks together into a single virtual network called an *internet*. Hosts on an internet communicate with other hosts as easily as if they were on the same physical network. In this section, we describe the Internet Protocol (IP), which forms the basis for the DARPA Internet.

Gateways are one of the fundamental components of the Internet. Gateways accept packets from one network and forward them to hosts or gateways on another. In Fig. 3-2, host A communicates with host B by sending a datagram to gateway G. Gateway G then forwards the datagram to B. Conceptually, internets act as point-to-point networks in which gateways are the nodes and networks are the links. Packets are forwarded from gateway to gateway until they reach a gateway on the destination network, which delivers the packet to the specific destination. Internet service is *unreliable* because delivery is not guaranteed. Packets may be lost, duplicated, or delivered out of order. The service is called *connectionless*, because each datagram is processed independently from all others.

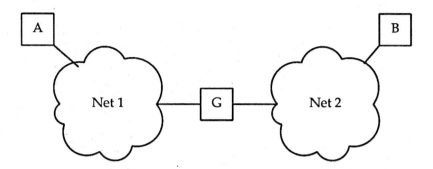

Fig. 3-2. Two networks connected by a gateway

Our simplified description ignores two problems: different network technologies use different frame formats and network addresses are not globally unique. Internets solve these problems by defining a universal packet called an *Internet datagram*. Internet datagrams strongly resemble the frames of physical networks. Indeed, a primary goal of the Internet architecture is to provide a virtual network in which hosts can exchange datagrams with any other host.

Internet Addressing

The Internet architecture is based on the idea that every host has its own unique address. *Internet addresses* are composed of two parts, a network portion and a local portion. The network part of the address specifies which network the host resides on, and the local part identifies the specific host on that network. Internet addresses closely follow the model where hosts connect to networks and networks are combined into internets. A central authority assigns addresses, guaranteeing that no two machines have the same addresses.

The Internet designers were not sure how the Internet would grow. Some researchers envisioned an Internet consisting of a few networks having many hosts. Others foresaw many networks, with a smaller number of hosts connected to any one network. As a compromise, Internet addresses accommodate both large and small networks. They are fixed in size at 32 bits but can be one of three types. Moreover, addresses are self describing; the most significant bits of the address define the type of an address (see Fig. 3-3.) *Class A* addresses support many hosts on one network: The high-order bit is zero, followed by a 7-bit network portion and a 24-bit host portion. In *class B* addresses, the high order bits are one-zero, followed by a 14-bit network number and a 16-bit host portion. *Class C* addresses begin with a leading one-one-zero, followed by a 21-bit network portion and a 8-bit host part. By convention, Internet addresses are given in "dotted notation," where the address is listed as four, dot-separated decimal numbers. For example, 10.0.0.51 and 128.10.2.1 are class A and class B Internet addresses, respectively.

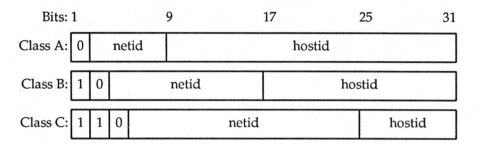

Fig. 3-3. The three formats of Internet addresses

Transporting Datagrams

Internet Protocol datagrams are the universal packet of the Internet, and all Internet hosts and gateways understand how to process them. To send an IP datagram, the sending machine *encapsulates* the datagram inside a network frame for transmission across a directly connected network. That is, the IP datagram is placed in the data portion of the frame, and the frame's type field is set to "type IP." After the network delivers the frame to the destination, the receiver uses the ·type field to *demultiplex* the frame to the software that processes IP datagrams. Because all networks carry frames, it should be clear that, in principle, every network can carry IP datagrams.

Mapping Internet Addresses to Physical Addresses

One problem arises when a host wishes to send datagrams to a host or gateway on its directly connected network: What physical address should the sender use to send datagrams to a specific Internet address? A mechanism that maps Internet addresses to physical addresses is needed. In some cases (e.g., proNET-10), physical addresses are small enough that they fit in the host part of an Internet address. Thus, an interface's physical address can be encoded in its Internet address. In other network technologies (e.g., Ethernet), physical addresses are larger than Internet addresses, making it impossible to encode physical addresses within them.

The Address Resolution Protocol (ARP) is a special protocol designed to solve the problem of mapping between Internet and physical addresses. When a machine needs to know the physical address corresponding to an Internet address, it broadcasts to every node on the network a frame that contains an ARP request that asks: What is the physical address for IP address X? The machine having the requested Internet address sends back a reply that contains the desired physical address. The requesting machine then caches the response, and future mappings for the address occur quickly.

Internet Datagrams

Although they resemble network frames, Internet datagrams differ from network frames in several important ways. The header format is given in Fig. 3-4. Like network frames, datagrams contain both the sender's address and the address of the intended recipient. A 16-bit checksum provides error detection for the datagram header. The checksum does not include the data portion of the datagram and uses 16-bit arithmetic to compute the one's complement of the one's complement sum of the header. An 8-bit type field identifies the type of data that the packet carries and is used to demultiplex the datagram to higher-level protocol software. An 8-bit TTL field squelches looping datagrams. Finally, the header can include a variable length list of options. Thus, the header is not of fixed size, and its length is given in the *length* field. The 16-bit length field allows datagrams to be up to 65,535 octets in size, although in practice they are usually much smaller. The *version* field must be 4.

1	9	17	25	32

version	IHL	TOS	Length	
Identification		Flags	Offset	
TTL		Type	Checksum	
Source Address				
Destination Address				
Options			Padding	

Fig. 3-4. Format of an IP datagram header

To indicate where the header ends and data begins, the header includes a field containing the length of the Internet header (IHL). The header length specifies the number of 4-octet units in the header. Thus, the data begins at an offset of 4 × IHL octets from the beginning of the datagram. Because IP headers consume a minimum of 20 octets, the data portion can contain no more than 65,515 octets of data.

Recall that datagrams are encapsulated within network frames for transmission through a network. Different network technologies place various limits on the size of the largest frames they carry. What happens if the maximum frame size is smaller than the size of the IP datagram? One possible solution limits the datagram size to that of the smallest frame. Such a solution is unattractive, however, because network performance is more efficient when using large packets. Another alternative, dictating specifications of network technologies and forcing them to conform to some minimum standard, is unattractive because it places restrictions on who can be part of the internet.

Internet designers solved this problem by allowing datagram sizes to be independent of frame sizes. When a datagram must be sent through networks that carry small frames, gateways *fragment* the datagram into several smaller datagrams such that each fragment fits within a frame. A fragmented datagram is still a complete datagram, but the destination machine must recombine the individual fragments back into one datagram before passing it to higher-layer software. Each fragment duplicates the header of the original datagram but includes only part of the data. When a datagram must be fragmented, the gateway sets the more fragments (MF) bit in the *flags* field of the header for each fragment except the last and updates the fragment *offset* field to indicate where the fragment fits in the original datagram.

The Internet software at the destination machine checks incoming datagrams for fragments. If the MF bit is not set, and the frag offset field is zero, the datagram contains the first and last fragment — that is, the datagram was not fragmented at all. If either the MF bit is set or the frag offset field is nonzero, the incoming datagram is a fragment that must be combined with its other fragments. One piece of information is still missing: How can the destination associate a fragment with its siblings? Fragmented datagrams from different sources are distinguished by source address. But what about datagrams sharing the same source? The *ident* field in the header identifies siblings of a fragmented datagram. Each sibling fragment of a datagram has the same ident field. The sender assigns a different identification value to each sent datagram. Typically, the sender maintains a counter that it increments when it sends a datagram.

Finally, datagrams can request special processing, such as low delay or high throughput, by setting the type-of-service (TOS) field. Currently, few gateways implement type of service requests, although there is considerable consensus that such gateways should be deployed soon.

Routing

When a host has a datagram to send, one of two actions takes place. If the host is on the same network as the destination, the host encapsulates the datagram in a network frame and sends it directly to the destination. Otherwise, the datagram is sent to a gateway on the directly connected network.

Forwarding datagrams through an Internet is a complex task because the sender and destination may be separated by many gateways and networks. To simplify the task, the forwarding operation is divided into two steps. First, gateways route the datagram based only on the network portion of its destination address. Then, once the datagram reaches a gateway that connects to the destination network, the gateway delivers it directly to the destination.

To forward datagrams properly, gateways must have knowledge about the topology of the Internet. Typically, gateways store topology information in the form of a *routing table*, with entries keyed on destination IP addresses. Each entry in the table consists of a destination address, gateway address, and pointer to the directly connected network the gateway resides on. When a datagram arrives at a gateway, the gateway consults the routing table and selects the interface the datagram should be sent on. The gateway then invokes the output routine of the interface, passing the datagram and destination Internet address as arguments. If the datagram is destined for a host on the directly connected network, the destination argument will be the destination address in the datagram. Otherwise, the destination will be another gateway.

Usually, gateways run dynamic, distributed *routing protocols* that exchange information about the current state of the network. As the topology changes, the gateway updates its routing tables to reflect current topology. One popular routing protocol is the *Routing Interchange Protocol* (RIP) used by the UNIX routing daemon *routed*.

ICMP

The Internet Control Message Protocol (ICMP) allows gateways and hosts to exchange bootstrapping information and report errors encountered while processing datagrams. Although ICMP uses the basic transport of IP as if it were a higher-level protocol, ICMP is an integral part of IP and must be implemented by every IP module. Gateways send ICMP messages when they cannot deliver a datagram or to direct a host to use another gateway. Hosts send ICMP messages to test liveness of the network.

One useful diagnostic utility is the UNIX `ping` program, which sends ICMP *echo request* messages to a specified machine. Upon receipt of an echo request, the destination returns an ICMP *echo reply*. Ping provides two benefits: It checks that a target machine is up and functioning properly, and it tests the path leading to the destination. Ping tests both hosts and gateways.

Hosts and gateways generate ICMP error messages when they encounter difficulty processing a datagram. If a gateway must discard a datagram for lack of resources, it sends a *source quench* to the datagram's source. If a gateway cannot deliver a datagram because the destination is down or no route exists, it returns a *destination unreachable* to the sender. ICMP error messages include the Internet header of the datagram that triggered the error. On receipt of an ICMP error message, a host inspects the returned header to determine which destination is causing the difficulty.

◆ Transmission Control Protocol ◆

In the previous section, we showed how the Internet Protocol provides a virtual packet-switched network. Hosts connected to the internet can exchange datagrams with any other host in the Internet. This section focuses on the Transmission Control Protocol (TCP), a protocol that transforms the raw datagram oriented service of IP—in which datagrams may be lost, duplicated, or reordered—into a full-duplex, reliable character stream.

At the highest level, application programs often need to send large quantities of data from one computer to another. One goal of the Internet Protocols is to provide powerful, easy-to-use communication facilities that allow programmers to write such applications. One convenient service is *reliable stream service,* which takes a stream of 8-bit octets and presents it to the remote application in exactly the same order generated by the sending application. Stream service is well understood—many applications process files sequentially.

TCP provides reliable stream service between applications running on different machines. It provides applications with an error-free, full-duplex communication channel. TCP handles all the details of recovering lost packets and insuring the integrity of the data. Applications using TCP *open* connections to remote applications, send and receive data, and *close* the connection when they have finished their exchange. Typically, one application acts as a *server*, waiting for remote applications to open connections to it, while the other is an active *client* that actually initiates communication.

TCP divides the input stream into *segments* small enough to fit inside IP datagrams. IP then carries the individual datagrams to the destination TCP. To overcome the unreliability of the internet delivery service, TCP uses the *acknowledgment-with- retransmission* paradigm. Each segment contains a sequence number that identifies the data carried in the segment. Upon receipt of a segment, the receiving TCP returns to the sender an *acknowledgment* that identifies which segment was received. If the sender does not receive an acknowledgment after waiting a short while, it assumes that the data was lost and retransmits it.

Sliding Window Protocols

TCP belongs to a class of protocols called *sliding window protocols* because a *window* identifies data that the sender has transmitted, but the receiver has not yet acknowledged. When the sender receives an acknowledgment for data not previously acknowledged, the window *advances*, exposing new data to transmit. Fig. 3-5a shows a sliding window protocol with four packets in the sender's window, and Fig. 3-5b shows the sliding window after the sender receives acknowledgments for packets 1 and 2.

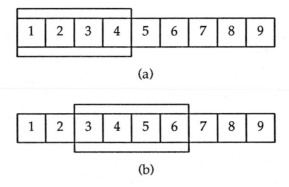

(a)

(b)

Fig. 3-5. A sliding window protocol

The simplest form of a sliding window protocol is called a *stop-and-wait protocol* because only one packet can be in transmission at a time. The sender transmits a single packet and then stops and waits for its acknowledgment. The disadvantage with stop-and-wait protocols is that they do not take full advantage of network capabilities. For instance, most networks can carry data in both directions simultaneously, yet the stop-and-wait protocols transmit data in only one direction at a time. First the packet travels to the destination, then its acknowledgment travels back.

To improve throughput, the sender increases the size of its window, allowing it to have multiple packets in transmission simultaneously. Conceptually, each packet is transmitted and acknowledged separately. While the throughput of stop-and-wait protocols is fixed at one packet per round trip time, the throughput of sliding window protocols is determined by the window size divided by the round trip time.

TCP Segment Format

The format of a TCP segment is given in Fig. 3-6. Like IP datagrams, the segment header contains 20 octets of fixed fields, followed by a list of 0 or more options. The 4-bit *offset* field indicates where the header ends and the data begins. The offset is given in 4-octet units, and the options list is padded to make the header length an even multiple of 4 octets. The segment header does not include a length field; the length of the segment is determined from the length of the data part of the IP datagram carrying the segment. The remaining fields are discussed in the following subsections.

1	9	17	25	32

Source Port		Destination Port	
Sequence Number			
Acknowledgment Number			
Offset	Reserved	Control	Window
Checksum		Urgent Pointer	
TCP Options			Padding
... up to 65,515 Octets of Data ...			

Fig. 3-6. Format of a TCP segment

Ports

If applications are to communicate, they must be able to name one another. That is, an application must be able to specify *who* it wants to communicate with. From TCP's perspective, TCP software must be able to demultiplex arriving segments to their corresponding connections. One possibility is to use the source and destination IP addresses of the two endpoints. IP addresses are not enough, however, because we want to allow multiple TCP connections between the same hosts. TCP uses *ports* to solve the addressing problem. Each end of a TCP connection is identified by its IP address and a 16-bit port number. One point that should be noted is that it takes *both* ends of a connection to identify specific connections uniquely.

Ports name services, and clients typically connect to servers at *well-known ports*. Well-known ports are fixed and rarely (if ever) change, making them safe to use as constants in programs. Moreover, a central authority registers well-known ports, assuring that no two services have the same port number. Standard applications such as mail and remote login all use well-known ports.

Often, an application does not care what port numbers it uses. Specifically, the client opening a connection cares only about the port number of the remote server. Thus, it may use any unused port number for its source port. This does not mean that the source port is unimportant, however. The remote TCP uses both the source and destination port numbers to identify connections. Indeed, a server can support an unlimited number of connections using the same *local* port number, because the remote ends of the connections will have different Internet address and port number combinations.

Sequence Numbers and Segments

Applications hand TCP a stream of octets that TCP divides into a sequence of segments small enough to fit into IP datagrams. To maximize flexibility, TCP associates sequence numbers with each octet of data rather than with segments themselves. One advantage of this style concerns retransmissions. If several segments are lost, TCP can coalesce into a single segment all the data originally sent in separate segments, reducing the number of retransmissions.

TCP uses 32-bit sequence numbers. The *sequence number* field in the segment header gives the position within the data stream of the first data octet in the segment. On receipt of a segment containing data, the recipient TCP returns an acknowledgment. TCP uses *cumulative* acknowledgments. Rather than identifying the data just received, the acknowledgment gives the position within the data stream of the lowest-numbered octet that the receiver has not yet received. That is, the *acknowledgment* (ACK) field identifies the highest sequence number for which all earlier data has been received. Thus, if one segment is lost, and subsequent ones reach the destination, returned acknowledgments point to the missing segment, even though some higher-numbered data has been received.

TCP is allowed to break up the octet stream any way it chooses, and it may delay sending data in order to collect data from subsequent write calls into a single segment. Reducing the number of segments is important because it decreases the cost of processing data. Likewise, the receiving TCP may also buffer data before passing it up to the application, allowing it to pass efficiently data received in multiple segments to the application in one operation.

Some applications, especially those that provide interactive service, send single characters at a time. If TCP delays sending interactive data, responsiveness of the application might be unacceptably reduced. TCP solves this problem by providing applications a way to signal TCP that it should flush out any data in its buffers. The signaling mechanism is a *push* option used when applications write data. The push option directs the sending TCP to transmit all data in its buffers. In addition, the sending TCP sets the *push* bit in the *control* field of the segment header, which forces the receiving TCP to pass any buffered data to the remote application. Note that the push operation does not provide a way to specify record boundaries; it simply forces any buffered data to be delivered to the remote application.

Establishing Connections

To support the client-server model of communication, TCP provides applications two types of connection open operations. Server applications issue *passive opens* when they are willing to accept connections from remote applications. Clients connect to servers by issuing *active opens* that specify the remote server they wish to connect to.

TCP uses a three-way handshake to establish connections (see Fig. 3-7). TCP uses the SYN bit in the control field of the segment header to establish initial sequence numbers. The first segment of the handshake sets the SYN bit in the control field. The first SYN segment does not acknowledge any data. TCP uses the ACK bit in the control field to indicate when the *acknowledgment* field is meaningful. The ACK bit is unused only when the connection is being established. The second segment sent has both the SYN bit and the ACK bit set; the ACK field acknowledges receipt of the first SYN. The third segment simply acknowledges the second segment. Usually, a client opens a connection to a server that has issued a passive open. However, the three-way handshake is cleverly designed to function properly even if both ends simultaneously issue an active open.

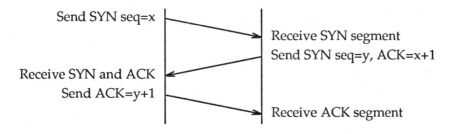

Fig. 3-7. The three-way TCP handshake

The three-way handshake serves two important purposes. First, it guarantees that both ends of the connection are ready to send and receive data. Second, it establishes initial sequence numbers to use. Each end of the connection chooses its own initial sequence number. Sequence numbers do not need to start at 1; in fact, they rarely do.

Terminating Connections

When two applications have finished exchanging data, they *close* the connection. When an application program tells TCP that it has no more data to send, the sending TCP sets the FIN bit in the control field of the segment header and transmits any remaining data. The remote TCP acknowledges the FIN and signals the application that no more data is available (e.g., through UNIX's end-of-file mechanism).

Recall that TCP connections are full duplex, carrying data simultaneously in both directions. When the sending TCP closes a connection, it is prohibited from sending any more data. The remote TCP may continue transmitting, however, and the sender must continue to accept data until both ends of the connection issue closes. A connection in which data is allowed to flow only in one direction is called *half-open*.

TCP uses the FIN mechanism to terminate connections gracefully. In some cases, however, a connection cannot be closed gracefully. For instance, consider the case where a host at one end of a connection fails. After the host reboots, all state information about active TCP connections will have been lost. If a TCP segment from a previous connection arrives, the receiving host will be unable to process it. Using the FIN mechanism in such cases is not appropriate, because the remote application could not distinguish those connections terminated by a crashed host from those in which the remote application issues a close. TCP uses the *reset* (RST) bit of the control field to terminate aborted connections. Whenever a segment arrives that is not intended for a current connection, TCP returns a segment with the RST bit set. When TCP receives a segment with the RST bit set, it terminates the connection.

Maximum Segment Size Option

TCP segments can be of arbitrary size so long as they fit within IP datagrams. Although IP can carry segments up to 65,515 octets long, many computers do not have the resources to process segments of such size. More importantly, few networks can carry IP datagrams of such size (yet). Thus, IP will fragment large segments into many small datagrams for transmission across a network. At first glance, fragmenting large datagrams appears acceptable. In practice, fragmentation can cause significant problems.

One example exploits a common weakness in network interface design. Specifically, some interfaces cannot process back-to-back frames that arrive with short interframe gaps. When the second frame arrives, the interface is still processing the first and the second frame is lost. When TCP sends a large segment, IP may fragment the datagram carrying the segment into several smaller datagrams. Moreover, IP sends the fragments in quick succession, resulting in a burst of back-to-back frames on the network. Although TCP will eventually retransmit the unacknowledged segment, the sequence of events repeats itself, and a complete segment never reaches the destination. Eventually, the TCP connection times out.

TCP uses the *maximum segment size* (MSS) option to negotiate an appropriate segment size. The MSS option specifies the maximum segment size that the receiver is willing to accept. The MSS option may be used only when a connection is established, and it is valid only in segments in which the SYN bit is set.

Flow Control

One issue that all transport protocols must consider is flow control. End-to-end flow control ensures that the receiver has sufficient buffer resources to accept the data sent by the sender. In the absence of flow control, if the sender is on a supercomputer and the receiver is on a small personal computer, the sender could easily overwhelm the receiver with data.

TCP uses *flow-control windows* to solve this problem. In addition to an acknowledgment, the TCP segment header contains a *window* advertisement field that specifies how many octets of data the receiver is prepared to accept. The sending TCP uses the receiver's advertised window for its send window. If the receiving TCP runs out of buffers, it reduces the advertised window to 0, and the sending TCP stops sending data. Once the receiving application consumes the buffered data, the receiving TCP advertises a larger window, and the sender begins transmitting data again.

Checksum

The TCP header contains a 16-bit checksum used to verify the contents of the segment header and data. The checksum is unusual because it includes fields from the IP header. As part of the checksum calculation, TCP prepends a *pseudoheader* to the segment that contains the source and destination Internet addresses. Use of the pseudoheader ensures that a segment has reached the correct destination. Fig. 3-8 shows the format of the TCP pseudoheader. The *protocol* field is type "TCP," and the *length* field gives the length of the TCP segment.

1	9	17	25	31
Source IP Address				
Destination IP Address				
Zero	Protocol	Length		

Fig. 3-8. Format of the pseudoheader

To compute the checksum, the sending TCP prepends the pseudoheader to the segment, appends enough octets containing 0 to pad the segment to a multiple of 8 octets, and computes the checksum over the entire result. As with other Internet checksums, TCP uses 16-bit arithmetic and takes the one's complement of the one's complement sum. The receiving TCP performs a computation similar to that of the sender, extracting information for the pseudoheader from the IP datagram that carried the segment.

Urgent Pointer

TCP has an *urgent* mechanism that allows the sending application to direct the receiving application to accept some urgent data. The sending application notifies the sending TCP at what point in the data stream the urgent data ends. If the urgent pointer marks data that the receiving application has not yet seen, TCP tells the application to go into urgent mode, and the application processes the urgent data. TCP uses the 16-bit *urgent pointer* field to notify the receiving TCP of the urgent data. The urgent field is meaningful only if the URG bit of the control fields is set. The *urgent* field is an offset relative to the sequence number, and the actual location of the urgent data is given by adding the the two fields.

To see the utility of the urgent facility, consider a TCP connection being used to carry interactive traffic between a terminal and a computer. Characters that start and stop output (e.g., Control-S and Control-Q) might be considered urgent because the receiver should process them as soon as possible. For maximum effectiveness, the *urgent* facility is used together with the push mechanism.

Retransmissions

One of the most important ideas in TCP is that the receiver returns acknowledgments for correctly received segments and that the sender retransmits segments that do not solicit an acknowledgment. Conceptually, the sender starts a timer when it transmits a segment. When the timer expires, the TCP retransmits the segment. One interesting question is what value the sender should use for its *retransmission timeout* (RTO). If the timeout is too short, the sender retransmits segments that are delayed rather than lost, wasting network resources. If the timeout is too long, throughput declines when a segment is lost because the sender remains idle waiting for the timer to expire. Ideally, the retransmission timeout closely matches the actual value of the RTT.

To cope with widely varying network delays, TCP maintains a dynamic estimate of the current *round trip time* (RTT). The RTT is the time that elapses between the sending of a segment and the receipt of its acknowledgment. Because RTTs vary tremendously, TCP averages measured RTTs into a *smoothed round trip time* (SRTT) that minimize the effects of unusually short or long RTTs. To track long-term changes in the RTT, the SRTT calculation gives recent measurement more weight than older measurements. Thus, as the measured RTT changes, so does the SRTT. The algorithm for computing the SRTT follows:

$$SRTT = (\alpha \times SRTT) + ((1 - \alpha) \times RTT)$$

where α is a smoothing factor that determines how much weight the new measurement is given. When α is 1, the new measurement is ignored; when its value is 0, the new value replaces the previous estimate. Typical values for α lie between 0.8 and 0.9.

The SRTT is an estimate for the average round trip time. However, the RTT may vary significantly between successive segments due to queuing and transmission delays. To take into account normal variances in delay, TCP also calculates the *mean deviation* of the measured RTT from the predicted value. The mean deviation (MDEV) is the average of the difference between the measured RTT and SRTT. MDEV provides a close approximation to the standard deviation but requires less computation. Like the RTT calculation, TCP calculates a smoothed value (SMDEV) as follows:

$$SMDEV = (\alpha \times SMDEV) + ((1 - \alpha) \times MDEV)$$

The final value for the retransmission timeout (RTO) is given by:

$$RTO = SRTT + 2 \times SMDEV$$

When the sending TCP transmits a segment, it sets its retransmission timer value to RTO.

One interesting phenomenon arises when measuring the RTT of segments that are lost and retransmitted. Specifically, the sender has no way of determining whether an acknowledgment refers to the retransmitted segment or to its first transmission. If it incorrectly assumes that the acknowledgment corresponds to the first transmission, the measured RTT will be too large. If it incorrectly assumes that the acknowledgment refers to the retransmission, the sender underestimates the RTT value. Underestimating the RTT leads to the wasteful condition where the sender retransmits each segment twice. Early implementations of TCP suffered from this problem; newer implementations do not feed RTT values for retransmitted segments into the SRTT calculation.

Congestion Avoidance and Control

One of the design goals of TCP/IP was a technology that operates over widely varying network technologies. Indeed, TCP operates across networks having multi-megabit-per-second bandwidths or networks that use low-speed, 1200-baud lines. One consequence of this ability is that TCP must dynamically adjust to varying network conditions. In the previous subsection, we showed how TCP adjusts to changes in network delay. In this subsection, we show how TCP adjusts to changes in the available bandwidth of Internet paths.

When the underlying networks permit it, applications using TCP can achieve throughputs in excess of megabits per second. TCP attains high throughput by generating and sending segments at high speeds. If TCP transmits segments too fast, however, gateway buffers fill and network delays increase. Finally, gateways become so overloaded that they must discard datagrams and the Internet becomes *congested*.

Recall that TCP is a sliding window protocol. TCP increases its throughput by increasing the size of its send window. When the network is congested, however, the sender must *decrease* its transmission rate. TCP reduces its transmission by shrinking the size of its send window.

For congestion control purposes, the sending TCP maintains a *congestion window*. The congestion window differs from the flow-control window because the flow-control window indicates how much data the receiving TCP is able to accept, but says nothing about what the underlying network path can process. The congestion window specifies how much data the underlying network path can carry. The sending TCP always uses the smaller of the two windows to govern its transmissions.

Adjusting the window to reflect current network conditions is a difficult task. When an application opens a TCP connection and begins transmitting data, other connections sharing the network will see an increase in congestion. When an application finishes transmitting its data, network load decreases; other applications should increase their window sizes to make use of the newly available capacity.

TCP adjusts to changes in available network bandwidth by slowly increasing the size of its congestion window when it thinks additional bandwidth is available and shrinking the window by a large amount when it believes the network is congested. Moreover, the rate at which the sender enlarges its window is low enough that it can always believe that the network is uncongested; if the network is congested, TCP detects the congestion and immediately shrinks its congestion window. There are two parts to the algorithm that increases the size of the congestion window. *Slow start* governs expansion of the window when the sender is recovering from a lost segment. Once the sender is transmitting data at the right speed for the network path, *congestion avoidance* takes over. We begin with a discussion of congestion avoidance.

When the sending TCP is transmitting data at or near the network path's capacity, increasing the window size suddenly would lead to congestion. If the window size were never changed, however, TCP would be unable to take advantage of bandwidth that becomes available when another connection closes. During the congestion avoidance phase of the algorithm, the sender increase the size of the congestion window *cwnd* by 1/*cwnd* whenever it receives an acknowledgment that uncovers new data. This slow increase increments the size of the congestion window by one segment every round trip time. Thus, the congestion window increases linearly with time.

The next problem is how the sender can detect congestion. When a gateway drops a datagram, it returns an ICMP source quench to the datagram's source. Unfortunately, not all gateways return ICMP source quenches. Moreover, the source quench itself might be lost. To overcome these problems, TCP assumes that *all* lost segments are lost because of congestion. When the sender's retransmission timer expires or it receives an ICMP source quench, TCP assumes that congestion is present.

When the sending TCP detects congestion, it halves the value of the congestion window and stores it in a temporary variable *ssthresh*. It then sets the congestion window *cwnd* to 1 and begins the slow start algorithm. During slow start, the sender increases *cwnd* by the size of one segment whenever it receives an acknowledgment that uncovers new data. Slow start doubles the window size at a rate of once per transmitted window, that is, once per round trip time.

Thus, the slow start portion of the algorithm enlarges the window exponentially. Once the size of the congestion window exceeds *ssthresh*, however, the window enlargement algorithm reverts back to congestion avoidance.

Slow start addresses a phenomenon common to sliding window protocols that use cumulative acknowledgments. Whenever a single segment is lost, the sender retransmits it and waits for its acknowledgment. When the acknowledgment arrives, it acknowledges not only the retransmitted segment but also the entire window of data, uncovering a full window of new data. If the sender transmits the entire window at once, the resulting packet burst might overload a gateway. Indeed, if the sender just retransmitted a lost segment, the network is probably congested and is in no condition to accept a burst of datagrams, raising the probability that datagrams will be discarded. Slow start guarantees that no more than two segments will be transmitted at any one time.

The variable *ssthresh* merits explanation as well. When the sender retransmits a segment, it sets *ssthresh* to half the value of the congestion window. If a gateway discards a datagram, it must be congested. Before the segment was lost, the sending TCP was happily transmitting at the rate given by the current congestion window. Most likely, network congestion increased because a new connection began transmitting. Thus, the sender can expect to lose half the bandwidth to the new connection. Hence, the congestion window should be set to half of what it was before. Slow start quickly brings the transmission rate to half that before the segment was lost.

Slow start and congestion avoidance work well in a congested network. If the network is not congested, however, performance decreases because TCP assumes that all lost segments result from congestion. Thus, if a segment is damaged during transmission, TCP unnecessarily reduces its transmission rate.

◆ User Datagram Protocol ◆

Not every application finds it convenient to use the reliable stream oriented service of TCP. Some applications want datagram-oriented communication that understands record boundaries. Distributed file systems, for instance, find it natural to operate at the file-page level. The User Datagram Protocol (UDP) provides datagram oriented service. UDP provides connectionless, unreliable delivery service using IP to carry messages among machines. Indeed, UDP provides little more than IP; it adds the ability to distinguish between multiple destinations on a machine and provides checksumming to ensure data integrity. It does not use acknowledgments or retransmit lost datagrams.

Unlike TCP, UDP is not a complete transport protocol. Most important, it does not provide congestion control or flow control. Applications that use UDP must contend with the issues themselves. In short, it provides applications with the minimal facilities needed to access the raw delivery service of IP. Applications typically use UDP as a building block for more specialized protocols. The domain name system, which we will discuss shortly, and Sun's NFS are based on

UDP.

Like TCP, UDP uses 16-bit port numbers to identify the destination of a datagram. UDP port numbers are completely independent from TCP ports because the type field in the IP datagram header distinguishes TCP segments from UDP datagrams. Fig. 3-9 shows the UDP header. The *length* field gives the length in octets of the datagram's header and data. Like TCP, UDP prepends a pseudoheader to the datagram when it computes the checksum. As shown in Figure 3-8, the pseudoheader contains the source and destination IP addresses, the IP protocol type UDP, and the length of the UDP datagram.

1	17	32

Source Port	Destination Port
Length	Checksum

Fig. 3-9. Format of a UDP header

◆ Domain Name System ◆

In the previous sections, we described Internet addresses and how the Internet delivery service uses them to route datagrams to their destinations. In addition, we showed how the TCP and UDP checksum calculation used Internet addresses in pseudoheaders for extra protection against misrouted datagrams. In this section, we show how application programs use the *domain name system* to find the Internet addresses corresponding to machine names. Indeed, few persons want to use Internet addresses directly; they are much too hard remember.

History

In the early days, the Internet consisted of a few dozen sites, and new machines joined the Internet infrequently. Finding the Internet address of a machine was easy; the names and addresses of all machines were kept in a central database called `hosts.txt`. A central site managed the database and distributed copies of it to all other sites. As more sites adopted the TCP/IP protocols, however, it became clear that a centrally managed system was not adequate. First, the number of sites were increasing rapidly, raising the overhead of distributing database updates from a central site. Second, sites began requesting frequent updates to the database that the central site could not process in a timely fashion. Finally, the Internet was evolving from a small set of sites having a few large time-sharing systems to a large number of sites, each having networks of workstations. The Internet had to prepare for a future in which every user had their own machine.

The domain name system (DNS) is a hierarchical, distributed naming system designed to address the problem of explosive growth. It is hierarchical because the name space is partitioned into subdomains, which can themselves be further divided. The DNS is distributed because management of the name space is delegated to local sites that are responsible for maintaining their part of the database. Because local sites control their portion of the database, they can change names and add new machines easily. Programs called *name servers* manage the database. When a client requests the IP address for a machine, it queries the name server at the site responsible for that part of the database. Finally, to offset the effort required to adopt the new system, the DNS was designed to be extensible and to support other types of operations.

Name Space and Resource Records

Conceptually, the DNS name space is a tree, and *domain names* are nodes in the tree (see Fig. 3-10). The tree has a *root*, and a *fully qualified* domain name is identified by the *components* of the path from the domain name to the root. Components are arbitrary strings of up to 63 octets in length; the length of a fully qualified domain name is limited to 256 octets. By convention, a domain name is written as a dot-separated sequence of components, listed right to left, starting with the component closest to the root. The root is omitted from the name. Thus, `wrl.dec.com` and `cs.purdue.edu` are fully qualified names in Fig. 3-10.

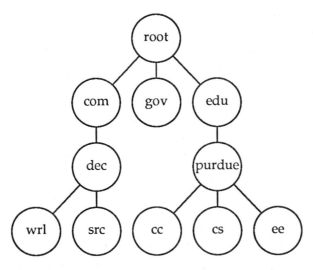

Fig. 3-10. Conceptual structure of domain name space

The DNS links data items called *resource records* with domain names. Resource records (RRs) contain information such as internet addresses or pointers to other name servers, and many RRs can be associated with the same domain name. As shown in Fig. 3-11, each RR has five components. First, an *owner* field identifies the domain name of the RR. A 16-bit *type* field describes the abstract resource contained in the RR. For instance, type A RRs contain host addresses, while type MX RRs identify *mail exchangers*, machines that accept mail. A 16-bit *class* field identifies the protocol family of the *type*. For example, RRs for Internet objects use class IN, whereas the ISO objects might use class ISO. A 32-bit TTL specifies the maximum time in seconds that a server may cache a RR that a name server returns in a query. The DNS relies heavily on caching to reduce repetitious queries. Finally, the *data* field holds the actual information. The type and class of a RR determine the size, contents, and format of the data field.

OWNER
TYPE
CLASS
TTL
DATA

Fig. 3-11. Five parts of a resource record

Table 3-1 shows a sample subset of the RRs found in domain cs.purdue.edu. To simplify the display, each RR's owner field omits the trailing .purdue.edu. The class of all RRs is Internet. The first two RRs, which identify the CPU and OS of two machines, are of type HINFO. The next two RRs, which specify the Internet addresses for the machines arthur and medusa, are of type A. The last two RRs are MX records. MX records contain a 16-bit preference value, followed by the name of a machine willing to accept mail for the domain. When a client wishes to send mail to a site, it contacts mail exchangers in order of their preference until it finds one that it is available. MX records provide a flexible way to identify multiple machines that accept mail for a site.

TABLE 3-1. Sample resource records for domain cs.purdue.edu

arthur.cs	3600	HINFO	Sequent S81 DYNIX(R) V3.0.8
medusa.cs	3600	HINFO	Sequent S27 DYNIX(R) V3.0.8
arthur.cs	3600	A	128.10.2.1
medusa.cs	3600	A	128.10.2.4
cs	7200	MX	10 arthur.cs
cs	7200	MX	20 medusa.cs

Name Servers

Name servers are programs that manage parts of the DNS name space called *zones*. The DNS name space is divided into *zones of authority*, and name servers have complete control of the names and RRs within their zones. A name server is said to be *authoritative* for all names in its zone of authority. Name servers can delegate authority to other name servers for *subdomains*. This allows a large domain to be split into smaller subdomains that are easier to manage. For instance, large universities might have subdomains for each of its schools or departments.

Name servers are linked by pointers. When a name server delegates authority, it maintains pointers to the name servers that manage the subdomains. Following a trail of pointers, fully qualified names can be resolved starting at the root. When the root name server is presented with a domain name query, the server is either authoritative for the name or has delegated responsibility for the name to another server. In the first case, the root answers the query directly. Otherwise, it returns a pointer to the authoritative name server for the requested name. Thus, the DNS can follow the components of a fully qualified domain name to an authoritative name server for the domain name. One benefit of following pointers to reach name servers is that the shape of the tree does not depend on the underlying topology of the Internet.

To improve the reliability of the DNS, name servers for each zone must be replicated at least twice. To minimize the impact of network and gateway failures, backup name servers are located at different sites. Typically, one server is designated the *master*, and the others are designated *slaves*. Slave servers periodically contact the master server to get updates to the zone database. Updates are called *zone transfers*. The distinction between master and slave servers is relevant only for processing zone updates; both slave and master servers are authoritative for their domains.

Queries

Clients use *queries* to extract information from name servers. Queries containing questions are carried to name servers in UDP datagrams. The DNS supports two types of queries. When a client issues *recursive queries*, the server must contact any other servers needed to satisfy the questions. Usually, clients issue *iterative queries*. If the server cannot itself answer a query, it returns pointers to other name servers that can, and the client issues any necessary follow-up queries. Recursive queries are useful for small systems that cannot support a complete DNS implementation, but iterative queries are preferred because they place less load on a server.

```
┌─────────────────────────────┐
│          QUESTION           │
├─────────────────────────────┤
│           ANSWER            │
├─────────────────────────────┤
│          AUTHORITY          │
├─────────────────────────────┤
│          ADDITIONAL         │
└─────────────────────────────┘
```

Fig. 3-12. Four parts of DNS query

Fig. 3-12 shows the general outline of query formats. A *question section* contains the type and class of the desired RR and requests iterative or recursive queries. The server returns the matching RRs in the *answer section*. When a server cannot answer a query, it fills the *authority section* with pointers to name servers that can. Finally, the server uses the *additional section* to append "hints" that might suppress follow-up questions. If the server fills the authority section with pointers to other name servers, for instance, it also places the internet addresses of the servers in the additional section under the assumption that the client will need the address to contact the server.

Resolvers

Resolvers are programs that query name servers on behalf of clients. Applications typically access resolvers through a subroutine or system call. Usually, the resolver is located on the same machine as the client and contacts any name servers needed to satisfy a request. One important goal of the resolver is to reduce the load on name servers by caching the results of frequently asked questions. By handling the requests of all the users on a machine, the resolver builds a cache that reduces the number of queries that it sends to other servers and helps the resolver answer queries quickly.

Application Software

One drawback of the DNS is that applications based on the original `hosts.txt` database have to be modified to use the DNS. In particular, simply modifying key procedures (e.g., the routine for mapping host names to addresses) is not sufficient. Because of its distributed nature, the DNS cannot always retrieve the requested information. Thus, applications have to deal with the concept of *soft errors*. Soft errors indicate that a request cannot be completed at the current time but should be issued again later. Mailers, for example, should not discard mail when it encounters soft errors. They should queue the message temporarily, and try again later.

◆ Application-Level Services ◆

So far, we have described how Internet protocols transform a collection of networks into a single virtual network. The real benefits of internetworking, of course, result when applications use the network to provide services that foster rapid exchange of information and give users access to remote resources. In theory, users are no longer limited to working on a single machine; they can access files located on remote machines, execute commands on remote machines, and exchange mail with other persons on the internet. In this section, we describe three important services that address these desires: remote login, file transfer, and electronic mail.

Remote Login

Before networking, users were restricted to working on those machines to which they had physical access. In network environments, transport protocols provide *virtual* connections that replace the need for direct physical connections. Remote login service is the logical extension of the model in which terminals physically connect to one machine. The user executes a client program that establishes a TCP connection to a server on the remote host, and the client sends keystrokes to the server and reads responses that the server sends back.

The Internet provides a simple remote terminal protocol called *TELNET*. TELNET allows a user at one site to establish a TCP connection to a login server at another, and it passes keystrokes from one machine to the other. Although not as sophisticated as alternative protocols, it is widely implemented. TELNET provides three main services. First, it defines a *network virtual terminal* interface standard upon which applications programs can be built. Second, it provides a way for a client and server to negotiate options and provides a standard set of options. For instance, one option specifies 7-bit ASCII or 8-bit binary data. Finally, TELNET treats each end of the connection symmetrically. Instead of designating one end of the connection as the terminal, either end can be a program.

Conceptually, a client application communicates with the TELNET process on the local machine that transfers the data to the remote TELNET server, and the remote application accepts data from the TELNET server on its machine (see Fig. 3-13). To hide the details of the interface between an application and TELNET, UNIX provides an abstraction called a *pseudo tty*. Applications use pseudo ttys as if they were real terminal devices, but they are actually implemented in software. Often, applications are completely unaware that they are using a pseudo tty rather than a real device.

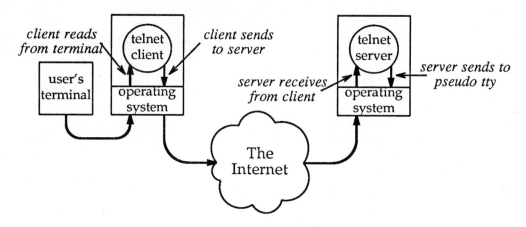

Fig. 3-13. The path of data in a TELNET remote terminal session

rlogin

Berkeley UNIX provides a remote login service, rsh, that understands a set of trusted hosts. It allows system administrators to define a set of machines over which file-access permissions and login names are globally shared and dispenses with the need for users to present passwords each time they access remote resources. In addition, users can grant other users access to their accounts by naming the account and remote machine of the other user.

Having transparent access verification makes it easy to use network services. With the rsh remote shell utility, for instance, users can execute commands on remote machines almost as easily as on a local machine. For instance, issuing:

```
% rsh arthur ls
```

executes the UNIX ls command on machine arthur. rsh uses the invoker's account on the remote machine and executes commands in the account's home directory.

rsh's related service, rlogin, is the UNIX equivalent of TELNET. Because the rsh protocols assume that both ends of the connection are UNIX environments, they are more general purpose than protocols like TELNET. Unlike TELNET, for instance, rlogin understands terminal control functions like flow-control characters (e.g., Control-S and Control-Q). The client rlogin process stops and restarts output immediately, while TELNET introduces annoying delays because it sends control functions to the remote server for processing.

rsh also preserves separate file descriptors for *standard input, standard output*, and *standard error*. It uses two TCP connections, one for standard input and output, and another for standard error. Thus, issuing:

```
% rsh arthur cat /etc/motd > temp
```

redirects the output from the `cat` command to the file `temp` (on the local machine). Finally, `rsh` and `rlogin` export much of the user's environment to the remote machine, including such information as the user's terminal type.

File Transfer

The Internet protocols include a file-transfer protocol called *FTP*. FTP permits authorized users to log into a remote system, identify themselves, list directories, and send and receive files. Although FTP is often used to transfer files interactively, it is actually designed to be used by programs. It can transfer simple text files or executable binaries.

FTP is more complex than protocols like TELNET. First, FTP allows third-party transfers, where one machine initiates a transfer between two other remote machines. Second, FTP uses two separate TCP connections, one for control commands and the other for data. Finally, FTP uses the TELNET protocols for its command channel. The main advantage of using TELNET for the control channel is that it provides an authentication system that the client uses to identify itself to the remote server.

Through a service called *anonymous FTP*, FTP makes it possible for sites to easily distribute software to other sites. In UNIX, a systems administrator creates a special account having login id "anonymous" that requires no password to use. Users copy the files that they want to make available into the special directory `/usr/ftp/pub`. Using FTP, anyone in the Internet can retrieve files that have been placed in the special directory. Of course, clients that use anonymous FTP are given access only to files located in the public directory.

Electronic Mail

Electronic mail is probably the most popular network service. Indeed, many users only use networks to exchange mail. Mail is a popular service because it provides fast, efficient transfer of information. Individual users can send private correspondence to one another or converse with groups of persons sharing a common interest.

Mail differs from other applications we have discussed because it does not have to be interactive. When the user has a message to send, but the destination site is not reachable, mail software should accept the message and queue it for later delivery. Thus, there are two conceptual parts to an electronic mail system. A *front-end* program accepts mail from a user and places it in a *spooling area*, while a *delivery* program removes messages from the spooling area and delivers them to the remote destination. UNIX has several front-end mail programs, including `mail` and the Rand *MH* Message Handling System. The UNIX daemon `sendmail` delivers mail to remote sites.

Before we describe how the Internet delivers mail, we must discuss a related issue—mail addresses. Mail addresses identify to the mail system to whom a message should be delivered. Although addresses in some mail systems are rather complex, Internet mail addresses are quite simple. They all have the form:

```
local-part@domain-name
```

where `local-part` is the name of a mailbox at the site `domain-name`. Although it is tempting to think of `domain-name` as the name of the machine to which the message should be delivered, the Simple Mail Transfer Program (SMTP) actually queries the DNS for MX records matching `domain-name`. Because there might be multiple MX records for a given domain name, `domain-name` represents a site rather than a specific machine at that site.

Usually, mailboxes identify the account of a specific user. However, mailboxes can also be *aliases* for one or more other mailboxes. Thus, mailboxes are often used to identify a service rather than a specific person. For instance, the Internet uses the convention that "postmaster" is an alias for the system administrator in charge of mail. Finally, mail addresses can also refer to groups of recipients. One such mail list is *unix-wizards*, which is the Internet counterpart of the USENET newsgroup `comp.unix.wizards`.

The Internet uses the *Simple Mail Transfer Protocol* to transport messages across a network. The SMTP protocol is surprisingly simple because it deals only with transferring messages between two machines and is designed to run on a reliable stream protocol such as TCP. SMTP provides reliable mail delivery because it is an end-to-end protocol; it uses TCP to communicate directly with the destination machine. When a message cannot be delivered immediately, it remains at the sending host until SMTP can deliver it. End-to-end reliability is important because it allows the sender to check whether the message has been delivered. This differs from other mail delivery systems (e.g., UUCP) that forward entire messages one machine at a time. In message forwarding systems like UUCP, the only way the sender learns that a message has been delivered is when (and if) the recipient sends back a reply.

SMTP is a command-response protocol, in which the sender identifies itself and the intended mail recipients, and then sends the body of the message itself. All SMTP commands generate response messages, which consist of two parts: a three digit code used by programs, followed by arbitrary text meant for humans. Responding to each command is important because it keeps the sending and receiving SMTPs synchronized with one another and permits the receiving SMTP to reject specific commands. For example, the receiving SMTP can selectively indicate those recipients that are invalid.

Fig. 3-14 shows an example transfer between machines `per-cival.cs.purdue.edu` and `gwen.cs.purdue.edu`. The sender's commands are preceded by an `S:`, while the recipient's responses are prefixed by `R:`. The `HELO` command introduces the sender to the receiving SMTP. The `MAIL` command identifies the sender of the message, while the `RCPT` commands specifies to whom the message should be delivered.

```
R: 220 gwen.cs.purdue.edu Sendmail 5.54/3.16 ready
S: HELO percival.cs.purdue.edu
R: 250 gwen.cs.purdue.edu Hello percival.cs.purdue.edu
S: MAIL From:<narten@cs.purdue.edu>
R: 250 <narten@cs.purdue.edu>... Sender ok
S: RCPT To:<comer@cs.purdue.edu>
R: 250 <comer@cs.purdue.edu>... Recipient ok
S: RCPT To:<raj@cs.purdue.edu>
R: 250 <raj@cs.purdue.edu>... Recipient ok
S: DATA
R: 354 Enter mail, end with "." on a line by itself
S: ... sends body of mail message ...
S: .
R: 250 Ok
S: QUIT
R: 221 gwen.cs.purdue.edu closing connection
```

Fig. 3-14. Sample SMTP transfer

Note that the sender and recipients do not have to correspond to the machines that are actually performing the transfer. Finally, the DATA command initiates transfer of the message. A period (.) on a line by itself signals the end of the message. The sender does not consider a message delivered until the receiving SMTP sends back an OK to the end of the data. If for some reason the transfer fails before the sender receives the OK, the sender assumes that the message was not delivered and resends it later. Finally, if the recipient discovers that it cannot deliver a message that it has already accepted, SMTP specifies that the recipient return an error message to the sender (via SMTP).

♦ User Interface ♦

Up to now, we have concentrated on the principles and concepts underlying the TCP/IP protocol suite without giving details on how applications use the protocols. We have delayed our discussion because the Internet protocol specifications do not prescribe an exact interface between applications and the protocol software, and the specific details vary from one system to another. In addition, many systems choose to implement the protocols inside the operating system kernel, making the resulting user interface operating system specific. In this section, we present one possible interface, that provided by the 4.3 edition of Berkeley UNIX.

Sockets

Dating back to the original UNIX, applications use a common framework to access both devices and files. Before an application performs input or output (I/O) operations, it calls open(), passing the file or device to be used as an argument. The open call returns a *file descriptor* that the application uses in future operations. Once the file or device has been opened, the application issues read() and write() calls to transfer data. When the transfer is complete, the application calls close() to terminate the exchange.

Because network protocols are more complicated, the file system model of I/O is not general enough to support network operations. For instance, the read/write model assumes that all data is stream data. In a network environment, applications may want to send variable-size datagrams. *Sockets* are a generalization of the UNIX file access system designed to incorporate network protocols. One important difference between sockets and files is that the operating system binds file descriptors to a file or device when the open call creates the file descriptor. With sockets, applications can specify the destination each time they use the socket. Finally, when sockets were first proposed, it was not clear that the TCP/IP protocols would be universally accepted. Thus, sockets permit applications to choose among several different network protocol families (e.g., TCP/IP or Xerox XNS) as well as among different protocols within the same family (e.g., UDP or TCP).

Applications issue calls to the socket() routine to create sockets. The call has the form:

```
s = socket(family, type, protocol)
```

The family argument specifies the protocol family, while the type argument specifies the abstract type of the communication desired. Valid types include stream and datagram. The protocol field specifies the specific protocol desired (e.g., TCP or UDP). At first glance, the type and protocol arguments appear redundant. However, some protocols cannot be described uniquely by the abstract service they provide. The Internet protocols, for instance, specify several different routing protocols at the same level of the protocol stack as TCP and UDP. In such cases, applications use the protocol argument to specify a specific protocol. When protocol argument is 0, the socket() routine selects the protocol based on type. All three arguments to the socket routine are integers; we will explain shortly exactly how applications map high-level names to their integer counterparts.

Addressing

To support multiple protocol families, UNIX represents all addresses within a common framework. The sock_addr structure consists of two parts: a sa_family field that identifies the protocol family of the address and a sa_data field that contains the actual address encoded in a format understood by the specific protocol family:

```
struct sockaddr {
      short sa_family;   /* address family            */
      char  sa_data[14]; /* up to 14 octets of address */
};
```

In the Internet family, transport addresses are 6 octets long: 4 octets for the Internet address and 2 octets for the port number:

```
struct sockaddr_in {
      short sin_family;  /* address family      */
      short sin_port;    /* 2 octet port number */
      long  sin_addr;    /* 4 octet IP address  */
      char  sin_data[8]; /* unused              */
};
```

Applications issue calls to gethostbyname() to find the Internet address of a host. The call follows:

```
hostent  =  gethostbyname(name)
```

The argument name is a string containing the name of the machine. gethostbyname() maps the request into a DNS query that it sends to the resolver running on the local machine. The call returns a pointer to a hostent structure that contains the requested addresses. The fields of the hostent structure follow:

```
struct hostent {
      char *h_name;       /* official name of host */
      char **h_alias;     /* list of aliases       */
      int  h_addrtype;    /* address type          */
      int  h_length;      /* length of address     */
      char **h_addr_list; /* list of addresses     */
};
```

The h_name field is the official, fully qualified domain name. The h_alias field is a null-terminated list of alternate names for the machine. The h_addrtype field specifies what protocol family the address belongs to, and the h_length field specifies the length of an address. The h_addr_list field is a null-terminated array of addresses for the host. The related routine gethostbyaddr() takes an Internet address as an argument and returns a corresponding hostent structure.

The first version of Berkeley UNIX was implemented before the DNS was in place. Thus, the original routines for mapping between names and Internet addresses did not return soft errors. For backward compatibility, current versions of the routines still return NULL if the request cannot be carried out. To determine the reason for a failed request, applications must inspect the global variable h_error. Upon return from the call, h_error indicates whether the request failed due to server timeouts, or whether the DNS returned an authoritative answer that the name does not exist.

Sometimes, it is necessary to use Internet addresses rather than machine names. UNIX supplies a set of routines for manipulating internet addresses. The inet_addr() and inet_network() routines take strings representing internet addresses in dotted notation and return numbers suitable for use as internet addresses in sockaddr_in structures. The related routine inet_ntoa() takes an internet address and returns a pointer to an ASCII string containing its dotted representation.

Applications issue calls to getservbyname() to find the integer port number of a service. The call follows:

```
servent = getservbyname(family, service)
```

Both arguments are strings. The family argument specifies the protocol family (e.g., tcp or udp), while service is the name of the service (e.g., smtp or telnet). The routine returns a pointer to a servent structure that contains the desired port number. The fields of servent follow:

```
struct servent {
        char *s_name;      /* official name of service */
        char **s_aliases;  /* list of aliases          */
        int  s_port;       /* 16-bit port number        */
        char *s_proto;     /* protocol family           */
};
```

The s_name field is the official name of the service, and s_aliases is a null-terminated list of alternate names for the service. The s_port field is the service's 16-bit port number, and s_proto is the name of the protocol family. The related routine getservbyport() takes a port number and protocol family as arguments and returns a servent structure.

The getprotobyname() routine takes the string form of a protocol type (e.g., tcp) and returns a pointer to a structure that contains the low-level integer encoding of the protocol. The call follows:

```
protoent = getprotobyname(protocol)
```

The protoent structure follows:

```
struct protoent {
        char *p_name;     /* official name of protocol */
        char **p_aliases; /* list of aliases           */
        int  p_proto;     /* protocol type             */
};
```

The p_name field is the official name for the protocol, while p_aliases is a null-terminated list of alternate names. The p_proto field is the integer encoding for the protocol type that can be used as the third argument to the socket() call. The related routine getprotobynumber() takes the low-level protocol number as an argument and returns its corresponding protoent structure.

System Calls

When an application initially creates a socket, the socket is called *unbound* because it has no addresses associated with it. Communication cannot take place on an unbound socket because it is impossible to name the process that owns the socket. Using network terminology, the operating system cannot demultiplex packets to the correct socket. The bind() routine binds an address to the local end of the socket. The call follows:

```
result = bind(socket, sockaddr, sockaddrlen)
```

Argument socket is the socket being bound, and sockaddr is a pointer to the address to which the socket should be bound. Argument sockaddrlen is the size of the address. The related call connect() takes the same arguments but binds an address to the remote end of the socket. If the socket is for a TCP connection, connect() initiates the three-way handshake. For connectionless protocols such as UDP, the operating system simply records the destination address in a control block associated with the socket.

Servers accept connections from remote clients and cannot use connect because they do not usually know the address of the remote client until after the client initiates a connection. Applications use the listen() and accept() system calls to perform passive opens. Applications call listen() to indicate that they wish to accept incoming connections. The form of the call is:

```
result = listen(socket, backlog)
```

Argument backlog specifies how long the queue of unprocessed connection requests can become before additional connection requests are discarded. listen() only indicates that an application is willing to accept connection requests; applications call accept() to accept them. The form of the call is:

```
new_socket = accept(socket, from, fromlength)
```

Argument from is a pointer to a sockaddr structure, and fromlength is a pointer to an integer containing its length. When the call to accept() returns, from contains the address of the remote end of the socket, and new_socket is in a connected state.

UNIX supplies three ways to send data on a socket. The send() call is similar to the write() call used to write to files, but it has one additional argument. The call follows:

```
result = send(socket, message, length, flags)
```

The message argument is a pointer to the data to be written, while length indicates the data's length. Applications use the flags field to send flags to the underlying protocol. Applications using TCP, for instance, use flags to signal the presence of urgent data. send() can be used only by sockets that are in a connected state.

Applications use sendto() when they want to specify the remote destination for each send. The call follows:

```
result = sendto(socket, message, length, flags, dest, destlength)
```

The first four arguments are the same as for the send() call, while dest is a pointer to the sockaddr structure, and destlength is its length. Applications typically use sendto() when they answer datagram queries sent by arbitrary clients because successive replies are sent to different destinations.

Applications use sendmsg() when the data they are sending does not reside in contiguous memory locations. The call has the following form:

```
result = sendmsg(socket, messagestruct, flags)
```

messagestruct is a structure that contains the destination address and describes where the actual data is located.

Along with routines for sending messages, UNIX provides three analogous calls to receive data. Applications call recv() to read data from a connected socket. The call follows:

```
result = recv(socket, message, length, flags)
```

The arguments are the same as for the send() call; UNIX places data into the buffer pointed at by message.

Applications call recvfrom() to receive messages on an unconnected socket. Because unconnected sockets do not have a remote address bound to them, the call also returns the address of the remote application that sent the message. The call follows:

```
result = recvfrom(socket, message, length, flags, from, fromlength)
```

The two additional arguments `from` and `fromlength` are pointers to a `sockaddr` structure and its length.

The `recvmsg()` routine is the analog of `sendmsg()`. The call follows:

```
result = rcvmsg(socket, messagestruct, flags)
```

Argument `messagestruct` is a structure that describes where UNIX should place the received data. The primary benefit of the `rcvmsg()` call is that an application can specify that data be placed in noncontiguous memory locations, possibly avoiding future copies.

Applications call `shutdown()` when they want to shut down all or part of a full-duplex connection. The call has the form:

```
result = shutdown(socket, how)
```

Argument `how` specifies which direction of the connection should be shutdown. When `how` is 0, additional receives are disabled. When `how` is 1, additional sends are disallowed. Finally, if `how` is 2, additional sends and receives will be disabled.

Applications issue `close()` calls to close a socket. The call has the form:

```
result = close(socket)
```

Example Client

The following C program illustrates the 4.3 BSD UNIX interface to TCP. The client uses TCP to connect to a well-known server, echo. The Internet echo server accepts connection requests and echos back all data sent by the client.

```c
/*
 * client.c - Open TCP connection to echo server on remote machine.
 * Copy all data read from standard input to the remote client and
 * echo response read from server to standard output.
 */
#include <stdio.h>
#include <sys/types.h>
#include <sys/socket.h>
#include <netinet/in.h>
#include <arpa/inet.h>
#include <netdb.h>
#include <ctype.h>

extern int  h_error;
main (argc, argv)
int    argc;
```

```
char *argv[];
{
  struct sockaddr_in  sin;        /* socket address */
  struct servent *ps;             /* server entry   */
  struct hostent *ph;             /* host entry     */
  int    s;                       /* TCP socket     */
  int    len;                     /* length         */
  long   address;                 /* IP      address */
  char   buf[BUFSIZ];             /* data buffer    */
  char *host;                     /* remote host    */
  /*
   * check for single command line argument.
   */
  if (argc != 2) {
    fprintf (stderr, "Usage: %s destination\n", argv[0]);
    exit (1);
  }
  /*
   * Find Internet address of host.
   */
  host = argv[1];
  if (isdigit (host[0])) {        /* dotted IP address? */
    if ((address = inet_addr (host)) == -1) {
      fprintf (stderr, "%s: invalid host name %s\n", argv[0], host);
      exit (1);
    }
    sin.sin_addr.s_addr = address;
    sin.sin_family = AF_INET;
  }
  else
    if ((ph = gethostbyname (host)) == NULL) {
      switch (h_errno) {
        case HOST_NOT_FOUND:
          fprintf (stderr, "%s: no such host %s\n ", argv[0], host);
          exit (1);
        case TRY_AGAIN:
          fprintf (stderr, "%s: host %s, try again later\n",
              argv[0], host);
          exit (1);
        case NO_RECOVERY:
          fprintf (stderr, "%s: host %s DNS error\n", argv[0], host);
          exit (1);
        case NO_ADDRESS:
          fprintf (stderr, "%s: No IP address for %s\n ",
              argv[0], host);
          exit (1);
```

```
            default:
              fprintf (stderr, "Unknown error: %d\n", h_errno);
              exit (1);
        }
    }
    else {
      sin.sin_family = ph->h_addrtype;
      bcopy (ph->h_addr, (char *) & sin.sin_addr, ph->h_length);
    }
/*
 * Get port number of echo server.
 */
if ((ps = getservbyname ("echo", "tcp")) == NULL) {
  fprintf (stderr, "%s: unknown service echo\n", argv[0]);
  exit (1);
}
sin.sin_port = ps->s_port;
/*
 * Open a socket.
 */
if ((s = socket (AF_INET, SOCK_STREAM, 0)) < 0) {
  perror ("socket");
  exit (1);
}
/*
 * Connect to the remote echo server.
 */
if (connect (s, (struct sockaddr *) & sin, sizeof (sin)) < 0) {
  perror ("connect");
  exit (1);
}
/*
 * Until end of file, copy data from standard input to echo
 * server and echo copy echo server's response to standard out.
 */
while (fgets (buf, BUFSIZ, stdin) != NULL) {
  if (write (s, buf, strlen (buf)) < 0) {
    perror ("write");
    exit (1);
  }
  if ((len = read (s, buf, BUFSIZ)) < 0) {
    perror ("read");
    exit (1);
  }
  if (write (fileno (stdout), buf, len) < 0) {
    perror ("write");
```

```
        exit (1);
    }
  }
}
```

Example Server

The following C program implements the Internet echo server. The server accepts TCP connections to the echo port, echoing back all data received over the connection. When it accepts a connection, the server forks a subprocess that handles the echoing of data, and waits for additional connections. Because the port number for the echo server falls within the range of port numbers reserved for UNIX, the server requires root privileges.

```c
/*
 * server.c -  TCP echo server. Create subprocess to
 *             handle each incoming TCP connection.
 */

#include <sys/types.h>
#include <sys/socket.h>
#include <netinet/in.h>
#include <arpa/inet.h>
#include <netdb.h>
#include <errno.h>
#include <stdio.h>
#include <ctype.h>


extern  errno;

main (argc, argv)
int    argc;
char *argv[];

{
  int    s;                   /* network socket */
  int    fd;                  /* TCP connection */
  int    len;                 /* length        */
  struct servent *ps;         /* server entry   */
  struct sockaddr_in  sin;    /* socket address */
  char  buf[BUFSIZ];
  /*
   * Get port number of TCP echo service.
   */
  if ((ps = getservbyname ("echo", "tcp")) == NULL) {
```

```
      fprintf (stderr, "%s: cannot get echo service\n", argv[0]);
      exit (1);
   }
   sin.sin_addr.s_addr = INADDR_ANY;
   sin.sin_port = ps->s_port;
   /*
    * Create the socket.
    */
   if ((s = socket (AF_INET, SOCK_STREAM, 0)) < 0) {
     perror ("socket");
     exit (1);
   }
   /*
    * bind address to local end of socket.
    */
   if (bind (s, (struct sockaddr *) &sin, sizeof (sin)) < 0) {
     perror ("bind");
     exit (1);
   }
   /*
    * Accept connections from remote clients.
    */
   listen (s, 5);
   while (1) {
     if ((fd = accept (s, (struct sockaddr *) &sin, &len)) < 0) {
       perror ("accept");
       exit (1);
     }
     /*
      * Create child process to perform work.  Server
      * waits for additional connections.
      */
     if (fork () == 0) {
       while ((len = read (fd, buf, BUFSIZ)) > 0)
         if (write (fd, buf, len) < 0) {
           perror ("write");
           exit (1);
         }
       exit (0);
     }
     close (fd);
   }
}
```

◆ Future Directions ◆

The DARPA Internet is growing at an explosive rate. In the early 1980s, it consisted of a few dozen sites. By the fall of 1988, it consisted of an estimated 40,000 hosts on 500 networks, with an estimated growth rate of 15 per month. The engineering and research questions raised by such rapid expansion are complex. One question that is raised is whether the current routing mechanisms will operate with substantially more hosts and networks. Ongoing research is looking at new routing protocols that can scale to thousands of network.

As the Internet has grown, it has become more difficult to monitor its functioning. Today, many parts of the Internet fall under different administrative authorities, making it difficult to track down problems. *Network monitoring* is an area that focuses on providing network administrators with facilities to monitor and control the activity of gateways and networks. Recent efforts have led to the standardization of the *Simple Network Management Protocol* (SNMP), which allows network managers to monitor the activities of hosts and gateways. SNMP defines a set of objects to monitor and provides clients with the mechanism needed to set and inspect the contents of objects in remote hosts and gateways. Defined objects include such items as routing table entries and counts of ICMP errors sent and received.

As always, new technologies stimulate interest in exploiting available capabilities. Historically, long-haul networks used low-bandwidth communication links. The advent of fiber optic communication technologies, however, promises high-bandwidth, low-error communication links spanning long distances. One question raised by fiber technologies concerns gateway architecture. With low-bandwidth links, gateways have sufficient processing power to switch packets at rates that keep all links saturated with traffic. As the link bandwidth increases, gateway processing power becomes a bottleneck. Can gateways be made fast enough to switch packets at speeds needed to keep multi-megabit-per-second communication lines saturated?

With high-bandwidth paths becoming available, some applications already demand their use. Two interesting areas of research require high-bandwidth throughput. One activity focuses on providing real-time video graphics. Thus, a scientist might run an application at a remote supercomputer that generates high-resolution graphics output displayed on a local workstation. Another area of research focuses on providing digital voice. Finally, *multimedia document systems* focus on integrating text, video, and sound, allowing users to send and receive documents that contain drawings, video clips, and voice clips. Transporting the large amounts of data required to achieve high-resolution graphics and digital voice in real time demands high throughput between applications.

One interesting project conducted at MIT is looking at a new transport protocol that provides high throughput. The protocol, called *NETBLT*, focuses on reducing the impact that lost datagrams have on throughput. NETBLT uses a novel technique called *rate-based transmission*. Instead of using windows and acknowledgments to govern the transmission of packets, an external clock triggers transmission of packets. In addition, NETBLT uses negative acknowledgments to indicate specific packets that were not received.

Another area of intense interest is high-performance transaction protocols that efficiently support the remote procedure call (RPC) paradigm. Applications that access remote file systems, for instance, might request individual pages of a disk file. The application sends a request datagram to the file server that identifies the file and pages desired. Usually, the request is small and fits in a single datagram. The file server sends back a sequence of response packets containing the requested data. The *Versatile Message Transaction Protocol* (VMTP) developed at Stanford is a protocol that provides high performance transaction processing. It provides the efficiency of UDP, yet applications can also specify reliable delivery using acknowledgments and retransmissions. It derives its high performance by sending only as many packets as are necessary. Unlike TCP, for instance, VMTP does not return an acknowledgment for every data packet.

NFS AND RPC

Louis A. Delzompo
Product Line Manager, Networking Products
Sun Microsystems, Inc.

◆ Introduction ◆

Information is recognized as an organization's most valuable asset. In many forms, information is spread throughout an organization and kept within divisions, departments, work groups, and individual user's files. In today's automated world, this usually means that this information is stored and processed on a wide variety of computer systems. Local Area Networks (LANs) were seen as a way of tying these disparate systems together. Unfortunately, information sharing on a LAN was handled in much the same way as paper-based systems: by duplication. This resulted in wasted disk space, poor data integrity, and low information content.

One approach to the problem was the creation of a distributed operating system. This required that all systems run the same operating system, which in practice was just not feasible. The Network File System (NFS) is an independent network service that is designed to be operating system and machine-type independent.

This chapter discusses both NFS and the Remote Procedure Call (RPC) mechanism upon which it relies from the standpoint of the protocol and the UNIX implementation. Familiarity with UNIX commands and TCP/IP-based networking is assumed. The information contained in this chapter is targeted at a user who has some responsibility for setting up and maintaining a network of computer systems as well as those who need to make use of such a network.

♦ Background and History ♦

The Network File System was developed by the computer vendor Sun Microsystems and introduced in late 1984. Since that time, NFS and the underlying Remote Procedure Call (RPC) platform it is based upon have been licensed and implemented to run on over 110 different computer platforms. By Sun's estimate, well over 100,000 computers run NFS, making it one of the most popular networking mechanisms in use.

The NFS allows the file systems of remote computer systems to appear as if they were attached to the user's own local computer. A file system is an organized set of data files, which under UNIX appear as a part of a directory structure. Users of IBM-style personal computers familiar with some of the more popular PC networking products such as Novell's Netware or IBM's PC-NET may wonder what makes NFS special. NFS's design makes it unique among these various networks. From the start, NFS was designed to be machine and operating system independent so that a given computer system could supply files to many different computer types.

NFS was first implemented under Sun's 4.2BSD (Berkeley System Distribution)-based operating system called SunOS. Several ports of NFS to non-Sun environments came soon thereafter. The very first port was to a VAX 11/750 running 4.2BSD. Since Sun's operating system was also 4.2BSD based, the entire port took about 2 man-weeks to complete. Soon thereafter, NFS was ported to UNIX System V.2 on a 11/750, PC-DOS on an IBM PC, DEC ULTRIX on a Micro-VAX II, and DG/UX on the Data General MV/4000. At the Uniforum conference in February 1986, 16 different vendors on five different operating systems demonstrated the ability to share files over an Ethernet.

Today, NFS runs on many more operating systems and computer types. Because of its origins, NFS remains closely aligned with UNIX and the future of the operating system. It is this close alignment that makes NFS so popular within the UNIX community.

♦ Overview ♦

NFS is a mechanism for sharing of computer-based information among computers of many different manufacturers over one or more networks. This sharing is accomplished by allowing users shared access to a set of files called a file system. An individual user's file system can be composed of one or more remotely mounted file systems that appear as a single set of files to the user. The concept of a mount deserves some explanation. mount is a UNIX command used to make a local disk available for use. NFS extends the concept of mount to allow system administrators and users to access files and directories remotely on their machines.

An individual computer system can be thought of as a client, a server, or both. In the client/server model, a client application running on the local computer makes a request of a remote service running on a remote computer. The local computer is called a *client*, and the remote computer is called a *server*. If the local machine is configured with a hard disk drive and makes that resource available to other users on the network, then that system is *both a client and a server*.

NFS is operating system independent by design. To accomplish this design goal, NFS uses a *Remote Procedure Calling* mechanism called RPC. An RPC is very much like a local procedure call in terms of how it behaves and how it is used. Via RPC, a local routine can call and bind to a remote service, have the service perform some task, and read the results. RPC uses another set of routines, the eXternal Data Representation (XDR) library, to account for differences in the internal data representations of different CPU architectures. XDR represents a "standard" data representation that all machines can understand. The NFS protocol is defined as a set of remote procedures, their arguments, results, and effects. The NFS network service can thus be thought of as a library of remote procedures that can be used to access remote files.

Another design feature of NFS is stateless operation. The procedure calls made by NFS contain all the information necessary to complete the call, and the server does not keep track of past requests. This makes crash recovery very easy since no recovery procedures need to be carried out in the event either a client or server crashes. NFS is designed to be communications system independent through its use of the RPC mechanism. Most implementations of NFS make use of the DARPA User Datagram Protocol (UDP) on top of the Internet Protocol (IP). UDP is a very low overhead protocol designed to exchange relatively small pieces of data (9 kilobits maximum) called *datagrams* very quickly. UDP is an unreliable transport mechanism, but the stateless nature of NFS allows UDP to be very effective.

◆ Hardware and Software Requirements ◆

NFS and RPC/XDR can be implemented on a wide variety of hardware and software platforms. Operational requirements vary based on the implementation. The UNIX-based implementations provided by Sun Microsystems are designed to function over a UDP/IP-based LAN or any number of LANs connected by a wide area network. Direct support is provided for both Ethernet/IEEE-802.3 and MAP (Manufacturing Automation Protocol)/IEEE-802.4 LANs. Any network can be supported as long as the appropriate UNIX communication device driver is provided.

Almost any hardware platform can be configured as an NFS client. Diskless work stations are typically configured to run in such a manner. NFS, RPC, and XDR require very little memory above that required by the UNIX operating system itself. A NFS server is typically a fast machine of some type with a large amount of attached disk space. Depending upon the number of clients on the server, the server can be anything from an entry-level engineering work station to a large mainframe computer.

The focus of this book is upon UNIX networking, but NFS and RPC are available on a wide variety of operating systems. To date, NFS has been ported to 4.2BSD, 4.3BSD, XENIX, System V Release 2 and 3, ULTRIX, VAX/VMS, UNICOS (Cray), UTS (Amdahl), AIX (IBM), VM (IBM), MS-DOS, and a host of others. Almost any operating system that recognizes the concept of a file can host NFS.

◆ Protocols, Layers and Error Detection ◆

OSI Model

The International Standards Organization (ISO) is an international standards-making body. In the area of communications, ISO has established a standard communications model called the Open Systems Interconnection or OSI model. The OSI model consists of seven layers, each of which may consist of a type of protocol and addressing method. The goal of the model is to specify that developers of communication products structure their products consistently. Each layer in the OSI model serves a purpose for the layer above it. The seven layers and their functions are provided in Fig. 4-1.

OSI Layers

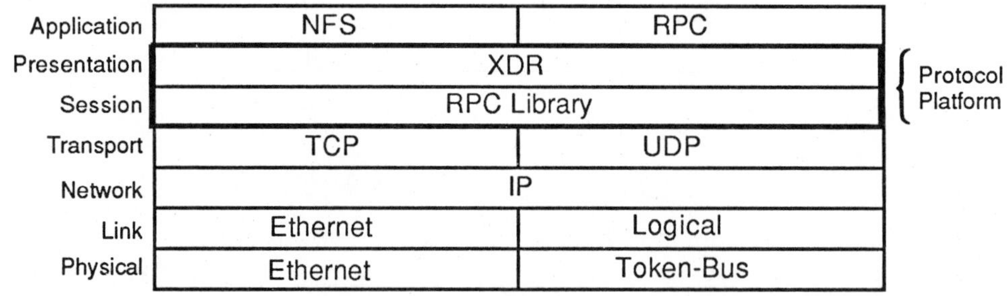

Application	NFS	RPC
Presentation	XDR	
Session	RPC Library	
Transport	TCP	UDP
Network	IP	
Link	Ethernet	Logical
Physical	Ethernet	Token-Bus

Protocol Platform (Presentation, Session)

Fig. 4-1. The seven layers of OSI

In discussing NFS and RPC, we focus on the top two layers-application and presentation. However, it is useful to view how all the layers are constructed in the UNIX environment in which NFS and RPC operate. Typically, the Physical layer is either Ethernet (IEEE-802.3) or Token-Bus (IEEE-802.4). The Link layer protocol is either Ethernet Link or IEEE-802.2 Logical Link Control. The Network protocol is the Internet Protocol (IP). The Transport protocol used by NFS is the User Datagram Protocol (UDP). NFS requires no Session layer functions so this layer is null. At the Presentation layer, NFS makes use of eXternal Data Representation (XDR) encoding. Within the Application layer itself, the NFS view of the world is subdivided into two sublayers—the NFS protocol and the RPC protocol.

Virtual File Systems

To implement NFS, we needed a way to add support for a networked file system to the existing UNIX file system. The goal was to make network files and UNIX files look identical to an application program. The challenge was more complex in that there could be envisioned any number of additional file systems that need to be supported. The answer in the case of Sun's 4.2/4.3BSD-based SunOS was to separate the file system interface from the file system implementation itself. The new file system interface defined by Sun to implement NFS is called the *Virtual File System (VFS)/Virtual File Node (VNODE)* interface.

The structure of the VFS/VNODE architecture is displayed in Fig. 4-2. As you can see from Fig. 4-3, the old UNIX INODE interface is replaced by the VNODE interface. INODEs are still used, but only in the case of the UNIX file system VFS. The file system interface within the kernel is kept at a high level of abstraction.

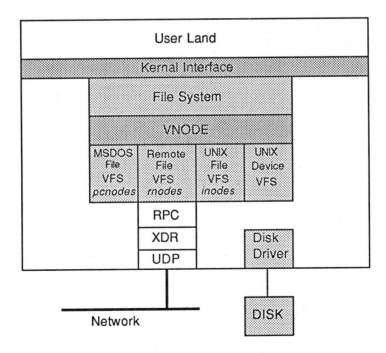

Fig. 4-2. VFS/VNODE architecture

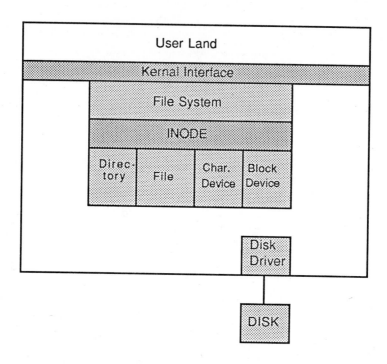

Fig. 4-3. UNIX INODE interface

You can also see from Figs. 4-2 and 4-3 that just as there is a UNIX file system, so too is there a NFS file system. Instead of INODEs, the NFS file system manipulates RNODEs, but the concepts are similar. (See Fig. 4-4.) The NFS file system is described in detail later following section.

The VFS/VNODE interface allowed Sun to create a uniform file system interface within the kernel of SunOS. This abstraction made it possible to achieve the goal of supporting multiple file system types in a generic fashion. Further, it allowed Sun to make network files and UNIX files look identical to an application program.

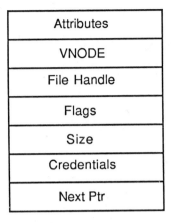

Attributes
VNODE
File Handle
Flags
Size
Credentials
Next Ptr

Fig. 4-4. RNODEs

All system calls that manipulate files or file systems were modified to perform operations on an abstracted uniform file system interface. These system calls now manipulate VFSs and VNODEs. A *VFS* is a data structure that is created whenever a file system is mounted. The VFS data structure is represented in Fig. 4-5. A *VNODE* is a data structure that represents either an open file or directory. The VNODE data structure is represented in Fig. 4-6. Each VNODE associated with a given file system is included in a linked list attached to the VFS for that file system.

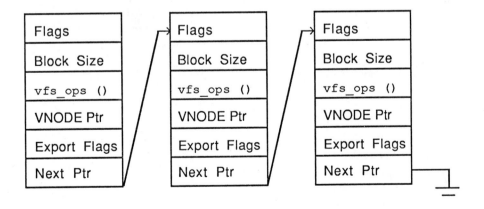

Fig. 4-5. VFS data structure

Flags
Type
Reference Count
VFS ptr (VFS VNODE is in)
VFS ptr (VFS mounted here)
vn_ops ( ) Ptr
Private Data Ptr

Fig. 4-6. VNODE data structure

Actual operations on data are carried out by the appropriate procedures within the file system that controls that data. The VFS and VNODE data structures provide the linkage between the abstract uniform file system interface and the "real" file system that accesses the data. During the mount process, the VFS data structure is created as well as the VNODE that identifies the mount point. A pointer to the mounted-on VNODE is placed within the VFS data structure. Since the mount operation identified the type of file system, the kernel passes the work of creating the VFS data structure and the mounted-on VNODE data structure to the appropriate file system. Within the VFS structure and the mounted-on VNODE structure is a pointer to the set of procedures within the file system that implements the standard set of VFS or VNODE manipulation operations. When an operation on a VFS or VNODE is attempted, the kernel redirects the operation to the appropriate file system (UNIX, NFS, etc.) for completion.

The linkage between VNODE and the appropriate data structure within the "real" file system is a pointer within the VNODE. This pointer, called the *private data pointer*, is created by the appropriate file system. In the case of the Berkeley UNIX file system, the pointer points to an INODE data structure. In the case of NFS, the pointer points to an RNODE data structure. You can now see how the linkage from abstract file system to real file system is made.

Other operating systems include similar functionality to VFS/VNODE. One of the more interesting is the File System Switch (FSS) included by AT&T in UNIX System V-based operating systems. From a functional standpoint, AT&T's FSS and Sun's VNODE interfaces are not different. However, since many other UNIX-based operating systems have implemented VNODEs and the operation of NFS is streamlined when VNODEs are present, Sun and AT&T have agreed to include the VNODE interface in the next release of System V, called System V Release 4. It is worth noting that IBM's AIX operation system includes the VNODE interface.

Old UNIX File System Interface

The old 4.2BSD file system included an interface that allowed applications to manipulate file system objects via system calls into the kernel. This interface, called INODE, recognized directories, files, character-oriented devices, and block-oriented devices as valid objects. This interface, although functional, did not allow for the addition of other file system objects without the relinking of an application.

VNODE and VFS

How NFS works. By allowing machines to share information on a network, NFS performs two major tasks—exporting file systems and mounting file systems. *Exporting,* is the process by which a local machine notifies other machines on the network of the availability of specific file systems for mounting. When the server boots, the `rc.local` shell file runs the `exportfs` command. The `exportfs` command reads the `/etc/exports` file and notifies the UNIX kernel which directories the server is willing to provide access to and what access restrictions (if any) are specified. The mount daemon (`rpc.mountd`) and several NFS daemons (`nfsd`) are started by the same `rc.local` shell script. These daemons suspend after starting and await a request.

　　When the client boots, the `mount` program reads its `/etc/fstab` file. The `mount` program in turn requests the appropriate remote server or servers to provide access to the directories the client has specified in `/etc/fstab`. The mount daemon on the server receives the request and determines if the requested file system is available to the client. If it is, the mount daemon returns a file handle to the client system's kernel. The *file handle* is a piece of data that the client will use to identify the file system to the server whenever any further access is required. The file handle is opaque to the client, that is the client uses the file handle without interpreting the contents of the file handle. It is essentially an address that is understood by the server only. (See Fig. 4-7.)

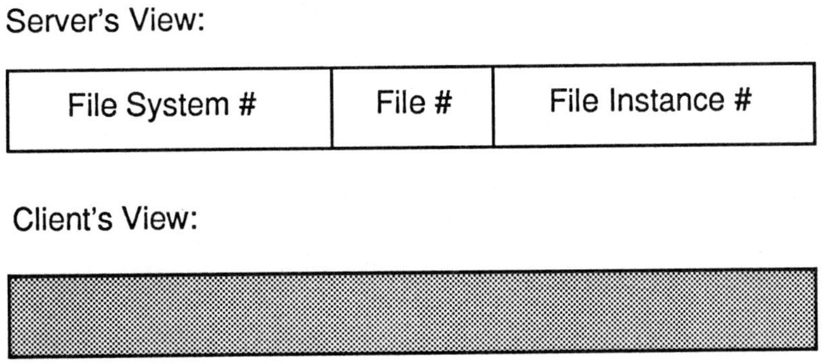

Server's View:

File System #	File #	File Instance #

Client's View:

Fig. 4-7. File handle

Once the client receives the file handle, the client system's kernel passes on the mount request through the uniform file system interface. Since the file system to be mounted was identified as an NFS file, the NFS file system on the client is instructed to create a VFS data structure and a mounted-on VNODE data structure. The NFS file system on the client creates the VFS and the mounted-on VNODE and supplies a pointer to an RNODE. Fig. 4-4 illustrates the RNODE data structure. After the VNODE is created, the NFS file system creates the RNODE using the file handle supplied through the mount operation.

As data on the server is accessed by the client, the NFS daemons on the server will look at the file handle to determine where the actual data is stored. During normal operation, the NFS daemons will continue to validate that the client has the appropriate access rights to the data. The following sections describe the underlying architecture of NFS in more detail.

NFS Virtual File System. The NFS filesystem is a set of operations that allows the manipulation of remote files and directories. These operations are performed on RNODE. RNODEs are data structures that contain the state of the file or directory. As the generic file system operations are passed down through the VFS and VNODE interfaces, the NFS file system is called upon to carry out these operations. Since the actual file or directory is not actually present on the local host, the NFS file system must provide a mechanism to carry out these operations. This mechanism is the NFS protocol.

The NFS protocol is a set of procedures that uses the RPC mechanism to contact the appropriate NFS server on the the remote host, which provides access to the actual file or directory to be manipulated. Since the actual file or directory may be contained within an operating system that is very different from that of the client, we needed a way of identifying the file or directory in an abstract manner. The file handle was created to provide that identification.

To the client, the file handle is an opaque piece of data. That is, the client does not understand the structure of the file handle. The client refers to the file or directory to be manipulated by passing the file handle to the remote system. The remote computer system does understand the structure of the file handle and in turn uses it to perform the required operation.

It can now be seen that the process of moving from an abstract view of the file system to a more concrete view of the file system is possible. It can also be seen that the file handle is a powerful structure that allows a client to keep a consistent view of the structure of its file systems.

Mount Protocol

The mount procedure is a method for converting an operating system specific path name into a file handle. Some operating systems do not provide useful mappings for the UNIX-directory-oriented file system organization. Since this is the case, the mount procedure is defined in a separate protocol from NFS itself. Most implementations use the UNIX mount procedure, which converts a UNIX path name into a NFS file handle. If the operating system upon which an NFS server is based can provide a reasonable way of converting UNIX directory path names into some local file system organization, then the UNIX mount protocol can be supported. If not, then a different mount command must be provided to provide access to that server. This does not affect the transparency of NFS, since NFS deals only with file handles and not with path names.

The UNIX mount command has been extended to allow for the mounting of remote file systems. This extended mount command allows a user to specify the file system type and the remote host name in addition to the name of the file system to be mounted. The mount command uses the uniform file system interface by calling the procedure vfs_mount(). If the file system is an NFS type, then vfs_mount() will call the nfs_mount() procedure. The nfs_mount() procedure makes a remote procedure call to the mount daemon on the remote host specified in the mount command.

The mount daemon returns a file handle for the remotely mounted file system that in turn is used by the nfs_mount() procedure to get the file system attributes and to build the VFS, VNODE, and RNODE structures for the file system being mounted. The VNODE is the abstract view of the file and points to the RNODE, which contains the more concrete view of the file. More information on the actual use of VNODEs and RNODEs in a file access is contained in the next section.

The mount server daemon is an RPC-based service that upon booting registers itself with the RPC server on the remote host and awaits mount requests. Whenever a mount request is identified by the RPC server, the RPC server makes a call to the correct procedure within the mount daemon. The mount daemon consults the /etc/hosts file to map hostid to the hostname and then checks the /etc/exports file to determine whether the requesting host is authorized to mount the requested file system. If the host is authorized, the mount daemon makes a getfh() system call to obtain the file or directory's file handle and returns the file handle to the local host.

File Access

The file handle for the top level of the directory structure being mounted is provided as part of the mount operation. From there on out, the client can traverse the directory structure on the server, manipulate the directory structure, and access files contained within that directory structure by using file handles supplied by the server.

Files are manipulated and accessed by using the set of procedures that comprise the NFS protocol. Many of these procedures map one for one with VNODE procedures, but in some cases the VNODE procedures are implemented using several NFS procedures. The set of procedures that makes up the protocol follows:

- `null()` is provided by all RPC-based services for use as a debugging aid.

- `getattr()` returns the file attributes for the file specified by the filehandle used to identify the file.

- `setattr()` is used to set file attributes on the remote system.

- `lookup()` returns the filehandle and attributes for the specified file "name" in the directory "dir" passed as arguments.

- `readlink()` reads the data in the symbolic link as identified by the file handle supplied.

- `read()` reads data from the remote file.

- `write()` writes data to the remote file.

- `create()` creates a file on the remote host.

- `remove()` deletes a file on the remote host.

- `rename()` renames a file on the remote host. This must be done in a manner that does not violate the stateless nature of the NFS protocol.

- `link()` creates a link to a file on the remote host.

- `symlink()` creates a symbolic link to a file on the remote host.

- `mkdir()` creates a directory on the remote host.

- `rmdir()` removes a directory on the remote host.

- `readdir()` reads the contents of a directory on the remote host.

- `statfs()` gives the attributes of the filesystem that contains the file (file handle) passed as an argument.

The actual specifications for the procedures that make up the NFS protocol can be obtained from Sun Microsystems or off the USENET public network. The procedures are defined in RPC language, and the data structures used by the procedures are defined in XDR format. RPC language is a C-like language used as input into Sun's RPC Protocol Compiler utility. This utility can be used to output the actual C language, including code necessary to implement the protocol. XDR is a machine-independent way of representing data and is used both to describe the data structure and to encode the data to be passed.

Except for the mechanisms of making a remote procedure call, the process of gaining access to a remote file can now be understood. An example of accessing a file on a 4.2BSD file system located on a remote host is shown in Fig. 4-8. The application on the local or client host makes a systems call into the uniform file system layer. To process the call, the UNIX kernel does a lookup into the VFS/VNODE layer to determine the location of the necessary file system procedure. Since the file is a remote file, the VNODE pointer is set to identify the

NFS file system. The kernel is directed to the specific procedure within the NFS file system that will process the request. In this case, the procedure turns out to be a call to a remote procedure located on the server host. Using the RPC mechanism, the client NFS file system requests the server NFS file system to perform the requested function. This request is received by the NFS daemon on the remote host. The NFS daemon then processes the request by using the VFS/VNODE interface to find the appropriate local file system to get the data. In this example, the appropriate file system is a 4.2BSD based file system on the server. It could very well have been another NFS file system that went out to yet a third host for file access. The 4.2BSD filesystem on the remote host gets the requested data and returns the answer to the NFS daemon, which in turn passes the results back through the RPC mechanism to the local host.

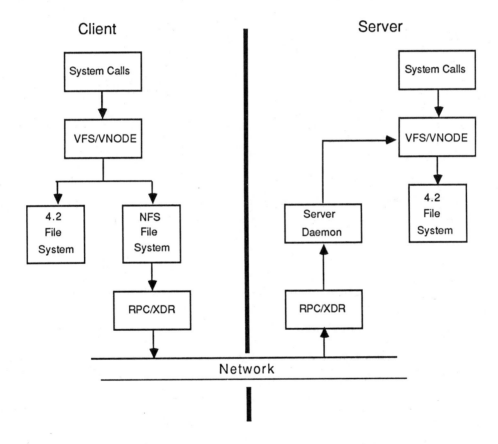

Fig. 4-8. Accessing a file on 4.2BSD

From the perspective of the application, there is no difference between accessing a file off a local disk and accessing a file on the remote host. The NFS protocol preserves the semantics of the UNIX file system access for the most part, allowing a high level of transparency. Exceptions to UNIX file access semantics are detailed in Sandberg (1986) and noted in a following section. Later sections discuss the RPC paradigm and how NFS makes use of RPCs.

UNIX File Access Semantics

The designers of NFS made every attempt to preserve UNIX file access semantics without modifying the server or the protocol when implementing NFS. UNIX allows open files to be removed to allow programs to hide temporary files. NFS converts an attempt to remove an open file into a rename file and then leaves it to the client kernel to remove the file after it is closed. It is also possible to change the access permission on a file after it has been opened, effectively locking out the current user. Since the local file system only checks access privileges on an open, this process works. In the case of NFS, access permissions are checked on every NFS call for security reasons. So, NFS saves the client credentials on an open and uses them to check later client accesses. Some interactions were not possible to guard against since it is not possible to coordinate access to a single file on the server from two different clients. An example is that even though one client has a file open, a second client can remove the file, making all future requests by the first client fail.

Error Detection

Error detection in NFS cannot be discussed without some mention of the stateless nature of the NFS protocol. To say that NFS is stateless implies that each and every operation is independent of the completion of another. To provide a specific example, every NFS write operation is treated as a separate event. This was done to ensure that if a server on the network crashed during an NFS operation, the client of that server could simply wait until that server came back online. Once the server was available, the client could continue from where it left off. In other words, complicated recovery mechanisms are not necessary.

To facilitate this type of operation (as well as allow NFS to work over a wide variety of networks), NFS was designed to require only datagram service from the underlying communications transport mechanism. The transport chosen was UDP. However, UDP does not provide a mechanism for the sequencing of blocks. Thus, NFS was designed to incorporate these functions. So, although NFS is not a transport system in the traditional sense, it incorporates many of the error detection features of a transport mechanism to allow it to operate over the widest range of actual networks.

♦ Remote Procedure Calls ♦

Remote Procedure Calls are a method of interprocess communication over a network. The benefit of RPCs is that they allow a programmer to program at a higher level of abstraction than most network interprocess communication mechanisms. This abstraction means that the programmer need not learn a new syntax to create a distributed application or network service such as NFS. In many cases, the programmer can effectively ignore the underlying communications transport mechanism and its implementation.

This section begins by covering the RPC interface to an application, the XDR layer, and the communications transport. This is provided for completeness and is not entirely necessary to understand how NFS uses RPCs. Next, the actual process of making an RPC is discussed along with the concepts of program/version numbering and authentication. The XDR layer is discussed briefly to show how RPC uses XDR routines to *marshall* data on a network. Marshalling data refers to the process of encoding data in a format suitable for transfer across a network. Finally, the use of RPC's in distributed programming is discussed.

RPC Application Interface

The RPC application interface can be thought of as containing three layers. Each layer offers a different amount of flexibility and complexity. The top layer is called the RPC service library. This interface is totally transparent to the applications programmer. In this case, the programmer makes a procedure call to one of a set of library routines. These routines are in fact implemented by RPCs. As RPC routines are added to a site or network, the programmer can make these routines available to all application programmers by adding a high-level language front end to the routine. To be entirely correct, this top layer is a way of using RPC routines and not actually a part of RPC itself.

Many vendors provide a set of RPC services in a library that can be called from other programs or used as stand-alone services. An example of this is the Sun Microsystems RPC SERVICE LIBRARY described in the SunOS Release 4.0 commands reference manual. For further information contact Sun directly.

The second layer of RPC interface is the actual RPC interface itself. This layer allows a programmer to call a remote procedure without worrying about the details of the underlying network transport mechanism. However, this abstraction is implemented by keeping the interface simple. There are only three system calls provided as part of this interface. The first call is `registerrpc()` which allows a routine to obtain a unique identification number. The second is `callrpc()` which is used by client applications to execute a given remote procedure call. The third is `svc_run()`. A network service makes this call after it registers itself using `registerrpc()` to inform the RPC dispatcher that it is ready to receive requests.

The lowest layer of RPC allows a programmer to exert more control over how a procedure is carried out. For most serious programming, it is necessary to use this layer. The programmer can control the use of timeouts, choose an appropriate communications transport mechanism, allow for flexible error handling, and support multiple authentication methods within the procedure. Programming at this level is complex, but necessarily so. Programmers who use this level of interface will find that they can use all the power and flexibility of the Berkeley UNIX sockets interface. This capability is provided while still working within an architecture that allows the resulting procedures to be very easy to use.

Vendors have attempted to increase the flexibility of RPCs of the higher-level RPC interfaces without decreasing the simplicity. Sun Microsystems has created a utility called the Remote Procedure Call Protocol Compiler, which can automatically create the lines of code necessary to implement a particular RPC protocol or procedure. Users of this utility describe the service or protocol in a high-level language called RPC language and then execute the utility. The output is C language source code that can be included in either the client application or the server.

This utility can be used to bridge the gap between the lowest layer of RPC and the simple `callrpc()` interface. Since RPC is an extension of the procedure call paradigm, it is possible to create environments with very high levels of abstraction that use RPC as an underlying communications mechanism. While none of these environments are commercially feasible yet, significant research is going on in this area. Some of these topics are discussed in the section on distributed programming.

RPC-to-XDR Interface

The XDR library is a set of C language routines that convert data types into and out of a standard data representation called *XDR-encoded data*. Various data structures are defined in XDR language. Then the data in a machine's internal representation or encoding is converted into XDR encoding through a process called *serialization*. The reverse process is called *deserialization*. The XDR library itself is described in more detail later.

This section is concerned with the interface from RPC to XDR. Since the purpose of a remote procedure call is to pass arguments to a remote procedure and receive the results, some data must be passed in both directions. Depending on the type of procedure, this data can either be a small or large amount. The XDR routines necessary to convert the required data are specified as part of the RPC. In addition, depending on the type of communications transport being used, a different type of XDR stream will be specified. An XDR stream is used to specify the type of device that XDR will be sending the serialized data to. With these two pieces of information, the RPC can use the appropriate XDR routines it needs.

The RPC library uses an XDR memory stream type to encode and decode data from a datagram or connectionless-oriented communication transport such as UDP/IP. In the case of virtual circuit or connection-oriented communication transports, the RPC library uses an XDR record stream to send and receive data. Since most current implementations of the RPC library attempt to remain one step removed from the communication transport programmatic interface, you must understand the Berkeley UNIX sockets mechanism.

Sockets are an interprocess communications mechanism introduced in the 4.2BSD release of UNIX. The RPC library implemented on top of 4.2/4.3BSD makes use of two different types of sockets. The first type is a *datagram socket*; it is used to interface to datagram-oriented transports. The datagram socket behaves very much like a block I/O device, which is why the XDR "memory stream" is used to interface to a datagram socket. The second type of socket used by the RPC library is called a *stream socket*, which provides an interface to virtual-circuit-oriented transport mechanisms. A stream socket behaves very much like a UNIX byte stream or file, so the XDR "record stream" type is used to interface to a stream socket. More information on XDR stream types is included in the XDR section.

Communications Transport

The RPC interface to the underlying transport layer is inherently transport independent as specified. This is an absolute necessity due to the variety of transport mechanisms currently in use. However, each underlying communication transport mechanism that a specific implementation of RPC will want to use will most likely have a completely independent programmatic interface. The choice of programmatic interface will limit any one particular implementation of the RPC specification to a certain number of communication transports.

The implementation of RPC in the most widespread use is the 4.2/4.3BSD implementation. This implementation was built to ensure as much transport independence as possible. This is done in two ways. First, the RPC library interacts with the communication transport indirectly via the Berkeley sockets mechanism. Also, to simplify the implementation of RPC on operating environments that do not support sockets, the library code that calls the socket interface is isolated in a separate set of files. These files can be replaced or modified to support other interface mechanisms. Evidence of this is the Lachmann Associates implementation of the RPC library on top of AT&T UNIX System V STREAMS interface.

The 4.2/4.3 implementation allow RPCs to use TCP/IP, UDP/IP, and "raw" sockets. Other implementations are possible, and several more are currently being explored. These "coming attractions" include XNS, ISO, and the System V and BSD shared memory interfaces.

RPC Process

The process of making a remote procedure call is very much like that of making any procedure call. Assuming the simple case, whenever an application needs a service performed, it initiates an RPC. The client application passes a set of arguments to the RPC library that includes a host name, remote program name, version of the remote program, procedure number within the service library, actual parameters to be operated upon by the service, and XDR definitions for the parameters and the results to be returned.

Several of these arguments can be in variables that are supplied by some other source. In the case of the host name, it not normally advisable to hardcode one particular host. Either the host name can be passed as an argument to the client application, the client can consult a network database or directory service, or the client can broadcast on the network for a host name. Each of these methods implies a more dynamic nature to the location of the host to be used to process the service. The program name, version, and procedure number as well as the definition of the parameters to be passed to the remote host are most often obtained by consulting an appropriate documentation source.

The service program can be started automatically using the UNIX `inetd` facility or manually at system boot time by some shell script. The server program calls the RPC library to register itself with the RPC library dispatcher, receive arriving RPC messages, and return results. Registration associates the program with a particular program, version, and procedure number. The RPC library dispatcher remembers this association and dispatches RPCs to the remote program as they come in. The server program also notifies the RPC library dispatcher of which XDR routines to use as filters for the incoming and outgoing data.

As the client becomes ready to send a message, it calls the client-side RPC library. The client RPC sets up an RPC by first encoding the arguments passed to it with the appropriate XDR filter routines. The library then passes the message over the network via a socket and blocks the client until a reply is returned. On the server, the RPC dispatcher receives the client call from a socket, decodes the XDR encoded arguments, and calls the remote program. The service runs and, when complete, returns control to the RPC dispatcher. The dispatcher then encodes the results and sends the reply back over the network via a socket. The client RPC library receives the reply, decodes the results, and unblocks the client program.

Note a few things about this process. First, the entire process is very similar to the procedure calling paradigm. The client program makes a procedure call, blocks, and receives a set of results. On the server, the service procedure is called and returns some results. In many cases, the programmer may not be aware of the fact that RPC is present. It is the levels of abstraction that can be built on top of RPC that represent the real power of distributed computing.

The RPC libraries make heavy use of a unique 96-bit ID that contains the program number, version, and procedure number. The program number identifies a particular group of procedures defined as a service. For example, the procedures that make up NFS are identified by program number 10003. The version number identifies the version of the protocol that the client is using. This allows a particular protocol or set of procedures to be extended and modified while still providing backward compatibility. The procedure number specifies a particular procedure within the program number grouping. Program numbers are meant to be globally unique numbers. Users wishing to create their own network services can obtain a globally unique program number from Sun Microsystems at the following address:

RPC Administrator
Sun Microsystems
2550 Garcia Avenue
Mountain View, CA 94043

There are a couple of commonly agreed to conventions for RPCs. An RPC should take only one argument and return only one result. Also, procedure zero of any service takes a null argument and returns a null result. The latter convention is useful for debugging and administration chores. Other conventions may come into widespread use at some point. It is conceivable that other procedures like the null procedure may be specified to improve the administration or ease of use of all network services.

Beyond the simple use of RPC already described, the RPC library provides several additional features, some of which were just alluded to. Normally, the server does not perform access control. It assumes the client has a right to use its service. Using the features of the lower-layer RPC interface, programmers can generate credentials to be used to authenticate that the client has appropriate access rights to the remote service. In this case, it is up to the server to be set with the appropriate credentials to look for. Broadcasting was described as a method of obtaining the host name to use in a particular RPC. A client can make a broadcast request to procedure zero (the null procedure) for every server on the network. The server to reply first is likely to be the one most lightly loaded and should be used to process the "real" request.

A remote service can also be told to call back a client whenever a certain event has occurred. In this case, the client application will not block awaiting a reply but will, in this case, register itself with the local RPC dispatcher as awaiting a message. The original client, in fact, reverses its role with the server. This can become useful in several different types of applications including network management and systems administration. The lower-level interface of RPC presents some interesting opportunities for users wishing to provide value-added network services to their organizations.

The Portmapper

Communication transports such as TCP/IP provide a method of interprocess communication whereby messages are delivered across a network to a particular address. In the case of TCP/IP and many other protocols, this address identifies a unique host and a unique location on that host called a port. A *port* is a logical communications channel between one machine and another machine. By waiting for messages on a particular port, an application need not be concerned with how a particular message got to the machine. By knowing the individual port that an application is waiting for messages on, another application can communicate with it. Ports are useful in a heterogeneous sense as well. By simply knowing the port number to send a message to, the remote program need not know how the remote computer system's operating system identifies that particular application.

The *Portmapper* is a network service that provides a client with a standard way of looking up the port number for any remote program available on a server. The Portmapper on any one particular machine maintains a database of port-to-program number mappings. Services on that host update the portmap, and clients query the portmap via the Portmapper. To find the port for a particular network service, the client will send an RPC message to that server's Portmapper. Since the Portmapper is always listening at a well-known port number, the client need not solve the problem of how to find the Portmapper. The Portmapper will return the correct port for the program number in question.

Like all RPC services, the Portmapper is implemented by a set of procedures that can be called over the network. The procedures are 0, null; 1, set (add entry); 2, unset (remove entry); 3, getport; 4, dump (get all entries); and 5, callit (call the remote procedure). It is possible to do an indirect RPC through the Portmapper using callit. The reply to the indirect call will be made directly to the client and not through the Portmapper to improve efficiency. Within the standard RPC library are calls that provide access to all of the Portmapper routines.

XDR

The purpose of the XDR standard is twofold. The first is to provide an architecture-independent method of representing data to be passed on the network. The second is to provide a method of converting an architecture's own internal data representation into and out of XDR-encoded format. XDR is necessary because of the proliferation of machines in the marketplace that have different internal representations for the same data type. The example most often used is integers. Most machines share the concept of a byte or word to describe an integer. However, some machines store the byte or word with the leftmost bit or byte being the most significant and others with the rightmost bit or byte being the least significant. So, while the communications transport mechanism will take care of getting the data to the remote machine, the remote machine may not interpret the data correctly.

Just what exactly is XDR? XDR is a data representation standard, a data description language, and a C library package. XDR is used as a network standard way of representing data. An alternative would be for every machine on the network to understand the representation of every other machine and convert data received from a particular host into its internal representation. This method has the advantage that, when the sender and the receiver have the same internal representation, the conversion step is not necessary and could improve performance. However, as the number of hosts on the network grows, it is far easier to write one set of routines to convert into and out of XDR format than to add a set of routines to each existing server.

The UNIX XDR library converts data into and out of XDR format by providing a set of C language procedures. These are two different types of procedures. Some XDR procedures create and manipulate objects called *streams*. Note that streams in this context have little to do with AT&T STREAMS. Other XDR procedures convert and transfer data to and from the streams. The set of procedures that convert data into and out of XDR encoding are called *filters*.

An XDR stream is a standard interface to a particular type of media. In the context of NFS, we think of network files as the media, but XDR is extensible to a wide range of media. For example, it may be advisable to store data on magnetic tapes in XDR-encoded format if that data may ever be read by a machine with a different internal representation of data. This would ensure that the machine reading the data would be able to understand and interpret the data. The benefit of a stream is that since the stream deals with the actual media, only one type of filter need ever be written for any data type. The filter interacts with the stream interface and the stream itself interacts with the media.

There are three types of streams supplied in the UNIX XDR library. The three are standard I/O, memory, and record. The standard I/O stream connects a filter to a C language standard I/O file. This is useful for programs such as databases or spreadsheets where the data being written may be accessed by several different machines of a different type. The memory stream connects a filter to a block of memory that might be shared by two processes. The main use of memory streams is to provide communication over datagram-oriented transports since the memory stream can write data to a memory area such as a buffer. When the buffer fills, the block can be passed as a unit to the transport. The final stream type is record oriented. This type of stream allows a filter to pass/receive en/decoded data that is delimited into records. This is useful for virtual circuit-oriented protocols since the filter must be able to identify the data being sent. It is possible for programmers to construct their own stream types for dealing with additional media types. This is beyond the scope of this material.

The process of converting data from an internal representation into a canonical form such as XDR is called serializing or marshalling the data. XDR filters are the mechanism for actually serializing and deserializing the data. A call to an XDR filter both converts the data to be transferred and transfers the data. The UNIX XDR library contains three types of filters for dealing with most C language data types. These filters are broken into three categories—primitive, composite, and pointer. There are primitive filters for the following data types: char, int short, unsigned short, int, unsigned int, long, unsigned long, float, double, and void. Each filter is a procedure called with two parameters, a pointer to the stream to be used (called a stream handle) and a pointer to the data to be encoded (called an item handle).

The composite filter types are string, byte array, unsigned + byte array, any array, unsigned + any array, and enum + union. There are also two pointer filters that are used to construct pointers—`xdr_pointer` and `xdr_reference`. The latter is used when the value of a pointer to be passed is known to be nonnull in all cases. If this is not the case, then `xdr_pointer` is used since an XDR Boolean data type is encoded along with the data to be transferred to identify whether the pointer is null. It is also possible to construct custom filters using the XDR language to describe new data types in terms of data types the XDR library knows how to deal with. This process is beyond the scope of this material. For more information, refer to the Sun Microsystems *Network Programming* manual, which contains the specifications for XDR.

Distributed Programming

The popularity of personal computers and engineering workstations has legalized the concept of distributed computing. *Distributed computing* is a model of computing whereby all users have access to their own computer. However, the ability to network these computers to each other and to powerful systems such as mainframe computers and supercomputers has brought on a new model of computing. *Network computing* is characterized by the availability of multiple computers for a single user. In other words, each application may call upon the capabilities of any number of computer systems at any one point in time. The resource used is the one best suited, relatively, for that task at that time.

To make a network computing a reality, applications must be designed to take advantage of many computers at once. These *distributed applications* parcel various computing tasks out to remote systems for processing. The process of determining where the tasks run, which tasks to distribute, and whether the application is suitable for distribution is complicated. The process of building a distributed application is called *network programming*. One method of network programming is the use of RPC and XDR.

RPC and XDR provide a framework for the development of both distributed applications and network services. RPC is used to provide a message service between applications or tasks within an application. XDR is used to provide network-wide data consistency. The preceding sections have given some insight into the potential of RPCs and XDRs. The similarity between RPCs and standard procedure calls is the heart of this potential. Since calls to an RPC can be hidden inside a standard call to a library, all the underlying power of the RPC interface can be exploited.

Today, examples of true distributed applications are rare. The creation and use of network services is more common. NFS is but one example of a particular type of service. Computer system performance monitoring tools have been created that communicate with RPC-based services on each machine in a particular network. They allow the tool user to determine the performance characteristics of any machine on the network. Other services include window systems and terminal emulators, which use RPC-like capabilities to communicate between application servers and users.

In the future, many applications will become distributed. Several application areas lend themselves well to distribution. Applications that require access to a database of some type are migrating to a model where the user interface is local to the user and the database access routines are on a remote server. This model leverages the graphics and ease-of-use features of a workstation-like device and the increased security and control of a large server environment. Other examples are calendar scheduling, transaction processing, and computer-aided design and manufacture. The underlying similarity of all these application areas is that the application requires a rather broad set of computing services and that the opportunity for increased functionality through the use of two or more computer systems was readily apparent.

Other applications are not as clearly suited for distribution. However, as more and more specialized processors are created, the likelihood that a particular application can benefit from distribution increases. You are encouraged to continue to research this area on your own and to experiment with the design and deployment of distributed applications.

◆ Administration ◆

The administration of an NFS environment starts with the proper setup and maintenance of the network platform that NFS and all other RPC services rely upon. In most cases, this implies that the LAN has been physically installed correctly, that the DARPA-based network software has been set up properly, and that the proper files have been edited.

The installation of NFS as a server on a particular machine may involve one or more of the following steps. If the machine is to operate as an NFS server, it must be identified as one. Once identified, the server's disk drives must be defined and the location of the shared file systems must be supplied in the /etc/exports file. The /etc/exports file is also used to specify the access permissions of the file systems the server will export or share with clients. If the local machine is to be used as a client of other machines on the network, the local /etc/fstab must be edited. This file allows the local machine to mount file systems from remote servers on the network.

The administrator may need to create mount points on the local machine for file systems that are to be mounted from a remote machine. A *mount point* is a directory in the UNIX file system hierarchy. Mount points can be directories that are either empty or full. If full, the NFS mount procedure will effectively hide the contents of the local directory. In some cases, this may be a way of ensuring that the local system can continue to function even if the connection to the network is lost.

Once NFS is running, changes to the way the local system is to be used may require changes. New systems that need to make use of local data as clients of the local machine may be added to the network. New users that may require access to new file systems may be added to the local machine. Or, the level of security required by either the organization or the local users may change. In most cases, changes such as these require the editing of local files and in some cases changes to the way the NFS server processes operate.

In general, to be a NFS server, the local host must export certain file systems for use by other systems on the network. How this exporting takes place is controlled by the /etc/exports file and the exportfs command. The configuration of the local host as an NFS server is specified by the contents of the /etc/exports file. Exportation is accomplished by the exportfs command. Both the file and command are described in detail later.

If the local host is to serve machines of a different architecture, the system administrator should install binary copies of whatever programs are required by the remote system in the /usr directory in an appropriate file system.

A different set of activities is required to configure the local host as an NFS client. First, appropriate mount points must be created on the local host. If you use the mkdir command, the system administrator will create directories in the UNIX file system to act as mount points. A diskless machine will require a different set of mount points than a local machine, but the process is similar. After the mount points are created, the local /etc/fstab file must be edited to specify the locations of the remote file systems that are to be mounted. Again, diskless computer systems will have a different /etc/fstab file from systems with a disk drive, but the process is similar. The contents of the /etc/fstab file are described in detail later.

The process of mounting a remote file system is accomplished using the mount command. In most cases, the mounting of all remote file systems specified in the /etc/fstab file is done at boot time via a shell script. End users need never use the mount command unless they want to make a change or addition to the file systems in use.

The following sections describe the commands, files, and daemons used by NFS and other RPC services to carry out their work and to be configured. Note that vendors who supply NFS on various computer systems may have provided shell scripts to simplify or streamline the installation and administration process. This text assumes that no such shell scripts are supplied.

The process of adding a client to an NFS server depends upon whether that client is diskless or has a local disk. Since only the most recent NFS revisions support diskless clients, research this process with your NFS supplier. The process of adding a diskful client is straightforward. It is necessary to have superuser privileges on the server. To become a superuser, you must either log in as root or use the su command to change your user name to root. After becoming a superuser on the server, you must add the client's Internet address to the /etc/hosts file and the client's Ethernet address to the /etc/ethers file. Then determine if the appropriate access privileges have been granted to the client in the /etc/exports file. If not, edit the file. Detailed information on the structure and contents of the three files mentioned is included in the following sections.

System Files

The use and administration of the files necessary to have a functional NFS environment in the UNIX environment are described next. Ten system files either affect the operation of NFS or are necessary for NFS to operate. The files and their main purpose follow:

- `/etc/fstab` describes files to be mounted.

- `/etc/mtab` contains a list of currently mounted filesystems.

- `/etc/exports` contains a list of filesystems that are available for mounting by remote systems.

- `/etc/xtab` contains a list of the currently exported filesystems for the local machine.

- `/etc/hosts` contains a list of the known hosts on the network.

- `/etc/netgroups` contains a list of network-wide groups that can be used as a shorthand in the remote mount permission-checking process.

- `/etc/inetd.conf` contains a list of daemons that the Internet `inetd` daemon will invoke when it receives a valid request.

- `/etc/protocols` contains a list of all valid protocols in use on the network.

- `/etc/services` contains a list of services available on the network.

/etc/fstab

In the context of NFS, the `/etc/fstab` file is used to describe which file systems are to be made available to be remotely mounted. The `/etc/fstab` file is normally used at boot time to make available all the file systems the users of a machine are likely to use. The `rc.boot` file also usually contains the `mount` command with the `-a` option. This causes the operating system to attempt to mount all devices and file systems in the `/etc/fstab` file. The file can be thought of as a way of hiding some of the administration of networked files from the end user, since the users may never have to use the `mount` command. Besides `mount`, the file is used by several system utilities to determine the file systems on which they need to perform their operations.

The `/etc/fstab` file consists of a set of entries of the form:

filesystem directoryname type options freq pass

The *filesystem* entry is the name of the remote file system to be mounted. The format for this is *remote hostname:remote pathname*. The *directoryname* entry is the path name of the directory on which the remote file system is to be mounted or made available. The two path names need not be similar or bear any relation to one another. For example, the remote directory `/usr/harry` can be made available on the local system as `/usr/remote/tom`.

The *type* entry is the type of file system. In this case, we are concerned primarily with NFS file systems, so the entry is `NFS`. Examples of other valid entries are `4.2` and `swap`.

The *options* entry contains a list of mounting options separated by a comma. The options accepted for NFS are an implementation issue, but several options are normally provided on all implementations. You can control the mechanism by which a `mount` request is retried if it fails on the first try. The process of retrying can occur in either the foreground or the background by specifying either `bg` or `fg`. In addition, the number of retries can be specified via the `retry=`*N* option.

Another set of options is used to control how NFS responds to situations where the client cannot maintain contact with the server for any reason. The `retrans=`*N* option specifies the number of retransmissions NFS will attempt before it posts a "Server not responding" error. The `timeo=`*N* option specifies the time in tenths of a second before NFS will timeout on a request. The `soft/hard` option tells NFS what to do in case the maximum number of retransmissions is exceeded. If you wish NFS to continue to try the request until the server responds, set the option to `hard`. This has the effect of halting the application until the server responds. Thus, setting the option to `soft` will allow NFS to return an error to the application. Frequently, this causes an application to terminate, but it will allow users to attempt to do some other work. A compromise between the two options is to set the `intr` option in conjunction with `hard`. This server may become unavailable only temporarily while a user is not active on the local machine. By specifying `hard,intr` as options, users will not have to restart their applications when they return.

A final set of options controls users' ability to write to a file system. The `rw` option tells NFS to mount the file system in read/write mode, allowing users full access to the remote files with whatever privileges their user name and group allow. The `ro` option tells NFS to mount the file system in read-only mode. This allows users to read files and execute programs in the remote file system, but not write to, delete, or move files in that file system.

The *freq* entry specifies the number of days between dumps. This is normally set to 0 for NFS-mounted file systems since it is assumed that the remote computer system is responsible for maintaining backup files. The *pass* entry is used to tell the file system check utility, `fsck`, which pass to check the file system on. Again, *pass* is normally set to 0 since the remote computer system is again responsible for ensuring file system consistency.

Note that the order in which the entries appear in `/etc/fstab` determines how `mount`, `umount`, and `fsck` process the file systems. Each utility processes the file systems in the exact order they appear in the `fstab` file. For example, mounting a file system and then mounting another file system as a parent will have the effect of negating the first mount. An example `/etc/fstab` follows:

```
/dev/sd0a / 4.2 rw 1 1
/dev/sd0g /usr 4.2 rw 1 2
viper:/usr/luigi /usr/luigi nfs bg,rw,hard 0 0
viper:/usr/ct /usr/ct nfs bg,rw,hard 0 0
chacha:/usr/ops/bin /usr/ops nfs bg,rw,soft 0 0
server:/usr/games /usr/games nfs bg,ro,soft 0 0
```

/etc/mtab

The `/etc/mtab` file contains a list of the file systems currently mounted by the local computer system. This list is valuable as information for system administrators and users who need to determine which file systems are actually available. The `mount` command issued as `mount` returns the contents of this file to a user. This file is accessed by programs via the `getmntent()` call.

/etc/exports

The `/etc/exports` file contains a list of the file systems on the local computer system that are to be made available to remote computer systems via NFS. The process of making a file system available for remote access is sometimes called *exporting*. Thus, the `/etc/exports` file determines whether the local computer system is an NFS server. The NFS daemon, `nfsd`, is told which file systems to accept `mount` requests for by the `exportfs` command. Normally, this is done when the local computer system boots. `exportfs` is usually included in the `rc.local` shell script.

The `/etc/exports` file is organized as follows:

directoryname option, option ...

directoryname is the path name of the local directory or file that is to be exported. Several options are normally supported, but they may vary depending on which implementation is used. Options exist to control the type of access granted, the remote computer systems who are granted access to this particular file system, and the way requests from root users and unknown users on remote machines are handled.

The `ro` option exports the file system as read-only for all remote computer systems. The `rw=`*hostnames* option allows a file system to be exported read-only to most remote computer systems, but read-write to some. The *hostnames* entry has the form *hostname : hostname : hostname....* Mount access is specified via the `access=`*client* option. The *client* entry can either be a host name or a netgroup. A *netgroup* is a group of hosts grouped together for ease of reference. Each *client* entry is checked in the `/etc/netgroup` file first and then the `/etc/hosts` file. Only those clients listed in either the `/etc/hosts` or `/etc/netgroups` file will be allowed to mount the specified file system. All others can either be excluded or given a default uid to allow controlled access to files.

Requests from unknown users can be controlled via the `anon=`*uid* option. If a file access request comes from an unknown remote user, the local system will use the uid specified by *uid* as the effective uid for that access. Thus, a certain amount of anonymous access can be allowed. Setting uid to a value of -1 disables anonymous access. Similarly, access to a local file system by a remote user having root privileges can be controlled. The `root=`*hostnames* option can be used to give root access only to root users on the specified hosts. Root users are always considered anonymous by NFS unless they are included in the `root=` option.

/etc/xtab

The `/etc/xtab` file contains a list of the currently exported file systems for the local machine. In this case, the machine is exporting a set of file systems (i.e., acting as an NFS server). This file is provided to allow programs to determine which file systems are currently available for mounting by remote client computer systems. This information is placed in the `/etc/xtab` file by the `exportfs` command when it runs. It is used by the mount daemon, `rpc.mountd` to determine which remote computer systems it should accept `mount` requests from. The file contains a list of entries in the same form as `/etc/exports`. The `/etc/xtab` file is accessed by programs via the `getexportent()` call.

/etc/hosts

The `/etc/hosts` file contains a list of the known hosts on either the local network or the larger set of hosts on the DARPA Internet. (The larger set would include the local network.) The file contains a single line per host with the Internet number of the host, the host name, and any aliases for that host. The file is used by a number of utilities. The `exportfs` command checks the `/etc/hosts` or `/etc/netgroup` file in order to determine the Internet numbers of the hosts named in the `/etc/exports` file. `exportfs` in turn provides the NFS daemon, `nfsd`, with those Internet numbers.

/etc/ethers

The `/etc/ethers` file contains a list of the 48-bit Ethernet addresses for all the known hosts on the network. Each host is listed in the file as a single line that contains the Ethernet address in the form $x:x:x:x:x:x$ and the host name. Each x is a hexadecimal number between 0 and FF representing 1 byte of the network address. The host names in the `/etc/ethers` file should be the same as those in the `/etc/hosts` file. The purpose of the `/etc/ethers` file is to provide the actual Ethernet address of a particular host to those programs that need it.

/etc/netgroups

The `/etc/netgroups` file contains a list of network-wide groups. These groups are used in the remote mount permission checking process. The file's entries have the form

groupname member member ...

Each *member* entry contains three fields—*hostname, username,* and *domainname.* If any of the three fields are blank, then anything will be considered a match for that field. If any of the fields contain something besides a letter, digit, underscore, or blank, then nothing will be a match for that field. Typically, a dash is used to indicate this. This may be useful when a host is to be included in some netgroup, but no users on that host are to be members.

Netgroups can be an efficient shorthand for systems administrators who wish to make certain file systems on all servers available to a wide group of users or hosts. Using a netgroup will save the time of entering individual names into each machine's /etc/exports file directly.

/etc/inetd.conf

The system file /etc/inetd.conf is the configuration file for the Internet server daemon inetd. This daemon will start other network service daemons on the local host on behalf of a client request. The format of the configuration file is a list of daemons that inetd will invoke when it receives an Internet request over a socket. Each line of the file has the following fields:

service type-of-socket protocol waitmode uid name-of-daemon arguments

service is the name of the daemon to be invoked. The service must be listed in the file /etc/services. RPC-based services are listed in the same manner, but the version number of the service is appended to the end of the name with a slash (e.g., /1 for version 1). The *type-of-socket* field can be either stream for stream, dgram for datagram, raw for raw, rdm for reliably delivered, or seqpacket for sequenced packet socket. The *protocol* field identifies the protocol to be used. The protocol must be listed in the file /etc/protocols. An RPC service must be listed as follows: rpc/*type of protocol*.

The *waitmode* field can be either nowait for services that release the socket until a timeout, or wait, for those that need to hold on to the socket. RPC service are normally nowait. The *uid* field is the user name under which the service should run, either root or a user name. The *name-of-daemon* field is the path name of the daemon to be invoked, and the *arguments* field are the parameters to be passed to the daemon upon invocation.

/etc/protocols

The /etc/protocols file contains a list of all valid protocols used in the DARPA Internet. Any protocol referenced in the /etc/inetd.conf file must be listed here. The file contains a list of protocols by name with their official protocol number and any alias they may have. This file is essentially a leftover from the days when no reliable name server existed. It is probable that this file will be replaced in UNIX with a name server such as the Berkeley Internet Domain service (BIND) or ISO X.500.

/etc/services

The /etc/services file contains a list of daemons that are available over the Internet or on a user's own network. The file contains a list of services, the port and protocol by which the service can be reached, and any aliases that can be used to identify the service. Like the /etc/protocols file, the /etc/services file is a UNIX relic that should be replaced with a name service.

Sun Yellow Pages Name Service

The Yellow Pages is a distributed name service supplied by Sun Microsystems with its SunOS operating system to simplify the administration of a network of computer systems. A name service serves a function similar to a database in that given a key value it provides a value for that key. Most often, name services are used as a means of translating names into network addresses.

Yellow Pages databases are called *maps*. The Yellow Pages is typically used to eliminate the need to update local files on individual machines on the network by replacing the local files with maps. These maps are accessible by any machine within a particular Yellow Pages domain. A *domain* is a set of Yellow Pages servers that are designated as serving a particular set of machines on the network.

Yellow Pages is a distributed service in that within any domain there can be several Yellow Pages servers, one of which is designated as the master server and the others as slaves. As the master server's maps are updated, the master server will transmit these changes to the rest of the slave servers within a domain through a process called *pushing*. The command yppush is used to instruct a Yellow Pages server to make its maps available to the other servers. Typically, yppush is contained in a cron file to ensure periodic updates. However, the network administrator can force a push at any time.

Yellow Pages simplifies the administration of an NFS environment by replacing many of the local files such as /etc/hosts, /etc/group, and /etc/passwd with maps. Thus, as changes are made to the configuration of the network, the administrator will only have to make the change once per Yellow Pages domain. The format of a Yellow Pages map is identical to that of the file which it replaces except that instead of being ASCII files, Yellow Pages maps are dbm3 files for faster access. Each of the Yellow Pages maps used by a particular server are contained as subdirectories in the directory /var/yp.

The administration of Yellow Pages itself is considered beyond the scope of this book. However, the presence of Yellow Pages on a network changes the way many of the files used to administer NFS are used. The main difference is that instead of consulting the local file, programs normally (with a few exceptions) consult the Yellow Pages maps instead. The files NFS uses that are augmented when Yellow Pages is in use follow.

/etc/hosts is consulted only when booting. After that the Yellow Pages hosts map is used. The /etc/ethers file is never used as is also the case with

/etc/netgroups. The /etc/protocols file is never used as Yellow Pages provides the same data. The /etc/services file is also no longer used.

One other file of interest that Yellow Pages replaces or augments is the /etc/passwd file. Programs will consult the local /etc/passwd file first. If there is a + or – entry in the file, then the Yellow Pages map is consulted.

In summary, Yellow Pages can serve a very useful purpose. In the case of the automount capability described at the end of this chapter, the Yellow Pages service can be used by the automount service to provide the location of file systems on the network. Thus, the entire sharable resources of the network can be made transparently available to all automount users.

If you are interested in learning more about the Yellow Pages service, consult the Sun Microsystems documentation entitled *Network Programming*.

Daemons

/usr/etc/nfsd. The command /usr/etc/nfsd is used to start a number of UNIX daemons on the NFS server to handle client file system access requests. The command has the form

    /usr/etc/nfsd [*number of servers*]

The number of servers is a function of the amount of load a server is expected to handle. A rule of thumb is to start with four daemons and adjust the number upward if needed. The nfsd daemon serves as a user application entry point into the kernel-based NFS server. Support for multiple daemons provides for parallelism and improves overall response time.

/usr/etc/biod. The /usr/etc/biod command is used to start a number of asynchronous block I/O daemons on an NFS client. The biod daemons allow a client to make read-ahead and write-behind requests to a remote file system. The biod buffers these requests on the client to improve the overall performance of NFS. The biod command has the form

    /usr/etc/biod [*number of daemons*]

Again, a good rule of thumb to start with four biod daemons and adjust upward if necessary.

/usr/etc/rpc.mountd. The mountd daemon responds to requests from remote computer systems to mount a local file system. mountd is an RPC-based service that performs three services. First, mountd checks the /etc/xtab file to determine which file systems are available for mounting by what machines. If the file system is available for mounting by the machine making the request, mountd processes the request and allows the remote computer system to begin making NFS access requests by providing the initial file handle for the file system that was mounted. Finally, rpc.mountd provides information on which file systems are mounted by which remote computer system via the `showmount` command. The `mountd` daemon is normally started by the `rc` script when the local computer system is booted.

/usr/etc/inetd. The `inetd` daemon is a service that will invoke network service daemons when it becomes aware of a request for that particular service. `inetd` reads a configuration file upon startup, `inetd.conf`, and then listens for connection requests for each service specified in the configuration file. It does this by identifying the Internet ports by which the services will be communicated with. Whenever a connection request is present on any of those ports, `inetd` will invoke the correct service. The configuration file specifies any arguments that should be passed to the service upon startup. Once the service has completed its work, `inetd` continues to listen for any more requests. This service reduces the load on any given machine by lowering the number of processes that are awaiting communication requests at any one time. Alternative methods for how a service operates have been considered from time to time. A rule of thumb is that if a service is required on a frequent or regular basis, it should stay available at all times. Other services that are used more infrequently can be started via `inetd`. NFS is an example of a service that stays available. In addition, multiple NFS server processes (`nfsd`) are kept available to allow for maximum throughput.

Commands

There are five major commands and four primary daemons used in the administration and operation of an NFS environment. These commands are described in detail in the following pages. In brief, the commands and daemons follow:

- Daemons

  - `nfsd` is used to start a number of UNIX daemons to handle file system requests.

  - `biod` is used to start the block I/O daemon on a client system.

  - `rpc.mountd` is used to start the mount daemon on the server system.

  - `inetd` is used to start the Internet `inetd` daemon.

- Commands

  - `exportfs` is used to make a file system available for mounting; it usually runs at boot time.

  - `mount` is used to instruct a remote mount daemon to mount a file system.

- showmount is used to determine which remote systems are using file systems on the local system.
- rpcinfo retrieves service information from the specified RPC routine on the network.
- nfsstat retrieves service information from the local NFS server daemons.

/usr/etc/exportfs. The exportfs command is used to export, or make available for mounting, a set of local file systems. This command, usually run at boot time by the rc.local script, reads the information contained in the /etc/exports file and places a list of currently exported file systems in the /etc/xtab file. exportfs can be run at any time by the superuser to make changes in the export list or the characteristics of the exported directories. The command has the form

/usr/etc/exportfs [*options*] *directoryname*

Simply typing the command /usr/etc/exportfs will print a list of the currently exported file systems.

Major options are -a for export all directories listed in the /etc/exports file, -u for unexport all directories, -v for verbose operation, and -i for ignore the /etc/exports file options and use the options provided in the command line. The options supported by exportfs are the same as those supported by /etc/exports.

/usr/etc/mount. mount is the command used to attach a remote file system to a point in the local directory structure. The general form of the mount command is

/usr/etc/mount [*switches*] [-t *type*] [-o *options*] [*filesystem*] [*directory*]

In the UNIX operating system, the mount command is used for mounting local disk drives as well as NFS file systems. If the command includes a *filesystem* of the form *hostname*:*pathname*, then the mount command will assume it is a NFS file system. The *directory* parameter is the path name of the point in the local directory structure where the remote file system is to be attached (mounted). All mounted file systems are kept in the file /etc/mtab. Entering the mount command with no parameters will display a list of mounted file systems. mount has several switches. One of the most useful is -a for mount all. mount will attempt to mount all the file systems listed in /etc/fstab. Another useful switch is -p for print a list of mounted file systems suitable for use in /etc/fstab. This is useful if the user has mounted some file systems using the mount command that are not included in /etc/fstab. The listing of mounted file systems can be used as a replacement for the existing fstab file. Other

switches include −v for verbose and −r for mount the file system read-only.
−r is a shorthand for −o ro, which specifies read-only mounting as an option
and not as a switch.

Options specifying how file systems are mounted (e.g., *type*, bg, and fg)
are used in the same manner as the /etc/fstab. Refer to the /etc/fstab
section for more information on how these options affect the mount command.

showmount. The /usr/etc/showmount command is used to determine which
computer systems have mounted a file system on a host. This command is very
useful for system administrators who need to determine which remote computer
systems depend upon a host before they shut down that host. Also, the information can be used as a debugging aid if the host in question is experiencing problems. Finally, the information can simply be logged as a way of accounting for
use.

The command has the form

/usr/etc/showmount [-ade] [*host*]

The default for *host* is the host name of the local computer system. The −a switch
tells showmount to display all remote mounts in the form *host:directory*. The
−d switch prints only the list of remotely mounted directories and the −e switch
prints the list of all exported file systems.

showmount communicates with the mountd daemon on the host specified
via a remote procedure call to determine the information it needs. mountd will
maintain this information and will preserve the information during crashes in
the file /etc/rmtab.

rpcinfo. The command rpcinfo is used to get information on RPC-based network services such as NFS. Each RPC-based network service has a unique program number and version associated with it. Using one of three methods, the
rpcinfo command can communicate with any network service on the network
and determine whether the services are operational. In addition, rpcinfo can
determine whether the services are operational on the correct host or hosts.

The primary method used by rpcinfo is to make an RPC call to procedure 0 of the specified program on the specified host using either the UDP or
TCP transport. Procedure 0 of any RPC program is a required null procedure
that will return only if the RPC service is operational. Thus, a user or system
administrator can determine if the host in question is capable of providing a
given service. The syntax for this method is

rpcinfo -u/-t *hostname programnumber* [*version*]

where −u is for UDP and −t is for TCP.

Sometimes, users are interested in determining all RPC services available
on a given host. This is accomplished by using rpcinfo to query the Portmapper on the host in question. Every RPC service must register itself with the

Portmapper upon coming up. Thus, the Portmapper will return a list of all RPC services on a host when queried. The syntax for this method is

    `rpcinfo -p` *hostname*

Finally, users may be interested in determining all hosts capable of providing a given RPC service. You can obtain this information by instructing `rpcinfo` to make an RPC broadcast using the UDP transport. All RPC services with matching program and version numbers will respond to the broadcast request. Users can thus determine all hosts capable of providing a given service. More often, a systems administrator will use the command in this manner to determine if all the hosts that should be running a RPC service are in fact running the service. The syntax for this RPC broadcast is

    `rpcinfo -b` *programnumber versionnumber*

If the version number is not specified, `rpcinfo` will attempt to find all versions of the specified RPC service.

    Remember that NFS is, in fact, an RPC service and will respond to `rpcinfo` requests for information.

nfsstat. System administrators and others use the `nfstaat` command to obtain certain usage statistics for both the NFS and RPC interfaces to the UNIX kernel on the local host. The command will display either server- or client-side statistics. This command, although somewhat useful for all users, is really designed to be used by a system administrator since the information displayed will give an indication of how efficient the local machine has been in servicing its requests and how often bad requests have been seen. A high number of bad requests will indicate that there is either a failure in the underlying communications mechanism (network interface, network software, etc.) or a particularly buggy client on the network.

    `nfsstat` will display the total number of RPC calls made and received and the number of bad calls made and received. Information on RPC timeouts and how often an RPC service had to wait for a chance to communicate to an remote service is also provided. Both sets of information are useful in determining the relative health of the network and the local system. When used with some of the other administration commands, `nfsstat` can be an extremely useful tool for a network administrator.

Performance and Reliability

Mount Problems. The `mount` procedure consists of at least 13 different steps. These steps have already been described. Since the `mount` process is critical and something that should in most instances be hidden from the user, any problems that occur in the process are bound to cause confusion. Most `mount` problems stem from improper setup and configuration. There are only a few times when the basic configuration for mounting will need to be set or updated. At installation time, the setting is usually done correctly. Problems normally occur when a change must be made to the configuration.

Most errors stem from improper /etc/fstab setup. Either the file system to be mounted is listed incorrectly or the options specified are wrong. Other errors occur when the file system to be mounted does not exist on the specified remote host, or the mount point directory does not exist on the local host.

Errors can also occur during normal operation of the network. In a network, computers systems come up and down with some degree of regularity. These can be planned or unplanned events. If a server dies or is otherwise unavailable, the error message "server not available" will appear. This is fairly straightforward to troubleshoot. However, the mount daemon or NFS daemon may not be available on the remote host. A system administrator must take steps to restart the failed daemons if this is the case.

Program Hangs. Remember that NFS file systems can be mounted either hard or soft. The difference is in the way server problems affect the operation of applications. Since NFS is stateless, a server that has crashed and then rebooted will have no adverse affect on the operation of an application. The exception to this, of course, is response time. If an NFS file system is mounted hard and the server crashes, the program will hang during file operations until the server comes back up. This could be a problem for some users since the application that has hung may not be the most important application on their host. Mounting a file system soft will cause the application to timeout and then abort. This will free up the user to carry on other work that does not require access to the down server.

When an application hangs during a file access, it is useful to check to see if the server the file system is mounted from is down. If the server is not down and the application is still hung, there might be a problem with the NFS daemons on the remote host. A systems administrator can try killing the NFS daemons and restarting them to see if this improves operation of the application. Killing the NFS daemons will have no adverse affect on any user of the file system so this is a safe option to try. If this does not improve the situation, there may be problems on the network that are preventing the client from gaining access to the server. The next step would be to troubleshoot the network being used.

Performance. Many things can affect NFS performance. The capacity and performance of the disk subsystems on the server are the most important of these. The faster the access provided by the server's disk controllers, the faster NFS will perform. It is also useful to keep the server from getting too bogged down. Keeping the application load on the server to a reasonable amount to allow NFS to have as much CPU time as it needs is a good idea. Other things that affect performance are the network and the block I/O daemons on the client. If the network is an Ethernet, it is useful to run the netstat utility whenever performance seems a bit sluggish. The netstat -i command will display the number of retransmissions from the local host onto the wire. A retransmission rate greater than 5% indicates that there is something wrong with either the local interface or the Ethernet tap. It is possible for the retransmission rate to be caused by an extremely congested network, but normally if the rate is higher than 5% then the interface is the cause.

Always avoid overloading the network. There are few rules of thumb that will apply in general, but it is worthwhile to keep the number of nodes on any Ethernet segment as low as possible. Fifty busy hosts are usually enough to start slowing down the network. Keeping the network segmented correctly is a good idea. The block I/O daemons (biod) are used to cache file handles and other data that are used to speed up access times. Checking to see that the biod daemons are not hung on the local host is a good technique to use when performance is slow. Killing the daemons and restarting them should clear any problems.

The interaction between NFS and other types of network services is not clear. Logic dictates that a few network applications will increase the amount of network traffic and affect NFS performance. Network window systems such as X Windows are designed to allow interactive graphic applications to be supported in a distributed environment. Specifically, the X system allows an application to be located on a server and the part of the application that paints screens and interacts with the user to be on a remote device such as a workstation. This setup, while highly functional, is expected to place a heavy load on any LAN. Thus, the number given as a rule of thumb should be viewed more conservatively.

Security. Security within an NFS environment is twofold. First, NFS maintains compatibility with UNIX credentials and enforces them across a network. This credential checking was described in the previously during the discussion on mounting and NFS file access request handling. Essentially, an NFS server requires a UNIX credential to be passed in each RPC message. The UNIX credential contains the user's user ID, group ID, and a list of groups to which that user belongs. The NFS server then saves its own credential and takes on the credential of the remote user as it attempts to access the requested file or file system. Thus, the security that UNIX provides is maintained. Clients of non-UNIX machines must generate a UNIX credential when accessing a UNIX-based server. This can be done by passing the contents of a file, or by adopting the default user ID nobody.

For the UNIX-credential-passing method to work correctly, remote users cannot have access to the root password on their local hosts. If they do, it is an easy matter to impersonate another user through the su *username* command. This command changes the effective user ID to *username*, allowing the remote user to defeat effectively the UNIX-credential-passing capability. The latest release of NFS, NFSSRC 4.0, includes a new feature for secure networking that plugs this security hole. This new scheme, called "Secure NFS," uses a new secure RPC mechanism to pass the real user ID of the requester and not the effective user ID. The scheme goes one step further by authenticating the NFS client. Through this authentication, the server is assured that the real user ID being passed is coming from a trusted source. Thus, the su *username* security hole has been filled.

For a more detailed discussion of the security mechanisms included in Release 4.0 of NFSSRC and RPCSRC, see *Security Features Guide*, part Number 800-1735-10, of the Sun Microsystems documentation set.

◆ Future Directions ◆

Support for Diskless Work Stations

The NFS mechanism of making remote file systems appear as if they were local has broader application than just remote data access. It is possible to make the root and swap partitions of a diskless workstation available via NFS as well. Diskless computer systems are configured with a CPU board, network interface, real memory, a network interface, and a small amount of bootstrap code in Read Only Memory (ROM). This bootstrap code is mainly used to find a server from which to download a copy of the computer system's operating system and networking code. The contents of the ROM can vary considerably from machine to machine. In some cases, it might be possible to have a version of the operating system kernel in ROM.

In the case of UNIX, however, the operating system is designed to be loaded into main memory from a disk drive. This loading is called *bootstrapping* since the machine must somehow figure out how to bring the operating system up without an operating system. In NFSSRC 4.0, Sun Microsystems added a mechanism called NETdisk, which is used to boot a diskless workstation and download the operating system. Once the operating system is loaded, all paging and swapping to the server from the client is done via NFS. This has the ability to make the server from which a client boots a different make of computer system than the client. An example would be a UNIX-based diskless workstation booting from a VMS-based VAX. The advantage of this method is that users are free to reuse their existing computers to support their new computers. Also, the system administration personnel need only be familiar with one method of diskless workstation support.

The NETdisk mechanism relies upon an RPC service called `bootparams`. This service, invoked by `inetd` or by a user, will respond to boot requests from hosts with Internet addresses that it has in its configuration file `/etc/bootparams`. The `bootparams` service gives the client system its host name and enough information to locate its root partition, swap partition, and dump partition. These partitions can be located anywhere on the network and can be accessed by the diskless workstation via NFS. The diskless workstation will download its kernel via its normal bootstrap mechanism. Then the kernel will talk to the bootparams service to find its root, swap, dump partitions.

This new use of NFS has interesting support and administration ramifications. Also, the issue of licensing has come up as a potential stumbling block since most operating systems are licensed to be kept only on a particular type of computer system. Storing the operating system on a server of a different make may violate some licensing agreements. It is anticipated that this issue may take some time to work itself out.

NFS Version 3.0 Protocol

NFS Version 3.0 is a proposed change to the NFS protocol currently being discussed in several user and vendor group environments by Sun Microsystems. As Sun is the owner of NFS, it can implement changes to the protocol when it wishes. However, since NFS has received widespread use in many environments, Sun has committed itself to changing the protocol only after public review.

If you wish to learn more about the proposed changes to the NFS protocol, contact Sun Microsystems:

NFS Administrator
2550 Garcia Avenue
Mountain View, CA 94043

The proposed changes are by in large in response to requests from both vendors and users. The changes are in keeping with the initial goals of the NFS service to be a simple and transparent file access method. Clients who wish to add specific functionality to their particular implementations are now allowed to. This does not mean that these implementations will be nonstandard, only that they can provide additional capabilities above and beyond what is the default.

♦ References ♦

R. Sandberg, *The Sun Network File System: Design, Implementation, and Experience*, Sun Microsystems, 1986.

R. Sandberg, *Sun Network File System Protocol Specification*, Sun Microsystems, DRAFT, 6/12/86.

N. J. Livesey, *Open Network Computing*, Sun Microsystems, June, 1987.

R. Sandberg, *A New UNIX Filesystem Layout to Support Diskless Clients*, Sun Microsystems, 1/30/87.

Network Programming, Sun Microsystems, 5/9/88.

Streams

Douglas Harris
Department of Mathematics, Statistics, and Computer Science
Marquette University

◆ Introduction ◆

The fundamental work in adapting UNIX to new hardware environments, or in adapting new hardware to UNIX, consists largely in providing appropriate device drivers. If the new hardware is similar to the old, then existing drivers can readily be adapted. The driver developer must merely take into account the manner in which data is communicated with the hardware device and the manner in which asynchronous signals such as interrupts are communicated. Since drivers are implementing system calls and often must respond to very low-level interrupts, they must interface intimately with the UNIX kernel. Typically, they are compiled into the kernel code, or linked with it at boot time.

With the advent of windowing, a new form of driver, often called a *pseudodriver*, has come into prominence. It may not interface with hardware directly but may need to interface with other drivers. Such a pseudodriver may be used to present an interface that appears to several processes as an ordinary teletype device while being actually an interface to a real teletype, or to a network, thus multiplexing output from several user processes onto a single physical connection and demultiplexing input from that connection to the user processes.

Similarly with the advent of networking, a new form of driver, often called a *software driver*, is used to stand between user system calls, or even kernel calls, and various network devices. A software driver is typically also a pseudodriver, since it usually does not talk to hardware directly. It often implements one or more layers of a networking protocol family, or acts as a filter to convert between data representations on different machines or devices. Since networking protocols are typically structured into protocol layers, we may need to stack several such software drivers, each handling a particular layer of the protocol.

Such a driver cannot properly be written as part of a single hardware driver, since the proper distribution of its output to the appropriate network device may not be known to the user. And of course the writing of such a driver as a "single piece of code" would be unimaginably complex (well, some of us have limited imaginations, in the original UNIX tradition) and would need to be continually redone as standards committees and vendors redefine those protocols. Finally, the particular networking interfaces for an individual machine vary from boot to boot of that machine, as new products and protocols become available, and these interfaces vary dynamically during the operation of the machine, as particular networks to which they are connected change their operational status. Managing these changes through opening and closing devices, in order to change their connections, would be disruptive and impossible to manage efficiently and securely.

Another new requirement for windowing and networking is that it may not be desirable to specify the hardware device to which it refers. (e.g., when a system call such as read is issued). We can at least imagine having a number of devices open to write upon, choosing the appropriate device for the window or network destination, and performing the usual write call. The only penalty paid here, other than the requirement that "routing" be determined by the user, is that of having a number of devices open in our file descriptor table. But there is nothing similar in basic UNIX for the read system call, and we must resort to timer-driven polling, or user-level message passing, or some other more arcane device. The traditional UNIX device interface is inadequate for such reads and is not ideal for such writes.

The tradititonal UNIX device interface, and generally the *system call interface* (the place where the user meets the kernel), has also become inadequate for carrying the information required for windowing and networking. Some of the information is purely data to be carried more or less intact to "the other end," performing perhaps only data representation filtering. Some of the information is for control purposes, describing needed routing or setting the windowing parameters. The read/write interface does not deal well with this since it has no provision for considering boundaries between control and data packets or for dealing with in-line control signals. Such matters are handled in the traditional interface with the ioctl call, which allows the passing of more or less arbitrary but fixed-size data structures between user and kernel for purposes of control (sometimes for passing data). This leads to a bewildering collection of customized ioctl calls for each device, and for each vendor's systems. There is no overall description of the dialog expected on the two sides of the interface. Control signals embedded in the data cannot be handled at all with this arrangement since read/write/ioctl are separate system calls. Finally, to handle protocol stacks, it is necessary to pass messages back and forth between different levels of a driver. This requires each level at least to know the messages that the other levels expect to send and receive, in order to pass them correctly, or to leave them alone.

The STREAMS I/O system provides a background for developing and installing such drivers, allowing them to be structured in simple and understandable (well, almost) modules and allowing these modules to be modified dynamically while the system is operational. In particular, it unifies the interface between the kernel and the user, specifying rather exactly the forms of dialog that can occur. In what is perhaps a form of *Occam's Razor* (entities should not multiply beyond necessity), it continues the traditional and conceptually well-understood (despite the picture already painted) user/kernel interface of `open/read/write/ioctl/close` system calls and adds two additional calls—`putmsg` and `getmsg`—for handling the combined control/data messages required for windowing and networking. It also provides simple specifications for the `ioctl` dialog, which preserve the traditional features, while allowing flexibility and modularity in driver development.

♦ Descriptions ♦

STREAMS was created by Dennis Ritchie, the cocreator of UNIX, and first described in an article "A Stream Input-Output System" in the October 1984 *AT&T Bell Laboratories Technical Journal.* It became an integral part of System V UNIX Release 3.0, which was first made publicly available in June, 1986. It will continue to be an integral part of System V UNIX and the base for all kernel driver development. It will be present in System V Release 4.0, the "unified" release of UNIX expected in 1989.

Ritchie described the STREAMS interface as a "flexible-coroutine-based design [which] replaces the traditional rigid connection between processes and terminals or networks" (and describes it as running on "about 20 machines in the Information Sciences Research Divison of AT&T Bell Laboratories"). The currently distributed version of STREAMS provides essentially the interface described in the paper but adds a provision for multiplexing several modules into one. Ritchie discusses this problem, and states "... a general multiplexing mechanism could help ..., but again, I do not yet know how to design it."

A *stream* is a collection of units called "modules," providing at one end, the *head*, a user/kernel interface following a prescribed protocol, and at the other end, the *driver*, providing what is usually very similar to a traditional device driver. The modules between the head and the driver serve as filters, transforming data as required; as servers, implementing particular data communication protocols; or as routers, choosing lower streams for routing data in and out of various devices and choosing upper streams for routing data to and from various processes. Any module may send and receive messages of its own, representing control requests or responses or error indications. The head and driver ends of a stream are fixed when it is opened, but modules may be dynamically pushed onto a stream as needed or popped from a stream when no longer required. Multiplexing is handled by allowing one stream to be linked under another, with the lower stream running at its head special routines defined within the upper stream.

The standard releases of System V now contain all the code required for STREAMS, and many of the standard drivers make use of it. In particular, the `poll` system call and related calls for signal handling are implemented using STREAMS to provide the "multiple read" capability already discussed. All networking interfaces are based on STREAMS, especially the Transport Level/Transport Provider Interface that is the System V programming interface to network transport protocols. Vendors of networking products have written, and are writing, STREAMS interfaces for those products. Several have reported substantial simplification of their development tasks, especially that of maintaining a variety of protocol suites and of adapting to changes in standards, or adopting new standards, as the networking and windowing fields explode. The famous comment in Tanenbaum's *Computer Networks* that "the nice thing about so many standards is that you can choose the one you want" is an exact description of the flexibility that STREAMS allows.

Conceptually, and ignoring special issues related to the head and driver ends of a stream (all these issues are discussed in great detail later), the flow of information through a stream is very simple. A stream is a stack of modules, each of which can be considered in the *downstream*, or head-to-driver, direction, and in the *upstream*, or driver-to-head, direction. The module has a *write side* of procedures relating traffic going downstream, and a *read side* of procedures relating to traffic going upstream. The write sides of modules are formed into a list, singly linked in the downstream direction, and the read sides are formed into a similar list, singly linked in the upstream direction. The whole configuration also forms a doubly linked list, since each side can immediately find the other, thus allowing ready movement across as well as up or down. (Fig. 5-1.)

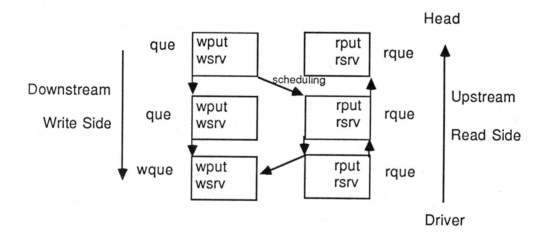

Fig. 5-1. Module Linkage in a Stream

Each side may have a `put` procedure, which performs simple transformations of the message, and then either passes the message on by executing the `put` procedure of the next side in the direction of traffic, or links the message onto its own queue for later processing. Occasionally a side may "reply" to a message by giving it to its other side for transmission in the opposite direction. Each side may have a *service* or `srv` procedure, which goes through a message queue of stored messages (usually those stored by its `put` procedure) and either passes them on or restores them. A `srv` procedure may also reply to a message. The `put` procedure of a side is executed by the previous side and runs to completion without sleeping. The `srv` procedure of a side is executed by the STREAMS scheduler, when it finds the side on its scheduling list, and it also runs to completion without sleeping. A side is placed on the scheduling list, or *enabled*, by the `put` or `srv` procedure of itself or of another side. The STREAMS scheduler runs rather simply. Whenever it is enabled, which is usually as a system call that is prepared to return to the user, it runs through its scheduling list and executes each `srv` procedure in turn. This guarantees that each enabled `srv` procedure will be run before the system call returns. This is essentially the only guarantee that STREAMS provides.

♦ Constructing a Stream ♦

Before considering STREAMS in detail, lets review the usual UNIX character-oriented device driver. This driver is a single object code module (`mydriv.o`) in which C functions are defined to perform the system calls `open`, `read`, `write`, `ioctl`, and `close`, taking arguments as described in Section 2 of every UNIX manual. The connection between the system calls and these functions is made through the the standard character-device switch table `cdevsw[]`, which is indexed by the major number of a device. The system calls use `cdevsw[]` to find the C function that should be used for that device. This is, in fact, exactly the way in which streams are incorporated administratively into UNIX System V.

A field `dstr` has been added to `cdevsw[]`. This field is intended to point to a structure that describes the construction of a stream. A NULL value for this pointer indicates that a device is an ordinary non-STREAMS device to be handled in the usual way. Thus, when the kernel `open` sees a nonzero pointer, it sets up to invoke special fixed STREAMS versions of `open` and `close` (and, in fact, of `read`, `write`, and `ioctl`). The value of `dstr` is the location of a `STREAMTAB` structure:

```
STREAMTAB
{
  QINIT *st_rdinit;      /* definitions for the read  side    */
  QINIT *st_wrinit;      /* definitions for the write side    */
  QINIT *st_muxrinit;    /* definitions for the mux head read */
  QINIT *st_muxwinit;    /* definitions for the mux head write */
}
```

The routines described in the QINIT structure are part of the kernel-linked driver code:

```
QINIT
{
  int (*qi_putp)();      /* Put     procedure location */
  int (*qi_srvp)();      /* Service procedure location */
  int (*qi_qopen)();     /* Open    procedure location */
  int (*qi_qclose)();    /* Close   procedure location */
  int (*qi_qadmin)();    /* Admin   procedure location */
  MODINFO (*qi_minfo);   /* Basic information struct   */
  MODSTAT (*qi_mstat);   /* Basic statistics  struct   */
}
```

```
    MODINFO
    {
      ushort mi_idnum;
      char   *mi_idname;
      short  mi_minpsz;  /* Min packet size accepted */
      short  mi_maxpsz;  /* Max packet size accepted */
      ushort mi_hiwat;   /* Hi water count           */
      ushort mi_lowat;   /* Lo water count           */
    }
```

```
MODSTAT
{
  long  ms_pcnt;  /* Count of calls to put   for this queue */
  long  ms_scnt;  /* Count of calls to srv   for this queue */
  long  ms_ocnt;  /* Count of calls to open  for this queue */
  long  ms_ccnt;  /* Count of calls to close for this queue */
  long  ms_acnt;  /* Count of calls to admin for this queue */
  long *ms_xptr;  /* Location of private statistics struct  */
  long  ms_xsize; /* Size of private statistics struct      */
}
```

The STREAMTAB structure itself need be the only variable accessible by name

outside the driver module itself. In other words, the remainder of the variables
may be declared static or may be local to particular routines. The name of the
STREAMTAB structure must be *STRinfo*, where *STR* is the name of the stream
configuration file stored in /etc/master.d (or its System V, Release 3.2
equivalent). The special STREAMS open() procedure now carries out the following actions:

- It allocates a pair of QUEUEs for the stream head, and fills these with the
  standard stream head QINIT structures.

- It allocates a pair of QUEUEs for the driver and fills these with the
  QINIT structures described in the STREAMTAB. (It ignores the multiplexed structures for now.)

It links the two QUEUE pairs (hereafter know as rque and wque) shown
in Fig. 5-2.

It copies the high and low water marks from the appropriate MODINFO
structs into the driver queues (and appropriate fixed values for the head queues).
Note that it is very common to reference the same MODINFO structure for both
rque and wque.

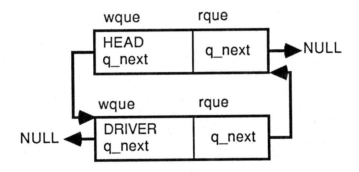

Fig. 5-2. The link between QUEUE pairs

Now various setup routines are executed. In particular, if the QINFO structures for rque specified an open routine this is now performed. It is called in a
manner very similar to the way the usual driver open routine is called:

```
ropen(q_p, dev, flag, sflag)
```

where q_p points to the read queue that points to the open routine, dev is the
device number, flag is the one the user open system call provided, and
sflag is the clone open flag, which is discussed later.

The final result is the lovely collection of plumbing shown in Fig. 5-3. It attempts to symbolize all you need to know about streams.

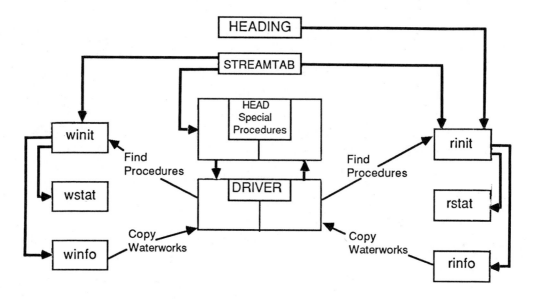

Fig. 5-3. STREAMS initial plumbing

♦ Queues ♦

The basic structural description of a stream is that it is a collection of pairs of *queues*, doubly linked in a special way. Each *queue* is an instance of the data structure:

```
QUEUE
{
  QINIT *q_qinfo;
  MSGB  *q_first;
  MSGB  *q_last;
  QUEUE *q_next;
  QUEUE *q_link;
  caddr_t q_ptr;
  ushort  q_count;
  ushort  q_flag;
```

```
    short   q_minpsz;
    short   q_maxpsz;
    ushort  q_hiwat;
    ushort  q_lowat;
}
```

QINIT is as defined in the previous section, and MSGB is as defined in the next section.

The queue pairs are made up of a read side and a write side. Their memory is allocated in one double-sized chunk, with the read member at the lower address. A bit in the q_flag indicates whether a particular queue is on the read side or the write side. It is a trivial matter for either queue to find the other by a constant positive or negative pointer offset (sizeof(QUEUE)), an operation that can often be incorporated by the compiler into a machine instruction.

The read queues in a collection are linked into a singly linked list by their q_next pointers, with a NULL value at the end. The write queues are linked in the same manner but in the opposite direction. It is now a simple matter to move upstream following the read pointers, or to move downstream following the write pointers, or to change directions at any point. The queue pair that contains the first read queue (and last write queue) is the *head* pair, and the queue pair that contains the last read queue (and first write queue) is the *driver* pair (Fig. 5-4).

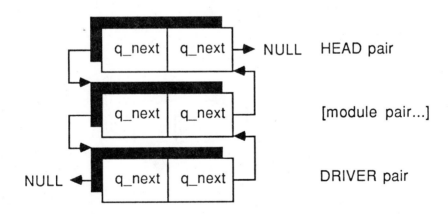

Fig. 5-4. Upstream and downstream linking of queues

Before you tire of the use of "queue," we will consider two other important terms formed from the above structures. Within each queue (read or write), we can link messages (described next) into a singly linked list using the q_first and q_last pointers, so that messages can be added at either end. The *message queue* belongs either to a read queue, which we shall call an rque, or the message queue which we shall call a wque (Fig. 5-5).

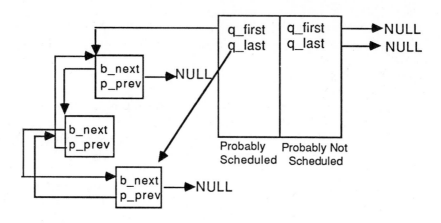

Fig. 5-5. The Message queues

Finally there is the *STREAMS scheduling queue*, formed as a singly linked list using the q_link pointers (see Fig. 5-6). In this case, STREAMS itself keeps track of the head of the list (for the purpose of traversing the list in order) and of the tail of the list, for adding queues to the STREAMS schedule. This queue then forms a first-in, first-out queue. The purpose of the q_link pointer in each queue is to allow the STREAMS scheduler to move quickly to the next item.

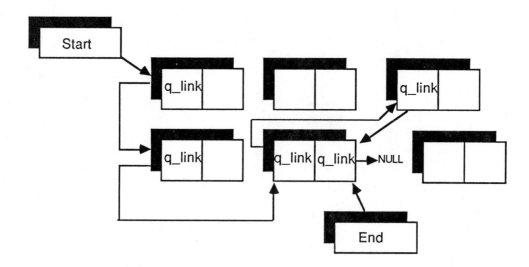

Fig. 5-6. The scheduling queue

◆ Messages ◆

The MSGB and DATB structures are the basis for the construction of messages.

```
MSGB
{
  MSGB *b_next;  /* Next in the message queue */
  MSGB *b_prev;  /* Previous in the message queue */
  MSGB *b_cont;  /* Next in the message itself */
  BYTE *b_rptr;  /* Where to read next msg byte */
  BYTE *b_wptr;  /* Where to write next msg byte */
  DATB *b_datap; /* The data that goes with this message */
}


DATB
{
  DATB *db_freep; /* For internal use */
  BYTE *db_base;  /* Beginning of data buffer */
  BYTE  db_lim;   /* End (+1) of data buffer */
  BYTE  db_ref;   /* A ref count for sharing blocks */
  BYTE  db_type;  /* The type of the data block */
  BYTE  db_class; /* For internal use - a weighted size */
}
```

The "type of a message" is the value of the db_type field of its first data block (e.g., m_p->b_datap.db_ type). The following allowed values (defined in sys/stream.h) are classified according to required source or destination. An asterisk indicates a priority message.

Unrestricted:

     M_DATA
     M_PROTO   used to establish a service interface
   *M_PCPROTO
     M_CTL   used to pass information inside STREAMS
   *M_FLUSH

Sent by Head:

     M_IOCTL

Sent to Head:

     M_SIG   causes a signal to user
     M_PCSIG

M_IOCACK	specifies return and error values for IOCNAK
M_IOCNAK	returned by module or driver
M_HANGUP	sent by driver when it cannot continue
M_ERROR	
M_PASSFP	
M_SETOPTS	

Sent to Driver:

    M_BREAK
    M_DELAY
    *M_START
    *M_STOP

The structure of a typical message queue is shown in Fig. 5-7.

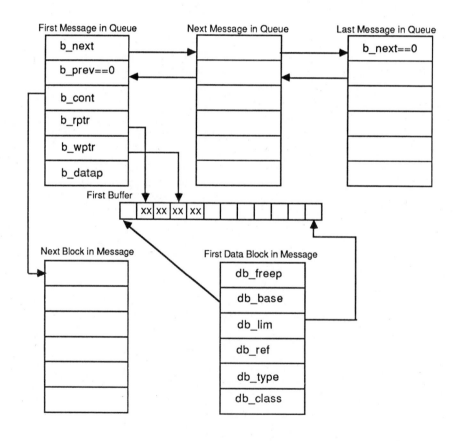

Fig. 5-7. The structure of a message

♦ Buffers ♦

The topic of buffer handling could readily consume several chapters (although not in a text by this author). Since the techniques (or black arts) involved are presumably familiar to anyone who has reached the kernel, we will limit our discussion to describing the standard utilities provided by STREAMS for this purpose. One tool, the `bufcall`, is somewhat unusual, and very useful, in that it allows a module that needs buffer space and cannot obtain it to ask to be scheduled when space is available. Since it is also a tool for creating deadlock (something that kernel hackers avoid since it tends to displease users), it is a dangerous tool. So is the kernel.

Before we continue, lets review the structure of, and especially the terminology of, messages. A message is composed of linked *message blocks*, and each message block points to a *data block descriptor*, which points to a *data buffer*. Many message blocks can point to the same data block descriptor, and the descriptor carries a *reference count* to indicate how many.

```
MBLK *
allocb(size, pri)
```

This is the basic tool for buffer allocation. It attempts to do what its name implies, to allocate a message block and data block descriptor and a data buffer of (at least) `size` bytes. It returns a NULL upon failure and the message block address upon success. Since there may be many reasons for requesting buffer space, and it is always a limited resource, STREAMS asks that a priority be placed upon the request.

The possible priority values are:

- `BPRI_LO`—for output from the user and other purposes for which we do not lose data if we do not obtain a buffer.

- `BPRI_MED`—for general purpose control and data buffers.

- `BPRI_HI`—for urgent control messages; use sparingly.

```
MBLK *
copyb(mb_p)

MBLK *
copymsg(mb_p)
```

These call `allocb` to copy a single message block, or an entire message, returning the address of the (first) message block upon success and NULL on failure.

```
MBLK *
dupb(mb_p)

MBLK *
dupmsg(mb_p)
```

These call `allocb` to create a message block, or an entire set of message blocks, pointing to the existing data block descriptors, and increments the reference count in each such descriptor.

These calls are used when more than one message queue must reference a message block or message. For example these calls could be used when a TCP is saving an entire segment for retransmission, and an IP is chopping it into fragments for transmission over a particular link. In general they should not be called if any of the users of the data will be changing it.

```
int *
pullupmsg(mb_p, len)
```

This call is used to create a single message block out of an entire message. It should only be used when all the blocks in the message are of the same type; typically all but the first block in a message will in fact be `M_DATA` blocks. The call will fail if `len` bytes are not available in the message.

```
MBLK *
unlinkb(mb_p)
```

This call removes the first block from a message and returns a pointer to the first block in the result or NULL if there was only a single block. It does not free the removed block, since the caller may have further use for it. The original `mb_p` points at the removed block, and its `b_next` and `b_prev` pointers are now NULL.

Negotations with the buffer pool are handled with the following two functions.

```
int
testb(size, pri)
```

This asks if a buffer of at least the size specified can be allocated at the requested priority. The test is advisory only, since it does not actually perform the allocation.

```
int
bufcall(size, pri, function, funcarg)
```

This call is usually performed when an `allocb` request has failed. It asks that `function(funcarg)` be called when a buffer becomes available at the requested size and priority. Its success is advisory only, and should generally be tried only once in order to avoid possible deadlock. Failure of `bufcall` indicates that STREAMS generally is in trouble and cannot allocate even enough space for this request.

Typical usage of `bufcall` is appending a header to an existing message. A `srv` procedure attempts to `allocb` a buffer for the header. If this fails, the message is put on the current message queue, and `bufcall` is called with `qenable` as the function and the current message queue as the argument. If `bufcall` succeeds the `srv` procedure will eventually be called, because `qenable` was executed. If `bufcall` fails, the message can be freed and appropriate recovery action invoked. To avoid spinning on the request in case of repeated failure, a count should be kept of attempts with failure when a maximum has been reached.

♦ Modules ♦

A *module* is a pair of QUEUEs and is added to an already opened stream by a special `ioctl` executed on the stream by a user, with the name of the module as a parameter. The procedures that are part of a module are kernel-linked code; thus, a module is part of the kernel. A special table, similar to `cdevsw[]` and `bdevsw[]`, has been added to describe the modules that are configured with a system. The table is called `fmodsw[]`, and an entry in `fmodsw[]` consists of a module name and a STREAMTAB pointer. The `fmodsw[]` entry itself is derived in the same manner as device entries from a configuration file in `/etc/master.d`. Since a module is part of the kernel and very similar to a driver, there is usually a manual entry for a each module.

The standard release of System V Release 3.1 (for AT&T 3B2 computers) comes with the following modules or drivers, each of which has a manual page.

- `clone`—*STREAMS* driver already discussed

- `sp`—*STREAMS* pipe driver for connecting two stream heads

- `timod`—Basic module for the AT&T Transport Library Interface

- `tirdwr`—Module to allow `read/write` calls to be done above `timod`

To place a module `mymod` onto the stream given by `strfd`, perform:

```
ioctl(strfd, I_PUSH, "mymod")
```

Note that the kernel variable NSTRPUSH is the limit on the number of pushes for a single stream.

This `ioctl` allocates one pair of `QUEUE` structures and fills them from the `STREAMTAB` structure pointed at by the `fmodsw[]` entry for `mymod`. It then links these into the stream, just below its head as shown in Fig. 5-8.

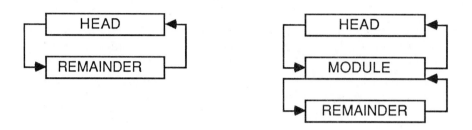

Fig. 5-8. Module linkage into a stream

It then calls the `ropen` and `wopen` procedures of the module, if any. The module then participates in the flow of messages through the stream, acting appropriately on those messages it understands, enqueuing and dequeuing messages as required.

On occasion, we wish to remove a module from a stream into which it is linked. There is an `I_POP` `ioctl` for this purpose, but it requires that the module to be popped be the one just below the stream head. Thus, to pop a module requires that we first pop those modules that lie above it in the stream, that is, those modules that were `I_PUSH`ed onto the stream at a later time. They can, of course, be pushed back onto the stream if their function is still required.

The `I_POP` function is performed by the system call:

```
ioctl(strfd, I_POP)
```

which calls the `rclose` and `wclose` routines, if any. It then waits 15 seconds for the module to drain if necessary, and frees the allocated data structures. Note that although it appears that a driver is just a module with fancy procedures, a driver cannot be `I_POP`ed. That is, every stream must have a driver at bottom.

There are also two `ioctl`s, `I_LOOK` and `I_FIND`, that allow us to discover the module contents of a stream.

```
ioctl(strfd, I_LOOK, name_p)
```

returns the name of the module just below the head of the stream or returns empty if no module has been pushed since the driver is not a module.

```
ioctl(strfd, I_FIND, name_p)
```

looks on the list of modules that have been pushed for the given name. It returns success if the module name is there and failure if it is not.

The I_LOOK ioctl is typically used when we need to verify if a particular service interface will be presented to a stream user. For TLI, we might want to know if the timod module is at the top of the stream, thus presenting that particular interface. Similarly, we might want to know if the tirdwr module is at the top, in order to have a pure read/write interface presented.

The I_FIND ioctl is typically used when there is a function that needs to be performed in the stream and should be performed only once. Thus, for a stream that is translating between UNIX and MS-DOS, we might wish to have a module that converts between LF line termination and CR/LF termination, and this should be done only once.

◆ Heads ◆

A stream head consists of QINFO entries, just like those for a module, together with a special head structure that we will not consider further. The only difference between the QINFO structures for a head and those for a module is that those for a head are fixed, are supplied at open time by the STREAMS system itself, and must handle certain types of message that may be ignored in other modules. Of course, they also are the only place in a stream where data crosses from system space to user space; thus, they deal with user context that is not otherwise accessible in a streams module.

The STREAMTAB configuration for a head is shown in Fig. 5-9.

rput	rsrv	rque	ropen	rclose
YES	NO	YES	NO	NO

wput	wsrv	wque	wopen	wclose
NO	YES	YES	NO	NO

Fig. 5-9. Typical head STREAMTAB configuration

Although a stream head has no open or close procedures, standard procedures are invoked on open or close of a stream. These can be thought of as including the processing that the module procedures would normally carry out. In particular, the stream open procedure must be careful to ensure that there is only a single stream open for each particular major/minor device number; it does this by looking through the file table for another inode with the same combination of device numbers.

The Read Side: read and getmsg System Calls

There are two basic system calls that relate to the read side of a stream: read and getmesg.

read(strfd, dat_p, dat_n). The read call removes messages from the head rque, blocking until its count dat_n is satisfied, or the read cannot be continued. It should encounter only messages of M_DATA type. In particular, if an M_PROTO/M_PCPROTO message is encountered, the error EBADMSG is returned. A zero length message is returned to the rque, to act as an end-of-file indicator until the stream is closed.

Note that a bug in STREAMS as delivered so far is that a message of nonzero length, in which the first block has zero length, is treated as a zero-length message. Thus, great care is required when manipulating messages where a zero-length first block is removed before the message is passed to the head.

getmsg(strfd, ctl_p, dat_p, flag_p). The getmsg removes messages from the head rque, blocking if there are no more messages. It should encounter only M_PROTO, M_PCPROTO, and M_DATA messages, returning these into ctl_p and dat_p as appropriate.

Only a single PCPROTO message is stored; others that arrive are discarded until the current one has been removed with getmsg. As noted in "Messages and Data Blocks," a PC_PROTO message serves as a "fast ACK," and we expect only one activity at a time that requires such an ACK.

In additition to M_DATA and M_PROTO messages, the rput procedure must handle many other message types that arrive upstream. It may pass appropriate information to the user, possibly in the form of the return value of a system call and possibly or also in the form of a signal sent to one or more processes. Examples follow:

- M_IOCACK, M_IOCNAK—If ioc_id of this ioctl message is that of the outstanding ioctl, return appropriate response to user. (See ioctl.)

- M_ERROR—

  - All system calls that reference this file descriptor, except poll and close, will fail, with errno set to the first data byte of this message.

  - Set POLLERR if the stream is being polled.

  - Send M_FLUSH/FLUSHRW downstream.

  - Wake all processes sleeping on a system call to the stream.

- M_HANGUP—

  - Fail all `write` and `putmsg` system calls, with ENXIO error.

  - Fail all `ioctls` that send messages downstream.

  - Set POLLHUP if the stream is being polled.

  - Send SIGHUP to the process group if the stream is a controlling terminal.

  - Once the head `rque` is empty, return EOF on `read`, and return both buffers empty on `getmsg`.

- M_SIG, M_PCSIG—

  - The first data byte of the message specifies a signal.

  - If the stream is a controlling terminal, send it to the process group.

  - If signal is SIGPOLL then send it to any process that has registered to receive poll signals from this file descriptor using `ioctl(strfd, I_SETSIG, ...)` to do so.

- M_SETOPTS—See the following section on options setting.

- M_FLUSH—

  - If FLUSHR is set, then flush `rque`.

  - If FLUSHW is set, then turn off FLUSHR and `qreply` the message.

The Write Side: `write` and `putmsg` System Calls

This side runs with a server and no `put` procedure. The service procedure is scheduled by back-enabling from downstream.

`write(strfd, dat_p, dat_n)`. This call has almost exactly the same behavior, from the user's point of view, as the usual non-STREAMS `write` call. Data is packaged into M_DATA messages, observing packet size limits given in the initial MODINFO structure. Zero-length packets are created and sent in the same way as other packets.

`putmsg(strfd, ctl_p, dat_p, flags)`. Here, two separate messages are put, with contents specified totally by the user.

Most messages other than the `M_DATA` and `M_PROTO` messages sent by `write` and `putmsg` result from user-executed `ioctl` system calls. The most common of these is:

```
ioctl(strfd, I_STR, ioctl_p)
```

where `ioctl_p` provides a command code, a timeout value, and possibly data to be sent with the command.

For the details of the actual structures see "`ioctl`."

The `ioctl` message is sent downstream with a unique ID. The head waits for a response, which may be a positive or negative acknowledgement, or a timeout.

◆ Drivers ◆

A *driver* can always be thought of as a module that must follow a special set of rules. It is described in `cdevsw[]`, not `fmodsw[]`. It is not pushed onto a stream, or popped from a stream, but is rather linked at the bottom of the stream when the stream is initially opened and removed only when the stream is finally closed. Like a module, it may or may not have its own `open`, `close`, `put`, and `srv` procedures, but they must follow more stringent requirements than those in an ordinary module. The write side of a driver, for example, cannot merely pass on any message it does not understand, since there is no module underneath to pass it to. In particular, the proper functioning of the STREAMS `ioctl` system call depends upon a guarantee that the write side of the driver will reply on the read side with a positive or negative acknowledgment of any `ioctl` that reaches it. Similarly, the proper functioning of the STREAMS flush mechanism depends upon the write side of a driver to "turn around" a `M_FLUSH` message that requests a flush of the read side of the stream.

Of course, a driver may contain special interrupt-handling routines that interface closely with the hardware. As part of this handling, or perhaps by polling, a driver may be expected to discover exception conditions or errors and possibly to notify a user process of such conditions. In particular, a driver might be expected to notice a "hangup" or "disconnection" condition and notify its head of this.

From the point of view of networking, the most interesting characteristic of a driver is that it can appear to have several streams connected upstream from it or several streams connected downstream from it. The mechanisms involved in these two cases are discussed later, as multiple devices and multiplexed drivers. From the pure STREAMS perspective, the situation is somewhat asymmetric; STREAMS allows one driver to be placed under another, but not above. This is not unreasonable since the user, who presumably controls everything the computer does, is after all "on top" of it all. In particular, control flows from the top and not from the bottom.

Driver Write Side Procedures

On the write side, drivers are most often interrupt driven, where the device interrupts whenever its transmit buffer is empty, and the interrupt routine then arranges to `get` and `write` to the device as much data as it can. Thus, the scheduling of writing is not really the prerogative of STREAMS, so a service procedure is often not appropriate. However, it is desirable for flow-control purposes to exert back pressure upstream; thus, a service queue is useful. The typical `QINFO` structure on the write side is shown in Fig. 5-10.

wput	wsrv	wque	wirq
YES	NO	YES	YES

Fig. 5-10. Typical driver write `QINFO`

Note that `wput` is executed by the previous module or the stream head. In that context, the proper queue pointer is known to the caller. The `wirq` routine, on the other hand, is executed in interrupt context and knows only the minor number (in a typical interrupt configuration) of the device. It will, therefore, need to use a private data structure of the driver, such as `mindev`, to find the queue pointer from the minor device number.

`wput` must recognize all `M_FLUSH` messages and turn them around:

```
/*
  Typically other message types, such as M_IOCTL,
  are also handled here
*/
switch(m_p->b_datap->db_type)
{
case(M_FLUSH):
  if (m_p->b_rptr & FLUSHW)
  {
    flushq(q_p, 0);           /* Flush all messages in my wque */
  }

  if (*m_p->b_rptr & FLUSHR) /* Should other side be flushed? */
  {
    flushq(RD(q_p), 0);       /* Flush all messages in my rque */
    *m_p->b_rptr &= ~FLUSHW;  /* Make sure head doesn't reject */
    qreply(q_p, m_p);         /* Shoot it up the read que      */
  }
  else
  {
    freemsg(q_p);
  }
```

```
    break;

    /*
    ---
    other cases
    ---
    */
    }
```

wput must recognize all M_IOCTL messages; these may be intended either for the write side driver or an upstream write module that did not recognize the message. Thus, wput must return M_IOCACK or M_IOCNAK. There is, of course, a timeout at the stream head that will also handle unrecognized ioctls, but (especially for situations where it is hard to determine an appropriate timeout setting) it is preferable to have a guaranteed notification from the stream itself of the disposition of an ioctl:

```
case(M_IOCTL)
{
  if (successful_ioctl)
  {
    m_p->b_datap->dbtype = M_IOCACK;
    iocp->ioc_count       = /* appropriate value, often 0 */
  }
  else
  {
    m_p->b_datap->dbtype = M_IOCNAK;
    iocp->ioc_error       = errno_desired /* usually EINVAL */
  }
  qreply(q_p, m_p);
}
```

Before continuing please review the flow section later in this chapter. For the data part of a message the following is typically used.

```
wput(q_p, m_p)
{
  if (device_is_available)
  {
    write_out_msg_data;
    free(m_p);
  }
  else
  {
    putq(q_p, m_p); /* This will not schedule the empty  */
       /* q_p->qputp. We depend upon wirq to getq(q_p) later on. */
```

```
      /* This will also handle QFULL for upstream writers  */
  }
}



    wirq(dev)
    {
      /* Uses mindev[dev] to find the write q_p  */

      while (can_write_to_dev)
      {
        if (m_p=getq(q_p))
        {
          if (m_p->b_datap->dbtype==M_DATA)
          {
            write_out_msg_data;
            free(m_p);
          }
          else
          {
/* Handling depends on other types that wput allows
   on the que.
   In particular some M_IOCTL messages typically
   must be handled here, and appropriate ACK/NAK
   messages returned
*/
          }
        }
      }
    }
```

Driver Write Side Signals

The write side of a driver must handle (if only by ignoring) certain signals that relate only to drivers. These are special cases of M_CTL message processing, which must be designed individually for each module in the context of any stream on which the module expects to be pushed. The special cases are:

- M_BREAK requests transmitter to send a standard BREAK signal.

- M_DELAY requests transmitter to delay output a specified time.

- M_STOP requests transmitter to stop sending.

- M_START requests transmitter to start sending.

The only aspect in which such code is special is in deciding whether it should be handled in some way by the `wput` procedure or enqueued for the `wirq` procedure to discover and handle. This decision must be made on the basis of the actual interface between the driver and the transmitter.

Driver Read Side Procedures

It is perhaps most common that the read side operates without flow control, merely freeing an arriving packet that cannot be put on the stream. This is, of course, especially common in networking applications, where higher levels expect such behavior from lower levels. We will outline typical read sides with and without flow control.

We will assume an interrupt handler `rirq`, runs when the device indicates that data has arrived. Just as with the `write` interrupt routine, it knows only the minor device number when run, and must extract its queue pointer from a private data structure in the driver that is not part of any stream (see "Minor Devices"):

```
rirq()
{
  /* Use mindev[dev] to find q_p */

  if (canput(q_p)) /* Failure of canput will not backenable */
                   /* anything since there is no rque         */
  {
    putnext(q_p, m_p);
  }
  else
  {
    free_(m_p);
  }
}
```

The `QINFO` configuration is shown in Fig. 5-11.

rput	rsrv	rque	rirq	ropen	rclose
YES	NO	NO	YES	YES	YES

Fig. 5-11. Typical driver read configuration

The `rclose` routine must store queue pointers in `mindev` and store `mindev[dev]` in the read queue private data area.

The configuration with flow control is different: We must use `rque` to exert pressure on the driver from upstream and use a `rsrv` that is back-enabled by loss of that pressure:

```
ropen()
{
  ....
  noenable(rque); /* This makes sure that rsrv is not scheduled */
       /* by putq */
}



rirq()
{
  /* Use mindev[dev] to find q_p */

  if (canput(q_p))
  {
    putnext(q_p, m_p);
  }
    ...
  {
    putq(q_p, m_p); /* rsrv will not be scheduled,          */
                    /* but QFULL will be appropriately handled */
}

rsrv() /* Scheduled only by back-enabling from upstream */
{
  Standard getq/canput/putnext procedure;
}
```

This gives the `QINFO` configuration shown in Fig. 5-12.

rput	rsrv	rque	rirq	ropen
NO	YES	YES	YES	YES

Fig. 5-12. Typical driver read configuration with flow control

The `ropen` routine must initialize queue pointers and the `mindev` structure and also make sure that `rsrv` is scheduled only by backpressure by disabling it initially.

Driver Read Side Signals

The driver read side commonly detects conditions from the receiver that should demand the special attention of the stream head or of the user who is reading or polling the stream. In particular, events may require the following messages to be sent upstream, and the behavior indicated will be taken by the head routines. A driver read must be able to handle the following events.

- M_SIG, M_PCSIG, M_HANGUP, M_FLUSH—Specifies a signal to be given to the group of processes that this stream controls (if it is a controlling stream). Specifies special behavior of the head, and possibly a signal. Can specify read or write flushing as already discussed; note that a driver, just like a head, may by this means specify with a single message flushing of the entire stream on read and write sides.

- M_SETOPTS—Can set high and low water marks for the head or specify special behavior of the read system call on this stream.

- M_ERROR—The stream is locked up, and no more system calls are accepted.

♦ Flow Through a Stream ♦

Flow through a stream has a basic pattern that is modifiable at will for special situations. It can best be described as follows.

Starting at the head for messages going downstream, or at the driver for messages going upstream, each module executes the put procedure of the next with the message as argument. This passes the message through the queue. (Actually, the message stays fixed; all that is passed is its address.) Each put procedure may process the message before passing it on; such processing is done "on the fly" without waiting on any other event or resource.

Several conditions can disrupt this smooth and rapid flow. Processing may need to be done before the message is handed on, as in the case of a message that should be preceded with its length (where the length is to be determined by counting until an EOD flag is seen), or a wait may be required until a particular event occurs, as with a driver where we may need to wait for an interrupt to occur. In such cases, STREAMS allows the message to be placed on the local message queue; a procedure to remove it and pass it on will execute after the appropriate event has occurred. In the case of the length accumulator, when the put procedure finally sees the EOD, it can remove the accumulated message from the queue, attach the length value to the front, and put the new message onto the next queue. In the case of the interrupting driver, its interrupt routine will remove the message from the local message queue.

Another more general possibility is that the stream ahead (upstream or downstream, depending on your direction of travel) may be blocked, without your knowing why. STREAMS provides a form of flow control that is very useful here. It is a form of "advisory" flow control, where each queue is expected to ask about conditions ahead and take appropriate action. However, it is not prevented from passing a message on if it so desires. The usual paradigm for such flow control in STREAMS is for a queue to ask if it can put a message on a queue ahead and to enqueue it on its own message queue if the answer is no. To avoid a possible infinite wait, the queue ahead remembers that there was a `write` request for it. When enough data has been removed to make space available, it asks STREAMS to schedule the service procedure of our message queue. This may sound rather complex, but it is really rather simple given the doubly linked nature of a stream. It is used in almost every STREAMS driver of consequence at some point or another. This process of enabling a queue behind one that has just had data removed is called *back-enabling*; the term appears repeatedly in the remainder of this chapter.

Notice, in particular, that since a STREAMS head is equipped with a write service procedure, it is reasonable to employ flow control on writes to the stream, and that flow control may very well propagate back to the head from the driver interrupt routine.

The STREAMS *utility functions* (or *macros*—take a careful look at `sys/streams.h` for your system to learn which) that implement these procedures are shown in Table 5-1.

TABLE 5-1. STREAMS utility functions

Utility	Function
canput (q_p)	Checks ahead and note if we must wait
putnext (q_p)	Executes the put procedure of our neighbor
putq (q_p, m_p)	Place on the msg queue of q_p
putbq (q_p, m_p)	Place back on the msg queue of q_p
getq (q_p)	Remove from the msg queue, enable a waiter
canenable (q_p)	Check if enabling is allowed
noenable (q_p)	Flag that enabling is not allowed
enableok (q_p)	Flag that enabling is allowed
qenable (q_p)	Place onto the scheduling queue

We will describe these functions in detail, but first, lets look at the cononical `put` and `srv` procedures:

```
/* Canonical put procedure */
/* Perform on_the_fly work, and handle priority messages */

if (canput(q_p->q_next)
{
  putnext(q_p, m_p);    /* Its yours */
}
else
{
  putq(q_p, m_p);       /* I enjoy having it around */
}
```

One common situation is to use the `putq` function as the `put` procedure of a queue. Thus when a neighbor does `putnext` to such a queue, they are merely laying it on my message queue for my `srv` procedure, or another procedure, to process later on.

```
    /* Canonical srv procedure */
    while (m_p = getq(q_p))
    {
      if (canput(q_p->q_next))
      {
          last chance processing...;
          putnext(q_p, m_p);
      }
      else
      {
          putbq(q_p, m_p);  /* Which may schedule me again */
      }
    }
```

The while loop makes sure that the `srv` procedure handles every message on the message queue. The STREAMS scheduling algorithm depends on such behavior and may never provide a second chance. Of course back-enabling may also be used.

◆ STREAMS Utility Functions ◆

A little description of the flow-control information associated with a queue is required.

Each queue has a:

- High water mark, `q_hiwat`.
- Low water mark, `q_lowat`.
- Current count, `q_count`.

The following bits are part of the queue's state, given by `q_flag`:

- QFULL—Normal data should not be enqueued.
- QNOENAB—The queue should not be scheduled.
- QENAB—The queue has been scheduled.
- QWANTW—The last `canput` found the queue FULL.
- QWANTR—The last `getque` found the queue EMPTY. (Or the module/driver to which the queue belongs was pushed.)

Now we can describe our functions as:

- `enableok(q_p)` resets QNOENAB.
- `noenable(q_p)` sets QNOENAB.
- `canenable(q_p)` tests QNOENAB.

They operate in the following manner:

```
MSGB *
getq(q_p)
/*
   Returns NULL if message queue is empty
   Returns a single message otherwise
   Back-enables a waiting server
*/
{
  if (message queue is empty)
  {
    set QWANTR
  }
  else
  {
    remove message from message queue
    decrement q_count
    reset QWANTR
    if  (q_count < q_hiwat)
    {
      reset QFULL
    }
  }
```

```
    if ((q_count <= q_lowat) and QWANW is set)
    {
      rest QWANTW
      if (there is a queue behind with a service procedure
      {
        qenable that queue (the first one back)
      }
    }
}
putq(q_p, m_p)
{
  link m_p in according to its priority
  /*
    Note that this link is done
    whatever the q_count may be
  */
  update q_count

  if (q_count >= q_hiwat)
  {
    set QFULL
  }

  if (priority msg OR (canenable(q_p) AND QWANTR)
  {
    qenable(q_p)
  }
}



qenable(q_p)
{
  if (QENAB is reset)
  {
    link queue into scheduler list
  }
}



canput(q_p)
{
  if (q_p is empty)
  {
    return FALSE
```

```
    }

    Search forward from q_p until you find
    a queue with a service procedure

    if (found and FULL)
    {
      set QWANTW
      return FALSE
    }
    else
    {
      return TRUE
      /*
        Either there was no such queue ahead OR
        the first one found was not FULL
      */
    }
}



putnext(q_p, m_p)
{
    (q_p->next_p.qi_putp(m_p));
}



qreply(q_p, m_p)
{
    putnext(OTHER(q_p), m_p);
}
```

♦ **ioctl** ♦

As mentioned in the introduction, device driver writers exercise their imaginations in writing ioctls for a device. This situation is under some control with STREAMS, although some seem to believe it is worse. There is a fixed set of ioctls, specified in the manual under streamio, and the behavior of these is fixed. However, one of them, the (ill-famed) I_STR ioctl, lets creative freedom reign again in that it specifies only how to send arbitrary M_IOCTL messages into the stream and to receive replies to them.

Even this `ioctl` has a specified behavior. STREAMS describes how such messages must be treated, in particular the way in which the stream to which they must send a response message. It also provides for a timeout in case this response does not arrive. STREAMS also specifies that a module that does not recognize a particular `M_IOCTL` message (which, in fact, does not recognize any message that passes through) must pass it on and that a driver must respond posivitively or negatively to each `M_IOCTL` that reaches it.

This behavior allows modularity. We can write modules to respond to specific `ioctl`s only and guarantee that those `ioctl`s can reach them wherever they reside in the stream. At the same time, we can guarantee a response despite whether a recognizing module is present in the stream.

In the `I_STR` ioctl system call, the user provides an `STRIOCTL` structure:

```
STRIOCTL
{
  int   ic_cmd;      /* a code that a downstream module will  */
          /* recognize */
  int   ic_timout;   /* value in seconds to wait for response */
  int   ic_len;      /* size of accompanying data            */
  char *ic_dp;       /* location of accompanying data          */
}
```

and issues the call

```
ioctl(stream_fd, I_STR, &strioctl);
```

The head constructs an `M_IOCTL` message that consists of one `M_IOCTL` block linked to zero or more `M_DATA` blocks. The `M_IOCTL` block has as its data contents an `IOCBLK` structure:

```
IOCBLK
{
  int    ioc_cmd;    /* Value provided as STRIOCTL.ic_cmd   */
  ushort ioc_uid;    /* Value provided from user context    */
  ushort ioc_gid;    /* Value provided from user context    */
  uint   ioc_id;     /* Value assigned uniquely with the msg */
  uint   ioc_count;  /* Value provided by STRIOCTL.ic_len   */
  int    ioc_error;  /* Value meaningless with M_IOCTL      */
  int    ioc_rval;   /* Value meaningless with M_IOCTL      */
}
```

The expectation is that some module will recognize `ioc_cmd` as the message passes through its `put` and/or `srv` procedures, carry out the command, fill in appropriate new values, and return the `IOCBLK` (or a new block of similar structure) to the head as a `M_IOCACK` or `M_IOCNAK` message. This recognition is guaranteed by the specifications for STREAMS drivers since, if nothing else, a driver will certainly return an `M_IOCNAK`.

The value of `ioc_error` is set by the responder as the value of `errno` that it wishes the stream to establish before the `ioctl` returns. A nonzero `errno` can be established with either `M_IOCACK` or `M_IOCNAK` return messages. In the former case, the meaning of a nonzero `ioc_error` is that some module recognized and acted upon the `ioc_cmd`, but that an error condition occurred; in the latter case, the meaning is that no module recognized the `ioc_cmd` and thus `M_IOCNAK` came from a driver. Data can be supplied with an `M_IOCACK` (indicated by a nonzero value of `ioc_count`) but not with `M_IOCNAK`.

The value of `ioc_rval` is just the value the responder wishes to have returned to the user; typical UNIX usage is, of course, 0 if no error occurs (`M_IOCACK` with `ioc_error==0`), and -1 if an error occurs (either response type with `ioc_error!=0`).

A timeout condition, of course, produces its own response value of -1 and its own error message, as shown in Fig. 5-13.

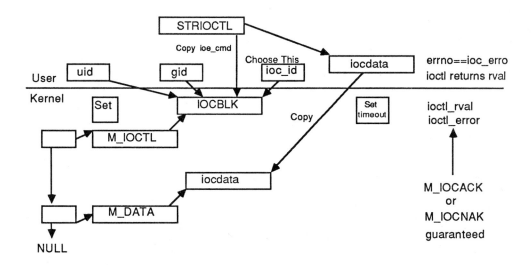

Fig. 5-13. `ioctl` flow through a stream

Some additional `ioctl`s have already been encountered:

- `I_PUSH`, `I_POP`, `I_LOOK`, and `I_FIND` were discussed under "Modules."

- `I_FLUSH` was discussed under "Heads."

◆ Linking ◆

In many cases, especially those involving networking, we need to have entire streams stacked upon one another. This is especially true in the case when a stream is required to communicate with a number of hardware drivers, as in the case of IP connecting to its various datalink drivers. In this case we say that the stream requires "fan-out," and a detailed discussion of this situation is given below. It is also a common situation that a number of devices, from the user point of view, must connect to a common controller or share data structures in some way. Similarly, a number of TCP users need to connect to the common IP driver just discussed. This situation is often handled using a variation of the ordinary UNIX minor devices configuration. We say that the stream requires "fan-in," and a detailed discussion is provided under the "Minor Devices" section that follows.

Our purpose in this section is to see how STREAMS allows the stacking of streams to accomplish the above purposes. For example we might have a number of TCP streams, stacked above a single IP stream, stacked above a variety of link driver streams.

STREAMS does not directly allow us to stack multiple streams on top of a single lower stream. But by creating a multiple driver stream on top, and linking the lower stream under a particular one of these multiple drivers (called its control stream), we can accomplish our objective, and the construction is very similar to the familiar one in which one minor device is "more equal than the others."

In this section we concentrate our attention upon the linking of two streams, one on top of the other, with the upper stream controlling the lower stream. Each will be an ordinary STREAMS driver, although each must have a few special features appropriate to its role.

The driver intended to become the upper stream should have at its driver end what is called a multiplexing driver (some would call this a pseudo-driver). Such a driver can be identified by having nonempty specifications in its STREAMTAB entry for the two QINIT structures st_muxrinit and st_muxwinit, which will be used to replace the init structures in the head of any stream linked below it. Thus the upper stream at its lower end runs the QINIT procedures usually found in a driver, although they are specifically written to do multiplexing. It also has special multiplexing procedures which will be installed just "underneath" it, which can take advantage of special knowledge of the upper drivers, especially of data structures and variables that may be defined within the upper driver object code.

Each lower stream has the usual STREAMTAB specified procedures at its lower end. At its upper end, where STREAMS normally places its own special routines, it runs the procedures provided by the multiplexing driver. These procedures should appear to the lower procedures to operate in the same way that the ordinary head procedures operate.

The single special facility that STREAMS provides to create such a multiplexed stream, is the `I_LINK` `ioctl`, and its companion, the `I_UNLINK` `ioctl`.

The first step in constructing a "stacked stream" is to open the upper stream in the usual way. Then open the lower stream, push on any modules that will be required, and issue the `I_LINK` `ioctl`. This removes the lower stream from its original head, and its file descriptor can now be closed if desired. The head routines are replaced by the `st_mux[rw]init` routines from the `STREAMTAB` entry of the upper stream. One might suppose that some sort of linkage of upper and lower queues would occur, but this would severely limit the flexibility of the multiplexer. Thus STREAMS now sends a special `M_IOCTL` message, with `ioc_cmd` set to `I_LINK`, down the upper stream, carrying as data a special `LINKBLK` structure that tells the upper stream where to find the lower stream queues and provides a unique MUX ID that can be used to identify the lower stream in routing and later in dismantling this portion of the multiplexer configuration:

```
LINKBLK
{
   QUEUE *l_qtop;
   QUEUE *l_qbot;
   int    l_index;
}
```

The `ioctl` `I_LINK` System Call

```
ioctl(upstreamfd, I_LINK, lowstreamfd)
```

is the system call that creates the link. The `upstreamfd` on which it is done becomes the "control stream" for this multiplexed configuration, and when it is closed the configuration is automatically dismantled.

Typically the upper driver (the multiplexing driver, it is usually called) will have a `wput` procedure that recognizes the special `M_IOCTL/I_LINK` message that is sent by STREAMS after the initial configuration is complete. The information in the `LINKBLK` are then stored in a private data structure. The lower head procedures are actually part of the object code module that defined this private data structure, so they are also able to access it to find the upper queues, and the upper queues access it to find the lower queues.

The driver routines in the lower driver know nothing of the link, and nothing of the upper driver(s); in particular the interrupt routines do not need (or have) this information. This aids greatly in producing a modular and reusable lower driver package. The lower driver procedures are designed to operate with a standard head above them, and the multiplexer routines that are specified with the upper driver emulate these head routines, as far as their interface with the queue below them. This setup has an additional advantage, in that lower driver testing and debugging can proceed without the upper driver being involved at all.

There are two `QINIT` pairs that determine the behavior of the structure being created. The `QINIT` pair for the original driver specify the bottom procedures for the upper driver, and the `QINIT` pair in the multiplexing entries for the original driver specifies the upper procedures for the lower driver. Generally when several links are made below a given driver, we have these multiplexing procedures replacing the head of each lower driver, and the single multiplexing driver pair communicating with them.

Typical configurations for these `QINIT` pairs are shown in Figs. 5-14 and 5-15.

wput	wsrv	wque	wirq		
YES	NO	YES	NO		

rput	rsrv	rque	ropen	rclose	rirq
NO	NO	NO	YES	YES	NO

Fig. 5-14. The multiplexing driver

wput	wsrv	wque	wirq		
NO	YES	NO	NO		

rput	rsrv		rque	ropen	rclose	rirq
YES	NO		NO	YES	YES	NO

Fig. 5-15. The multiplexed driver

Typical flow through the write side is for the upper `wput` to store its message on its own queue, and `qenable`, the lower `wsrv`; it saved the appropriate address from the original `LINKBLK`. That lower `wsrv` may also become enabled through an interrupt as usual. When the lower `wsrv` runs, it searches round-robin fashion through all upper `wques` (only one so far, but the upper driver may be multiple as well as multiplexing). Remember that the lower `wsrv` is really part of the code belonging to the upper driver, and so it also can access the stored `LINKBLK` information.

Typical flow through the read side is for the lower `wput` to attempt a `putnext` just above the upper read queue and to toss the incoming message if it cannot perform this `putnext`.

♦ Minor Devices ♦

The `open` activity so far described occurs each time a stream is opened for the first time from the `cdevsw[]` table. If the stream is merely reopened, none of this setup need be done, and STREAMS merely executes any `open` routines shown in the `QINFO` structure, as well as the `open` routines for any modules that have been pushed at the time of the reopen. But what is the situation regarding opening "minor" devices? The `cdevsw[]` entry refers only to major device number, of course, and for ordinary devices the minor device number is passed to the open procedure as a parameter. This procedure is also followed with STREAMS. The queue allocations and so on are all done using the `STREAMTAB` entries specified in `cdevsw[]`, that is, specified by the major device number. But the allocations are done individually for each minor device, so that each opened minor device refers to a separate stream.

There are now two ways in which a "major" device appears as a single entity. The first is that each minor version of it shares exactly the same structure (unless and until modified by the open routines, or by user calls); the second is that there is only a single kernel-linked set of routines for a particular major device, and thus the minor devices potentially share the data structures specified in those routines. The situation is very similar to that for non-STREAMS device drivers, recalling however that those have developer-specified routines "at the head" there is room for more diversity in minor device opens, even potentially a separate open routine for each minor device. In STREAMS it is usually the function of the driver `ropen` routines to maintain any data structures needed to keep track of minor devices.

The most common method of handling minor devices is to use an array of appropriate structures, indexed by the minor device number. This is the traditional UNIX method of handling multiple copies of a device, and it is highly applicable in the present setting.

Note that a particular queue may be encountered in two very distinct ways. During normal flow of data along a stream, the queue is encountered as a `q_next` pointer value, and we may need to find out its minor device number in order to index the table of minor devices to obtain needed values. During interrupt routine execution, the interrupt routine will be provided with the minor device number as an argument, and from this the appropriate `rques` and `wques` will have to be found. Thus the table of minor devices will have to contain these queue addresses.

The preceding constraints tell us the minimum contents of a `qopen` procedure when minor devices all present. Note that the `open` routine for a queue is called with the address of the queue and the minor device number as arguments. We first define a minor device table to hold whatever values we need:

```
STRUCT mindev[NDEV]
```

Usually this can be declared as part of the configuration file for the device, i.e., in the `/etc/master.d` file with global parameter values possibly taken from

/etc/master (or its System V 3.2 equivalent).

```
qopen(q_p, dev, flag, sflag)
{
```
check that mindev[dev] *has not been initialized,*
i.e., that this minor device is not already open

Store q_p *(or* OTHERQ(q_p)*, or both) into* mindev[dev]

Store &mindev[dev] *into* q_p->q_ptr, *the private data structure*
```
}
```

In a typical driver there is only an ropen procedure, which does all of the open work for both sides. In this case we will also wish to store &mindev[dev] into the partner's private data structure OTHERQ(q_p)->q_ptr.

Clone Open

The usual paradigm for finding an available minor device is to try opening them in numerical order until one is found that was not already open. With STREAMS a much simpler procedure is easily performed. There is a special STREAMS driver called *clone*, supplied with STREAMS versions of System V, and it allows a special open called a *clone open* that produces an unopened minor device and creates an inode for it. The developer of the desired driver has to allow for this special type of open, which is actually rather simple to do.

In a clone open, we actually open the clone device, passing as minor number the major number of the driver we really desire to open. The clone driver uses this major number to access cdevsw[] on its own and find the appropriate STREAMTAB entry. It then calls the open procedure for that device, with the special CLONEOPEN flag set, and if the developer has allowed for this possibility in the open routines, an unused minor number is produced and returned as the value of the open. The clone driver now receives this value, and uses it to construct a new inode in the same way that "unnamed inodes" are constructed for pipes. Placing this new inode into the file table in place of itself, the "open of the clone device" now returns, and appears to have been an "open of a minor device."

6

TLI

Douglas Harris

Department of Mathematics, Statistics, and Computer Science
Marquette University

◆　The ISO-OSI Model　◆

The International Standards Organization (ISO) has produced the well-known Reference Model of Open Systems Interconnection (ISO-OSI, or just OSI). This model conceptually divides interconnection into seven layers:

- application

- presentation

- session

- transport

- network

- link

- physical

and describes an interconnection method in terms of messages passing between these layers and actions that occur in the layers.

The *Transport Layer Interface*, or TLI, is an interface at the top of the transport layer, or in ISO-OSI terms, between the session and the transport layers. The ISO terminology of layer-to-layer communication describes messages passing between entities in those two layers. The upper layer entity is called the *user*, and the lower layer entity is called the *provider*, with four types of messages passed:

At the client/talker:

1. **request**: user to provider, asking that a certain task be done.

2. **confirmation**: provider to user, providing the result of the task.

At the server/listener:

3. **indication**: provider to user, describing some event that has occurred.

4. **response**: user to provider, responding to an indication.

For example, the process of creating an end-to-end connection between transport users A and Z can be described as follows:

1. User A **requests** provider a to set up a connection with user Z.

    A. Provider a does whatever is required to connect with

    B. Provider z which is the provider for user Z.

2. Provider z **indicates** to user Z that user A wishes a connection.

3. User Z **responds** to provider z that a connection will be accepted.

    A. Provider z does whatever is required to connect with provider a.

4. Provider z **confirms** to user Z that user A is now connected.

In the standard terminology, once A and Z have become connected, they are user level peers, and similarly the providers a and z are transport level peers.

We shall attempt to describe interactions as much as possible using this terminology. Notice that a request may initiate actual transport of control or data information across a network, but it is equally possible that a provider can confirm a request without ever contacting its peer. Similarly an indication given by a provider is often initiated by the provider's peer, but it may equally well have been inititated by the local provider on its own.

♦ The Transport Layer Interface ♦

For those interested in end-to-end (or host-to-host) communication, the transport layer is perhaps the most interesting, and the most important, as the first layer from the bottom to guarantee reliable communication, and as the first layer from the top to require consideration of the actions taking place at both ends of the connection. ISO has itself developed standards for the transport layer (usually referred to as ISO/TPn, where n can be 0, 1, 2, 3, or 4 and indicates the type of service specified in that standard). Other familiar standards are the Department of Defense (DoD) TCP/IP protocol suite; various public standards such as X.25; and commercial standards such as AT&T's Starlan transport provider, various Appletalk protocols, or Microsoft's Server Message Block (SMB) protocol.

Influenced by the ISO model, AT&T has constructed the UNIX system Transport Level Interface (TLI) as a progamming interface to any transport provider that follows the ISO-OSI precepts. The goal of the UNIX system TLI is to allow higher layers, applications in particular, to be developed and implemented independently of the details of the underlying provider. This means in particular that one can expect code conforming to TLI to run over any provider, requiring only linking with the TLI library appropriate to that provider. Furthermore, if the standard STREAMS based TLI library provided with UNIX System V Release 3.2 and beyond is used, code conforming to TLI can run with any STREAMS based provider without relinking. Thus we can merely perform what appears to be an ordinary UNIX open system call on the appropriate provider.

The requirements that a provider must meet to prepare a library of TLI routines are minimal. In fact there is a document, the Transport Provider Specification, spelling out these requirements. If the provider meets these specifications, then the programmer is protected from most of the details of the dialogue with the provider. When those details are relevant, for example when a message-oriented interface rather than a byte-stream interface is required, the TLI interface provides for determining the needed information from the provider and for negotiating setting of the options desired.

It is important that the TLI user understand these semantics carefully. TLI is an "interface to a transport provider," not a transport provider itself. The user of TLI specifies the transport provider to be used, which could be based upon the DoD TCP/IP protocol suite running over any network that supports IP, on a special protocol such as AT&T's Universal Receiver Protocol running over a Starlan local area network, or on a STREAMS library such as the AT&T Network Services Library, which runs using any stream on which the modules of the library can be pushed.

◆ Getting to Know Your Provider ◆

Although we have indicated that TLI code is written to be independent of the provider, that does not preclude us from attempting to take advantage of particular characteristics of the provider. In order to keep this interface between user and provider uniform, however, TLI has provided an appropriate data structure (TINFO) and routine (t_getinfo) for this purpose. The rationale for this mechanism is that a TLI program can look at the parameters provided and organize its activities appropriately, so that a single program can adapt itself to a wide variety of transports.

The `TINFO` data structure encapsulates all of the information TLI is willing to give the programmer regarding the provider:

```
TINFO
{
   addr;       /* allowed size of the transport address */
   options;    /* allowed size of the options field */
   tsdu;       /* allowed size of a transport service data unit */
   etsdu;      /* allowed size of an expedited transport service
                  data unit */
   connect;    /* allowed size of a connect request */
   discon;     /* allowed size of a disconnect request */
   servtype;   /* type of service provided */
};
```

The primitive for requesting this information is `t_getinfo`:

```
int
t_getinfo(tep, infores_p)
TINFO *infores_p;
```

Usually the fields of the result structure `infores_p` show size limits as indicated in the definition. However, it is possible that a particular field does not apply for the provider currently in use, or that it has no limit. Interpretations are given in Table 6-1.

The connect/disconnect length fields of `infores_p` show whether data can accompany connect/disconnect requests; this might be useful to show a peer the reason behind such a request. The actual values used here would be up to the implementor.

The service type indicates whether the provider is merely for end-to-end datagrams, or if it can provide a real transport connection, and, in the latter case, whether it provides graceful or graceless connection facilities.

The codes for service type are:

- `T_COTS`: Stream transport, graceless disconnect.

- `T_COTS_ORD`: Stream transport, graceful disconnect (also called orderly).

- `T_CLTS`: Datagram transport (also called connectionless).

TABLE 6-1. TINFO structure values

Element	Value	Meaning
addr	>=0	maximum size is value of this field
	-1	no maximum size
	-2	address size cannot be set by user
options	>=0	maximum size is value of this field
	-1	no maximum size
	-2	options cannot be set by user
tsdu	0	tsdu is unsupported
	>0	maximum size is value of this field
	-1	no maximum size
	-2	this provider does not transport normal data
etsdu	0	etsdu is unsupported
	>0	maximum size is value of this field
	-1	no maximum size
	-2	this provider does not transport expedited data
connect	>=0	maximum size is value of this field
	-1	no maximum size
	-2	connect cannot carry data
disconnect	>=0	maximum size is value of this field
	-1	no maximum size
	-2	disconnect cannot carry data

Variations in the type of service are typically provided by opening different devices. For example with AT&T 3B1/3B2 Starlan based TLI, /dev/starlan provides stream transport, and /dev/starlandg provides datagram transport; with AT&T 3B15 TWG/TCP/IP based TLI, /dev/tcp provides stream transport, and /dev/udp provides datagram transport; with Micom/Interlan TCP/IP UNIX V.3 we have /dev/it for stream and /dev/is for datagram transport; and with Excelan EXOS TCP/IP Network Software for UNIX/386 we have /dev/xt and /dev/xtd.

Table 6-2 gives representative T_INFO values.

TABLE 6-2. TINFO service values

TINFO element	AT&T 3B15 WIN/TCP		AT&T 3B2 STARLAN		AT&T 3B1 STARLAN	
	/dev/tcp	/dev/udp	/dev/starlan	/dev/starlandg	/dev/starlan	/dev/starlandg
addr	16	16	255	16	255	255
option	-2	-2	32	32	32	32
tsdu	0	0	-1	1462	-1	1462
etsdu	1	-2	-2	-2	-2	-2
connect	-2	-2	128	-2	128	-2
discon	-2	-2	-2	-2	128	-2
srvtype	2	3	1	3	1	3

At the end of this chapter is a TLI program (showtli.c) that extracts appropriate information for a particular TLI transport provider; it was used to obtain the values given above.

◆ Negotiating Options with Your Provider ◆

Since TLI code is expected to be portable to a variety of systems and to be independent of its provider, it should come as no surprise that TLI provides primitives for adapting to the capabilites (or lack thereof) of a provider at run-time. In TLI there is a service primitive t_optmgmt, and options negotiation proceeds by using it to get and set values of a T_OPTMGMT structure:

```
typedef t_optmgmt
{
  NETBUF opt;
  long   flags;
}
T_OPTMGMT;

int
t_optmgmt(tep, reqop_p, resop_p)
T_OPTMGMT reqop_p;
T_OPTMGMT resop_p;
```

The negotation proceeds as follows:

1. The `reqop_p->flags` specify a request, and

2. The `resop_p->flags` specify an indication or confirmation.

The `T_NEGOTIATE` provider looks at `reqop_p->opt`, decides, and returns `resop_p->opt`.

The `T_CHECK` provider indicates support for the option by setting `resop_p->flags` to `T_SUCCESS/T_FAILURE`.

The `T_DEFAULT` provider returns default in `resop_p->opt`.

As an example of options negotiation, the sockets-based AT&T WIN/TCP 1.1 uses a modification of the *sockets* options negotiation familiar to devotees of the Berkeley variant of UNIX. `opt.buf` points to a

```
struct
{
  unsigned short name;
  unsigned short val;
}
```

where `name` can be one of the BSD socket option values:

```
SO_DEBUG
SO_REUSEADDR
SO_KEEPALIVE
SO_DONTROUTE
SO_USELOOPBACK
SO_LINGER
SO_DONTLINGER
```

and `val` is unused, except when name is `SO_LINGER`.

◆ States and Events ◆

The TLI description of a transport connection is given in terms of *transport end-points* (TEP). A TEP has a *current state* (whose value is available to the user) and a *current event* (whose value is also available to the user). The behavior of a TEP is described completely as that of a "finite state machine." That is, the TLI specifications describe how events cause a TEP to change its state and describe those events that can occur when the TEP is in any particular state. The programmer uses the TLI routines to request and respond to changes of the state of the transport provider. Table 6-3 lists the states of a TEP.

TABLE 6-3. TEP states

TEP state	Meaning
T_UNINIT	The embryonic state in which there is no user
T_UNBND	The TEP has a user, but the TEP has no name
T_IDLE	The TEP has a name, but nothing to do
T_INCON	The TEP is waiting to connect to another TEP
T_OUTCON	The TEP is trying to connect to another TEP
T_DATAXFER	The TEP is communicating with another TEP
T_OUTREL	The TEP is trying to disconnect from the other TEP
T_INREL	The TEP is waiting to disconnect from the other TEP

The state of a TEP can be found at any time as the value returned by the t_getstate primitive:

```
t_getstate();
```

The events that can occur at a transport endpoint are listed in Table 6-4.

TABLE 6-4. TEP events

TEP event	Meaning
T_LISTEN	A connect indication arrived
T_CONNECT	A connect confirmation arrived
T_DATA	A data indication arrived
T_EXDATA	An expedited data indication arrived
T_ORDREL	A release indication arrived
T_DISCONNECT	A disconnect indication arrived
T_UDERROR	An error occurred in a datagram
T_ERROR	An error occurred in the provider

The current event can be found at any time as the value returned by the t_look primitive:

```
t_look();
```

◆ Changing the State (Gracefully) ◆

The 12 TLI primitives that direct changes of state are listed in Table 6-5.

TABLE 6-5. State changing primitives

TLI function	Action
t_open()	Give me a TEP
t_bind()	Name my TEP
t_listen()	Wait for a connection indication from some TEP
t_accept()	Respond to connection indication from some TEP
t_connect()	Request connection to a specified TEP
t_snd()	Request data be sent to the other TEP
t_rcv()	Wait for a data indication from the other TEP
t_sndrel()	Request disconnection from the other TEP
t_rcvrel()	Wait for a disconnection indication from the other TEP
t_unbind()	Give up my TEP's name
t_close()	Give up my TEP

Table 6-6 showing the state table of how events cause changes of state is arranged as follows: the events are on the left, the states are on the top, and an entry in the body of the table is the *next state* that results when the event occurs while the TEP is in the state at the top of its column. If there is no entry in a particular column, the event should not occur while in the state corresponding to the column; this means to the programmer that the corresponding function request should not be issued while the TEP is in that state.

TABLE 6-6. Changing states

	State change						
TLI function	T_UNINIT	T_UNBND	T_IDLE	T_INCON	T_DATAXFER	T_SNDREL	T_RCVREL
t_open()	T_UNBND						
t_bind()		T_IDLE					
t_listen()			T_INCON				
t_connect()				T_DATAXFER			
t_accept()				T_DATAXFER			
t_snd()					T_DATAXFER		T_RCVREL
t_rcv()					T_DATAXFER	T_SNDREL	
t_rcvrel()					T_IDLE		
t_unbind()			T_UNBND				
t_close()		T_UNINIT					

♦ Addressing ♦

TLI in and of itself does not provide a standard for transport addresses but rather a standard for *providing* transport addresses. Namely, TLI routines that must deal with addresses deal with them merely as a string of bytes (in UNIX tradition, these are of course called `chars`, but as usual this in no sense means that they are ASCII characters—or even EBCDIC characters for that matter). Addresses for TLI then are a certain number of bytes: the transport provider is welcome, and indeed expected, to turn these into addresses appropriate for its world. It is up to the implementor of a particular application written in terms of TLI functions to provide byte strings that the provider will convert appropriately.

The primitive for providing transport addresses in TLI is `t_bind`, and it uses the `T_BIND` structure to communicate addreses with its provider.

```
typedef struct t_bind
{
  NETBUF   addr; /* Size limited by T_INFO.addr */
  unsigned qlen; /* Maximum number of queued
                    connection indications */
}
T_BIND;
```

`qlen == 0` supposedly is allowed for a server that expects only one client. However, some implementations do not handle this well, so `qlen == 1` is safer for this situation. `qlen > 1` is only appropriate for a passive listener that expects many clients.

```
int
t_bind(tep, bindreq_p, bindres_p)
int tep;
T_BIND bindreq_p;
T_BIND bindres_p;
```

The function can return:

TBADF:	tep does not refer to a TEP.
TOUTSTATE:	t_bind not issued from the T_UNBND state.
TBADADDR:	T_BIND.addr is not legal.
TNOADDR:	T_BIND.addr could not be allocated by the provider.
TACCES:	T_BIND.addr is not allowed for this user.

TBUFOVFLW: `bindres_p.addr` is too small for the address to be returned.

TSYSERR: A system error occurred during the call to `t_bind`.

In the AT&T WIN/TCP 1.1 implementation of TLI, an address buffer is a structure of the following form:

```
struct sockaddr_in
{
  short sin_family;          /* Must be AF_INET */
  unsigned short sin_port;   /* user port      */
  struct in_addr sin_addr;   /* host address   */
  char sin_zero[8];          /* unused - zeroed */
}

struct in_addr
{
  unsigned long s_addr;
}
```

In the AT&T 3B1/3B2 Starlan implementation, addresses are ordinary character strings such as the usual UNIX node name, perhaps with a dotted postfix. A function is provided to convert such a name into something appropriate for the provider, and the user need only be sure to perform that conversion before giving the address structure to the provider. For example the usual node name of the machine (e.g., "marque") is used to connect with a login server, and the usual node name with the postfix ".serve" (e.g., "marque.serve") is used to connect with a special command server.

The names used in this implementation are compatible with names as used in NetBios, and in fact interoperate with those names.

♦ Listening and Connecting ♦

Now that we know our own name (or that of our endpoint), communication will be even more interesting if we have someone else to communicate with. The paradigm followed in finding a partner is the familiar *client-server* model; more appropriate, perhaps, it can be called the *talker-listener* model.

The TLI model contemplates a client-server form of connection and of disconnection. That is, it expects that a server be listening before a client tries to connect with it. In this model you cannot talk unless you know there is a listener; more exactly, you can speak even though there is no listener, but there will be no confirmation of the conversation, and it will fail. It is possible that the listener will also talk, but initially the listener is purely passive, and the talker can become active only when a listener confirms that the talk is being heard.

An analogy with the telephone service is apt: you cannot call someone who is not listening for the phone to ring. In fact the layer most commonly used above TLI in AT&T software is called the "Network Listener Service," and its major function is to provide a listener which will then fork a desired server. To continue the telephone analogy, this listener corresponds to a secretary who then rounds up the intended recipient of the call.

These matters are described in the usual terminology as *types of service*, and the service as just described is called *Connection-Oriented Transport Service*, or COTS. We establish a connection from client to server (talker to listener) and a two-way conversation can then take place, in *reliable byte stream* mode; i.e., each byte that is sent is delivered, and the order in which bytes are sent is the order in which they are delivered.

There are several primitives involved in establishing a connection; each of them makes use of the T_CALL structure.

```
typedef struct t_call
{
  NETBUF  addr;
  NETBUF  opt;
  NETBUF  udata;
  int     sequence;
}
T_CALL;
```

The functions that use this structure can be divided into client and server functions.

On the client (or talker) side:

```
t_connect(tep, callreq_p, callcon_p)
T_CALL *callreq_p,
       *callcon_p;
```

callreq_p identifies the peer you wish to contact, and callcon_p identifies the peer that you did contact.

```
t_rcvconnect(tep, callcon_p);
T_CALL *callcon_p;
```

callcon_p identifies the peer that you did contact.

On the server (or listener) side:

```
t_listen(tep, callind_p)
T_CALL *callind_p;
```

callind_p->sequence identifies the particular queued connect indication.

```
t_accept(tep, step, callind_p)
T_CALL *callind_p;
```

`step` represents either the current TEP, or possibly a new TEP, in `T_UNBND` state, with which the connection will be made.   `callind_p` will be the same structure received in an earlier `t_listen`.

◆ Conversing: Sending and Receiving Data Units ◆

The primitives for the conversation itself are straightforward: the `t_snd` primitive is used to send data units, and the `t_rcv` primitive to receive them. Each of these can be used in blocking or nonblocking mode by use of the `O_NDELAY` flag when the TEP is `t_opened`.

```
t_snd(tep, buf_p, buf_n, flag)
```

`tep` is the transport endpoint file descriptor, `buf_p` is the location of the data, `buf_n` is the length of the data, and `flag` carries `T_MORE` and `T_EXPEDITED` requests.

```
t_rcv(tep, buf_p, buf_n, flag_p)
```

`tep` is the transport endpoint file descriptor, `buf_p` is the location of the data, `buf_n` is the length of the data, and `flag_p` carries `T_MORE` and `T_EXPEDITED` indications.

Transport Service Data Units

In the ISO-OSI protocols, descriptions of interaction are often given in terms of *Transport Data Units, Expedited Transport Data Units,* and similar terms. The transport protocol is thought of in part as a byte stream with no message boundaries, and in part as a collection of user messages.

A particular provider may place a limit (`T_INFO.tsdu/T.INFO.etsdu`) on the amount of data that a user may give to the provider in a single request. The user needs to know that maximum, so that the `t_snd` call may be appropriately prepared. The user may also wish to send a message longer than that maximum and will of course be required to send it in chunks not larger than `T_INFO.tsdu`.

Fragmenting: the T_MORE Flag

Two basic forms of reliable transport are supported by TLI. In *stream* transport we attempt to move a stream of bytes from peer to peer, preserving their order but no boundaries within, and in *message* transport we move a stream of messages (which are themselves indivisible strings of bytes), preserving the order of the messages. A particular provider may permit only one of these.

The mechanism established by TLI for message transport is the T_MORE flag, whose value can be set by the programmer in t_snd calls, or by the provider in the underlying transport, and whose value can be read by the programmer in t_rcv calls.

Thus to send a 980 byte message using t_snd calls of 120 bytes each, the user will t_snd 8 messages of 120 bytes, each with the T_MORE flag set, and t_snd one message of 20 bytes, with the T_MORE flag off.

The T_MORE flag is also used by the provider itself if it needs to or wishes to fragment the message or deliver it framed differently than the framing requested by the user.

A user's message (as far as TLI can deduce) is defined as follows: if T_MORE was set in the previous message and is not set in this message, then this is the last segment of the user message. if T_MORE was set in the previous message and is set in this message, then this is a continuation of the user message. if T_MORE was not set in the previous message and is not set in this message, then this message stands on its own.

Put more simply, if you do not care about boundaries, do not set T_MORE. It is still possible that TLI will fragment the message and that t_rcv will find T_MORE set, although you will not care.

At the receiving end a user (who cares about message boundaries) must always check the T_MORE flag in a t_rcv call; it is set if and only if the received data split a user message.

Expediting: the T_EXPEDITED Flag

To request that data sending be *expedited*, set the T_EXPEDITED bit in the t_snd. The actual interpretation of this is determined by the provider (and in fact part of the t_info information is whether expedited data transfer is provided at all). Only an interface for the service is provided by TLI.

If a t_rcv returns with the T_EXPEDITED flag set, this means the flag was also set by the sender, and presumably the provider did the right thing to get the data here. The TLI interface specification allows the user to see that the data packet that was just received was an expedited data packet, and further action is up to the user. Note that arrival of an expedited data packet may or may not provide some special indication at the receiving end in accordance with the provider implementation; the "official" way of discovering this is through the flag_p value returned by t_rcv.

◆ Terminating ◆

The basic state model given above describes disconnection in terms of the so-called *graceful disconnect*, which in fact is not part of the ISO-OSI model. That model contemplates instead what might be called the "disgraceful disconnect," or perhaps the *graceless disconnect*. If we were describing a telephone conversation, the "graceful" model is one in which one of the callers says "Goodbye" and stops talking but remains carefully listening until hearing "Goodbye" from the other end. The "graceless" model is one in which one of the callers hangs up the phone, fortunately with a bang so that the other caller at least knows there is no longer a listener. Every provider must support graceless disconnect, since nature may intervene even if the callers are trying to be polite; that is, the provider machine at one end, or the network connections in between, may crash, and the provider is expected to detect this and issue its own local disconnect indication.

The TLI interface itself does not prejudge the capabilities of the transport provider. In the `T_INFO` structure returned by `t_getinfo` there is a *service type* field to show these capabilities.

Service types for a transport provider are:

- `T_COTS`: stream transport with graceless disconnect only

- `T_COTS_ORD`: stream transport with graceful/graceless disconnect

- `T_CLTS`: datagram transport

The Graceless Disconnect

The graceless disconnect is supported by the `t_snddis` and the `t_rcvdis` primitives, as well as the `T_DISCONNECT` value returned by `t_look`, possibly invoked following a `TLOOK` error return from a TLI primitive.

```
t_snddis(tep, call_p)
```

Request (actually demand) disconnection from the TEP given in the `T_CALL` structure pointed to by `call_p`.

```
t_rcvdis(tep, disc_p)
```

Receive indication of disconnection from the other TEP. A reason may be given in the `T_DISCONNECT` structure pointed to by `disc_p`. These calls actually take us from any state to the `T_IDLE` state.

These routines must be used (especially if portability is an aim), since many providers do not support the `T_COTS_ORD` orderly release. Even for a provider that does support graceful disconnect, it is still possible that a graceless disconnect will occur. Your peer may exit prematurely, and the TLI always arranges a graceless disconnect in this case. Your peer may not wish to speak with you when you call, and the graceful way to say so is for your peer to request t_snddis from its provider. Thus every TLI program must be prepared to both send and receive this form of disconnect.

The indication is handled in the usual UNIX manner; a blocking call, such as t_rcv, is given an error return, with t_errno set to TLOOK. The user who looks via t_look is then given a T_DISCONNECT value for the event (see the next section).

A very common beginner's error with a T_COTS provider is to allow the disconnect to be sent before all the data has arrived at your peer. The peer may see the disconnect before it has seen the data, and thus will never see the data.

♦ Looking: Asynchronous Events ♦

One may well wonder in the preceding discussion of disconnection how it is that one user finds out another has disconnected, or for that matter how the other end has gracefully disconnected. Of course, in the "telephone" analogy, you "hear the bang" for a graceless disconnect, and "hear the Goodbye" for a graceful disconnect. But TLI does not wish to depend upon users recognizing problems in the data, or patterns in the data, to accomplish graceless/graceful disconnects, and thus it provides a way for the user to learn more certainly about events that the provider has detected. The method is the time-honored UNIX method of handling such matters: when an event such as some form of disconnect occurs, any TLI function that is currently pending is forcefully returned with an "error" indication, and a special error variable is set to a value which means "something has occurred in the provider, you had better take a look and see what it is." The error value returned is in fact called TLOOK, it is returned in the special value t_errno, and the TLI function t_look can be used to see what has occurred.

The following is typical code for a data receiver, which expects the other end to disconnect when all the data has been sent.

```
if (t_rcv() < 0)
{
  if (TLOOK == t_errno)
  {
    t_event = t_look();
    if (t_event == T_DISCON) /* Or T_ORDREL
                                for a graceful sender*/
    {
      t_rcvdis();              /* t_rcvrel() if graceful */
      exit(0);
    }
    else
    {
      printf("Some unexpected event occurred\n");
```

```
    }
    printf("t_rcv failed unexpectedly\n");
  }
}
```

◆ Sample Programs ◆

The following programs implement simple server/client pairs. In the first pair, a command is taken from the argument list of the client and sent to the server, which executes the command and sends the output back to the client. In the second pair, the command from the argument list of the client is sent to the server along with input that is passed to the command when executed by the server. A sample interactive session follows. The last program, showtli.c, lists TLI information given by the provider in the t_info structure.

In order to compile and link these programs, you have to be able to find the proper include files and libraries. On System V, Release 3, the TLI library is found in

```
/usr/lib/libnsl_s.a
```

nsl represents network services library, and the _s means that it is a shared library.

Some implementations, especially for earlier releases of System V, or other networking situations, use other header files. On the UNIX System V 3B15 Release 2.1.1 implementation:

```
/usr/netinclude/sys/tli.h
```

is the header file, and

```
/usr/lib/libnet.a
```

is the library. On 3B1/Starlan, the header files are

```
/usr/include/net/tiuser.h
/usr/include/net/sys/tiuser.h
```

and the library is

```
/usr/lib/libslan.a
```

```
/**************************************************************
/*
/*   PROGRAM: srvo.c
/*   Written by Douglas Harris, December 13, 1988
/*   To illustrate use of TLI routines
/*   A server which receives a command that produces output
/*   only and returns the output to its client
/*
/**************************************************************/

#include <signal.h>
#include <fcntl.h>
#include <stdio.h>
#include <sys/tiuser.h>

int t_errno;

main (argc, argv)
int argc;
char *argv[];
{
  FILE  *exec_p;
  char   dat_p[1024];
  char   cmd_p[1024];
  int    dat_n;
  int    s_tep;
  int    flags;

  struct t_bind *bindreq_p;
  struct t_call *callind_p;

  if ((s_tep = t_open("/dev/starlan", O_RDWR, NULL)) < 0)
  {
    t_error("S:open failed");
    exit(2);
  }

  bindreq_p = (struct t_bind *) t_alloc(s_tep,T_BIND,T_ALL);
  bindreq_p->addr.maxlen = 16;
  bindreq_p->addr.len = strlen(argv[1]);
  strncpy(bindreq_p->addr.buf, argv[1], 16);
  bindreq_p->qlen = 1;
  if (!lname2addr(s_tep, &(bindreq_p->addr)))
  {
    t_error("S:Name conversion failed");
    exit(3);
```

```
}

if (t_bind(s_tep,bindreq_p,NULL) < 0)
{
  t_error("S:Bind failed");
  exit(4);
}

callind_p = (struct t_call *) t_alloc(s_tep, T_CALL, T_ALL);

if  (t_listen(s_tep, callind_p) < 0)
{
  t_error("S:Listen failed\n");
  exit(5);
}

if  (t_accept(s_tep, s_tep, callind_p) < 0)
{
  t_error("S:Accept failed");
  exit(6);
}

if (t_rcv(s_tep, cmd_p, sizeof(cmd_p), &flags) < 0)
{
    t_error("S:Cmd Receive failed");
    exit(2);
}

if  (!(exec_p = popen(cmd_p, "r")))
{
  perror("S:File Open of %s failed\n", cmd_p);
  exit(3);
}

while ((dat_n = fread(dat_p, 1, sizeof(dat_p), exec_p)) > 0)
{
  if (t_snd(s_tep, dat_p, dat_n, 0) < 0)
  {
    t_error("S:Data Send failed");
    exit(4);
  }
}

if (ferror(exec_p))
{
  perror("S:File Read failed");
```

```
        exit(5);
    }

    sleep(2);

    if (t_snddis(s_tep, NULL) < 0)
    {
        t_error("S:Disconnect failed");
        exit(6);
    }
    pclose(exec_p);
    exit(0);
}
```

```
/****************************************************************
/*
/*   PROGRAM: oclient.c
/*   Written by Douglas Harris, December 13, 1988
/*   To illustrate use of TLI routines
/*   A client which sends a command that produces output only
/*   and receives the output from its server
/*
/*****************************************************************/

#include <signal.h>
#include <errno.h>
#include <fcntl.h>
#include <stdio.h>
#include <sys/tiuser.h>

int t_errno;
int t_lookno;

main (argc, argv)
int argc;
char *argv[];
{
  int c_tep;
  int flags;

  int dat_n,
      cmd_n;

  char add_p[1024],
       cmd_p[1024],
       dat_p[1024];

  struct t_call *callreq_p;

  if (argc < 3)
  {
    exit(1);
  }

  strcpy(add_p, argv[1]);
  argv++;
  argv++;

  for (; *argv; argv++)
  {
```

```
      strcat(cmd_p, *argv);
      strcat(cmd_p, " ");
   }
cmd_n = strlen(cmd_p);
cmd_p[cmd_n-1] = '\0';

if ((c_tep = t_open("/dev/starlan", O_RDWR, NULL)) < 0)
{
   perror("C:Cannot open tep");
   exit(2);
}

if (t_bind(c_tep, NULL, NULL) < 0)
{
   t_error("C:bind failed");
   exit(3);
}

callreq_p = (struct t_call *) t_alloc(c_tep, T_CALL, T_ADDR);
callreq_p->addr.maxlen = 16;
callreq_p->addr.len = strlen(add_p);
strncpy(callreq_p->addr.buf, add_p, 16);

if (lname2addr(c_tep, &(callreq_p->addr)) == NULL)
{
   t_error("C:name conversion failed\n");
   exit(4);
}

if (t_connect(c_tep, callreq_p) < 0)
{
   t_lookno = t_look(c_tep);
   if (t_lookno == T_DISCONNECT)
   {
     t_error("C:unanticipated event");
     exit(5);
   }
   t_error("C:connect failed");
   exit(6);
}


if (t_snd(c_tep, cmd_p, cmd_n, &flags) < 0)
{
   t_error("C:cmd snd failed");
   exit(7);
```

```
}

while((dat_n=t_rcv(c_tep, dat_p ,sizeof(dat_p), &flags)) > 0)
{
  if (fwrite(dat_p, 1, dat_n, stdout) < 0)
  {
    exit(8);
  }
}

if  ((t_errno != TLOOK) ||
     ((t_lookno = (t_look(c_tep)) != T_DISCONNECT)))
{
  t_error("C:receive failed");
  exit(9);
}

if  (t_rcvdis(c_tep, NULL) < 0)
{
  t_error("C:rcvdis failed");
  exit(10);
}
exit(0);
}
```

```
/**********************************************************
/*
/*   PROGRAM: srvi.c
/*   Written by Douglas Harris, December 13, 1988
/*   To illustrate use of TLI routines
/*   A server which receives a command that requires input only
/*   and receives the input from its client
/*
/**********************************************************/

#include <signal.h>
#include <fcntl.h>
#include <stdio.h>
#include <sys/tiuser.h>

int t_errno;

main (argc, argv)
int argc;
char *argv[];
{
  FILE  *exec_p;
  char  dat_p[1024];
  char  cmd_p[1024];
  int   dat_n;
  int   cmd_s;
  int   s_tep;
  int   flags;
  struct t_bind *bindreq_p;
  struct t_call *callind_p;

  if ((s_tep = t_open("/dev/starlan", O_RDWR, NULL)) < 0)
  {
    t_error("S:open failed");
    exit(2);
  }

  bindreq_p = (struct t_bind *) t_alloc(s_tep, T_BIND, T_ALL);
  bindreq_p->addr.maxlen = 16;
  bindreq_p->addr.len = strlen(argv[1]);
  strncpy(bindreq_p->addr.buf, argv[1], 16);
  bindreq_p->qlen = 1;
  if (!lname2addr(s_tep, &(bindreq_p->addr)))
  {
    t_error("S:Name conversion failed");
    exit(3);
```

```
}

if (t_bind(s_tep,bindreq_p,NULL) < 0)
{
  t_error("S:Bind failed");
  exit(4);
}

callind_p = (struct t_call *) t_alloc(s_tep, T_CALL, T_ALL);

if (t_listen(s_tep, callind_p) < 0)
{
  t_error("S:Listen failed\n");
  exit(5);
}

if (t_accept(s_tep, s_tep, callind_p) < 0)
{
  t_error("S:Accept failed");
  exit(6);
}

if (t_rcv(s_tep, cmd_p, sizeof(cmd_p), &flags) < 0)
{
    t_error("S:Cmd Receive failed");
    exit(7);
}

if (!(exec_p = popen(cmd_p, "w")))
{
  perror("S:File Open of %s failed\n", cmd_p);
  exit(8);
}

while((dat_n=t_rcv(s_tep, dat_p, sizeof(dat_p), &flags)) > 0)
{
  if (fwrite(dat_p, 1, dat_n, exec_p) < 0)
  {
    perror("S:fwrite failed");
    exit(9);
  }
}

if (cmd_s = pclose(exec_p))
{
  perror("S:Exec failed");
```

```
      exit(10);
   }

   if (t_rcvdis(s_tep, NULL) < 0)
   {
      t_error("S:Receive Disconnect failed");
      exit(11);
   }
   exit(0);
}
```

```
/********************************************************
/*
/*   PROGRAM: iclient.c
/*   Written by Douglas Harris, December 13, 1988
/*   To illustrate use of TLI routines
/*   A client which sends a command that requires input only
/*   and sends the input to its server
/*
/********************************************************/

#include <signal.h>
#include <errno.h>
#include <fcntl.h>
#include <stdio.h>
#include <sys/tiuser.h>

int t_errno;
int t_lookno;

main (argc, argv)
int argc;
char *argv[];
{
  int c_tep,
      flags;

  int cmd_n,
      dat_n;

  char add_p[1024],
       cmd_p[1024],
       dat_p[1024];
  struct t_call *callreq_p;

  strcpy(add_p, argv[1]);
  argv++;
  argv++;

  for (; *argv; argv++)
  {
    strcat(cmd_p, *argv);
    strcat(cmd_p, " ");
  }
  cmd_n = strlen(cmd_p);
  cmd_p[cmd_n-1] = '\0';
```

```
if ((c_tep = t_open("/dev/starlan", O_RDWR, NULL)) < 0)
{
  perror("C:cannot open tep");
  exit(1);
}

if (t_bind(c_tep, NULL, NULL) < 0)
{
  t_error("C:bind failed");
  exit(2);

}

callreq_p = (struct t_call *) t_alloc(c_tep, T_CALL, T_ADDR);
callreq_p->addr.maxlen = 16;
callreq_p->addr.len = strlen(add_p);
strncpy(callreq_p->addr.buf, add_p, 16);
if (lname2addr(c_tep, &(callreq_p->addr)) == NULL)
{
  t_error("C:name conversion failed\n");
  exit(3);
}

if (t_connect(c_tep, callreq_p) < 0)
{
  t_lookno = t_look(c_tep);
  if (t_lookno == T_DISCONNECT)
  {
    t_error("C:unanticipated event");
    exit(4);
  }
  t_error("C:connect failed");
  exit(5);
}

if (t_snd(c_tep, cmd_p, cmd_n, &flags) < 0)
{
  t_error("C:cmd snd failed");
  exit(6);
}

while ((dat_n = fread(dat_p, 1, sizeof(dat_p), stdin)) > 0)
{
  if (t_snd(c_tep, dat_p, dat_n, 0) < 0)
  {
    t_error("C:data snd failed");
```

```
      exit(7);
    }
  }

  if (!feof(stdin))
  {
    perror("C:fread failed");
    exit(8);
  }

  sleep(10);

  if (t_snddis(c_tep, NULL) < 0)
  {
    t_error("C:snddis failed");
    exit(9);
  }
  exit(0);
}
```

```
$ srvo mysrvo &
[1]    3622
$ oclient mysrvo cat /etc/group
root:NONE:0:root
other:NONE:1:daemon,lp
bin:NONE:2:root,bin,daemon
sys:NONE:3:root,bin,sys,adm
mail:NONE:6:root,uucp,nuucp,uucpadm
users:NONE:100:tutor,install
adm:NONE:4:root,adm,daemon,listen,net
$
$ srvi mysrvi &
[1]    3625
$ iclient mysrvi mail doug < /etc/group
$ cat /usr/mail/doug
From doug Tue Dec 13 16:34 CST 1988
root:NONE:0:root
other:NONE:1:daemon,lp
bin:NONE:2:root,bin,daemon
sys:NONE:3:root,bin,sys,adm
mail:NONE:6:root,uucp,nuucp,uucpadm
users:NONE:100:tutor,install
adm:NONE:4:root,adm,daemon,listen,net
$
```

```
/**************************************************************
/*
/*   PROGRAM: showtli.c
/*   Written by Douglas Harris
/*   to obtain TLI information on
/*   a particular transport provider
/*
/*   Usage: showtli provider
/*
/**************************************************************/

#include <signal.h>
#include <fcntl.h>
#include <stdio.h>
#include <sys/tiuser.h>

extern int t_errno;

main (argc, argv)
int argc;
char *argv[];
{
  int tep;

  struct t_info info;

  if (argc != 2)
  {
    printf("Usage: %s provider\n", argv[0]);
    exit(1);
  }

  if ((tep = t_open(argv[1], O_RDWR, &info)) < 0)
  {
    printf("Device %s is not a transport provider\n",argv[1]);
    exit(2);
  }
  else
  {
    printf("\n");
    printf("\n");
    system("uname -a");
    printf("------------ Device %s ------------\n", argv[1]);
    printf("MAX ADDR      % ld\n", info.addr);
    printf("MAX OPTIONS   % ld\n", info.options);
    printf("MAX TSDU      % ld\n", info.tsdu);
```

```
      printf("MAX ETSDU     % ld\n", info.etsdu);
      printf("MAX CONNECT   % ld\n", info.connect);
      printf("MAX DISCON    % ld\n", info.discon);
      printf("SERVICE TYPE  % ld\n", info.servtype);
   }

   t_close(tep);
}
```

Remote File System

Douglas Harris

Department of Mathematics, Statistics, and Computer Science
Marquette University

◆ Introduction ◆

As the work of any organization begins to be spread across a number of machines, it becomes important to be able to access portions of that data from any of the machines quickly and reliably. In some ideal sense, we wish to treat all this distributed data as a single collection and access it by a uniform set of commands and with a uniform set of administrative actions related to access permissions, data backup, etc. Thus, Distributed UNIX, in which the entire collection of machines on which the needed data exists is treated as a single whole, is an ideal setting for many organizations.

In such a setting, differences between machines and methods of accessing the data on each are invisible to users. This does not mean, however, that such differences are invisible to the administrators of the organization, or of the separate machines. Just as the details of disk storage may be very important to the administrator of an individual machine, and yet invisible to its users (as long as it is fast enough and reliable enough for their purposes), so the details of inter-machine connectivity are arranged by administrators and of little interest or importance to users, as long as they work.

An ideal situation might occur when all user programs worked in the same way. An even more desirable situation would occur when the same programs work without change, even without recompilation or relinking, despite whether the data on which they operate resides on a single machine or on several machines that are connected by a communications network of some sort. This ideal setup requires that the connections provided by the network be highly reliable and operate dependably without user intervention. Also, the semantics of file names, access permissions, and similar matters must be independent of the connections, once those have been set up by the administrators of the machines involved. Similarly, the arcane details of disk partitions, cylinder/track/sector mappings, and file system mounting must be invisible to the user once the administrator accomplishes them.

Thus, a reasonable approach to Distributed UNIX, at least as far as data is concerned, is to repeat what has been highly successful for dealing with storage on a single machine and to handle the problem of accessing data on various machines in the same way as the problem of accessing data on various (local) storage devices. In other words, a remote access is exactly the same as a local access, except that it involves a (more or less visible) communications network. Of course, a local access may in fact involve such access also, especially if we consider (as we may) such local devices as a SCSI bus to be a form of network.

AT&T's approach toward UNIX System V, Release 3.0 and beyond is to provide a *Remote File System* (RFS) that is an extension of the ordinary file system arrangement. An ordinary disk partition (*block special file* in UNIX parlance) is mounted much like an ordinary UNIX file system (actually a portion of that file system) is "remote mounted" onto a local directory. Once this mounting has taken place, all programs work exactly as they did before. A few differences may become apparent during operation. For example, remote file systems may become inaccessible more frequently than local ones. Typically, a local file system is accessible whenever the local machine is. If a particular disk drive is not operating, it is a hardware problem that should be solved immediately, and the machine may be taken off line until the drive is available.

A remote file system has more points at which a problem can occur. First, the local file system on the remote machine may suffer the difficulties just described. The administrator of that machine may then need to make the file system remotely available (the RFS term for this is to "advertise" the remote file system). Of course, we must consider the network itself, which may be down or disconnected from one or both of the two machines involved. Finally, the local administrator must mount the remote file system locally. If any of these actions do not occur, the file system is not accessible. At least two actions, those that the administrator must perform, are not usually considered to be required actions before the local machine can be brought up. Thus, remote file systems are sometimes deemed to be less reliable than purely local ones. This is clearly a function of the complexity of the systems, however. Once that is taken into account, such an arrangement needs be no more or less reliable than one involving equivalent resources handled purely locally.

Remote File System Release 1.0 was first introduced in 1986 with Release 3.0 of UNIX System V for AT&T 3B2 machines with Starlan network connections. It makes heavy use of STREAMS, which were also introduced at that time. The next release RFS 1.1, accompanying System V Release 3.1, was greatly enhanced. At this time, releases for other machines became available. In particular, with the release of a standard UNIX for Intel 80386-based machines that incorporated STREAMS, vendors of networking products could arrange for RFS to operate with those products, and RFS could run over Ethernet or any other network that could support a solid transport connection such as TCP/IP or NetBIOS. The standardization of such arrangements was simplified by relating RFS to the Transport Library Interface (TLI), which was also released with these versions of UNIX. The released RFS was implemented in such a way that it could operate over any transport provider that met the Transport Service Interface standards provided by AT&T.

In comparing RFS to other systems that allow access to remote data, it is important to understand that RFS is really Distributed UNIX. It operates by implementing *remote system calls* from inside the local UNIX kernel. That is, when a system call is performed in the local kernel and that kernel detects that it relates to a file (which in UNIX may, of course, be a device, pipe, etc.) that exists on a remote machine, then, using the transport provider from inside the kernel, the kernel arranges to have that system call continued on the remote machine and the appropriate results returned. There is little difference, other than perhaps with the complexity of the implementation, between this and the usual UNIX kernel activity. In particular, the user sees only the usual system call interface and does not know (and in fact, may find out only with the greatest effort) that the call is actually being executed remotely.

Other approaches to the problem typically involve trapping such activity at the library level and, thus, usually at least require relinking programs to use the new library and often require special syntax to specify that a file is located remotely. Matters such as file locking and data consistency with multiple file users must be dealt with explicitly at user level. Individual programmers must attend to such matters.

◆ Overview ◆

The world of RFS consists of a number of machines, each operating its own version of the transport provider. Each machine may have one or more collections of data, each one called a *resource*, that other machines may wish to access remotely. In RFS terminology, a machine may "advertise" a resource by means of the provider, and a machine wishing to access that data may "mount" the resource on one of its own subdirectories. From the point of mounting on, all further activity is invisible to every user (except, of course, the administrator who may have to perform miracles to keep this cloak of invisibility intact).

The administrator of an RFS machine makes sure the provider is operating correctly, advertises any local resources that it is willing to share (after establishing appropriate access controls), and mounts any resources advertised elsewhere that are needed on the local machine. The user merely uses the resources that have been mounted and does not deal with those that have been advertised at all, other than perhaps to use them locally. Of course, the operations of a local user, or for that matter those of a remote user, may modify the content of the resource, but they will do so in the usual UNIX ways. If the resource happens to contain (as a special file) a device, then that device is now accessible remotely. Thus, access to tape drives, modems, and similar items requiring special device handling and administration is done remotely in the same way that it is done locally.

The administration of RFS on a network (or several networks interconnected by gateways) can be quite complex. There is an RFS administrator for each separate machine, who by convention is the "root" administrator or "super user" of that machine (just as `root` is the administrator for local file systems). But it is reasonable that there be interrelationships between the various resources and some sort of global control over access permissions and resource availability. Thus, within the group of machines running RFS using a particular provider, we may subgroup these machines into *domains* (the proper term being "administrative domain" or "sphere of authority"), and allow much of the administrative work to be done by a *domain administrator*. In RFS, the domain administrator is determined by choosing for each domain a particular machine (which generally is in the domain, although it need not be) and having the administrator of that machine be the administrator of the domain.

Thus, RFS can be thought of as dividing the address space of a transport provider (each address represents one machine or *network node*) into subsets called domains and attaching to each domain one machine to serve as its *primary*. Technically, this is carried out by *name servers*; administrative activities tend to take the form of "who/what/where" queries and responses related to machines and resources; and the domain administration machine is the one that runs the domain name server for that domain. (There may also be secondary servers for backup, as we shall later see.) As shown in Fig. 6-1, we have 11 machines divided into four domains, with 3, 2, 4, 2 hosts, respectively.

node	member	domain	primary
node01	member1	DOMAINA	member2
node02	member2		
node03	member3		
node04	member1	DOMAINB	member1
node05	member2		
node06	member1	DOMAINC	member3
node07	member2		
node08	member3		
node09	member4		
node10	member1	DOMAIND	member1
node11	member2		

Fig. 6-1. Sample RFS network

Member names must be unique within the domain; domain names, unique for the particular provider.

The name of a primary may need to be qualified. Generally, the RFS name of a machine is given in the form *domain . host*.

◆ A Typical Problem ◆

Let's look at a (close to real-life) example of domains, resources, and permissions. We will use this example throughout this chapter to illustrate the concepts discussed, and it is a prototype for many situations you will encounter in setting up your own RFS.

A certain department of Mathematics, Statistics, and Computer Science (in an anonymous Upper MidWestern University—private, therefore poor) decides to distribute computing throughout its department, which is housed in two separate buildings connected by an Ethernet. There is a single system administrator for the entire setup. We shall consider only the major machines involved.

Computers are used by faculty, some of whom possess individual UNIX workstations, some of whom have PCs, and some of whom have terminals. There are several "superminis"; each is dedicated to the work of particular groups of individuals, although any faculty member has access to any of these machines since the group compositions are dynamic. They attempted to localize file storage related to a given activity, or to a given individual, on a particular machine. Storage redundancy is a result of administrative backup, not allowing individuals to leave copies of files in various inconsistent states in any directory for which they have write permissions.

Certain tasks are highly localized since they require special file collections, processors, or devices. In particular, although preparation of text for processing (troff or Tex) can be done on any machine (e.g., the vi editor is everywhere available), work such as previewing and printing that requires special software and font collections is done on a single dedicated machine, which may be accessed remotely. Furthermore, license agreements regarding the software may require that it be run only on a single machine. Similarly, mail handling, which involves not only routing but also system-wide aliasing, mailing list explosion or implosion, and similar activities, is done on a single machine on which all needed tables and specialized processors are kept. Printing is concentrated on a few machines, where the queues for particular forms or types of printer are maintained.

Considering only the major actors, there are six machines in our example. We identify them by their UUCP names rather than their Internet addresses. A list of the machines and the resources they need or supply follows:

- `compsys`—Approximately ten of the 30 faculty members have their main activity here.

- `marque`—The remaining 20 faculty members use this as their main machine.

- `textsys`—This machine stores font files, previewer code, and processors for `troff` and `Tex`. In particular, it has attached Blit terminals for previewing and editing, and laser and high-resolution dot matrix printers for output.

- `musys`—This is the "external" machine for the department. It handles USENET news and all external and much internal mail and serves administratively as the Internet gateway for the campus (a router is the physical gateway, getting instructions when needed from here).

- `facsys`—Administratively, this machine serves as a gateway to the "faculty" domain, which consists of individual faculty machines and machines used in the departmental offices or by departmental or computer systems administrators. On this machine are maintained dossiers for faculty, which must be updated by both the individual faculty member and also departmental secretaries; schedules for individual faculty, which must be consulted by others for the purposes of setting up meetings, compiling reports, or forwarding office visitors; and schedules related to the department, such as grade or grant deadlines, dates for colloquium presentations or departmental meetings, dates for university-scheduled examinations.

- `labsys` —Administratively, this machine serves as gateway to the "student" domain, which consists of individual laboratory workstations, machines used by teaching assistants or tutors, and one or more "student superminis." It is used as a repository for homework that students turn in and assignment schedules and course materials that faculty members churn out. It is also a machine through which students may obtain access to USENET news or to repositories of source code that require access control of various sorts.

These hosts are split among three domains:

- The `mscs` domain contains `marque`, `compsys`, `textsys`, and `musys`.

- The `mscsfac` domain contains `facsys` and other faculty machines we need not mention further.

- The `mscslab` domain contains `labsys` and other student machines we need not mention further.

We consider seven resources:

- MSCSNEWS is the USENET news spool directory.

- MSCSMAIL is the external mail directory.

- MSCSTEXT is the directory that contains troff/Tex materials.

- HOMEWORK is the work students turn in.

- SCHEDULE is the assignments faculty churn out.

- DOSSIER is faculty dossiers, and departmental bibliographies.

- CALENDAR is faculty and departmental calendars.

From the previous description of machines, you can determine on which machine each of these resources should exist and a get reasonable idea of which machine should mount each resource. Let's take a look now at permissions.

Anyone should be able to read MSCSNEWS. It probably should be writable only by news on the machine on which it exists. In particular, the news administrator of this machine will post news on behalf of authorized posters.

MSCSMAIL should contain the real mail directory for each faculty member. On the local machine, it should have in it a mail file owned by the faculty member and a group-owned file. Thus, the local machine should "know" each faculty member, and mail on each possible posting machine should map to mail on the local machine.

DOSSIER should have a directory owned by each faculty member, with files accessible only to that faculty member as user. In addition, a dossier group consisting of authorized individuals such as departmental administrators should have access to these files. Truly confidential information such as salaries (remember, it's a private university) is kept encrypted. Fortunately, the encryption time for such short strings of digits is not long.

Everyone can read MSCSTEXT. However, some files inside the resource may not be available to everyone in accordance with particular software license agreements.

HOMEWORK is writable by a "daemon user" on the machine that contains it and readable by any faculty member (in a different approach, possibly subdirectories are readable only by the faculty member in charge). The "daemon user" handles verification, timestamping, and similar details, and is contacted by the student in order to submit work.

SCHEDULE is writable by faculty members (possibly also teaching assistants) and readable by anyone.

As you go through this chapter, recall this example and think of how each topic relates to it and how it can be used to accomplish the above purposes. If you find a better approach than the one suggested, let me know.

◆ Provider ◆

The first choice to make in setting up RFS is that of the transport provider. This must be a device that conforms to the AT&T Transport Provider Interface (discussed in Chapter 6). This will be a STREAMS-based device in the /dev directory or an appropriate subdirectory. If a machine has several possible providers, a single one must be chosen on which to base RFS. That is, because of the intimate connections between the system calls in the kernel and the data structures of the provider, no provider-based routing is provided.

The RFS provider is defined by the dname command:

dname -N *providername*

In our example, a single provider has the same device name /dev/mu on every machine. Thus, root on each machine executes:

dname -N /dev/mu

at some time before starting RFS. This choice is stored on the node in the file

/usr/nserve/netspec

and is accessed by RFS as required.

In the AT&T implementation of TLI over Starlan for AT&T 3B1 machines, the transport provider is:

/dev/starlan

In the AT&T implementation of TLI over Starlan for AT&T 3B2 machines, the transport provider is again:

/dev/starlan

but this time it is linked to the file

/dev/net/mau/urp

In the WIN/3B implementation of TLI over TCP for AT&T 3B2/5/15 machines, the transport provider is:

/dev/tcp

In the Micom-Interlan implementation of TLI over TCP for 386-based machines, the transport provider is:

/dev/it

RFS does not provide "forwarding" or anything of the sort between different providers, even though each of them may be capable of running RFS. Thus, if you have a machine with an AT&T Starlan interface and a TCP/IP Ethernet interface, even though it could run RFS with either provider, it may run with only one provider at a time. Thus, if you wish to do RFS involving machines on both nets, you must find (or create) a single provider that covers both. For example, the TCP/IP might run over both nets, although at present few products of this sort seem to be available. Such a configuration would make your machine a gateway, since it would have two net interfaces. More likely, you would have a single interface and a gateway forward of the IP level between the nets. The provider will be TCP-based in this case. It is possible that TCP-based providers from different vendors are compatible at this level. Typically, if there is a difference, it is with the addressing and the responses that name servers return to queries. As vendor experience with RFS and TLI-providers increases, we hope there will be common agreement on this matter. Neither RFS nor TLI provides a standard for this. Currently, the only guaranteed solution is to stick with a single provider for your provider. The System V guidelines state only that the system RFS code will work with any provider that meets the Transport Service Interface, that is, that supplies the standard service interface to its STREAMS driver. Thus, RFS will run with the provider, but whether it can contact any other machine is subject to experiment.

◆ Naming ◆

A *domain* in the sense of RFS is a group of machines and resources whose RFS is administrated as a single entity. A particular machine can belong only to a single domain. The name of the machine must be unique within the domain, and the complete RFS name is written in the form *domain.host*. The *host* portion of the name is in fact the UNIX node name of the machine, typically established at boot time from `/etc/rc` files or commands and stored in the standard kernel `uts.nodename` structure.

A machine defines its domain by the command `dname`:

```
dname -D domainname
```

This choice is stored in the local file

```
/usr/nserve/domain
```

and this file is accessed by RFS as required.

A domain name consists of no more than 14 characters, in any combination of letters (upper and lower case), digits, hyphens, and underscores. In particular, a domain name cannot contain the dot (.) character in order to avoid ambiguity in using the *domain.host* naming convention.

The main characteristic of a domain is uniqueness of names within it. That is, host names need be unique only within a domain. Other names such as resource names similarly need be unique only within a domain. A related characteristic is that all members of a domain share a particular name service (discussed later).

In our sample problem we divide administratively into three domains: The `mscs` domain contains the backbone machines and is administrated appropriately for faculty research and course development. The `mscslab` domain contains the student machines, and is administrated appropriately for student coursework. Graduate students are assigned accounts in that domain and spend their energies attempting to become useful enough to be assigned an account in the `mscs` domain. The `mscsfac` domain contains machines related to the administration of the department and is administrated appropriately. In particular, it requires more security than the other machines, since it contains sensitive data relating to faculty members. The major machine in this area also serves as a gateway to individual faculty office machines, which are used primarily for communicating with faculty, rather than for dedicated research. Since this is the most secure of the three domains, it is also used as a repository from which `passwd` files and other administrative materials for all the domains are distributed.

The administrators of the six machines execute the following commands:

```
on mathsys:    # dname -N mscs
on compsys:    # dname -N mscs
on textsys:    # dname -N mscs
on musys:      # dname -N mscs
on facsys:     # dname -N mscsfac
on labsys:     # dname -N mscslab
on all:        # rfadmin -a mydomain.host
               Enter password for host:
               Re-enter password for host:
```

The rfadmin -a command enters an entry for *host* into /usr/nserve/auth.info/mydomain/passwd. This host must be defined on a primary for some domain. In order to start RFS this primary must be running. Administration must be done by root.

```
# nlsadmin -a 105 -c /usr/net/servers/rfs/rfsetup -y
# dname -D mydomain
# dname -N mqnet
# rfstart -p MASTER_ADDR
rfstart: Please enter machine password:
```

rfstart wants the password the domain administrator gave. Note my machine saves these, so from now on RFS just starts up at init level 3.

Now the primary advertises the `auth.info` files as the resource `DOMA`. Typically I copy these (to avoid frequent remote access), then I can unmount them.

`rfstart -v` means use these to verify every host on connect. For just `rfstart` remove any hosts you don't want to verify.

◆ Primary ◆

Each domain must have at least one name server, the "primary" name server, from which all domain administration is done. There can be any number of secondary name servers, whose function is to keep the name server running temporarily in case the primary fails. A secondary does not in any sense become a primary, however. The primary name server sets up the original configuration files from which all others are derived.

With deepest respect to AT&T, we shall call the primary name server for a domain the "master" or the "domain master." The use of this term in no sense implies that the master is involved in every transaction within the domain, or that the master need even be in operation in order for those transactions to occur. The mastery involved is mastery of the "name tables," and that is all. So if you are tempted to let the terminology impute more power than this to a domain master you are wrong and should not!

Every machine has a directory hierarchy for name service:

`/usr/nserve/`	Top directory.
`/usr/nserve/netspec`	Contains the device name of the provider; contents established by `dname -N`.
`/usr/nserve/domain`	Contains the name of the domain; contents established by `dname -D`.
`/usr/nserve/rfmaster`	Contains the name and net address of the master, of each "secondary" name server ("backup" name server), and the provider address of each member.
`/usr/nserve/auth.info/`	Information related to machine connection authorization and user access authorization.

`/usr/nserve/auth.info/uid.rules` and
`/usr/nserve/auth.info/gid.rules`

Show how to map remote uids and gids into local uids and gids.

`/usr/nserve/auth.info/`*domain*`/passwd`

Required for a host to enter *domain*.

`/usr/nserve/auth.info/`*domain*`/`*host*`/passwd` and
`/usr/nserve/auth.info/`*domain*`/`*host*`/group`
> Needed if uid/gid mapping is to be done by name.

We go to the master for authoritative information regarding addresses of domain members, passwords of hosts, name/uid correspondences on individual hosts if needed for authorization, or resources advertised by individual hosts within the domain.

A machine becomes master for a particular domain by declaring itself to be so in its own `rfmaster` file. This declaration is of course subject to dispute by other machines who may believe that there is another master for that domain.

A member of a domain upon startup is told where its master is in one of two ways:

`rfstart -p` *MASTER_ADDR*

is given the provider address of its master (thus if a machine has declared itself to be the master of the domain surreptitiously or mistakenly this host will not agree, and a fight will ensue).

A member of a domain that has previously been started will have obtained its `rfmaster` from the *MASTER_ADDR* given when it was first started, and presumably that `rfmaster` file will show its master residing at *MASTER_ADDR*. If in doubt when starting up a member, give the `-p` option.

The `rfmaster` file obtained by `rfstart -p` *MASTER_ADDR* is stored locally as `/usr/nserve/rfmaster` and used at boot time, as well as at other times.

◆ Connecting ◆

The first issue that arises in connecting nodes in RFS is how to find provider addresses from domain based names. Obviously the domain name servers perform this, and they obtain their initial information from a particular file. The file `rfmaster` on the primary name server for a particular domain has already been encountered as the official specifier of the primary and secondary name server for that domain. It specifies as well the official provider address of each member of the domain. It may contain information regarding other domains as well, although it is not the official source of that information.

To add nodes (machines, hosts, choose your own terminology) to a domain, we need to add a line to the `rfmaster` for that domain showing the provider address of the node and add an entry in the file of node passwords for that domain.

The `rfmaster` file is in `/usr/nserve/rfmaster` and may be edited with any text editor to install an address entry for a particular node. Note that the address entry required depends totally upon the provider. With some providers, such as AT&T Starlan, the address is the ordinary UNIX node name of the node, with the postfix `.serve`. Other providers, such as most TCP/IP based providers, require some variation of a TCP/IP address, involving at least a TCP port number and IP address. For RFS purposes, such an address is represented in `rfmaster` by a string of ASCII hexadecimal bytes in the order in which they should be entered into a TLI `netbuf` structure (see Chapter 5); syntactically this string is preceded by `\x`.

The file of node passwords is kept in `/usr/nserve` `/auth.info/`*domain*`/passwd` on the primary name server for that domain. The command `rfadmin`, run on the primary name server for a domain, prompts in the usual manner for a password which it then installs in the domain password file.

```
# rfadmin -a member
```

is the syntax of the command; its semantics were just described. The password for which it prompts must meet the usual UNIX rules for passwords, as enforced by the standard `getpass` function. In particular this command must be run by a process with a valid `/dev/tty` controlling terminal (and thus not over a network connection of the simple sort).

In our case study, the `rfmaster` addresses are a single byte representing an address for the `/dev/mque` provider, and this byte is shown in `rfmaster` as ASCII hexadecimal prefixed by `\x`.

```
mscs.mathsys  a \x24
mscs.compsys  a \x25
mscs.textsys  a \x2b
mscs.spool    a \x2a
mscsfac.spool a \x23
mscslab.spool a \x21
```

The password file is used for checking when a member executes the `rfstart` command, but only a warning is given if the password supplied by the member to the primary does not match the password held by the primary. Failure will occur only when an attempt is made to mount a resource advertised by some member of the domain, and it uses the primary name server to validate the password. Further discussion can be found under "Checking Permissions."

A member is removed from a domain by the `-r` option to the `rfadmin` command:

```
# rfadmin -r node
```

which will fail if the node given is not in the domain or is defined to be a name server for some domain or is currently advertising resources.

◆ Starting ◆

We are ready to start RFS on this particular node. Eventually, we will see this as a routine task and relegate it to `/etc/inittab`, where as we shall see it usually runs at `init` level 3.

First, we check that our machine has been named correctly:

```
uname -n
```

(`uname -a` for those who can handle it.) Now we check that the provider and domain have been specified:

```
dname -a
```

So far we know that we are *domain.host* and that we expect to use the provider network interface. Next, we check to see if the provider is running

```
nlsadmin -v net
```

and finally we check to see if the `rfsetup` server is available

```
nlsadmin -x
```

Before taking the fatal plunge, let's consider how we connect correctly into our domain. Although it might appear that setting the domain name with `dname  -N  or  having  an  existing  domain  name  in  the  file` `/etc/nserve/domain` had taken care of this, a subtle point regarding domain membership is obvious once explained.

Consider the situation in which two machines set their domain names to the same domain and on which each has an `rfmaster` file showing itself as the primary name server for that domain. When each one comes up under RFS, it will not contact any node other than itself for authorization or for any other form of name service. There will be no collision (unless the `rfmasters` show additional connections that may cause a collision). Each is the master of its own domain, and each domain has the same name. In other words, the network is split into two disjoint pieces. Similarly, suppose machine A considers itself to be the primary name server of a certain domain, and its `rfmaster` file shows machine B at a particular address to be a member. If machine B has different notions but does not conflict directly with A, there will be no collision of authority. In other words, a primary name server does not actively seek out its members and force them to acknowledge its authority when they join the network. Domain membership, and especially acknowledgment of the authority of a primary name server, is purely voluntary on the part of the member. It is at startup time that voluntary submission occurs.

To summarize, you become master of a domain by stating that you are in your own `rfmaster` file. You obtain members of that domain when they voluntarily request you to become the master. If you are a member, you become one by connecting with the master and following the `rfmaster` file on that master for your connections to the remainder of the network.

The safest way for a member to perform this procedure is to start up RFS by giving an explicit address for a primary name server, which will result in your obtaining a current copy of its `rfmaster` file. When the situation is stable, as it usually is, you may also start up RFS by depending upon your current copy of `rfmaster` to show the primary name server and its address, using these two pieces of information to contact the primary and refresh the `rfmaster` file.

If your node is to be the primary name server, the two methods are the same, and the contents of your `rfmaster` file are definitive.

The two forms of the command are:

```
rfstart [-v] -p MASTER_ADDR
rfstart [-v]
```

The flag `-v` specifies whether to perform connect and uid/gid checks for authorization as described in "Checking Permissions."

Once `rfstart` has successfully executed, we will see several results. In particular, daemons will run to perform various RFS activities. The most important daemons will have (something similar to) the following names:

- `rfdaemon`—A kernel daemon started by the system call `rfstart`.

- `recovery`—A kernel daemon started by the system call `rfstart`.

- `server ... server`—Kernel daemons managed by `rfdaemon`. The number of these may fluctuate between the limits `MINSERVE` and `MAXSERVE`, described in "Reporting."

- `nserve`—A user daemon for name service.

- `rfudaemon`—A user daemon for recovery.

We will not need to know much about these daemons, except perhaps to notice the activity of `server` and possibly to change to local taste the shell script `rfuadmin`, which `rfudaemon` invokes as required, describing local actions to cope with changes in the exterior environment. The `rfudaemon` and `rfuadmin` are described under "Recovering."

It is perhaps useful to explain the term "kernel daemon" used for `rfdaemon`, `recovery`, and `server`. A user daemon is a process started by some user, typically disconnected from any control terminal, and a leader of its own process group. It runs with permissions established for user processes, derived from those of its parent. In particular, we know its parent was started by forking a process that was executing a particular file; of course, the daemon may then execute its own file if it wishes. Line printer spoolers and the `cron` are user daemons. A kernel daemon, on the other hand, is created by the kernel out of code that exists inside the kernel. The kernel merely goes through the steps required to create a new process and does so. In particular, there is no file from which the daemon's running code was loaded (e.g., there is no "…/rfdaemon", "…/recovery", "…/server" text—in the sense of the loader—files that are being executed).

Note that the user daemon listen, which provides the NLS, must be running for any of this to work and that one or more copies of rfsetup may have been forked by listen if our machine is acting as a server.

To learn the host name of the primary name server for the domain enter

rfadmin

This returns host name of master for this domain.

To add member *host* to this domain use rfadmin -a. (You must be root on the primary name server of the domain.)

rfadmin -a *host*

This adds *host* to the rfmaster file. This machine must be shown as primary in the rfmaster file, and *host* must be unique in the rfmaster file. rfadmin prompts for a password; the password must satisfy the regular passwd restrictions.

To remove *host* from this domain use rfadmin -r. (You must be root on the primary name server of the domain.)

rfadmin -r *host*

This removes *host* from the rfmaster file and the *domain*/passwd file. The *host* node must exist, must not be a primary name server, and must not be advertising a resource. Note: The *host* node may in fact be a server for a mounted resource, and removing it from the domain will not affect this resource; it will affect only the ability of the next machine to mount the resource.

To transfer name server authority from the current name server use rfadmin -p. (You must be root on the primary name server of the domain.)

rfadmin -p

If run by a primary name server this gives authority to the first secondary available. If run by a secondary name server which has become the current name server by virtue of a crash, or of a transfer from the (soon-to-be former) current name server, this returns authority to the primary if it is available, otherwise to the next secondary available. In RFS Release 1.1 this invocation returns 0 if it succeeds, 2 if it fails because there is no server to pass control to, or 1 if it fails otherwise.

To start RFS activity on a particular node use `rfstart`. (You must be `root` on that particular node.)

 # rfstart -p *MASTER_ADDR*

This connects to *MASTER_ADDR* and obtains a copy of `rfmaster`. If `loc.passwd` is not set the prompts for a password and creates `loc.passwd`. Then it checks with the primary to see if `loc.passwd` matches the password stored on the master.

 # rfstart

This is the same as before but it uses the local copy of `rfmaster` to find the primary. A machine that is to be the primary must do `rfstart` with itself declared as the primary name server in its own `rfmaster` file.

In order for `rfstart` to succeed:

1. RFS cannot already be started.

2. The provider must be operational.

3. The primary name server must be up (or this machine is the primary name server).

4. This node must be entered in `rfmaster` on the primary name server.

5. The invoking user must be the super user.

`rfpasswd` registers a new password in `loc.passwd` and in *domain*/`passwd` on the primary name server.

`rfstop` stops RFS activity on this machine. If this machine is the master this gives authority to a secondary. In order for `rfstop` to succeed:

1. RFS must have been started.

2. No resources have been advertised.

3. No local resources have been remotely mounted.

4. No remote resources have been locally mounted.

◆ Advertising Resources ◆

As a full-fledged member of the RFS community, you may now wish to contribute your share to the resources available. From the syntactic (and for that matter the semantic, given the unique nature of files in UNIX) point of view, a resource is merely a local path name that ends in a directory name. To advertise the resource means to let other machines know about it and to allow them to mount everything that hangs under the directory on their own machine, with access determined by uid/gid mappings.

The command to advertise a directory is `adv`.

adv -r -d *"DESCRIPTION"* RSRC_NAME *resource* [*client*...]

The `-r` option specifies that the resource is to be made available to other nodes read-only. The `-d` option allows you to specify a short description (0–32 characters) of the resource.

RSRC_NAME is the name that other nodes will use to refer to this resource; it can be up to 14 printable ASCII characters and may not contain white space or the slash (/) or dot (.). By convention the characters are uppercase.

pathname is the full local path of a directory. This path cannot be advertised as any other resource and cannot contain a remotely mounted directory.

client... are the clients that can mount the resource, which can be specified as *host* (specific host in my domain), *domain* (any host in that domain), or *domain*.*host* (specific host in that domain).

In our hypothetical system, the mail machine `mscs.spool` will advertise:

```
# adv MSCSMAIL /usr/mail/mscs math comp mscsfac.spool
```

This machine is also the news machine, and news is to be read-only:

```
# adv -r MSCSNEWS /usr/spool/news
```

There are no node restrictions on mounting `MSCSNEWS`.

Unadvertising

A resource that has been advertised can be *unadvertised* (I wish television commercials were resources). First, we request its removal from the table held by the domain name server. Removing it will not affect existing mounts (use `fumount` for that, as discussed under "Mounting Resources"). Using `fumount` will prevent further mounts and will occur immediately since it also affects the local advertise table.

Only a local resource can be unadvertised; the administrator of one machine cannot control the resources advertised by another. The single exception to this rule, as one might expect, is that the domain administrator (e.g., `root` on the primary name server machine) can unadvertise any resource in the domain. This may become desirable when a member crashes, in order to prevent requests for mounting that will certainly be denied. This is not a desirable practice for a member that is running since it affects only the local advertise table. A member could conceivably believe itself to be advertising a resource that cannot be found by a potential client.

The syntax of `unadv` is unexceptional:

unadv *resource*

The command will fail only if the resource is not being advertised, that is, is not part of the local advertise table. If run on a domain member, an `unadv` command is sent to the primary name server as well.

Advertising and unadvertising a resource that happens to be a local mount point for a block special file does not affect our ability to mount or unmount that resource. It is possible, although not normally desirable, to mount a resource remotely on its own node so that the single machine serves as server and client for that resource. As much as is possible, this situation is treated in accordance with the semantics for a truly remote mount.

◆ Mounting Resources ◆

Now that I have done my duty and advertised some resources of my own (or even if I have not), let's look around and see what some of my friends have made available.

nsquery [-h] [*name*]

shows the resources that *name* has advertised. *name* is either a full domain name in the form *domain.host*, a host name that will be interpreted in the domain of the current machine, or a domain name (followed by a .) that will be taken to refer to every host in the domain. If no name is given, then every advertised resource known to the name server of the current domain is shown.

The `-h` option eliminates the header from the output, which is useful when preparing reports that carry your own headers, or when piping into a `grep` or `awk` command that will search for a particular resource.

Suppose you see a resource that you would like to mount. Use the ordinary UNIX `mount` command to obtain it:

/etc/mount -d *RSRC_NAME* *loc_pathname*

The only difference between this and the ordinary UNIX `mount` command is that the `-d` option is used and that a resource name is given rather than the name of a block special device on the present system. In the usual case of mounts of block special devices, the *loc_pathname* given in the command obliterates the special name (e.g., `/dev/dsk/0s2`). Similalry, *loc_pathname* given here obliterates *loc_pathname* as given on the server machine when the resource was advertised.

The -r option may be used to request a read-only mount.

In our hypothetical examples, let's look at some variations. The machines
mscs.comp, mscs.math, mscslab.spool, and mscsfac.spool each perform:

```
# /etc/mount -r -d MSCSNEWS /usr/spool/news
```

Notice that they mount over the local news directory, not running any news of
their own. Posting news is done (for those who are interested in where such
things come from) through a client on each machine that contacts a server daemon on mscs.spool after adding appropriate headers and doing minor content and permissions checking. In this way, news maintenance is done totally on
the single machine, and file locking for write need never be done (although RFS
can do this). Furthermore, since the daemon runs only at periodic intervals, read
cache invalidation seldom occurs; that is, readers who are perusing articles can
move around freely without incurring excessive networking overhead.

The machines mscs.comp and mscs.math each mount MSCSMAIL

```
# /etc/mount -d MSCSMAIL /usr/mail/mscs
```

allowing for /usr/mail/... directories on each individual node for local
mail. Mailing is again done by contacting a server daemon, so that writebacks to
the mail files that occur while reading the mail and writes that occur as new mail
is sent do not collide and so that routing information need be kept only on a single machine. Mail messages are treated by the mailer insofar as possible as single
files in a directory, rather than as text catenated with From>-type separators.
This simplifies maintenance dramatically.

The machine mscs.text mounts the advertised user directories from
mscs.comp and mscs.math under its own user space:

```
# /etc/mount -d USRCOMP /usr/compsys
# /etc/mount -d USRMATH /usr/mathsys
```

For $HOME directories on a direct login to textsys, a login directory is
provided for each user. (This could be a common directory such as /usr/tmp if
desired.) In the .profile of each user, the value of HOME is set to the
appropriate remote home provided it is accessible at the time. (If it is not accessible, the user is told, so that they can arrange their work accordingly. Content
placed in their local home is either temporary or moved to their remote home
once it is available.)

Here is a caution (although the phenomenon is nothing new to RFS) involving a directory that will become a remote mount point. If a user accesses the
directory and the mount has not been done or, on occasion, if the remote
machine and thus the mount goes down, some data may end up in the local
directory. Always check before mounting to see if there is any content. We shall
consider other interactions involving the standard RFS recovery process, and
administrative daemons later.

The unmount (umount for UNIX lovers) of a remote resource follows the usual UNIX patterns. There is an RFS twist, of course, in that a umount cannot be done if the resource is in use, and the users of the resource are very likely to be remote users. Just as in the case of a block special device, if an administrator wishes to umount, a notice should be sent to all users, including remote users. Those who do not respond to it in a suitable time frame (have you every mistakenly forced a umount of /usr directories in a room full of users with no warning?) are sent the infamous nonignorable kill signal. RFS, in its never-ending quest to preserve UNIX semantics, preserves these as well; what else could it do?

The polite form of the umount process begins with the fumount command, which unadvertises the resource (to avoid luring new remote users into a trap that is about to spring) and notifies a daemon on each client node that the resource is going to be unmounted, with a warning interval (grace period for the super polite). At the expiration of that interval (default 60 seconds), it actually unmounts the resource whether there are (were) remote users or not. This in turn triggers notices to the daemons on client nodes (if any are left) that the umount has in fact been done and, thus, that their users are attempting the impossible and should be dealt with appropriately. This daemon on each machine actually calls a shell script that can be customized with actions of varying degrees of severity, and messages of various degrees of tenderness, by the administrator of that machine according to the needs and tastes of its users. In particular, the daemon may help users get out gracefully, perform appropriate backup, or even wait until the resource is mounted again (after relinquishing their hold on it, of course). The standard daemon provides them with the appropriate warning messages, similar to those we have all seen before, and at the end of the period of grace kills the processes that did not obey.

Syntactically, we have:

```
umount    -d  resource

fumount  [-w seconds]   resource

fuser    [-k] resource
```

in which

- umount fails if *resource* is not mounted or is busy (a file is open or it contains some user's home directory).

- fumount fails if *resource* is not advertised and not remotely mounted.

- fuser lists the process uid of each process using *resource* and sends SIGKILL signals to each if -k is specified (multiple arguments can be given to fuser, but see the manual page for more details).

The daemon and the shell script mentioned above are discussed in detail under "Recovering."

rmount

The `rmount` shell script repeatedly tries to mount a resource. (It loops on `mount`.)

◆ Checking Permissions ◆

There are several layers of security available for RFS, each following one of the familiar UNIX paradigms. The security is intended primarily to protect resources, that is, files, and thus the most detailed protection consists of standard UNIX file `rwx` protections, broken down as usual into user/group/other categories. Obviously there must be some new twist, since user/group/other refers to uid and gid numbers established on a particular node. The new twist is that each node administrator can specify the way in which uid and gid numbers are to be mapped into uid and gid numbers for the node when it is used as a server, thus determining access rights to resources on the node that are mounted remotely. This mapping is also done in the inverse direction, so that users on the remote machine see the permissions in numbers that reference their own machine. This mapping by default is done very simply, and every remote user is mapped to a user guaranteed not to exist on the server, so that the default access becomes that accorded to "other" in the usual scheme. Much more involved mapping can be specified.

One layer above the uid/gid mapping check is a check that can be carried out when a client requests to mount a local resource. This check requires the remote machine to specify its password, which the local machine (or the primary name server of its domain acting on its behalf) checks against the password it was told the domain administrator of that machine assigned when it was added to the domain. Several variations of this check will be discussed shortly in this section.

Above those two checks is the general structure of RFS, with `rfmaster` files specifying addresses of nodes, addresses of name servers, and registration of nodes with primary name servers. In order to access any remote resource at all, a client must be recognizable to the name servers and will be contacted only at its official address. Obviously this system is only as strong as the root protections of the machines involved, but the only root protections that matter greatly are those of the primary name servers, and they should be well protected.

Mount Checking

When a (potential) server machine is started via the `rfstart` command, its administrator may or may not have requested the `-v` or verify option.

When the verify option has not been specified for mounting on the server, then nodes that have an entry in *domain*/`passwd` on the server will be verified using this entry, and other nodes will be allowed to connect without verification.

When the verify option has been specified for mounting on the server, then only nodes that have an entry in *domain*/passwd on the server will be allowed to mount its resources, and they will be verified as above.

Notice that it is the *domain*/passwd file on the server that controls this verification, rather than the one on the primary name server. These files may be, and often are, the same. But the local verification allows the server administrator tighter control, in that certain nodes can be removed from its own *domain*/passwd file, so that verification (if in effect) will not allow them to use the server's resources.

The client node may be required to supply a password for itself during the mount, as discussed above. This password is initially supplied by the node administrator when it starts RFS for the first time and is stored thereafter in the file /usr/nserve/loc.passwd and supplied when required to other nodes for verification. If this file becomes corrupted it may be removed after an rfstop, and the node rfstarted again, whereupon it will prompt for a new password.

◆ Authorization and Permissions ◆

Well, for those who thought handling /etc/passwd was fun, now you have a lot of them.

There is a *domain*/passwd file, and each host has an entry. It was created when the host did rfstart, with a copy into loc.passwd on the host (rfstart prompted for it).

When rfsetup runs, it asks the master nserve for this password and requires that this be sent from the machine. So if the machine does not know what to send, no mount takes place.

I have uid.rules and gid.rules. These show how permissions are to be mapped, by domain or host if desired. If I want to use names from individual hosts, these can be obtained from the master auth.info/*domain* directory.

If I want to let others use my password files for name mapping, I can copy them into auth.info/*domain*/*my_host_name*/ directory or mail them to the master administrator to do so. Typically that directory is accessible to root on my machine, and I do cpio -p of my own into there.

The mapping rules are as follows:

- If never set up, all remote uids map to 60001. There is no such account, so this is "guaranteed other."

- If any remote creates something it shows remote users that 60001 created it.

- If any local user creates something it shows remote users that 60002 created it.

- Thus I can get it only if "other" can, since I am 60001.
- Can map users: transparent means just keep the uid the same.
- Or can map individually or by group into some uid.
- Can exclude uid from mappings that will be set up (e.g., exclude 0 for root).

♦ Requirements from the Listener Service ♦

RFS depends upon an NLS service provided by the NLS listener for the provider of choice, so that provider must be running in order for RFS to operate.

The server forked by the listener is used most frequently when a remote machine wishes to mount a resource that the local machine has advertised. The service code for RFS is 105, and the server program is rfsetup, running with no arguments. As with any listener-forked server, it can of course discover the provider it is using, and the address of the client who caused it to be forked, as values of environment variables set before the fork/exec by the server.

The following steps should be taken to make sure that the listener is running and the server is available.

Make sure the provider is initialized:

1. Initialize the listener for this provider:

   ```
   nlsadmin -i mqnet
   ```

2. Define the listener address for this host on this provider:

   ```
   nlsadmin -l "mqmain.serve"
   ```

   (Also -t "mqmain" is often included, but that is not required here.)

3. Define the RFS server for this provider:

   ```
   nlsadmin -a 105 -c /usr/net/servers/rfs/rfsetup -y "rfsetup" mqnet
   ```

4. Start the listener:

   ```
   nlsadmin -s mqnet
   ```

♦ Running and Crashing ♦

Well, that's it. Now you are running RFS. Since its really just UNIX, relax, it runs itself. All you need to do is deal with problems.

Crashing can occur in several forms:

- My master crashes, that is, my name server goes down. This does not affect any advertising or mounts that already are in existence, but no new permissions, hosts, and so on can occur. If there is a secondary, not much else happens, and the primary is told when it comes back.

- One of my servers crashes. Well, my `rfudaemon/rfuadmin` try to handle this, remounting frequently, notifying users, etc.

- One of my servers stops, or wants to stop.   `rfudaemon/rfuadmin` handle this. They will do a `fumount`, and this corresponds to what occurs when you need to take a disk offline.

- One of my clients crashes or stops. Fine, one less customer to worry about (they don't pay anyway).

♦ Recovering ♦

A kernel recovery daemon, created by `rfstart`, handles much of the internal work of recovering from *failures* (unanticipated events) and *faults* (anticipated negative events) of various sorts. This daemon is not contacted directly by the local or remote administrator, and what it does is known only to those who have seen, and understood, the source code (possibly to those who wrote it as well).

A user-level recovery daemon called `rfudaemon`, as well as a kernel daemon started by `rfstart`, handles events that are (or are about to become) detectable by users. It usually is told of such events via a message from a local or remote RFS or from a remote user (usually `root`), and it runs the shell script `rfuadmin` with arguments appropriate to the event.

Where the current machine is a client of the resource *resource*, the events are:

- *DISCONNECT*: disconnect *resource*. A disconnect from the resource server was detected by the provider.

- *FUMOUNT*: `fumount` *resource*. The RFS kernel in the resource server detected `fumount`.

- *GETUMSG*. This could be any message from a user process on the resource server, although currently only `fuwarn` sends such a message: `fuwarn` *resource time*.

- *LASTUMSG*. This event results in the death of `rfudaemon` and is sent by the local RFS when it shuts down.

Typical behavior required of `rfuadmin` in the above situations (that is the behavior provided in the script supplied with the RFS software) is as follows:

- *DISCONNECT*:

  - Use `wall` to warn all users that *resource* is no longer accessible.

  - Use `fuser` to find all users of *resource* and `kill` them.

  - Use `umount` to unmount *resource*, so the kernel can clean up its structures.

  - Use `rmount` to try to remount *resource*.

    Typically this means we make repeated attempts to remount the resource, until we succeed.

  Note a difference here that is often remarked upon in statefull versus stateless systems. The resource will be unmounted, and calls that user programs are making to it will fail. When the resource is again mounted, user programs find all their files that referenced the resource closed and must reopen them and start again. With stateless systems, it is possible to keep trying an operation until it again begins to succeed. Since the state of the file was kept locally, not remotely, it is not lost during the crash.

- *FUMOUNT*: Action similar to above. We are still connected to the resource server in this case, and this may make a difference in the way we handle the reconnect attempts.

- *FUWARN*: This is exactly the same sort of thing that is done when the message "System going down in 60 seconds" is sent. The message "RESOURCE will be unmounted in 60 seconds" might be sent, and users are expected to take appropriate action.

- `rfuadmin` isn't run for *LASTIMSG*.

The preceding activities, needless to say, do not make any user happy, any more than a forced disk unmount would. The situation may be less drastic, since typically when a disk unmount occurs there has been a problem with the disk, and therefore perhaps with the data stored on the disk. With a remote mount the situation may have nothing at all to do with physically stored data, but merely mean a disconnected network cable or a node crash that has no effect upon stored data. Particular nodes can customize the script for as much interaction with users as is required.

There are a few points to notice regarding the `fuser` command. The first is that it does not find remote users with local files open; those users are presumably dealt with by `fuser` on their own machine. The second point is that `fuser` may not find all local users of a remote resource, since such a user may have only just begun. Such a user can be sent the SIGKILL signal directly.

◆ Reporting ◆

The regular UNIX "system activity reporter" `sar` (and friends) can be used to profile RFS activity in the same way as purely local disk and buffer activity are profiled.

The `-Dc` option to `sar` requests information on system calls resolved over the network.

```
# sar -Dc

textsys textsys 3.1 1 i386     05/12/89
```

00:00:00	scall/s	sread/s	swrit/s	fork/s	exec/s	rchar/s	wchar/s
10:00:00							
in	7	2	4		0.00	770	680
out	6	4	2		0.00	450	600
local	180	43	18	0.91	1.02	23076	9814
10:20:00							
in	0	0	0		0.00	0	0
out	0	0	0		0.00	0	0
local	4	1	1	0.05	0.10	336	203
10:40:00							
in	0	0	0		0.00	0	0
out	0	0	0		0.00	0	0
local	6	2	2	0.94	0.13	691	365
11:00:00							
in	4	1	2		0.00	376	322
out	3	2	1		0.00	178	202
local	132	30	11	0.78	1.39	11232	3822
Average							
in	3	1	2		0.00	104	39
out	2	2	1		0.00	92	40
local	81	19	8	0.67	0.74	9812	988

where an `scall` is any system call, `sread`, `swrite`, `fork`, and `exec` are those specific system calls, and `rchar` and `wchar` are counts of characters processed by `read` and `write`. Calls to this node as a server are described as `in`, calls from this node as a client are described as out, and local calls (reported usually by sar -c) are described as local. Thus we expect incoming scalls to be relatively high on a machine acting as a server, and outgoing scalls to be relatively high for a machine accessing remote resources frequently.

A measure of the efficiency of the scalls themselves is given through dividing rchars/s by sread/s, and wchars/s by swrite/s. This gives an average read/write size and may give an indication of whether or not changing the buffering strategy of an application or similar adjustments would be worthwhile.

In the presence of local caching, an outgoing scall may not require actual communication with the server machine. That is, this statistic counts scalls made for a resource on the server machine and not scalls executed on the server machine.

Remote execs obviously consume substantial resources, since they require the copy of the entire load module to the client machine. Use of the sticky bit may be appropriate, but note that the removal of the sticky bit on a client machine will have no effect until reboot.

The CPU utilization statistics, broken down into client/server usage, can indicate whether those resources are being inappropriately consumed by clients (or by local users playing rogue):

```
# sar -Du

textsys textsys 3.1 1 i386     05/12/89
```

00:00:00	%usr	%sys local	%sys remote	%wio	%idle
10:00:00	57	20	9	8	6
10:20:00	4	5	0	1	90
10:40:00	1	2	0	1	96
11:00:00	54	5	11	7	23
11:20:01	6	7	0	2	84
11:40:01	6	6	0	2	85
Average	21	10	3	2	64

Perusal of these numbers may give an indication that limits should be placed on remote usage, by mounting fewer resources or by slowing down their access through selective parameter tuning.

The following report, describing buffer pool activity, seems to become a familiar one when RFS is in use. Recall that an RFS mount is "really" just a mount of a disk drive, and that the UNIX kernel and its disk drivers are well known for making demands on the buffer pool. Then recall that RFS may involve a great deal of name service, and that name servers are also well known for making demands on buffer pools. Then double your careful estimates, and sacrifice your original set of the *Programmer's Manual*. None of these things will help.

```
# sar -Db

textsys textsys 3.1 1 i386     05/12/89
```

00:00:00	bread/s	lread/s	%rcache	bwrit/s	lwrit/s	%wcache	pread/s	pwrit/s
10:00:00								
local	5	72	92	2	8	77	0	0
remote	2	21	90	1	2	55		
10:20:00								
local	1	4	80	0	1	63	0	0
remote	0	0	0	0	0	0		
10:40:00								
local	1	5	83	1	1	60	0	0
remote	0	0	0	0	0	0		
11:00:00								
local	2	41	93	1	6	81	0	0
remote	1	12	91	1	3	64		
Average								
local	2	21	93	0	2	78	0	0
remote	1	7	87	1	1	61		

The fields are as described in the sar manual entry:

bread/s bwrit/s represent transfers between buffers and disk/net, lread/s lwrit/s represent accesses of the buffers, %rcache is the percentage of hits (1 - bread / lread) in percentage.

With files that have only readers, caching of course works as well as it can, and the %rcache is determined by the number of "new" reads that a client must make, since each block must be read from the server at least once. This statistic would be high in situations such as editing or shell level paging of files in which the same block is read again and again.

In our case study example we might expect a high %rcache on mscs.spool, at least as far as news reading is concerned. This could be the case not only because users tend to page back and forth through articles, but also if a number of readers tend to be reading the same articles at once (misc.comics just arrived). On mscs.textsys where files may often be copied intact the access pattern defeats caching totally, so %rcache might be lower, yet no amount of tuning would help.

The interpretation of %wcache requires a little more thought; fortunately, studying it may give us some information that we can use. As is usual with caching, writes are always sent to the server (the descriptive terminology is "write-through cache") and a bwrit entry means "I wrote something that was not cached." So a high %wcache means I frequently wrote over the cache, and thus the server frequently had to toss cache entries.

pread/s and pwrit/s are not reported by the -Db option.

There are two new sar options added for RFS. The -S option gives statistics on server activity, and the -C option gives statistics relating to cache consistency, that is, to how often the server was required to notify clients to toss cache entries.

```
# sar -S
```

```
textsys textsys 3.1 1 i386    05/12/89
```

00:00:00	serv/lo-hi 3 - 6	request %busy	request avg lgth	server %avail	server avg avail
10:00:00	6	100	33	0	0
10:20:00	3	0	0	100	3
10:40:00	3	0	0	100	3
11:00:00	4	67	8	33	2
Average	3	0	0	100	3

These figures can aid in determining proper settings of the kernel parameters MINSERVE and MAXSERVE. You may wish to consult a statistician trained in queueing theory first, however.

serv/lo-hi shows for each period the extreme numbers of servers running; typically the lowest number for each period will be MINSERVE.

The %busy statistic shows how often a request had to wait because all servers were busy. If this number is high we do not have enough servers (brilliant deduction); but assuming we are willing to increase the number of servers should we increase MINSERVE or MAXSERVE or both?

If the percentage waiting is high but the average number of servers used is low, this means we should raise MINSERVE, so that a larger number of servers is constantly available .

If the percentage waiting is high and the average number of servers used is high, we should raise MAXSERVE, since these waits are occurring when we have already gone beyond MINSERVE, which means it is in effect already raised.

If servers are almost always available, we have too many servers (got it again!); but do we have too many at all times, or too many at the peak? That is, should we make customers wait a little at all times, or only at peak times? If the number of total servers running is usually near MINSERVE, then lowering MAX-SERVE will have little or no effect, so we lower MINSERVE. If the number of available servers is high, we lower MAXSERVE, since many of the excess servers were not really needed.

```
# sar -C

musys musys 3.2 2 i386    05/12/89

00:00:00 snd-inv/s snd-msg/s rcv-inv/s rcv-msg/s dis-bread/s blk-inv/s
10:00:00     0.6      1.1       0.2       1.5        0.0        0.4
10:20:00     0.0      0.0       0.0       0.0        0.0        0.0
10:40:00     0.0      0.0       0.0       0.0        0.0        0.0
11:00:00     0.3      0.6       0.0       0.6        0.0        0.1

Average      0.2      0.9       0.0       0.7        0.0        0.2
```

The snd rates refer to my node as a server, with snd-inv indicating how often it sent (because of a change in the resource) a toss command to a block that was being cached by some client, and snd-msg indicating how often it wrote to a client at all. Similarly the rcv rates refer to my node as a client, with rcv-inv indicating how often it had a block cached unnecessarily (or at least not helpfully), and rec-msg indicating the overall message rate from the server. The ratios of these pairs of numbers then tell us what proportion of our message overhead is consumed by caching that has no effect.

To understand the next two numbers, you must first understand that when invalidation of a cache buffer related to a particular resource occurs, it is assumed that invalidation will be occurring regularly for at least a short while, so caching is turned off until the writing processes closes or until a certain amount of time expires (the value of the kernel parameter RCACHETIME).

The dis-bread/s rate refers to my node as a client and counts the number of bread calls that occurred when the cache was disabled; any of these would have been cached if caching had been on, so this number shows how often we were penalized by the automatic cache turnoff just discussed. This situation is improved by decreasing the RACHETIME parameter.

The blk-inv/s rate refers to my node as a client and indicates the rate at which invalidations occur.

♦ Statistics ♦

A useful summary is one of bytes transferred between local file systems and resources mounted by the client. The fusage gives several forms of such a report:

fusage [*resource_name*]

shows usage by client of this particular resource.

```
# fusage
FILE USAGE REPORT FOR textsys


   /dev/dsk/0s1           /


                          /
                              textsys          6936 KB

      /dev/dsk/0s3        /usr


                          /usr
                              textsys          4880 KB

   /dev/dsk/0s4           /usr2


                          /usr2
                              textsys          4930 KB
```

If one client's usage is consistently greater than the server's, the resource should probably be moved to the client.

The df command requires interpretation for RFS:

```
# df
/            (/dev/dsk/0s1    ):     36462 blocks       6700 i-nodes
/usr         (/dev/dsk/0s3    ):      5552 blocks       4264 i-nodes
/usr2        (/dev/dsk/0s4    ):     42026 blocks       9631 i-nodes
/news        (MSCSNEWS        ):     29740 blocks      20850 i-nodes
/usr/lib/news (NEWSLIB         ):       7542 blocks       8832 i-nodes
/comptmp     (COMPTMP         ):     57396 blocks      18910 i-nodes
/usr/mail/mscs (MSCSMAIL       ):       7542 blocks       8832 i-nodes
```

Recall that a resource, when resolved on the server, represents only a directory, which is most often not itself a local mount point. The remote df system call is implemented to perform a local df on the file system that contains the resource. Noting that there may be several resources within that file system, we might expect that each one will be listed in the output of the df (and if you understood the explanation you should expect that each one will show the same amount of free space). A valiant effort is made to bring the situation to our attention and to mark all listings after the first with an asterisk. Unfortunately in some current releases this marking is done only when the df is given without arguments, and not when individual resources are specified on the command line.

In our case study the resources MSCSNEWS and MSCSMAIL, which resolve on the server to /usr/spool/news and /usr/spool/mail, might both be directories in the file system /usr/spool.

Note for example on `textsys` if you really want `df` to be correct where users have individual file systems, then separate resources are required, i.e.,

```
/usr/math/a
/usr/math/b
/usr/math/c
```

if treated as `/usr/math` gets `df` for `/usr`; if treated as separate resources gets `df` for `/usr/math/[abc]` individually.

du

The `du` command works exactly as expected, and is just an ordinary (local or remote) system call. Unlike `df`, it refers to directories and not file systems. Of course its output may require some interpretation if there is a remote mount point in the tree underneath one of its arguments.

fumount

The `fumount` command is the most useful, perhaps. It lists the full path name and resource name of all (local) resources that are currently mounted, together with the domain name of the client. Note that this may show resources that are not currently advertised; these must have been advertised at the time the `mount` was done but may have subsequently been unadvertised.

```
fumount   [-h] [resource...]
```

As one might expect, if no resources are given then all mounted resources and their clients are listed. The `-h` option asks that the header not be printed, in case we wish to attach our own, or process the output of `fumount` through a `grepish` shell script.

8

OS/2 to UNIX LAN

Martin R. M. Dunsmuir

Director of Xenix Development
Microsoft Corp.

◆ Introduction ◆

Lan Manager/X is a systems software product that allows PCs running MS-DOS or OS/2 to use a UNIX system as a file server or host for distributed applications. From the workstation's point of view, a UNIX system installed with Lan Manager/X provides all the services of and behaves identically to an OS/2 system running OS/2 Lan Manager software. In addition, because Lan Manager/X runs on UNIX rather than OS/2, access can be provided to additional services, including transparent file access to other network servers accessible only from UNIX and gatewaying facilities to UNIX services such as printing.

Lan Manager/X is designed specifically to run on UNIX systems. Unlike many other file server products for UNIX, Lan Manager/X was designed from the start to require no kernel modifications to the host system and to be portable across a wide range of UNIX variants running on the full spectrum of hardware platforms from PCs to large mainframes. To achieve this goal, the architecture of the server is such that interfaces between Lan Manager/X and variable operating system features such as Interprocess Communication (IPC) mechanisms and network services are carefully compartmentalized. Nevertheless, the standard, or reference, implementation of Lan Manager/X is optimized for UNIX System V, Release 3, which is the most common variant in its marketplace.

Lan Manager/X has been licensed widely to both UNIX and non-UNIX vendors. The primary deliverable is a source code and binary targeted at UNIX System V/386, running on a Compaq Deskpro 386 or PS/2 platform. The reference port makes use of System V IPC mechanisms such as shared memory and uses the standard streams-based Transport Level Interface (TLI) to access the network. OEMs who license Lan Manager/X (it is marketed solely as an OEM product by Microsoft) have to adapt the reference code to their own platform. For System V vendors, this is a relatively simple matter. The effort involved in bringing the product up on other platforms depends upon that system's capabilities. To make life easier on Berkeley UNIX systems or systems that don't support TLI, the product comes already made with an alternative network interface to Berkeley sockets.

The rest of this chapter should help give the reader a good understanding of the features and architecture of Lan Manager/X. Before we embark on a detailed discussion, however, it is useful to understand the motivation for Lan Manager/X's development and its relationship to other PC-networking products both past and present.

◆ Historical Background ◆

Computer networks are nothing new; they have been around for 20 years or so. Early networks provided simple point-to-point file transfer and remote login services over low bandwidth links. These systems were complemented in the 1970s by local area networks (LANs), which provided very high bandwidth and standard communication protocols. However, because computers and network interfaces remained expensive and largely proprietary, the impact of networking outside research and specialized commercial spheres was limited. It is only since the arrival of cheap, standard, PCs that the commercialization of computer networking on a grand scale has become possible.

Although the original IBM PC was a poor platform for major system software by anyone's standards, it has been phenomenally successful as a base for single-user commercial applications. Today, about 30,000,000 PCs are installed worldwide ranging from small floppy-disk-based systems to powerful 286- and 386-based models, which rival the power of minicomputers. The major impact of the PC's success on the computer industry has been to steer it away from multiuser, multiterminal systems toward installations composed of desktop PCs for every user, with LAN links to minicomputers or mainframe hosts. After an initial loss of centralized control, with each PC being an island, corporate systems organizations are now moving to consolidate around an architecture that provides users with easy access to centralized services by employing PC networking.

The other clear result of the users' love affair with the PC has been to move systems manufacturers away from proprietary systems toward a regime in which there is a broad consensus on systems software standards. Manufacturers now compete on the basis of added value and price/performance where once they tried to lock the users into their solution. With few exceptions, manufacturers are turning to UNIX as the standard system software of choice for minicomputers.

◆ PC-to-PC Networking Standards ◆

A major goal for any software product that aims to tie PCs and other systems together is to disturb the software running on the PC as little as possible. The reason for this is that PC applications are notoriously sensitive to changes in the behavior of the underlying software, and users are extremely sensitive to any changes that would tie them to a specific vendor's solution.

Luckily, even before PC-to-UNIX connectivity became an issue, IBM and others had established standard mechanisms for tying PCs together over local area networks. PC NET is an extension to the original MS-DOS operating system, which allows the DOS file system to be distributed between PCs running a piece of client software known as the *redirector* and PCs running a special dedicated file server program. Since 1985, versions of MS-DOS have included redirector software, while the server has been available as an option. The simplest PC-UNIX product is, therefore, a UNIX subsystem that emulates the PC server and thereby allows PC clients to access it as a file server without any modifications to the MS-DOS operating system.

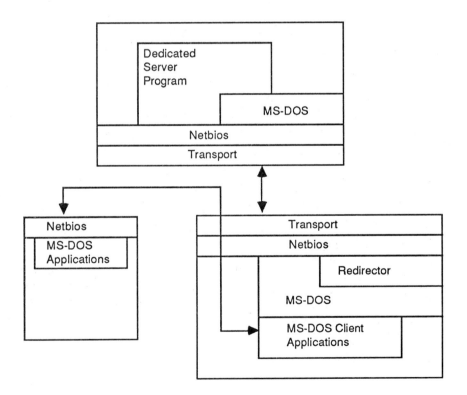

Fig. 8-1. PC-NET diagram from presentation

With the PC-NET redirector installed and enabled, the PC user sees additional DOS drives that reside, not locally, but on the file server. The software works by installing hooks in the code of MS-DOS to intercept all file system calls to network drives and to send them to the server rather than perform them locally. This redirection function is common to the client side mechanism of all network transparent distributed file systems.

To communicate with the server, the redirector uses a special file-sharing protocol that is piggybacked on top of the underlying transport software. The file-sharing protocol used by PC-NET is called the *Core Server Message Block* (or Core SMB) Protocol. Within the context of the commonly used OSI model, Core SMB is an application layer service.

One other aspect of the PC-NET software subsystem is crucially important to anyone wishing to achieve connectivity with a non-PC host. That is the interface between the redirector and the underlying transport mechanism over which the SMB messages are dispatched. In the PC world, and by virtue of IBM's early introduction of cheap networking hardware for PC interconnectivity, a standard interface is used almost universally for this purpose. This interface, called *NET-BIOS* (an acronym for Network Basic I/O System), defines the conventions for communication with any underlying transport software. We will have more to say about the details of NETBIOS later; however, it is important to appreciate that any server that wishes to connect with off-the-shelf PCs running PC-NET must faithfully replicate the PC's mapping of SMBs to NETBIOS requests and the mapping of NETBIOS requests to the underlying transport.

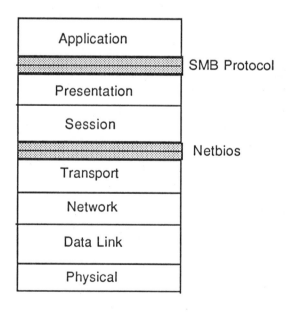

Fig. 8-2. OSI model with NETBIOS and SMB

Existing PC-Net Compatible Servers

Many system vendors have recognized the need to provide a server capability, compatible with PC-NET, on non-DOS systems. They recognize the potential of providing connectivity with the very large installed base of MS-DOS systems. These server subsystems can be divided into two groups, those implemented on UNIX and those implemented on proprietary operating systems. In the first group AT&T, Microsoft, IBM, Intel, and Hewlett-Packard are among the main protagonists. In the latter, DEC has a server for VMS; Hewlett-Packard, Tandem, Apollo, and others have implemented servers for their operating system platforms.

For each of these products, the goal has been the same: to provide a Core-SMB compatible file server that maps the MS-DOS file system on top of the host file system. In this way, data can be shared conveniently between programs running on DOS workstations and programs running on the host. Also, large disk storage requirements such as price, performance, and reliability can often be increased by using disk subsystems on central minicomputers.

Although Lan Manager/X is a new technology and not based on earlier UNIX servers, Microsoft has long been interested in tying PCs to UNIX systems. In the mid-1980s they developed a product called XENIX-Net for the Microsoft version of the UNIX operating system. This product supports a Core SMB server function and also provides UNIX-to-UNIX connectivity by using an extended SMB Protocol designed to support UNIX file system operations. Although XENIX-Net was never a strategic product, largely because UNIX-to-UNIX connectivity solutions have been dominated by Sun's NFS and AT&T's RFS, it has been invaluable in providing a technological base upon which the Lan Manager/X product development has drawn in developing PC-to-UNIX connectivity.

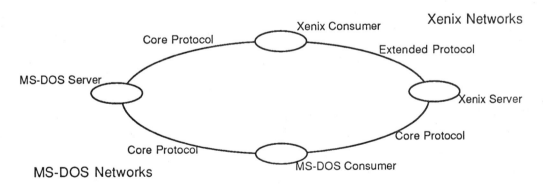

Fig. 8-3. XENIX-Net Diagram

♦ The Lan Manager/X Product Goals ♦

The Microsoft Connectivity Model

When Microsoft began developing OS/2 and its networking systems software to support that operating system, it developed a model of the networking software that would be needed to address that market. The Microsoft PC connectivity shown in Fig. 8-4 supports three tiers of systems.

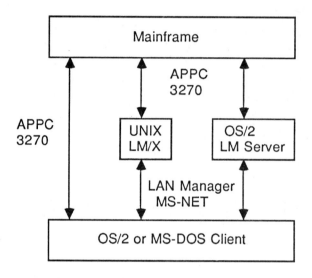

Fig. 8-4. Microsoft PC connectivity model

In the first or lowest tier, PC workstations run a combination of OS/2 and MS-DOS; these machines reside on the desktop. On the second tier, departmental minicomputers run UNIX and a few proprietary operating systems; dedicated servers also run OS/2. Finally, on the third tier, mainframe computers perform largely transaction-oriented functions.

This division of the computing base implies a number of connectivity functions between the tiers. These functions follow:

- *File Sharing*—There is a need for transparent access to files stored on departmental computers by programs running on OS/2 and MS-DOS workstations. This implies a transparent redirector facility under OS/2 and MS-DOS and also the provision of protection and name service functions by the file servers.

There is also a need for file sharing between machines at the departmental level. If these systems are running UNIX, the most common choices of software to provide this service are Sun Microsystem's Network File System (NFS), described in Chapter 4 and AT&T's Remote File System (RFS), described in Chapter 7.

- *Interprocess Communication*—To provide transparent access to files stored on departmental computers, a simple high-performance, peer-to-peer interprocess communication between programs running on workstations and server programs running on departmental servers (e.g., database and print servers) is needed. To provide file sharing between machines at the departmental level, a transaction-oriented IPC between programs running on workstations and departmental computers and programs running on mainframes is needed.

- *Miscellaneous Functions*—Many functions fall into this category; however, a consistent set of resource management and administration facilities, networkwide; is clearly needed. In addition, the network can potentially support functions such as remote boot, remote printing, and device sharing. Mainframe connectivity is addressed at all levels by specialized software supporting proprietary protocols such as IBM's 3270, 5250, and APPC.

The Goal of Lan Manager/X

Because Microsoft's goal is to have OS/2 and MS-DOS workstations on the desktop as well as be a strong player in the UNIX market, Lan Manager/X was conceived to fill the role of the file-sharing and IPC server at the departmental level.

Lan Manager/X is complementary and fully compatible with the OS/2 Lan Manager file server subsystem, which can also be used at the departmental level. Also, because Lan Manager/X is a server-only subsystem, it allows system vendors freedom of action in choices of UNIX-to-UNIX connectivity solutions.

◆ Protocol Support in the Lan Manager/X Server ◆

Before discussing the details of the server itself, we review the nature of the communication mechanism and the protocols used by Lan Manager/X.

The network protocol requirements of Lan Manager/X can be divided into two parts: the higher-level applications protocol used to support the file-sharing and interprocess communication functions of Lan Manager/X and the interfaces between Lan Manager/X and the underlying transport medium supported by the host system.

File-Sharing Protocols

The application-level protocols supported by the server are common to all servers that wish to communicate with the PCs running Lan Manager or PC-NET client software. Two protocols are supported: Core SMB and the Lan Manager Extended SMB (normally shortened to *Extended SMB*). Lan Manager/X does not provide support for the XENIX-Net extended SMB protocol. The Lan Manager Extended SMB Protocol is a strict superset of the Core Protocol and embodies all the functions of the latter as a subset.

The SMB Header. All SMB transactions between a client and the server involve exchange of standard messages. Both requests and responses consist of a standard SMB header and a variable length, function-dependent data field. The format of the SMB header is

```
struct{
    BYTE smb_idf[40];      /* Contains Oxff, 'SMB' */
    BYTE smb_com;          /* Command code */
    BYTE smb_rcis;         /* Error class code */
    BYTE smb_reh;          /* Reserved */
    WORD smb_err;          /* Error code */
    BYTE smb_reb;          /* Reserved */
    WORD smb_res[7];       /* Reserved */
    WORD smb_tid;          /* Tree ID */
    WORD smb_pid;          /* Caller's process ID */
    WORD smb_uid;          /* Caller's user ID */
    WORD smb_mid;          /* Multiplex ID */
    BYTE smb_wct;          /* Count of parameter words */
    WORD smb_vwv[];        /* Parameter words */
    WORD smb_bcc;          /* Number of bytes following */
    BYTE smb_data[];       /* Data bytes */
};
```

Note that the byte ordering of the transmission of SMB packets across the network always adheres to the conventions of the Intel microprocessor family. In particular, the least significant bytes of 16- and 32-bit quantities are transmitted first. The receiving software is responsible for performing any byte reordering required by the local architecture.

The first four bytes of the header always consist of the magic bytes 0xFF, followed by the the three bytes "SMB". This identifies the packet as an SMB. The command code identifies the particular type of request or response being transferred. All other fields should be self-explanatory, except for the treeID, processID, and multiplexID.

ID fields identify the source and destination of the request and are necessary largely because the SMB protocol uses only one virtual circuit between any given client and server. All requests are multiplexed over this connection. The software is responsible for handling the multiplexing and demultiplexing of each packet and routing it to the correct point for processing.

The *treeID* is used to identify a particular file-sharing connection between the client and the server. Each treeID is normally associated by the server with access to a particular resource such as a print queue or disk subtree.

The *processID* is used to identify a particular process within the client environment. Provided by the client, these IDs are used, for example, to help the server free resources when a given process terminates.

The *multiplexID* is unused in the Core Protocol; however, in the Extended Protocol, it is used by the server and client to identify subprocess environments, within client processes (e.g., threads). For example, under OS/2, one thread commonly performs a blocking, asynchronous, I/O operation, while other threads of the same process continue execution.

The *userID* is not used by OS/2 or DOS clients; its use is currently confined to the XENIX Extended Protocol.

Core and Extended SMB Protocols differ in two ways. First, they have different mechanisms for user validation and for mounting parts of the server file system in the client's file name space. Second, the Extended Protocol supports a variety of extra SMB transaction types for both file I/O and interprocess communication.

Protocol Negotiation and Dialects. How are SMB connections established between a client and a server? How does the server know whether a given client wishes to use the Core or the Extended Protocol?

The first SMB sent to the server, when a client wishes to establish a new connection, is the NEGOTIATE request. The NEGOTIATE request contains information regarding the choice of protocols the client is able to support and a variety of housekeeping and initialization data such as the time of day.

Each protocol that could be used to communicate between the client and the server is called a *dialect*. The client provides an array of strings, one for each dialect it supports. The dialect strings are passed in the data portion of the SMB. The server looks at this array and chooses the first entry it can support and returns the index of this entry to the client (indices start at 1, not 0). This protocol allows Core and Extended clients to be identified and allows a limited server to offer a compatible service to a more capable client. The dialect negotiation also allows a server to fine tune the protocol used between a variety of old and new versions.

For example, if an OS/2 client wishes to establish a connection it might send the three dialect strings `LANMAN1.2`, `LANMAN1.0`, and `PC NETWORK PROGRAM 1.0` in its negotiate packet. In response to this, a Core-only server would return the index 3, while an OS/2 or Lan Manager/X server might return 1 or 2, depending upon the highest-level revision of the Extended Protocol it supported.

The Core SMB Protocol

The Core SMB Protocol is used by MS-DOS clients running the older PC-NET or MS-NET redirector software. The functions supported by this protocol are summarized in Table 8-1. In this section we describe the user validation and file system mounting protocols used and also describe a few on the more important SMB file I/O transactions.

TABLE 8-1. Core SMBs

Function		Value	Action
#define	SMBmkdir	0x00	Create directory
#define	SMBrmdir	0x01	Delete directory
#define	SMBopen	0x02	Open file
#define	SMBcreate	0x03	Create file
#define	SMBclose	0x04	Close file
#define	SMBflush	0x05	Flush file
#define	SMBunlink	0x06	Delete file
#define	SMBmv	0z07	Rename file
#define	SMBgetatr	0x08	Get file attributes
#define	SMBsetatr	0x09	Set file attributes
#define	SMBread	0x0A	Read from file
#define	SMBwrite	0x0B	Write to file
#define	SMBlock	0x0C	Lock byte range
#define	SMBunlock	0x0D	Unlock byte range
#define	SMBctemp	0x0E	Create temporary file
#define	SMBmknew	0x0F	Make new file
#define	SMBchkpth	0x10	Check directory path
#define	SMBexit	0x11	Process exit
#define	SMBlseek	0x12	Seek
#define	SMBtcon	0x70	Tree connect
#define	SMBtdis	0x71	Tree disconnect
#define	SMBnegprot	0x72	Negotiate protocol
#define	SMBdskattr	0x80	Get disk attributes
#define	SMBsearch	0x81	Search directory
#define	SMBsplopen	0xC0	Open print spool file
#define	SMBsplwr	0xC1	Write print spool file
#define	SMBsplclose	0xC2	Close print spool file
#define	SMBsplretq	0xC3	Return print queue
#define	SMBsends	0xD0	Send single block message
#define	SMBsendh	0xD1	Send broadcast message
#define	SMBfwdname	0xD2	Forward user name
#define	SMBcancelf	0xD3	Cancel forward
#define	SMBgetmac	0xD4	Get machine name
#define	SMBsendstrt	0xD5	Send start of multi-block message
#define	SMBsendend	0xD6	Send end of multi-block message
#define	SMBsendtxt	0xD7	Send text of multi-block message

User Validation and File System Access. Historically the Core SMB protocol was used between MS-DOS clients and the MS-DOS server running PC-NET software. Although DOS is a single-user system and has no concept of users or user passwords, the Core SMB Protocol supports both unprotected and protected connections.

By default, all requests for network access are refused by a server; however, a server may identify certain parts of its file system tree as accessible by client machines. Each file system tree so identified is called a *share* (or *resource* in PC-NET parlance). The administrator of the server establishes resources by executing the NET SHARE command locally. This command associates a particular directory subtree with a network access name and an access attribute, which is an appropriate combination of read (R), write (W), and create (C) file access modes. For example, the command:

```
NET SHARE netname=c:\u\filetree password/RWC
```

associates the network name netname with the file system subtree rooted on the directory c:\u\filetree. Since MS-DOS has no concept of file protection based on local access privileges, this command gives unrestricted access to all files in the subtree for clients who can supply the correct network name and password.

On the client side, DOS or OS/2 users execute a net use command to associate a disk drive letter, with resources on any servers they want to access. For example:

```
net use e: \\svr1\netname password
```

would associate the drive e: with the share netname on server svr1. The syntax \\servername is the standard form of addressing a given network server. This syntax is used only during the net use command under PC-NET but may be used elsewhere under Lan Manager as discussed later. Once the connection (or *tree connect* as it is called) has been completed, the client may access files on the e: drive as if they were local, and the redirector takes care of translating all file I/O calls into SMB transactions.

All tree connections are established using the Tree Connect SMB. This SMB returns a treeID to the caller (see Fig. 8-5); this ID is used to identify all subsequent accesses to this network drive.

User Command:

```
net use x: \\server\service <password>
```

SMB Transactions:

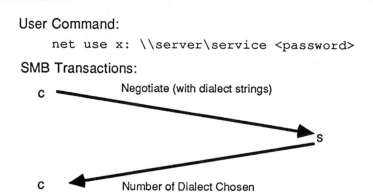

Fig. 8-5. Diagram of tree connect logic

File I/O. Once a tree connect has been performed we may want to do some file I/O. The Core SMB protocol provides a full set of transactions to support DOS file I/O system calls. An example file I/O transaction to open, read, write, and close a file is shown in Fig. 8-6. Initially the redirector sends an open SMB to the server, along with the correct treeID and the pathname of the file to be opened. If the file is accessible then the server opens the file locally and returns a fileID to the client. This fileID is similar in use to a UNIX file descriptor. Read and Write operations proceed as expected with the treeID and FileID being passed as parameters. Data is transferred in the Data field of the SMB. Closing the file is accomplished using the close SMB with the treeID and fileID being passed as parameters.

Using the lock and unlock SMBs where the offset and range of the lock are passed as parameters supports file locking. In the UNIX environment these calls can easily be mapped onto the UNIX file-locking primitives.

Program Code:

```
fh = open("x:\foo",O_RDWR);
n = read(fh, buffer, n);
write(fh, buffer, n):
close(fh);
```

SMB Transaction:

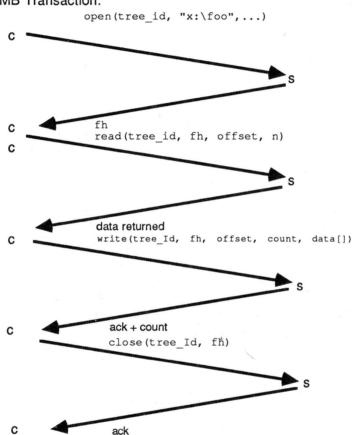

Fig. 8-6. File I/O

Remote Printing. Printing support is a special case of file I/O handled directly by the redirector. In the first instance, the server must offer a special type of share (e.g., prn). Then the user must execute a net use command to associate a DOS printer device name (lpt1:, lpt2:, or lpt3:) with this network name. For example:

```
net use lpt1: \\server\prn password
```

The treeID returned by this transaction is special and thereafter any data sent or spooled to the device lpt1: is transferred to the server by the redirector using special spooling SMBs. An example of this is shown in Fig. 8-7.

SMB Remote Printing Services

User Command:

```
net use lpt1:\\server\prn <password>
copy foo lpt1:
```

SMB Transaction:

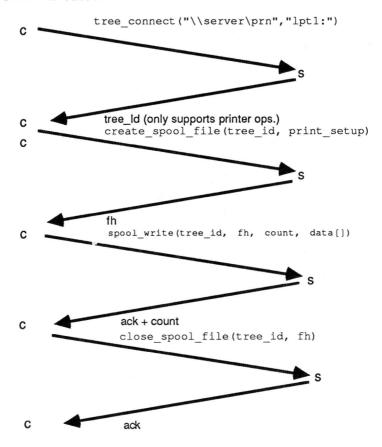

Fig. 8-7. Spooling example

The Extended SMB Protocol

The Extended Protocol differs from the Core Protocol in two respects. First, it supports a more sophisticated security and session validation scheme. Second, the repertoire of SMBs has been extended to support more efficient use of the connection for file I/O (e.g., chaining of SMBs) and also to allow for IPC. It is important to realize that the Core Protocol is a subset of the Extended Protocol and that Extended clients use many of the Core functions such as file I/O in their normal operation. The functions supported by the Extended SMB Protocol are listed in Table 8-2.

TABLE 8-2. Extended SMBs

Function	Value	Action
#define SMBlockread	0x13	Lock then read data
#define SMBwriteunlock	0x14	Write then unlock data
#define SMBreadBraw	0x1A	Read block raw
#define SMBreadBmpx	0x1B	Read block multiplex
#define SMBreadBs	0x1C	Read block (secondary response)
#define SMBwriteBraw	0x1D	Write block raw
#define SMBwriteBmpx	0x1E	Write block multiplex
#define SMBwriteBs	0x1F	Write block (secondary request)
#define SMBwriteC	0x20	Write complete (response)
#define SMBqrysrv	0x21	Query server information
#define SMBsetattrE	0x22	Get attribute expanded
#define SMBgetattrE	0x23	Get file attributes expanded
#define SMBlockingX	0x24	Lock/unlock byte ranges and X
#define SMBtrans	0x25	Transaction name, bytes in/out
#define SMBtranss	0x26	Transaction (secondary request/response)
#define SMBioctl	0x27	IOCTL
#define SMBioctls	0x28	IOCTL (secondary request/response)
#define SMBcopy	0x29	Copy
#define SMBmove	0x2A	Move
#define SMBecho	0x2B	Echo
#define SMBwriteclose	0x2C	Write and close
#define SMBopenX	0x2D	Open and X
#define SMBreadX	0x2E	Read and X
#define SMBwriteX	0x2F	Write and X
#define SMBnewsize	0x30	Set new file size
#define SMBcloseTD	0x31	Close and tree disconnect
#define SMBsessetup	0x73	Session Set Up & X (including user login)
#define SMBulogoff	0x74	User logoff and X
#define SMBtconX	0x75	Tree connect and X
#define SMBffirst	0x82	Find first
#define SMBfunique	0x83	Find unique
#define SMBfclose	0x84	Find close

User Validation and File System Access. The Extended SMB server must also support the Core SMB protocol, in which case the user validation scheme is identical to that already described. However, for clients who negotiate the Extended Protocol, the server may be operated in one of two modes. In *resource-level security mode* the server provides access identical to that provided by the Core Protocol; that is, resources are made available and the client who knows the resource name and the password acquires a set of default privileges. In *user-level security mode*, the server makes directory trees available, but in addition to the resource name it requires a valid user name and password to be supplied before access privileges are granted. User-level security mode is similar to the XENIX-Net mapping of resources to user names but by removing the direct association of user names and share names it is more flexible. Under Lan Manager/X, resource names are obtained from an Lan Manager/X specific resource file, and user names and passwords are validated against the UNIX password file.

User Command:

```
netlogon username <password>
net use x:\\server\service
```

SMB Transaction:

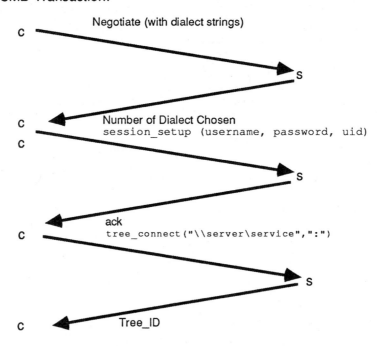

Fig. 8-8. Implicit UNC file I/O

On the client side, setting up a resource-level tree connection is identical to setting up a Core connection. However, when user-level security is being used, the syntax of the client operations is different.

On the Lan Manager client, before a user-level session can be established, the user must login to the server. This operation associates a user name and a password with his local machine. This information is initially stored locally and is encoded as a session setup SMB before the first tree connection is subsequently initiated with any particular server.

For the user, the advantage of the user-level security mode is that is allows tree connects to be made both explicitly in the normal way and implicitly during file operations. For this latter purpose, the `\\servername`naming convention is used. (This convention is also known as the *Universal Naming Convention* or UNC.)

For example if the user wishes to open a file `\u\file` residing in the share `filesys` on server `svr1`, it can be done either by first using the `NET USE` command to associate a drive letter with a remote resource, followed by a file operation or implicitly by opening the file. `\\svr1\filesys\u\file` in the file I/O call. This latter transaction sequence is shown in Fig. 8-8.

As we shall see, UNC is most useful for addressing IPC objects on a remote server.

SMB Chaining. One of the major performance bottlenecks of the Core Protocol is the fact that a network packet must be sent and received for every single SMB transaction. The Extended SMB Protocol improves on this by supporting the chaining of SMB requests and responses within a single packet. The maximum amount of chaining is limited only by the maximum packet size supported by the client and server. (This limit depends on the implementation and is agreed upon during the negotiate protocol.) All the SMBs shown in Table 8-2 including the words `and_X` can be chained. In addition, there are some special purpose combinations: `CLOSEandDISCONNECT`, `WRITEandCLOSE`, `LOCKandREAD`, and `WRITEandUNLOCK`. For example, the opening of the UNC addressed file `\\svr1\filesys\u\file` may involve the following chained sequence of SMBs in one packet:

```
SESSION_SETUPandX
    TREE_CONNECTandX
        OPENandX
```

The availability of other chained SMB transactions to the programmer depends upon the interfaces provided by the local operating system.

TRANSACTION SMBs. In addition to the standard File I/O SMBs, the Extended Protocol also supports a special type of SMB known as a TRANSACTION. This SMB allows a client to perform an operation on a symbolically named object residing on the server. No tree connect is necessary.

TRANSACTIONs are the foundation of all IPC, printing, and remote device capabilities provided to extended clients. The basic flow a TRANSACTION is sending the SMB to the server accompanied by its data arguments and receiving a response from the client. Support is provided for multiple data packets to be exchanged if the transaction such as a file spool operation will not fit into one packet.

Remote Device Support. One interesting example of the combination of file I/O and specialized SMBs is the support provided in the protocol for remote devices. A typical operation, setting the baud rate on a remote communications port, is shown in Fig. 8-9.

The client software opens the remote communications port \\svr2\dev\com2 and performs an ioctl call on that open device. This ioctl is encoded as a single IOCTL SMB request and response. Lan Manager/X supports such access to UNIX communications ports for client applications.

User Command:
```
net use com2\\server\comservices
setbaud com2 9600
```
SMB Transaction:

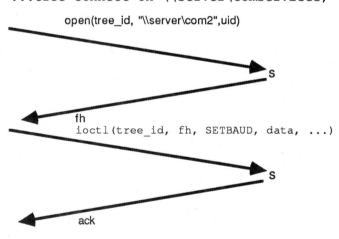

...tree connect on \\server\comservices,

open(tree_id, "\\server\com2",uid)

fh

ioctl(tree_id, fh, SETBAUD, data, ...)

ack

Fig. 8-9. Remote ioctl

DOS Lan Manager

When OS/2 Lan Manager and the Extended Protocol were developed it was considered important to be able to offer an improved service to MS-DOS clients as well. Although the basic Core services are supported for the sake of compatibility, it is possible, if you install the extended redirector on your DOS machine, to take advantage of many new Lan Manager features. The software that offers this enhancement is called DOS Lan Manager. Services provided by DOS Lan Manager include TRANSACTION support, user-level security, and SMB chaining (Table 8-3).

TABLE 8-3. Extended SMBs not used by DOS Lan Manager

Function	Value	Action
SMBreadBmpx	0x1B	Read block multiplexed
SMBreadBs	0x1C	Read block (secondary response)
SMBwriteBmpx	0x1E	Write block multiplexed
SMBwriteBs	0x1F	Write block (secondary response)
SMBecho	0x2B	Echo
SMBwriteC	0x20	Write complete (response)
SMBgetattrE	0x23	Get file attributes expanded
SMBioctl	0x27	IOCTL
SMBioctls	0x28	IOCTL (secondary request/response)
SMBwriteclose	0x2C	Write and close
SMBsetattrE	0x22	Set file attributes expanded
SMBulogoff	0x74	User logoff and X
SMBffirst	0x82	Find first
SMBfunique	0x83	Find unique
SMBfclose	0x84	Find close

Because DOS Lan Manager is a subset of the Extended Protocol and the Lan Manager/X server supports that protocol fully, DOS Lan Manager support falls out in the wash; however, keep in mind that two sorts of MS-DOS clients must still be supported by the server.

Interface-to-Transport Protocols

The SMB Protocol is an applications-level protocol and is independent of the underlying transport mechanism used to move data between the client and the server. Normally, the transport protocol used is an industry standard such as TCP/IP or one of the ISO/OSI protocols.

Since one of the major objectives of the Lan Manager/X implementation plan was to support a wide variety of transport mechanisms, the server does not interface with the transport software directly, but rather it uses its own interface.

Part of the effort of porting Lan Manager/X into a new UNIX environment is to reimplement the mapping of this interface onto the underlying network services.

In practice UNIX systems provide two standard interfaces to the network: Berkeley Sockets (usually interfacing with TCP/IP transport) and AT&T's TLI. The Lan Manager/X product comes with ready-made interfaces to these two mechanisms.

The NETBIOS Interface. As already described, in the DOS or OS/2 client environment, the interface between the redirector and the transport has been standardized around a functional interface that was originally defined by IBM and is called NETBIOS. Although NETBIOS can be implemented on top of any transport such as TCP/IP or ISO/OSI, the redirector is insulated from it by the NETBIOS interface. For each transport there must be a mapping, within the DOS or OS/2 network device driver, between NETBIOS functions and the real transport mechanism. Table 8-4 summarizes the NETBIOS functions.

For an Lan Manager/X server to communicate successfully with a DOS or OS/2 client that uses the NETBIOS interface, it is not sufficient to provide the same transport protocol alone. The mapping between NETBIOS functions and the underlying transport also must be faithfully reproduced. The result of this requirement has historically been a diversity of proprietary mappings and a concomitant lack of interoperability between PCs running over the same transport but using a different vendor's NETBIOS interface. Luckily, efforts are now well advanced to solve this problem by developing standard mappings between NET-BIOS and the two most commonly used transport protocols: TCP/IP and ISO/TP4.

TABLE 8-4. NETBIOS function summary

Function	Value	Action
NCBcall	0x08	Call
NCBlisten	0x09	Listen
NCBhangup	0x0A	Hangup circuit
NCBsend	0x0C	Send Data
NCBrecv	0x0D	Receive Data on circuit
NCBrecvany	0x0E	Receive data on any circuit
NCBsenddbl	0x0F	Send double data packet
NCBsenddgrm	0x10	Send datagram
NCBrecvdgrm	0x11	Receive datagram
NCBsendbcst	0x12	Send broadcast datagram
NCBrecvbcst	0x13	Receive broadcast datagram
NCBaddname	0x18	Add name
NCBdelname	0x19	Delete name
NCBreset	0x20	Reset transport
NCBadapstat	0x21	Adapter status
NCBsessstat	0x22	Session status
NCBcancel	0x23	Cancel asynchronous transaction
NCBaddgrnam	0x24	Add group name
NCBunlink	0x38	Unlink

The Lan Manager/X network interface is closely modeled after the functionality of NETBIOS. One of the tasks of adapting the server is to implement an appropriate mapping onto the underlying network services. Depending upon the nature of the local NETBIOS support, more or less work needs to be done in this regard. For example, many UNIX TCP/IP implementations now include the standard NETBIOS (or *RFC* as it is called) interface. In this case, the Lan Manager/X interface library can talk directly to these services. Where no such interface is provided, the implementor of Lan Manager/X must provide one, either at user level or in the kernel.

The Lan Manager/X Network Services Interface

The overall architecture of the Lan Manager/X server and its interfaces to the underlying network services are shown in Fig. 8-10.

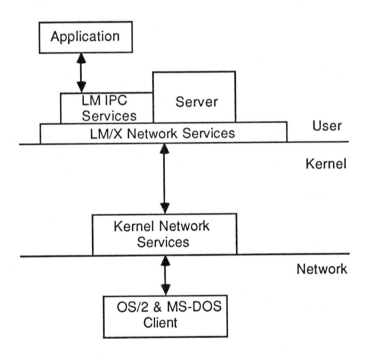

Fig. 8-10. Lan Manager/X diagram

The Lan Manager/X Network Services are summarized in Table 8-5.

TABLE 8-5. Lan Manager/X network services

Service	Action
nb_accept	accept a connection on a Netbios transport endpoint
nb_bind	bind a Netbios name to a transport endpoint
nb_call	initiate a Netbios connection to another Netbios session
nb_close	unbind a Netbios name from an endpoint and close the endpoint
nb_dgrecv	receive a Netbios datagram from a Netbios client
nb_dgsend	send a Netbios datagram to another Netbios host
nb_disco	hangup a virtual circuit
nb_dup2	duplicate a Netbios file descriptor
nb_exec	prepare Lan Manager/X for a UNIX exec in the caller
nb_fork	Fork a process using nblib
nb_listen	listen for connections on a Netbios transport endpoint
nb_open	create a Netbios transport endpoint
nb_poll	poll a group of Netbios endpoints for data
nb_recv	receive a single Netbios message over a virtual circuit
nb_send	send a single Netbios message over a virtual circuit

The network interface functionality can be divided into three categories: circuit initialization and name service, data transfer and polling services, and, finally, interface control functions.

Connection Initiation and Name Service. Before a UNIX program can engage in any network communication, it must initiate a connection with the local transport services. This is done, using the nb_open call. This call takes a service name (there may be more than one on any given host), an indication of whether a virtual circuit or datagram service is required and a flag to indicate blocking or nonblocking operation. For example:

```
fd = nb_open("tcp", STYPE_VC, O_NDELAY);
```

might establish a nonblocking, virtual circuit endpoint within a TCP/IP module. The call returns a UNIX file descriptor, which is used in all subsequent calls.

The next stage is to bind a NETBIOS local name to the endpoint. This is used by remote clients who wish to address this endpoint. For example, the call:

```
struct nbaddr *nbaddr;
strcpy(nbaddr->name, "LMXSVR1          ");   Note padding to 16 chars
nb_bind(fd, nbaddr);
```

would bind "LMXSVR1   " to a previously created endpoint. Once the name has been bound, the UNIX program may call other endpoints or, in the case of virtual circuits, listen and accept connections on its own address. For example, the sequence:

```
struct nbaddr *nbaddr;
nb_listen(fd);
newfd = nb_accept(fd, nbaddr);
```

would listen and accept connections on a virtual circuit. The address of the remote endpoint is returned in the nbaddr structure. Note that when a connection is accepted a new file descriptor is created, specifically for communicating with this client. An existing connection is closed using the nb_close call, which takes an existing endpoint file descriptor as a parameter.

Data Transfer and Polling. The data transfer calls provided by the interface are modeled after the standard UNIX read and write primitives. For virtual circuit connections the parameters of nb_send and nb_recv match read and write exactly. For datagram connections, an additional argument is included for the remote endpoint address since datagrams can be sent without the need for accepting connections. For example, the call:

```
struct nbaddr *nbaddr;
actual_length = nb_dgrecv(fd, buffer, max_length, nbaddr);
```

would receive datagrams with the size of the incoming packet returned in actual_length and the address of the sender returned in nbaddr.

In addition to data transfer, it is often necessary to be able to poll for incoming I/O without blocking in the calling process. This function is commonly provided on Berkeley UNIX by the select system call and on UNIX System V.3 by poll. On other systems, it must be implemented in some other way. In the Lan Manager/X environment, the nb_poll call is provided for this purpose: nb_poll takes an array of file descriptors as an argument and returns the status of them all simultaneously. A timeout is provided to prevent blocking in the system if no data is available on any descriptor. For each file descriptor, the system returns its status as a combination of the following:

- Data is ready to be read from the endpoint, or an incoming connection request has been received.

- Data can now be sent on this endpoint. (It has been accepted remotely.)

- An error has occurred.

Control Functions. The final pair of calls provided by the interface are nb_sync and nb_cntl.

nb_sync should be called whenever a file descriptor has been duped or has been subject to a fork or exec operation. It tells the underlying transport to prepare the endpoint correctly for further operations.

nb_cntl is used to control the blocking mode of an existing endpoint. Although the initial mode is determined by nb_open, it is often useful to be able to control this behavior during operation. For example, the call:

```
nb_cntl(fd, NB_BLOCK);
```

would set the mode of the endpoint pointed to be `fd` to blocking. On most UNIX systems, this maps onto a call to the `fcntl` system call.

◆ Lan Manager/X Functional Overview ◆

Functionally Lan Manager/X is divided into four major subsystems: connection management; file sharing, printer and remote device support; interprocess communication; and administration. In this section, we discuss these subsystems from the functional point of view. The next section discusses the architecture of the Lan Manager/X server and provides some details on how its features are implemented.

Connection Management

As already discussed, the Lan Manager/X server supports both the Core and the Extended SMB protocols. The definition of these protocols includes specifications of the method of initiating connections with the server and the validation of clients who wish to gain access. Lan Manager/X provides support for the Core concept of resources and supports both the user-level and resource-level security models of OS/2 Lan Manager. When the server is started, the administrator specifies whether it should operate in user- or resource-level mode. The details of these security modes are discussed here.

Two databases are maintained on the server to control connections: the share table and the UNIX password file `/etc/passwd`.

The Share Table. The share table is established at server startup and is maintained by the server. Entries are added to it and removed from it using the `net share` command. This command can be used to maintain four kinds of resources: file trees, printer queues, devices, and special resources.

File tree shares associate remote resource names with parts of the UNIX directory hierarchy. For example, the command:

```
net share userfiles=/usr/files
```

associates the network resource name `userfiles` with the directory tree rooted at `/usr/files` and will allow access to that tree to clients who provide the appropriate password information (see discussion that follows).

Printer queue resources are a generalized mechanism for providing access to the standard input of different UNIX commands from remote programs that use printer devices. For example, the command:

```
net share laser="/usr/bin/lp -dlaser"
```

associates the remote printer name `laser` with the UNIX lineprinter queue to a laser printer. If clients associate their printer devices with this name, then any data they send to that device will be routed to the remote printer.

Device resources provide a mechanism for accessing character devices attached to the server system. For example, access could be provided to a pool of modems. The advantage of the device resource mechanism is that it allows data transfer and control functions to be multiplexed between a number of similar devices on the server without the client needing to address the device it wants to use directly. For example, the command:

```
net share modems=/dev/tty01,/dev/tty02 -comm
```

In this case a resource called `modems` is established containing the UNIX communications ports `/dev/tty01` and `/dev/tty02`. The server allocates these devices in round-robin fashion to interested clients and performs data transfer and `ioctl` requests on their behalf.

Two special resources are provided in addition to the generalized file tree, printer, and device mechanisms. The first of these (`IPC$`) is used to specify that the server supports remote IPC and the second (`ADMIN$`) specifies that the server supports remote administration. Depending upon which of these features the server wishes to support, the share commands:

```
net share IPC$
```

or

```
net share ADMIN$
```

must have been executed. These resources are discussed in more detail in the sections on IPC and Administration.

To terminate a resource and delete its entry from the share table, the `net share` command is used with the special argument `-delete`. This command deletes the named resource from the share table and disconnects any tree connects currently associated with it. For example, to delete the resources established by the examples already cited, the following commands would be executed:

```
net share -delete userfiles
net share -delete laser
net share -delete modems
```

The Password File. The UNIX password file `/etc/passwd` is used to control access to server resources and to decide which uid will be used by the server to determine detailed access permissions to that resource. In addition, if a file resource name that does not appear in the share table is specified, then it is also looked up as a user name in the `/etc/passwd` file. If the user name is found, then the HOME directory of the user is assumed to be the root directory of the file resource whose name is `username`. For example, if the password file contains the entry:

```
fred:uBhhxlDvEh50E,60GD:371:50::/usr/fred:
```

then the client command:

```
net use f: \\server\fred
```

would give access to the file tree rooted on the UNIX directory `/usr/fred`.

The use of the password entry in the `/etc/passwd` file depends upon whether the server is operating in user- or resource-level security mode.

User-Level Security Mode

In user-level security mode, connections are associated with directory trees and UNIX uids.

For Core clients, the `net use` command passes the machine name, resource name, and resource password to the server (actually the machine name is provided explicitly by the client software; it is not specified directly by the user). The server first searches `/etc/passwd` to try to find the machine name. If it finds it, the uid of the connection is set to the uid of the UNIX user `machinename`. If this name is not found, then, depending upon the configuration of the server, either the uid is set to a default value, or the connection attempt is rejected. The connection will also be rejected if the password does not match that specified for the user `machinename`.

The actual resource to be used is taken from the resource name part of the connection request, and this name is looked up in the share table. If it is not found there, it is assumed to be a file resource and looked up in the `/etc/passwd` file. If the user `resourcename` is found in the `passwd` file, then the root directory of the connection is set to the HOME directory of this user; otherwise, the connection is rejected.

The effect of all this is to require each remote client machine to have an entry in the UNIX password file corresponding to its NETBIOS network name and for there to be an entry in either the share table or the `passwd` file for every resource. Also note that the same password, corresponding to the user `machinename` must be given with every tree connect request.

For Extended Protocol clients (e.g., Lan Manager), the procedure used to set up connections is the same as that used for Core clients, except that the user name and password used to determine the uid of the connection access are provided during session setup, when a `net login` command is executed by the client.

The user name and password, passed during the `net login` command, are used for every tree connect. The password field of subsequent tree connects to the server is ignored. For example, the Lan Manager commands:

```
net login fred password
net use d: \\server\userfiles
net use e: \\server\programs
```

cause the user `fred` to be validated against `/etc/passwd` in both cases. The resources, `userfiles` and `programs`, are associated with the network drives `d:` and `e:`, respectively.

Resource-Level Security Mode

In resource-level security mode, there is no difference between the Core and Extended Protocols. For each offered resource there must be an entry in the `/etc/passwd` file and possibly an entry in the share table. The resource name and the password, given in the `net use` command, are checked against the password file, and the resource itself is either that specified in the share table or, if it is not present there, then in the user's HOME directory corresponding to the resource name specified. Connections for which there is no entry in the password file are refused.

As a result different connections between a given client and server potentially have different uids associated with them on the server. As we shall see, this has ramifications for the design of the Lan Manager/X server program.

Connection Termination

Connections may be terminated by either the client or the server. If the server terminates a connection, this is seen as an error condition at the client's end. As we shall see, the server often times out idle connections, and it is the redirector's responsibility to resurrect them if the client becomes active again.

Client termination is usually performed using the `/d` option to the `net use` command. For example, the commands:

```
net use d: /d
net use lpt1 /d
```

terminate the connections associated with the network drive `d:` and the line-printer `lpt1:`, respectively.

File Sharing

File sharing is the heart of the Lan Manager/X server's functionality. Once a client has logged onto a server and performed tree connects to it, the files can be accessed using the standard DOS or OS/2 file I/O system calls.

The redirector must map I/O system calls into appropriate sets of SMB transactions; the server must map these SMB's into the appropriate UNIX I/O calls on the client program's behalf.

File Naming. Both UNIX, OS/2, and DOS share a similar file system hierarchy; however, there are a number of differences in file-naming conventions and detailed file I/O semantics that the server needs to consider.

On DOS and OS/2 machines, file names adhere strictly to an 11-character convention: Each file name consists of up to eight characters, followed optionally by a dot (.) and an extension of up to three characters. In addition, if the file being addressed does not reside in the current directory, then the components of the directory path used to reach the given file are separated by backslashes (\). Both UNIX and DOS reference current and parent directories as "." and "..", respectively.

Another difference that leads to problems is that DOS and OS/2 are case insensitive with respect to alphabetic characters (i.e., the files FOO and foo are considered identical). For example, the following are valid OS/2 file names:

```
file.c
prog.exe
\usr\fred\file.txt
```

Also, under Lan Manager, file addressing may implicitly require a tree connection to be made prior to the file being opened if the UNC naming convention is used. For example:

```
\\server\usr\fred\file.c
```

is the file `\usr\fred\file.c` on the server `server`. The UNC was already discussed.

Because of these differences, the server must convert the incoming file name to a valid UNIX format before the file name can be used locally on the server. Also, because the UNIX file system is case sensitive, has no extensions, and allows longer file names than OS/2, certain files on the UNIX system cannot be addressed by OS/2 or DOS clients.

File Name Mapping. Before a file name is sent to the server, it is manipulated by the redirector to put it into a canonical or standard form.

On the server, the following actions are performed to convert the file name to a usable UNIX format:

- All backslashes are converted to forward slashes.

- All uppercase letters are converted to lower case.

For example, an attempt by a client to open the file:

```
\USR\FRED\FILE.C
```

would result in the server attempting to open the UNIX file:

```
/usr/fred/file.c
```

in the UNIX directory tree associated with the client connection.

Unaddressable UNIX Files. Problems arise when DOS and OS/2 clients address UNIX file systems because many file names that are valid or unique on UNIX are unaddressable or lead to conflicts on DOS. For example: the files `Makefile` and `makefile` are unique on UNIX but are the same file name on DOS; the files `longfile1` and `longfile2` not only violate the 8.3 DOS naming convention but also lead to a conflict if their names are truncated for DOS's benefit.

Many SMB UNIX servers try to be clever and provide various name translation tricks to get around this problem, but these all lead to confusion for users on DOS and confusion and inconvenience for UNIX programs. The approach taken to this problem on Lan Manager/X is very simple. The client sees only those lowercase file names on the UNIX server that are valid on DOS (e.g., uppercase names); all other files are hidden in normal use from SMB clients. The rationale for this is that DOS and OS/2 users are primarily using Lan Manager/X as a DOS or OS/2 file server and are not normally interested in UNIX-only files. For clients who really want to see all UNIX files, special subroutine libraries and commands are provided to allow them to address all UNIX files. These mechanisms do not use the redirector for communication but rather a special IPC Protocol between client and server.

So, in the case of these two examples, the client would see only the file `makefile`; the files `Makefile`, `longfile1`, and `longfile2` are hidden by the server.

Directory Searching. One of the most common functions performed by users and programs under both UNIX and DOS is the desire to scan through the contents of a directory and find all the files that match a certain pattern. A good example of this on UNIX would be the command:

```
ls *.c
```

which lists all the files ending in `.c`. A similar command on DOS would be:

```
dir *.c
```

To support these functions, DOS and OS/2 provide the functions Findfirst, Findnext, and FindClose. Findfirst opens a directory and returns the name of the first file matching the pattern. Findnext is called subsequently to step through the directory and return names of the other files matching the pattern. Findclose closes the directory when the search is completed.

In response to these commands, the Lan Manager/X server converts the DOS wildcard used to specify the file names to be matched into a UNIX wildcard specification and uses the UNIX directory manipulation system calls (opendir, readdir, closedir, etc.) to obtain the data for the client. For UNIX systems that do not implement these system calls, the server may explicitly need to open and read the disk directory.

File Locking. In addition to data transfer operations on files, Lan Manager/X also supports file locking. When a file is locked, a specific region is unavailable for reading, writing, or both by other clients or local UNIX programs. To implement this functionality, Lan Manager/X maps DOS- and OS/2-locking calls onto the appropriate UNIX file-locking primitives.

Other File Operations. There are many other file operations that can be performed via the Lan Manager/X server:

- *Get/Set File Attributes.* Both DOS and OS/2 provide calls that allow the client to interrogate and set the attributes of a file. These functions are similar to those provided by the UNIX stat system call.

- *Changing File Size.* OS/2 provides a call to truncate or extend an existing file without I/O. This call is easily implemented using fcntl on UNIX System V.

- *File and Directory Creation and Deletion.* Both file and directory creation and deletion functions map directly onto UNIX system calls; however, in the context of the server, file deletion applies only to the link being directly addressed by the client. Of course, a file with more than one extant UNIX link will continue to exist. The SMB File Move request maps to a link followed by an unlink system call.

- *Program Execution and Termination.* In addition to normal file operations, the client may request that a program file resident on the UNIX file system be loaded for execution on the client. When this happens, the server provides the program image data to the client and locks the executable file until the client redirector provides an exit notification.

Other SMB operations that map conveniently onto UNIX file primitives are file flush, file seek, and the compound SMBs such as write and close.

Printer and Remote Device Support

As already explained, printer-spooling operations are associated with a special set of SMBs. Lan Manager/X handles these SMBs and routes the data to the appropriate UNIX printer spool program, as specified in the resource share command that was executed on the server to advertise the printer service. Print spool queue interrogation and control is provided via the administrative interface.

Access to remote devices is also performed using normal File I/O SMBs for data transfer and TRANSACTION and `ioctl` SMBs to allow control functions to be requested by client programs.

Interprocess Communication

Lan Manager/X provides UNIX interfaces to the OS/2 Lan Manager Interprocess Communication services. The purpose of providing these facilities on UNIX is to allow UNIX programs to act as servers or clients to programs running in the Lan Manager environment. This allows server programs running on UNIX to be called by programs running on OS/2 or DOS workstations using the standard facilities provided in those environments. When the Lan Manager/X IPC facilities are used, the client software cannot distinguish between a service running on Lan Manager/X and a service running on an OS/2 Lan Manager server.

Lan Manager/X provides two IPC facilities for communicating with OS/2 and DOS clients: named pipes and mailslots. The interfaces are not part of the base UNIX API and should not be confused with the standard UNIX facilities going by the same names (i.e., Named Pipes). Both named pipes and mailslots are used extensively by the Lan Manager to support System Administration functions. In the first release, Lan Manager/X supports only the server side of the Lan Manager IPC interfaces; however, client side services will be implemented in a future release. The effect of this is that server applications can be implemented on UNIX, and clients can call those services; however, programs on UNIX cannot call out to IPC-based applications on other Lan Manager compatible servers.

Named Pipes. Named pipes are full duplex IPC channels functionally akin to Berkeley Sockets. They have two ends: the server end and the client end. The *server end* is owned by the process that creates the pipe (using `LmxMakeNmPipe`) and the *client ends* are owned by client processes, on OS/2 or DOS, that attach to the pipe. Each endpoint is distinct and provides for bidirectional data transfer.

When a new pipe is created on the server, the caller specifies how many instances of that pipe can exist. It can then call `LmxMakeNmPipe` successively with the same pipe name to create multiple instances of the pipe; each instance is associated with a distinct named pipe UNIX file descriptor. Once a file descriptor has been obtained for a given instance, the server can listen and accept a connection on that instance using `LmxConnectNmPipe`. In this way, a server can support multiple instances of a pipe name, each with a different client attached. Table 8-6 summarizes the named pipe services.

TABLE 8-6. Named pipe services

Service name	Client side	Server
LmxMakeNmPipe	no	yes
LmxConnectNmPipe	no	yes
LmxDisconnectNmPipe	no	yes
LmxQNmPipeInfo	yes	yes
LmxQNmpState	yes	yes
LmxSetNmpState	yes	yes
LmxPeekNmPipe	yes	yes
LmxTransactNmPipe	yes	yes
LmxOpen	yes	yes
LmxClose	yes	yes
LmxRead	yes	yes
LmxWrite	yes	yes
LmxNmpSync	yes	yes
LmxCallNmPipe	yes	no
LmxWaitNmPipe	yes	no

A given pipe instance can be attached to only one client at a time; however, it is possible to terminate conversation with one client and accept a connection from a new client by using `LmxDisconnectNmPipe`, followed by `LmxConnectNmPipe`. A named pipe instance goes away when the last file descriptor associated with it is closed (Fig. 8-11).

Client

Server

Create a Pipe
```
fh + MakeNmPipe("\pipe\foo",...)
```

Listen for Connections
```
ConnectNmPipe(fh);
```

Open a Pipe on the Server
```
fh = DosOpen("\\server\pipe\foo",...);
DosWrite(fh,...);
```

```
Read(fh,...);
Write(fh,...);
```

```
DosRead(fh,...);
DosClose(fh);
```

Close and Remove Pipe
```
DisconnectNmPipe(fh);
```

Fig. 8-11. Named pipe example

Named pipes can be configured in two different operating modes: stream oriented and record oriented. In *stream-oriented mode,* no record boundaries are maintained, and the semantics are identical to those supported by UNIX pipes. In *record-oriented mode,* record boundaries are preserved across the network; attempts to read data smaller than the record size will fail. The other distinguishing feature of named pipes is the ability to read incoming data without removing it from the pipe.

Mailslots. Mailslots are unidirectional (half-duplex) communication channels like datagrams. Like named pipes, they have a distinct server and client side. The server program creates and owns the mailslot. Multiple clients can connect simultaneously to the same mailslot name, and there is no differentiation made between clients. Mailslots are record oriented, and records are delivered individually to the server. The only service available to clients is the ability to open, write-to, and close a mailslot in a single atomic operation. As with named pipes, a server process can perform a nondestructive read-ahead, if desired. Fig. 8-12 shows an example of connecting to a mailslot.

Client   **Server**

                                   Create Mailslot on Server
```
                              fh = MakeMailslot(fh, TIME_OUT);
```

Send Message, No Open/Close Necessary
```
DosWriteMailslot("\\server\mailslot\foo",message);
```
                                   Close and Delete
```
                              DeleteMailslot(fh);
```

Fig. 8-12. Mailslot example

Table 8-7 summarizes mailslot services.

TABLE 8-7. Mailslot services

Service name	Client side	Server side
LmxMakeMailslot	no	yes
LmxDeleteMailslot	no	yes
LmxMailslotInfo	no	yes
LmxReadMailslot	no	yes
LmxPeekMailslot	no	yes
LmxWriteMailslot	yes	no

Addressing Named Pipes and Mailslots. On OS/2, named pipes and mailslots live in pseudo-directories \PIPE and \MAILSLOT respectively and so they are addressed locally as \PIPE\NAME or \MAILSLOT\NAME. Remote pipes and mailslots are addressed by prepending the remote node name to these roots as \\SERVER\PIPE\NAME or \\SERVER\MAILSLOT\NAME. The only exception to this rule is that in the case of mailslots the NODE name may be specified as * in which case the message is broadcast to all machines advertising the mailslot name \MAILSLOT\NAME.

Under Lan Manager/X, the name specified during named pipe creation is not the name of a UNIX file but a string that is cached in the server and matched with incoming client connection requests. For convenience, this interface is case insensitive, and the server maps all alphabetic characters to uppercase. Also, the server maps forward slashes to back slashes in named pipe and mailslot names. The names used by server programs may omit the leading /pipe or /mailslot since it is clear from the context which is intended; however, if these prefixes are included, they are treated benignly by the server. For example, the named pipe:

    /mailsvr

would be advertised on the network as:

    \\SERVER\PIPE\MAILSVR

Support of Named Pipes by the Extended Protocol. All named pipe and mailslots are accessed over special tree connections to the shared resource IPC$. No explicit tree connect is necessary to this resource, however. When the first IPC request is made to a given server, the redirector makes the tree connect implicitly. The advantage of this approach is that a server can indicate to clients that it is supporting IPC by advertising the IPC$ resource in its share table.

Once the connection to IPC$ has been established, the client uses TRAN-SACTION SMBs to perform IPC operations. These transactions are defined in the protocol specification and may be regarded as a form of remote procedure call (RPC).

All system administration and user control functions, described in the next section, are performed as RPCs over a special named pipe, which is present on all servers, called \pipe\lanman.

System Administration and Information Services

In addition to services provided for application programs, the Lan Manager/X server offers the full range of Lan Manager system administration and user control functions. All these functions are implemented as Application Program Interfaces (APIs), which call into the server to get and set various data fields.

The services are divided into two classes: those that can be used by any users and those that require administrative privileges. These APIs are provided for clients via the use of the \pipe\lanman named pipe.

To gain administrative access to the server, it is necessary to have administrative privilege. Locally on UNIX this privilege reserved for the super-user. Remotely the administrative privilege is granted to users who can gain access to the shared resource ADMIN$. In user-level security mode, the ADMIN$ resource is automatically offered, but the user's privileges are determined during session setup. In resource-level security mode, it is necessary to know the password for the ADMIN$ resource and to perform an explicit tree connect to gain administrative privilege. (Although this tree connect always takes place, it is typically hidden from the user within the administrative applications used.)

ADMIN$ is actually a normal disk resource that is always associated with the root directory of the server system. This is useful because it allows remote clients to access directly Lan Manager configuration files that reside in certain fixed places in the server directory hierarchy. Administrative functions use a combination of named pipe IPC to \pipe\lanman and normal file I/O over ADMIN$ to perform their tasks.

User Interface to Administrative Functions. Although at the lowest level the administrative functions are accessed via the APIs shown in the following table, the normal access method used to get at these functions is one of the standard commands provided with the Lan Manager/X product. Two interfaces are provided: a simple line-based interface and an easy-to-use menu-based program. These interfaces are available both locally and remotely.

Administrative APIs where user and administative use are specified are listed in Table 8-8.

TABLE 8-8. Administrative APIs

API	Function	API	Function
0	RNetShareEnum	48	NetGroupDel
1	RNetShareGetInfo	49	NetGroupAddUser
2	NetshareSetInfo	50	NetGroupDelUser
3	NetShareAdd	51	NetGroupGetUsers
4	NetShareDel	52	NetShareEnum
5	NetShareCheck	53	RNetUserAdd
6	NetSessionEnum	54	NetUserDel
7	NetSessionGetInfo	55	NetUserGetInfo
8	NetSessionDel	56	RNetUserSetInfo
9	NetConnectionEnum	57	RNetUserPasswordSet
10	NetFileEnum	58	NetUserGetGroups
11	NetFileGetInfo	59	NetWkstaLogon
12	NetFileClose	60	NetWkstaLogoff
13	RNetServerGetInfo	61	NetWkstaSetUID
14	NetServerSetInfo	62	NetWkstaGetInfo
15	NetServerDiskEnum	63	NetWkstaSetInfo
16	NetServerAdminCommand	64	NetUseEnum

API	Function	API	Function
17	NetAuditOpen	65	NetUseAdd
18	NetAuditClear	66	NetUseDel
19	NetErrorLogOpen	67	NetUseGetInfo
20	NetErrorLogClear	68	DosPrintQEnum
21	NetCharDevEnum	69	DosPrintqGetInfo
22	NetCharDevGetInfo	70	DosPrintQSetInfo
23	NetCharDevControl	71	DosPrintQAdd
24	NetCharDevQEnum	72	DosPrintQDel
25	NetCharDevQGetInfo	73	DosPrintQPause
26	NetCharDevQSetInfo	74	DosPrintQContinue
27	NetCharDevQPurge	75	DosPrintJobEnum
28	NetMessageNameEnum	76	DosPrintJobGetInfo
29	NetMessageGetInfo	77	RDosPrintJobSetInfo
30	NetMessageNameAdd	78	DosPrintJobAdd
31	NetMessageNameDel	79	DosPrintJobSchedule
32	NetMessageNameFwd	80	RDosPrintJobDel
33	NetMessageNameUnFwd	81	RDosPrintJobPause
34	NetMessageBufferSend	82	RDosPrintJobContinue
35	NetMessagefileSend	83	DosPrintDestEnum
36	NetMessageLogFileSet	84	DosPrintDestGetInfo
37	NetMessageLogFileGet	85	DosPrintDestControl
38	NetServiceEnum	86	NetProfileSave
39	RNetServiceInstall	87	NetProfileLoad
40	RNetServiceControl	88	NetStatisticsGet
41	RNetAccessEnum	89	NetStatisticsClear
42	RNetAccessGetInfo	90	NetRemoteTOD
43	RNetAccessSetInfo	91	NetBiosEnum
44	NetAccessAdd	92	NetBiosGetInfo
45	NetAccessDel	93	NetServerEnum
46	NetGroupEnum	94	LNetServerEnum
47	NetGroupAdd		

For example, the command:

```
net share disk2=/usr/disk2
```

is actually an invocation of the net program that makes a `NetShareAdd` call to the server with the appropriate parameters.

The menu-based interface gives a more friendly interface to these functions and is the normal method of access to server control functions. The line-based interface is most often used in command scripts.

User Control Functions. The Administrative APIs that correspond to user control functions are shown above. These APIs can be used by any client applications that wish to interrogate the server on the user's behalf. The functions available allow the user to examine the server to determine its configuration and the resources it offers. They also allow the user to control activities that have been initiated on the client's behalf (e.g., printer jobs); they allow account information such as passwords to be changed; and they support the retrieval of useful information such as system messages and statistics.

Administrative Functions. The administrative interface is a superset of the user control interface. It gives the administrator full access to all the configuration data about the server and allows the server's parameters to be changed. Administrative functions include the following major sets of functionality:

- Configuration of resources offered.

- Control of user accounts and permissions.

- Real-time control of attached users and sessions.

- Setting of system messages and alerts.

- Control of printer and device queues.

- Interrogation of audit trail and error log data.

Other Services

In addition to the services already described, Lan Manager/X provides a number of miscellaneous services to the users and administrators of the system. These include the following functions:

- *Messaging.* This service uses the special messaging SMBs and allows applications to send messages to users who are attached to the system. If the client is running standard Lan Manager software, these messages will appear in a popup window on the user's workstation. For example, the administrator could use this facility to warn users of an impending system shutdown.

- *Alerts.* The alerter service is a function local to a given server. It is used by local applications such as the print spooler to send status information to the main server. The server uses this information to maintain a consistent view of the services it can offer and to generate messages such as "out of paper" to clients who are interested (using the messaging service).

- *Service Announcement.* One of the most useful functions provided to the user by Lan Manager is its ability to review the servers and services available on the network. This function is provided using mailslots. Each client who is interested in receiving information about available services creates a mailslot with a standard name (e.g., \mailslot\announce). All servers periodically broadcast information about the services, resources, etc., they are offering on this mailslot name. Any clients who are listening can receive this information and use it to build a table of information for the local user.

- *Audit Trails.* This service is available to administrators and allows them to log selectively all transactions that take place. In particular this function is used to log all file accesses and administrative and control functions invoked by attached clients.

- *Error Logging.* Errors that occur on the server are logged in a file and can be interrogated by the administrator of the system.

- *Statistics Gathering.* Servers can record I/O statistics and information relating to the dynamic aspects of their behavior. This information is very useful when tuning a server's parameters for best performance.

- *Profiling and Debugging.* When problems occur and during testing of a new server implementation, it is useful to be able to see the details of server operation at a low level. Facilities are available on the server machine to log detailed behavior and to provide debug information.

◆ Lan Manager/X Internal Architecture ◆

In the previous section, we discussed the functionality of the Lan Manager/X server in some detail. This section discusses the internal architecture of the Lan Manager/X server implementation on UNIX System V, Release 3.

Basic Structure of the Server

The structure of the UNIX server is shown in Fig. 8-13. It consists of a number of cooperating UNIX processes that communicate with each other via virtual circuits and shared memory. Basically, the server consists of one *daemon process* that controls the operation of the other processes in the system, a print spooler control process, and a dynamic collection of worker processes, one per attached client. Worker processes are responsible for directly performing all the file I/O and IPC requests associated with a given client. All the server processes that use virtual circuits either to communicate with other local processes, or to exchange SMB packets with clients, are built on top of the Lan Manager/X network interface.

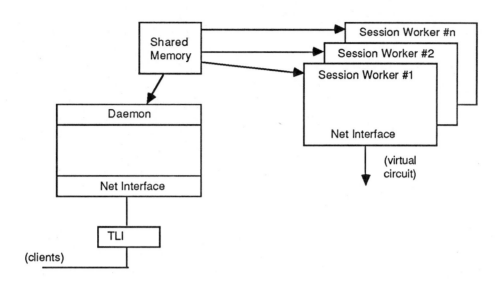

Fig. 8-13. Overall Lan Manager/X process structure

The server could be organized in many ways. However, the worker process per client process model was chosen for a two major reasons: It avoids complexity and minimizes kernel interaction. This leads to increased performance and reduced code complexity. Since Lan Manager multiplexes all traffic between a given client and server across a single VC, there needs to be a focal point for multiplexing and demultiplexing SMB requests. Also, if different functions are associated with different server processes, (e.g., file I/O is performed by one class of process and all IPC activities by another), then this necessitates an added level of synchronization complexity and interprocess communication to handle it. On UNIX, IPC and semaphore services require kernel intervention. Also, process scheduling overhead is generally expensive.

The Daemon Process

The daemon process is the first process to run when Lan Manager/X is started. It is responsible for loading and maintaining the server configuration data and remains active until the server is shut down. Shutting down the server is accomplished by sending a signal to the daemon—all other server processes are its descendants.

The daemon process establishes a shared memory pool that is used to communicate with all other active processes and especially workers. This shared memory pool resides at a fixed virtual address in all processes attached to it; this is important because it allows memory pointers into this region to be valid in all server tasks.

The daemon is primarily responsible for initiating and terminating client connections. The idle daemon blocks awaiting connection requests on a well-known network address associated with the server network name. When a new client requests a connection, the daemon accepts the connection and spawns a worker process to handle all subsequent requests on the VC linking the client and the server. Global data of interest to multiple clients and the daemon is maintained in shared memory. Care has been taken to design these data structures in such a way that a minimum of semaphore synchronization is needed to protect them.

Worker Processes

The worker processes are the heart of Lan Manager/X. They are responsible for implementing all functionality expected by remote clients. Whenever a new connection is established, a worker process is created to handle it.

Worker Timeouts. Normally, the worker process remains active until the client terminates the connection. However, in order that the system not be clogged with inactive workers, they may be timed out and their connections terminated involuntarily. When this happens, it is the responsibliity of the client to reestablish silently the connection if it becomes active again. Luckily, this feature is supported by Lan Manager redirectors and so there is no need to maintain state on the server for timed-out connections. The only exception to this is for Core clients. The older, MS-NET redirector does not support timeouts; for these clients, the worker must remain active indefinitely. For servers that support a large number of Core connections, this can be a problem.

Internal Structure of a Worker. The worker loops polling its virtual circuit for work, reading SMBs from the network, processing them and returning the results to the client. Unfortunately, because some transactions may block indefinitely on the server, it is not sufficient to use a single-threaded process model for the worker. Instead, each worker uses a nonpreemptive coroutine package to support a single thread of execution for each active SMB request. When a thread blocks on an activity, it posts an asynchronous I/O request and relinquishes control to the coroutine package, which continues to poll for completed I/O activities and reschedules threads in round-robin fashion as they become unblocked. Each thread has a separate stack and maintains data concerning its active request in a private buffer allocated for that purpose from a global pool. One of the major advantages of the coroutine implementation is that it dispenses with the need for expensive, kernel-mediated semaphore synchronization and does not incur any extra-process-scheduling overhead in the UNIX kernel.

Implementation of Lan Manager Security Features. In user-level security mode, each client is associated with a single UNIX uid and gid on the server. When operating in user mode, it is sufficient to set the uid and gid once when the worker is started, and the kernel will subsequently mediate file protection correctly for the worker on behalf of the client.

In resource-level security mode, a given client can be associated with a number of different user and group ids depending upon which tree connection is being used for the transaction. In this case, the worker must set its effective uid and gid on a per SMB basis. This functionality depends upon the underlying UNIX kernel supporting the set effective uid and gid system calls. On UNIX systems that do not support these calls, the server can operate only in user-level security mode. (These calls are a feature of Berkeley rather than System V UNIX, so pure System V systems cannot support resource-level security. We have implemented these extra calls in the System V kernel we have used for development.)

The UNIX Open File Limit. One of the other limitations of the worker per client model is the fact that the number of open files per process is limited in UNIX to a fixed number (normally 60). The effect of this limitation is that no client can have more that this number of files open at any one time. In practice, this is not a serious restriction, however, since 60 files is usually more than enough.

IPC Support. Lan Manager IPC support (i.e., named pipes and mailslots) is a critical functional element of Lan Manager/X; however, its support is more complicated that normal file I/O because it normally involves a second, user-supplied server process on the UNIX system. Remember the current version of Lan Manager/X supports only the server side of the Lan Manager IPC model. When a server creates an IPC object, it uses a special set of library routines for the purpose. These routines create a data structure that is shared memory containing information about the IPC object, including its name. There is one shared memory data structure for each instance of a given IPC object. These data structures logically belong to a worker process. For each IPC object, the IPC server process also creates a transport endpoint with a name derived from the object name and blocks accepting connections (Fig. 8-14).

When a worker receives a request for a connection to a given IPC object, they scan the shared memory area describing existing objects and then establish a local VC with the appropriate IPC server process. Since the acceptance of a connection by the IPC server implies the creation of a new VC, the IPC server is free to continue to accept more connections on the same object name later. Once the connection establishment has been completed, there are two VCs: one between the worker and the client and one between the worker and the IPC server. IPC transactions and data flow along these two VCs between the IPC server and the client process.

System Administration

System Administration is a special case of named pipe IPC. All administration and control functions are associated with the named pipe \PIPE\LANMAN. As a result, all worker processes automatically accept connections on this IPC object name, and no server process, with its associated second VC, is involved.

Administration functions are handled directly by the worker with appropriate communication, through shared memory, with the daemon process and other worker processes.

Local administration requests are also handled through this mechanism. They are the only case where a client-side IPC connection can be established locally on the server. A worker process is provided for this purpose, and its job is to accept local connections from administration commands and to perform the requested administration and control functions in the normal way.

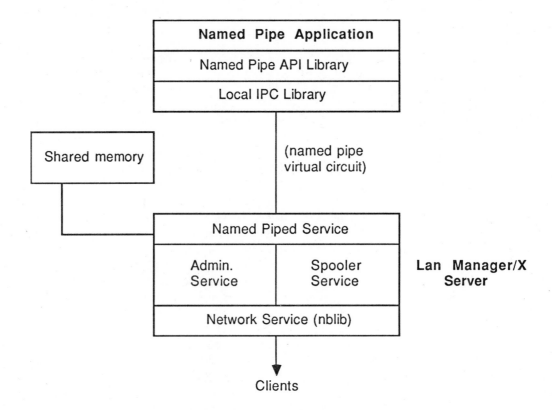

Fig. 8-14. Structure of an IPC connection

Spooler and Device Daemons

Special processes are associated with printer and device sharing. These processes are executed asynchronously by worker processes on behalf of clients.

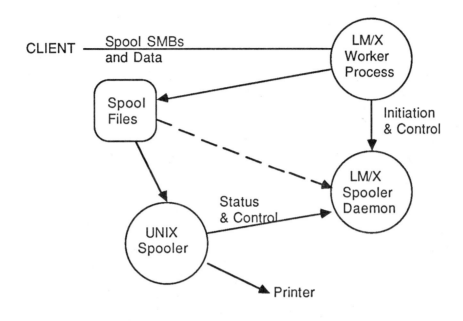

Fig. 8-15. Diagram of spooler structure

Printer and device-sharing daemons are responsible for routing requests to the appropriate UNIX programs and devices specified in the corresponding share table entries. In the case of printer requests, data is routed to the UNIX spooler subsystem. The spooler process maintains information about the status of current print jobs in shared memory so that it can respond to user control requests and so that clients can interrogate print job status correctly.

Messaging and the Announcement Protocol

The services of messaging, alerts, and the announcement protocol are provided by Lan Manager/X via a collection of small programs. These programs are either invoked directly or are executed by the server as necessary.

Portability Considerations

One of the primary goals of the Lan Manager/X development project was to create a server source code that was portable between a variety of different UNIX systems. To better achieve this end, the server is carefully constructed to isolate machine dependencies. In particular, care has been taken to compartmentalize the following functions within the code:

- *Network Services.* These are all provided through the Lan Manager/X Network Services interface already discussed. The server itself does not depend on other network-related functions.

- *Interprocess Communication.* The server is implemented using shared memory; however, the interfaces to the kernel services needed to create and manipulate shared memory have been compartmentalized for easier portability.

- *File Name Mapping.* Lan Manager/X implements the file name mapping functions between DOS and OS/2 conventions; however, the routines that perform these functions are carefully separated so that a different scheme could be implemented if desired.

- *User Account Information.* The Lan Manager/X server does not access the /etc/passwd file directly. It uses a special set of functions that return specific information and perform functions such as password validation. These functions could be easily reimplemented on a system that did not have the standard UNIX account database.

- *Byte Ordering.* Lan Manager/X adheres to the convention that all data transferred on the network uses Intel byte ordering. A set of routines is provided to convert data items with that ordering into the correct order for the host machine. These functions are used extensively within the server and can also be needed in network server applications.

- *National Language Support.* The current server assumes that all data contains eight significant bits and takes care not to mask or alter the high bit of character information such as file names in any way. For support of multibyte languages such as Japanese Kanji, hooks are available so that this support can be provided easily in the future.

♦ Performance Issues ♦

Performance is a critical factor in the success of any product. In the case of Lan Manager/X, some very concrete performance goals result from the fact that there are a large number of different SMB servers around with which Lan Manager/X can be compared. Getting comparative performance measurements is not simply a matter of collecting raw data, however; it is important to factor out performance elements that are not related to the performance of the server code itself. The most significant of these factors is transport overhead since the same server can run over a variety of network interfaces. Transport overhead can have a significant effect on server performance; typically, it accounts for a significant fraction of the total processing time for any transaction.

The primary Lan Manager/X performance goal was to be as good as or better than a comparable OS/2 Lan Manager server running over similar transport on a similar processor and with a similar memory configuration.

Several factors have contributed to meeting this goal. The process model discussed in the previous section was chosen largely on the fact that it kept kernel overhead to a minimum. Also performance critical sections of the server are carefully coded to encur the minimum of kernel overhead. When designing the server, raw file I/O performance was considered the most significant performance element, followed closely in importance by directory search and file attribute checking. Although industry benchmarks often measure more than this, three functions have the most impact on end-user perceptions and real performance.

◆ Future Directions ◆

The first release of Lan Manager/X is in the field; however, work is continuing. There are three major goals for future releases of the product: to continue to improve performance, especially in areas where the first release did not meet expectations; to add support for Lan Manager functionality missing from the first release; and, finally, to track extensions and changes to the Lan Manager product itself.

The major functionality missing from the first release is support for client-side IPC functions. Although it would be possible to implement client IPC above the kernel, it was felt that it is really a redirector function that should be accessible through the UNIX file system API. Since Lan Manager expects all network traffic, both server and client, to be multiplexed over a single virtual circuit, the major challenge associated with the implementation of an Lan Manager/X redirector is the need to support this multiplexing at the kernel level. SMBs destined for client programs on UNIX must be handled by the file system while SMBs destined for the UNIX server processes must be sent there. The plan is to make available a redirector that supports both client-side IPC and other Lan Manager services. This redirector would be provided as an installable file system (Fig. 8-16).

The major advantage of offering client-side services would be to enable remote administration functions by allowing UNIX users to act as clients to other servers on the network. The realization of remote administration support would allow a UNIX server to be the central administration point for a large network.

Lan Manager itself is not static; new extensions and modifications are being developed all the time. One of the major challenges for future development work is to maintain compatibility with earlier versions of Lan Manager and PC-NET while continuing to add this new function. Functions that are likely to be added soon are: generalized RPC, directory services, and new protocol extensions for higher-file I/O performance.

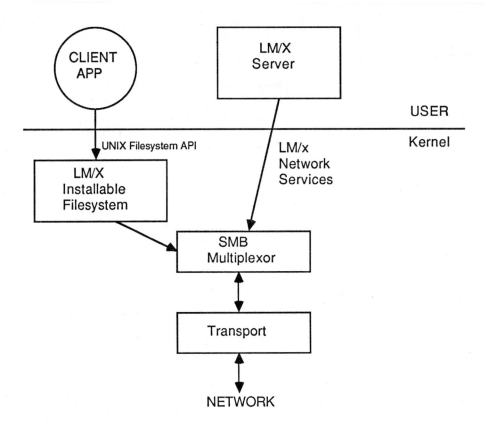

Fig. 8-16. Diagram of the client-side architecture

◆ Conclusion ◆

Lan Manager/X is a UNIX server that provides connectivity with PCs running OS/2 and DOS. As such, it is more closely related to the PC world than many other servers that have been implemented on UNIX. For example, both NFS and RFS had UNIX-to-UNIX connectivity as their primary goal. By allowing PCs to attach themselves to a UNIX system without any modifications being necessary to their systems software Lan Manager/X offers great potential for UNIX as a file and application server at the departmental level.

UNIX offers many services that are not available on the traditional PC server (e.g., support for electronic mail and gateways to other systems through UNIX based networking subsystems such as NFS). As a result, it will be possible to build services using the combination of Lan Manager/X, Lan Manager, and these other UNIX-based facilities that would otherwise have been impossible.

♦ Bibliography ♦

Microsoft Lan Manager Documentation, Microsoft Corporation, 1988.

> Documents the OS/2 and DOS Lan Manager family of products. The documentation consists of the following parts: a *User's Guide*, describing to end-users how to operate the Lan Manager Client Software; an *Administrator's Guide*, describing how to set up and administrate Lan Manager Servers and Clients; a *User's Reference Manual*; an *Administrator's Reference Manual*; and, for ISVs, a *Lan Manager Programming Guide and Reference*. This documentation is available with the Lan Manager retail software.

Lan Manager/X Porting Guide, Microsoft Corporation, 1989.

> The *Porting Guide* is part of the OEM documentation for Lan Manager/X. It provides the OEM with a detailed description of the structure of the Lan Manager/X server code and highlights the work necessary to bring up Lan Manager/X on a new UNIX platform. This document is available though the OEM marketing department at Microsoft Corporation.

Server Message Block, protocol specifications (Core, Extended, XENIX), Microsoft Corporation, 1986-88.

> These are detailed specifications for the file sharing protocols used by Lan Manager and XENIX-NET. They are available on request from the OEM marketing department at Microsoft Corporation.

PC Network, IBM Technical Reference, Part #6322916, 1982.

> This is a specification of the programming interface and data packet format to the IBM NETBIOS transport provided with IBM's PC Network Cards.

"An Introductory 4.3BSD Interprocess Communication Tutorial," *UNIX Programmer's Supplementary Documents*, Vol. 1, Computer Science Research Group, Computer Science Division, Dept. of EE and CS, University of California, Berkeley, CA 94720, 1986.

> This is a basic tutorial on the use of the sockets IPC mechanism. This document and others related to 4.3BSD are available from the USENIX Association, P.O. Box 2299, Berkeley, CA 94710.

"An Advanced 4.3BSD Interprocess Communication Tutorial," *UNIX Programmer's Supplementary Documents*, Vol. 1, Computer Science Research Group, Computer Science Division, Dept. of EE and CS, University of California, Berkeley, CA 94720, 1986.

> This is a more advanced tutorial on the use of sockets in network related programs.

4.3BSD UNIX Programmer's Reference Manual (URM), Computer Science Research Group, Computer Science Division, Dept. of EE and CS, University of California, Berkeley, CA 94720, 1986.

This volume contains detailed manual pages for each of the socket functions.

RFC 1001, *Protocol Standards for NETBIOS Service on UDP/TCP Transport: Concepts and Methods.*

This is a draft standard specification of the mapping of the NETBIOS functionality on top of the TCP/IP transport protocol.

RFC 1002, *Protocol Standards for NETBIOS Service on UDP/TCP Transport: Detailed Specifications.*

This is a draft standard specification of the mapping of the NETBIOS functionality on top of the TCP/IP transport protocol.

UNIX System V/386, Release 3.2, *Programmer's Reference Manual*, Section 3N, Prentice Hall, Englewood Cliffs, NJ, 1987.

Detailed manual pages for the STREAMS-related and TLI interfaces to the UNIX 5.3 kernel.

UNIX System V/386, Release 3.2, *STREAMS Primer*, Prentice Hall, Englewood Cliffs, NJ, 1987.

A overview of STREAMS concepts.

UNIX System V/386, Release 3.2, *Streams Programmers Guide*, Prentice Hall, Englewood Cliffs, NJ, 1987.

A detailed guide to writing STREAMS-based drivers and programs.

UNIX System V/386, Release 3.2, *Network Programmer's Guide*, Prentice Hall, Englewood Cliffs, NJ, 1987.

A detailed guide to writing programs to the Transport Level Interface (TLI).

Mapping the NETBIOS Interface to ISO Transport Services, document number TNB87-011. *NETBIOS Name Service Protocol Specification*, document number unknown.

These are analogous to the RFC specifications for the ISO transport world. Both these are published by the MAP/TOP organization.

9

Networking and the X Window System

Adrian Nye
O'Reilly & Associates, Inc.

◆ Introduction ◆

The X Window System (or simply X) provides a hierarchy of resizable windows and supports high-performance, device-independent graphics (see Fig. 9-1). Unlike most other window systems for UNIX that have a built-in user interface, X is a substrate on which almost any style of user interface can be built. But what is most unusual about X is that it is based on an asynchronous network protocol rather than procedure or system calls. This protocol basis has a number of advantages:

- Both local and network connections can be operated in the same way using the protocol, making the network transparent from the user's point of view and from the application programmer's point of view.

- The X protocol can be implemented using a wide variety of languages and operating systems.

- The X protocol can be used over any reliable byte stream, several of which are standard and available on most architectures.

- For most applications, using a protocol has little performance penalty because speed is limited by the speed of actually drawing the graphics than by the protocol over today's local area networks such as Ethernet.

It makes sense that networks and window systems should be used together. The window system allows the building of a user interface for applications. If it makes no distinction between local and network connections, the applications automatically provide a user interface to the network. The window system lets users get the benefit of access to remote computing resources using only the commands they use for running programs locally.

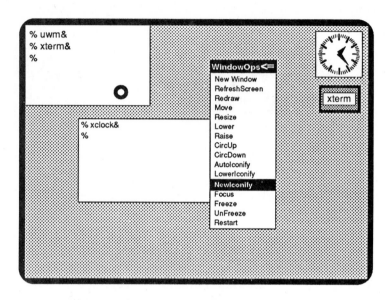

Fig. 9-1. A typical X Window System display

The protocol basis and concomitant portability of the X Window System is especially important today when it is very common to have several makes of machines in a single network. Until X, there was no common window system, and the common graphics languages that did exist did little to hide the differences between operating systems and graphics hardware. On the other hand, code that implements X is freely available and has shown itself to be extremely portable. Implementations exist for machines ranging from Atari personal computers to Cray supercomputers. The system is so hardware and operating system independent that properly written application software will compile and run on any system.

◆ History and Background ◆

The X Window System was designed and developed at the Massachusetts Institute of Technology (MIT). The primary reason for developing the system was that MIT was to be given many DEC and IBM workstations and needed a window system to make the displays more useful. Within MIT, X underwent several revisions to accommodate different types of hardware. X Version 10 satisfied the initial needs of MIT and was adopted by several vendors as a basis for commercial products. Though the system held promise, it had a few deficiencies. Since a number of universities and system manufacturers were taking a serious interest in X, a new version was designed to satisfy a wider community. X Version 11 was designed to be flexible enough to remain a standard for many years.

All the versions of the X protocol were designed by Robert Scheifler, who also wrote the software for the server used through Version 10. The C language library for X was designed and implemented by Jim Gettys and Ron Newman. X is still being maintained and improved at MIT, now under the auspices of the X Consortium, a group whose membership includes most major hardware manufacturers and several independent software vendors. A higher-level C language toolkit for building user interfaces has also been designed at MIT and DEC and has been accepted as a standard by the X Consortium.

X as a Standard

Though first released only a little more than a year ago, X Version 11 has already become a de facto standard supported by virtually every UNIX system manufacturer and is also available on several non-UNIX systems. There are several reasons why it has become a standard so quickly. Most important, it was well crafted to appeal to the widest possible segment of computer manufacturers. Its provision for extensions that will perform at the same level as its core capabilities lets manufacturers support any unique capabilities of their systems. The fact that the X Window System is designed not to specify a certain style of user interface avoided the problem of manufacturers being unwilling to accept a different user interface from the one used in their existing proprietary products. Also probably important was the fact that the system was developed at MIT instead of by a single company. Since MIT is not a computer hardware manufacturer, the intercorporate politics that might have taken place to fight one manufacturer's attempt at establishing a standard did not occur. Finally, it helped that MIT decided to provide the software virtually free to hardware vendors and the public, and many educational institutions and companies contributed code without restrictions.

The Benefits of X

The X Window System is widely recognized as good for the workstation industry. It benefits independent software vendors most directly, but it will also eventually benefit system manufacturers and users.

For independent software vendors, a common graphics language portable to many systems greatly lessens the effort required to offer a software product on a new machine. Reducing this porting load means more and better software should become available for all machines running the X Window System. It also becomes more cost effective to develop or port and maintain X applications that would not be possible otherwise because the market is the sum of all the workstations made by all companies.

For the user, the X Window System promises to make more applications available on more machines. It should change the current situation where most applications are available on only one machine. There is, however, one remaining problem for users, stemming from the fact that X does not mandate a particular user interface policy. If user interface standards are not widely adopted by manufacturers and independent software vendors, users will see a single workstation running three applications written using three different user interface conventions. They will all work fine together on the workstation, but the user is likely to get completely confused. This problem is widely recognized, and organizations such as the Open Software Foundation and the AT&T System V supporters coalition (recently named UNIX International) may provide the appropriate standards.

X is good for UNIX system manufacturers in general because more UNIX systems will be sold now that there is a common window system. This will be more true when one or two standard user interfaces for UNIX are established. X allows small system manufacturers to supply a window system that they could never afford to develop and places them on a more even footing with the big companies. Companies can still distinguish themselves from other manufacturers by optimizing the performance of their system and supplying extensions that provide unique features.

With that background, we'll begin describing the networking aspects of X.

◆ The Server and Client ◆

The use of the terms server and client in X are different from their use in other computing contexts and elsewhere in this book. To X, the *server* is the software that manages one display, keyboard, and mouse. One user is controlling the keyboard and mouse and looking at the display controlled by a server. The *client* is a program displaying on the screen and taking input from that keyboard and mouse. A client sends drawing requests and information requests to the server, and the server sends user input, replies to information requests, and error reports to the client. The client may be running on the same machine as the server or on a different machine over the network.

You are probably familiar with the concept of a *file server*, which is a remote machine with a disk drive from which several machines can read and write files. But in X, the server is the local system, whose resources the (perhaps remote) client programs are accessing. Fig. 9-2 shows a server and client and their relationship to the network.

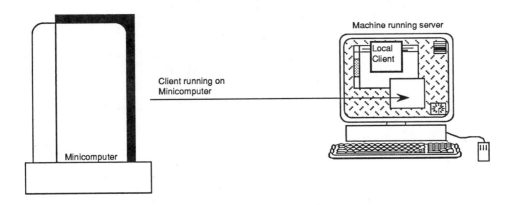

Fig. 9-2. The server and client

The X Window System is not limited to a single client interacting with a single server. Several clients may interact with a single server, which is the case when several applications are displaying on a single screen. Also, a single client can communicate with several servers, which would happen when an announcement program is displaying the same thing on several people's screens.

A client may be running on the same machine as the server if that machine supports multitasking, or the client may run on a different machine connected over the network. On multitasking UNIX workstations, it is normal to have some clients running locally and others operating over the network. Naturally, other users will probably have clients running on their own system and perhaps on yours as well, but most will be displayed on their own screens. With servers running on single-task systems such as IBM or compatible PCs and AT class computers, all clients must run on other systems over the network. The same is true of specialized X terminals that have the server software built into ROM, and have an integral Ethernet network interface. Fig. 9-3 shows a network with a number of servers, in which clients can run on any node and display on any other node.

X clients are programmed using various client-programming libraries that are available for X. Currently, these libraries are available in C and Lisp. The C libraries are the most widely used. They include a low-level procedural interface to the X protocol called *Xlib* and a higher-level toolkit written in object-oriented style called the *Xt Intrinsics*. The *Intrinsics* are used to build user interface components called widgets. Several widget sets that implement certain user interface conventions are available. The one supplied by MIT is called the Athena widgets. Fig. 9-4 shows how the various programming interfaces for C are combined to write clients that use the X protocol to communicate with the server.

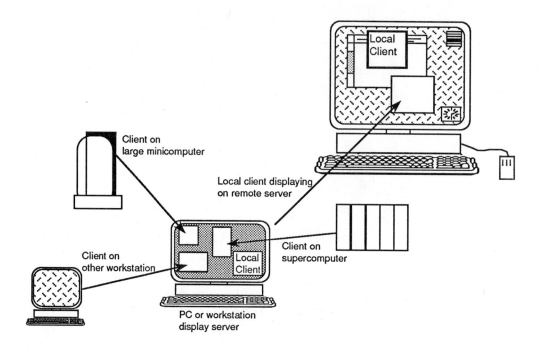

Fig. 9-3. A distributed X environment

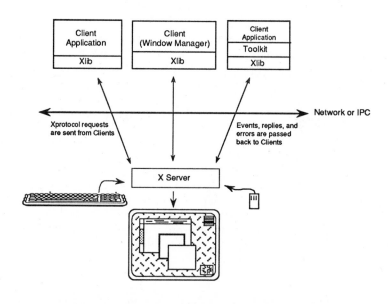

Fig. 9-4. The client programming libraries in C

These C language libraries were developed at MIT. Several other programming layers that use Xlib to interface to the protocol have been developed outside of MIT, some written in C and some in C++. As you can see from the figure, one is called Andrew and another InterViews.

◆ The X Protocol ◆

The X protocol is the true definition of the X Window System, and any code in any language that implements it is a true implementation of X.[†] It is designed to communicate all the information necessary to operate a window system over a single asynchronous bi-directional stream of 8-bit bytes.

Below the X protocol, any lower layer of network can be used, as long as it is bidirectional and delivers bytes in sequence and unduplicated between a server and a client process. When the client and server are on the same machine, the connection is typically based on local interprocess communication (IPC) channels; otherwise, a network connection is established between them.

The lowest level of network performance required is subjective, but in general it depends on how many clients will use the network and how busy each client will be in sending graphics requests over the network. Redrawing a normal 80 x 24 character terminal window using the X protocol would take exactly 2 seconds of network time at 9600 baud. This calculation takes into account that the X protocol requires some information in addition to the character codes that a hard-wired terminal requires. The actual calculation of the number of bytes of data required to refresh a single terminal window is

$$(L * (H + C + P))$$

where L is the number of lines in the terminal window; H is the number of bytes that describe which request this is, the length of the request, the window it is to be drawn in, the graphics context with which to interpret the request, and the position to place the text; C is the number of columns in the window; and P is padding to make sure the total request length including all header is a multiple of 4 bytes. The format of protocol requests is described in detail later.

If there are several terminals on the screen, which is the usual practice, refreshing the entire screen would probably take 10 seconds or more. To give you an idea of how efficient the X protocol is, a hard-wired terminal would take 80% as much time to refresh an entire screen of the same dimensions at the same serial speed.

The protocol is designed to be operated asynchronously because this allows much higher performance. Synchronous operating speed is limited by the time required to make a round trip, which on most currently available local area networks (LANs) is between 5 and 50 milliseconds. This speed is usually much less than the speed of the network in requests without replies. With client requests

---

[†]The X protocol is defined in a document entitled *X Window System Protocol, X Version 11* by Robert W. Scheifler. It is available as part of a book describing Xlib, the standard C language library for writing clients, through Digital Press, and in source form on the X distribution tape and from several sites on the ARPANET and from UUNET.

each containing 80 characters and a round-trip delay of 25 milliseconds, only 3200 characters per second can be drawn synchronously, while asynchronous drawing requests without replies could proceed much faster. The server also sends events asynchronously because this allows local polling for applications that must poll continuously for input. An example of such an application would be a game where the display is changing continuously, but user input is still sought. Otherwise, applications that must poll for input during continuous drawing would actually be forced to operate synchronously.

Numerous window systems under UNIX use file or channel descriptors to represent windows. This has several disadvantages compared to X's approach of multiplexing all the windows on a single network connection. There is often a limit to the number of such descriptors, and they can't be shared by clients on different machines and sometimes even on the same machine. Finally, the time order of communications through each descriptor is difficult to guarantee. The multiplexing of requests affecting different windows on the same stream allows the client to control the time order of updates, and similarly the multiplexing of events on one stream also guarantees that the correct order is preserved.

Normally, clients implement the X protocol using a programming library that interfaces to a single underlying network protocol, typically TCP/IP or DECnet. The sample implementation provided by MIT of the C language client programming library called Xlib uses *sockets* on systems based on Berkeley UNIX. Note: The *interfaces* defined in MIT's implementation of Xlib are standard, but the code is not. In other words, hardware vendors are allowed to change and optimize the library code for their systems as long as it matches the specification of Xlib provided with the MIT distribution of X software. MIT does not provide a routine for handling networking on systems based on AT&T's System V Release 3 UNIX. AT&T, in their proprietary implementation of Xlib, uses the System V native STREAMS, where a protocol module supporting any underlying network protocol can be "pushed" onto a stream, allowing Xlib to use any underlying protocol for which a module exists.

Servers often understand more than one underlying protocol so that they can communicate with clients on more than one type of network at once. For example, the DEC windows server accepts connections from clients using TCP/IP or from clients using DECnet. Currently, these are the only two network protocols commonly supported in X servers.

Division of Responsibilities

In the process of designing the X protocol, one of the ongoing decisions was the division of capability between the server and client, since this determines what information has to be passed back and forth. This decision was based on portability of client programs, ease of client programming, and performance.[‡]

First, hardware dependency is taken care of by the server, as much as possible. The server manages windows, does all drawing, and interfaces to the device drivers to get keyboard and pointer input. The server also manages off-screen

---

‡An excellent source of information about the rationale behind certain choices made in designing the protocol is The X Window System, by Robert W. Scheifler and Jim Gettys, *Association of Computing Machinery Journal Transactions on Graphics*, Vol. 5, No. 2, April 1987.

memory, windows, fonts, cursors, and color maps. The sample server code written at MIT contains a device-independent part and a device-dependent part. The device-dependent part must be customized for each hardware, and it is here that the characteristics of the hardware are translated into the abstractions used by X such as "colormap."

Having the server responsible for managing hierarchy and overlapping windows has few if any disadvantages. It would seem quite possible for the client to waste network time by requesting graphics to a window that is not visible, since the client knows nothing of the window position or stacking order. Such a request would have no effect since X does not preserve the contents of obscured windows. However, this situation is dealt with through an Expose event that announces when an area of window has become exposed. Clients draw only in response to the Expose event that signals that the window is visible. In X, it is the client's responsibility to send the appropriate requests needed to redraw the contents of the rectangle of a window specified in the Expose event. For the rare clients where this responsibility leads to a severe performance penalty, X servers may (but are not required to) have a backing store feature that lets the server maintain window contents regardless of visibility.

There are certain hardware variations that are impossible or unwise to hide in the server. The X server could attempt to insulate the client from screen variations such as screen size, color vs. monochrome, and number of colors, but each of these would come at some cost. Hiding the screen size would make it easier to program applications that require graphics of a consistent size independent of the screen resolution, but it would make it harder to identify and manipulate single pixels, and it would add a burden to the server code. Hiding whether the screen is color or monochrome and the number of planes would lessen the load on the client program for simple color use, but it would be harder to manipulate the color map in powerful ways or use tricks in color such as overlays. A decision was made to make client programming more complicated in order to make it more powerful. This is an area where the design of X differs from NeWS. NeWS does attempt to hide some of these factors, as we shall see in chapter 10.

The server takes steps to make the keyboard handling as uniform as possible on different machines, but it cannot completely hide variations in what symbols are actually embossed on the caps of the keys. For example, not all keyboards have Control and Meta keys. X handles this by providing several ways of handling the keyboard at different levels of abstraction. Each physical key has a code assigned by the server's device-dependent layer, which is reported in each key event. The server implementation also provides a table of key combinations and a resulting symbol, which is the meaning of that key combination. For example, if the A key was pressed while the Shift key was being held down, the key symbol in the table would represent "A". This table is managed by the server so that it applies to all clients, but the client library often maintains a copy of it so that the client can interpret events locally. The server does not use the table to interpret events before sending them to the client, which allows the client to interpret the keys in different languages or to use other event handling techniques if desired (a client might want to treat the keyboard as a musical instrument rather than use it for text, for example). X supplies a request (ChangeKeyboardMapping) for changing the key symbol table, which results in a MappingNotify event to be sent to all clients. Clients other than the one that called ChangeKeyboardMapping respond to this event by sending a (Get-KeyboardMapping) request, which gets the updated table.

Some decisions were made purely to simplify (or enhance) client programming. For example, coordinates in drawing requests are interpreted relative to the window being drawn into rather than the screen. This provides a virtual drawing surface or "window" and makes client programming easier because the client does not need to track the window position continually and calculate where to draw based on this position. This gives the server the burden of determining where actually to draw graphics on the screen based on window positions, while taking this burden off client programs. This in turn allows the server to support the window hierarchy without necessarily having to report all changes back to the client.

In other cases, decisions were made to increase performance. An example of this is the graphics context. The X *graphics context* (GC) allows the server to cache information about how graphics requests are to be interpreted, so this information need not be sent over the network from the client with every graphics request. This reduction in network traffic results in improved performance, particularly when the network is slow. Also, servers can be designed to cache GCs so that switching between them is fast and efficient. Finally, it is a happy coincidence that the GC usually makes client programming easier because it reduces the number of parameters needed in drawing calls.

The GC is one of several abstractions X maintains in the server; the most important others are the Window, Pixmap (an off-screen virtual drawing surface that must be copied into a window to become visible), Colormap, and Font. X calls these *resources*. The client refers to each resource in protocol requests using a unique integer ID assigned by the server. This ID is a 29-bit integer (high bits are unused to simplify implementation on architectures that employ garbage collection). IDs are chosen by the client, who uses a specific subrange specified by the server at connection time that guarantees that the IDs will be unique from all other IDs that can be created by other clients using the same server. The fact that IDs are not assigned by the server means that creating a resource does not require a reply by the server. This is very important in reducing the startup time of applications because creating each resource would otherwise waste at least one round-trip time.

The Window abstraction lets the server manage which parts of the screen are displaying which parts of which window and lets the server take care of applying the window attributes (e.g., the border and background) to each window. The X protocol includes requests that get information about resources so that the client is not completely in the dark. However, not every detail of each resource is necessarily accessible from the client side since some information of limited usefulness was left out of query replies to allow more flexibility in server code design. One example of this is that some of the window attributes cannot be queried (e.g., bit gravity, which is for redrawing optimization). Another is that the values in GCs can't be queried at all. Neither the window attributes that can't be queried nor the GC values are changed by any client other that the one that created them and set their parameters. Therefore, it does not add much burden to clients to require them to keep track of their own settings if they need the information later. Furthermore, programming the server to be able to provide this information places contraints on the server that could affect performance.

Packet Types

The X protocol specifies four types of packets that get transferred over the network. Requests are sent from the client to the server, and replies, events, and errors are sent from the server to the client.

- A *request* is generated by the client and sent to the server. A protocol request can carry a wide variety of information such as a specification for drawing a line, changing the color value in a color map cell, or inquiring about the current size of a window. A protocol request can be any multiple of 4 bytes in length.

- A *reply* is sent from the server to the client in response to certain requests. Not all requests are answered by replies—only the ones that ask for information. Requests that specify drawing, for example, don't generate replies, but requests that inquire about the current size of a window do. Protocol replies can be any multiple of 4 bytes in length, with a minimum of 32 bytes.

- An *event* is sent from the server to the client and contains information about a device action or about a side-effect of a previous request. The data contained in events is quite varied because it is the principal method by which clients get information. All events are stored in a 32 byte structure to simplify the queuing and handling of them.

- An *error* is like an event, but it is handled differently by clients. Errors are sent to an error-handling routine by the client-side programming library. Error packets are the same size as events, to simplify the handling of them.

A protocol request that requires a reply is called a *round-trip request*. Round-trip requests have to be minimized in client programs because they lower performance when there are network delays. This will be discussed in more detail in the section on client library implementation.

Notice that all the X protocol packet types are designed to have a length in multiples of 4 bytes. This simplifies implementation of the protocol on architectures that require alignment of values on 16- or 32-bit boundaries. As we will see, 16- and 32-bit values within the packets are always placed on 16- and 32-bit boundaries, respectively.

We will define the contents of each of these in more detail later.

♦ A Sample Session ♦

This section describes what happens over the network during a minimal application that creates a window, allocates a color, waits for events, draws into the window, and quits. This example uses three of the four types of X network messages as they would occur in an application. The fourth is the error, which we hope will not occur during the normal operation of an application. How errors are generated and handled and what the network message for an error looks like will be explained after successful operation is described.

Here are the network events that will take place during a successful client session, first shown in graphic terms in Fig. 9-5 and then described in text.

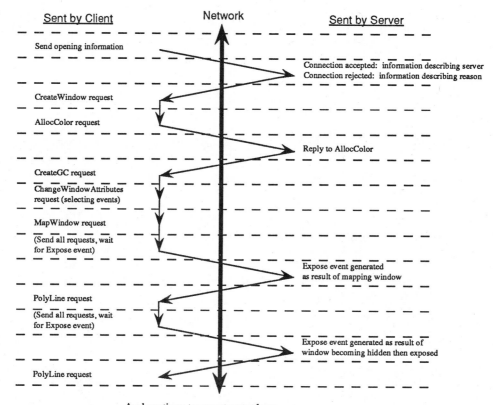

And continue to repeat event loop...

Fig. 9-5. A sample X Window System client session

- Client opens connection to the server and sends information describing itself.

- Server sends back to client data describing the server or refusing the connection request.

- Client makes a request to create a window. Note that this request has no reply.

- Client makes a request to allocate a color.

- Server sends back a reply describing the allocated color.

- Client makes a request to create a graphics context, for using in later drawing requests.

- Client makes a request identifying the types of events it requires (in this case, Expose, and ButtonPress events.)

- Client makes a request to map (display on the screen) the created window.

- Client waits for an Expose event before continuing. This sends the accumulated requests to the server.

- Server sends to client an Expose event indicating that the window has been displayed.

- Client makes a request to draw a graphic, using graphics context.

- Loop back to waiting for an Expose event.

In this session description, client requests are queued up by the client library before being sent to the server, and the client reading events trigger the sending. This is not actually a required characteristic of client libraries, but it improves performance greatly because it takes advantage of the asynchronous design of the protocol. Xlib works this way. This behavior allows the client to continue running without having to stop to wait for network access, until it would have to wait anyway for an event.

Note that many of the actions taken by the client in the session must be done in the order shown for the application to work properly. For example, Expose events must be selected before the window is mapped; otherwise, no event would arrive to notify the client when to draw. This becomes even more important when a window manager is managing the screen. Many window managers let the user decide on the size and position of a window before allowing it to be mapped, introducing a sizeable delay between when the client requests mapping the window and when the window actually appears on the screen ready to be drawn into. Only the Expose event tells the client when it is time to draw.

Colors are allocated very early in the session before creating the graphics context to optimize the use of protocol requests. To allocate a color, the client tells the server what color is desired, and the server responds by giving the client a *pixel value*, which is a number that identifies the closest color available (the exact color may not be physically possible on the screen, or all color map entries may already be in use by other clients). When creating the graphics context, this pixel value can be used to set the foreground color to be used for drawing. It is also possible to create a default graphics context before allocating the color, but then setting the foreground value in the existing graphics context would require an additional, unnecessary request.[†]

Opening the Connection

The client allows the user to identify the server it wants to connect to by specifying a host and display number. The display number is 0 on personal workstations because there is only one keyboard, pointer, and display connected to a single host. Multiuser workstations and time-sharing systems that support graphics terminals are rare today, but X leaves open the possibility that a single host could support two (or more) servers by having two (or more) sets of display, keyboard, and mouse.

The client-side library should provide an easy-to-use method for the user to specify which server to connect to. In the case of Xlib, the user specifies the server using the host name and server number separated by a colon, (e.g.,ghost:0). The networking utilities under Berkeley UNIX translate host names into network addresses using the file /etc/hosts or on some systems the yellow pages daemon.

For TCP connections, displays on a given host are numbered starting from 0, and the server for display N listens and accepts connections on port 6000+N. For DECnet connections, displays on a given host are numbered starting from 0, and the server for display N listens and accepts connections on the object name obtained by concatenating X$X with the decimal representation for N (e.g., X$X0 and X$X1).

Once the proper address is known, the client begins sending bytes that describe itself. Then the server sends back information describing itself if the connection is acceptable or describing what went wrong if the connection is refused.

Table 9-1 specifies the data that the client sends. Throughout this chapter, when the type for a certain piece of data is not defined by the protocol, it is not critical and is not shown.

The first byte of data identifies the byte order employed on the client's machine. The value 102 (ASCII uppercase B) means values are transmitted most significant byte first, and the value 154 (ASCII lowercase l) means values are transmitted least significant byte first. All 16- and 32-bit quantities, except those involving image data, are transferred in both directions using this byte order specified by the client. Image data is an exception and is described later.

---

†For more information about of the order of operations for most effective client programming, see *Xlib Programming Manual* by Adrian Nye, available from O'Reilly and Associates, Inc., 90 Sherman St., Cambridge, MA 02140.

TABLE 9-1. Byte stream sent by client to open connection

# Bytes	Type	Values	Description
1		102 (MSB first) 154 (LSB first)	byte-order
1			unused
2	unsigned integer		protocol-major-version
2	unsigned integer		protocol-minor-version
2		n	length of author-ization-protocol-name
2		d	length of author-ization-protocol-data
2			unused
n	list of unsigned integers		authorization-protocol-name
p			unused, p=pad(n)
d	list of unsigned integers		authorization-protocol-data
q			unused, q=pad(d)

Next, the client tells the server the version of the protocol it expects the server to implement. The major version is currently 11, and the minor version is 0 (this is true for Release 1, 2, and 3 of X Version 11). The version numbers are an escape hatch in case future revisions of the protocol are necessary. In general, the major version would increment for incompatible changes, and the minor version would increment for small upward compatible changes. The server returns the protocol version numbers it actually supports, which might not equal the version sent by the client. The server can (but need not) refuse connections from clients that offer a different version than the server supports. A server can (but need not) support more than one version simultaneously.

The authorization name indicates what authorization protocol the client expects the server to use, and the data is specific to that protocol. Specification of valid authorization mechanisms is not part of the core X protocol, as discussed later. In the mean time, most servers ignore this information.

The padding bytes are required because each network packet generated by X is always a multiple of 4 bytes long, and all 16- and 32-bit quantities are placed in the packet such that they are on 16- or 32-bit boundaries. This is done to make implementation of the protocol easier on architectures that require data to be aligned on 16- or 32-bit boundaries. Consequently, lengths of data in the X protocol are always specified in units of 4 bytes.

The server sends back the information shown in Table 9-2 if connection is refused.

TABLE 9-2. Byte stream returned by server on failed connection

# Bytes	Type	Values	Description
1		0	failed
1		n	length of reason in bytes
2	unsigned integer		protocol-major-version
2	unsigned integer		protocol-minor-version
2		(n+p)/4	length in 4-byte units of "additional data"
n	list of unsigned integers		reason
p			unused, p=pad(n)

The value of the first element is 1 if the connection succeeded or 0 if it failed.

Table 9-3 shows the stream of data returned when the connection is successful. The Xlib client programming library stores this information in the `Display` structure, and the pointer to this structure is passed as an argument to most Xlib routines. The routines then access this information internally when necessary. Xlib also provides macros for accessing a few of the more frequently used items, so that client programs don't depend on the particular implementation of the structure that contains this information.

To understand the returned connection information, you need to know that an X server can support multiple screens. An X server shows information to a single user, but perhaps through more than one physical or logical screen. An example of a use for two physical screens would be to be able to debug an application on a color and on a monochrome screen at the same time. The Sun sample server on color systems currently provides two logical screens on a single physical screen: one with the screen acting as monochrome, which is much faster, and the other with the screen acting in color. The user switches between the screens by moving the pointer off either side of the screen. No geometry of the screens is defined by the protocol, and how the mouse moves between the various screens depends on the server implementation.

The connection information describes each of the attached screens separately. Since there can be any number of attached screens, there is a section of the connection information that is repeated for each screen. Moreover, each screen can sometimes be used in a variety of ways. For example, a color screen can also be used to display windows in black and white. X calls the attributes describing a particular way of using the screen a *visual*. For each screen, there is information describing the one or more ways that screen can be used.

The concept of a visual has a number of advantages. If you know a certain window is going to be used in black and white only even on a color screen (e.g., a terminal emulator), it is much more efficient to treat it that way because it requires handling only 1 bit per pixel instead of up to 24. Some hardware can take advantage of this to improve performance dramatically.

TABLE 9-3. **Byte stream returned by server on successful connection**

# Bytes	Type	Values	Description
1		1	success
1			unused
2	unsigned integer		protocol-major-version
2	unsigned integer		protocol-minor-version
2		8+2n+(v+p+m)/4	length in 4-byte units of "additional data"
4	unsigned integer		release-number
4	unsigned integer		resource-ID-base
4	unsigned integer		resource-ID-mask
4	unsigned integer		motion-buffer-size
2		v	length of vendor
2	unsigned integer		maximum-request-length
1	unsigned integer		number of SCREENs in roots
1		n	number for FORMATs in pixmap-formats
1		0 (LSBFirst), 1 (MSBFirst)	image-byte-order
1		0 (LeastSignificant), 1 (MostSignificant)	bitmap-format-bit-order
1	unsigned integer		bitmap-format-scanline-unit
1	unsigned integer		bitmap-format-scanline-pad
1	KEYCODE (unsigned integer)		min-keycode
1	KEYCODE (unsigned integer)		max-keycode
4			unused
v	list of unsigned integers		vendor
p			unused, p=pad(v)
8n	LISTofFORMAT		pixmap-formats
m	LISTofSCREEN		roots (m is always a multiple of 4)

# of Bytes	Type	Values	Description
FORMAT			
1	unsigned integer		depth
1	unsigned integer		bits-per-pixel
1	unsigned integer		scanline-pad
5			unused
SCREEN			
4	WINDOW		root
4	COLORMAP		default-color map
4	unsigned integer		white-pixel
4	unsigned integer		black-pixel
4	SETofEVENT		current-input-masks
2	unsigned integer		width-in-pixels
2	unsigned integer		height-in-pixels
2	unsigned integer		width-in-millimeters
2	unsigned integer		height-in-millimeters
2	unsigned integer		min-installed-maps
2	unsigned integer		max-installed-maps
4	VISUALID		root-visual
1		0 (Never), 1 (WhenMapped), 2 (Always).	backing-stores
1	BOOL		save-unders
1	unsigned integer		root-depth
1	unsigned integer		number of DEPTHs in allowed-depths
n	LISTofDEPTH		
DEPTH			
1	unsigned integer		depth
1			unused
2		n	number of VISUALTYPES in visuals
4			unused
24n	LISTofVISUALTYPE		
VISUALTYPE			
4	VISUALID		visual-ID
1		0 (StaticGray), 1 (GrayScale), 2 (StaticColor), 3 (PseudoColor), 4 (TrueColor), 5 (DirectColor)	class
1	unsigned integer		bits-per-rgb-value
2	unsigned integer		colormap-entries
4	unsigned integer		red-mask
4	unsigned integer		green-mask
4	unsigned integer		blue-mask
4			unused

All this information describes the server in painstaking detail. It's impossible to describe all of it in detail here, but we'll touch on some of the more interesting parts.

The resource-ID-mask and resource-ID-base elements provide the information necessary for the client to generate IDs that are unique within the client but also unique from IDs generated in other clients. An ID must be unique with respect to the IDs of all other resources created by all clients, not just other resources of the same type and by the same client, because the server manages them all. The resource-ID-mask is a 32-bit value with at least 18 bits set. The client allocates a resource ID by choosing a value with some subset of these bits set and ORing it with resource-ID-base. To allocate the next ID, the client normally increments its value that is a subset of resource-ID-mask. This local allocation of IDs is important because it eliminates the need for round-trip requests when creating resources, which speeds the startup time of clients.

Maximum-request-length specifies the maximum length of a request, in 4-byte units, accepted by the server. This limit might depend on the amount of available memory in the server. That is, this is the maximum value that can appear in the length field of a request. Requests larger than this generate a `BadLength` error, and the server will read and simply discard the entire request. Maximum-request-length will always be at least 4096 (e.g., requests of length up to and including 16,384 bytes will be accepted by all servers).

The connection information repeats the block of information that described a screen the number of times necessary to describe all the screens connected to the server (it is assumed that all these screens act as a single display for a single user). One of the more interesting abstractions X introduces is called the visual. The visual is a server-created resource that describes a way of using color in a particular window. As we'll see in the `CreateWindow` request, a window is created with a particular visual, and this is a permanent aspect of the created window. Since there may be several different ways of using color on a certain screen, the block of data that describes a visual may be repeated several times for each screen. Each screen description includes the width-in-pixels, height-in-pixels, width-in-millimeters, and height-in-millimeters of the root window (which cannot be changed). This information can be used to tailor client operation according to the screen size and aspect ratio.

Each screen also has a default color map which contains at least two entries permanently allocated entries called `BlackPixel` and `WhitePixel`. These entries can be used in implementing a monochrome application on monochrome or color screens. The actual RGB values of `BlackPixel` and `WhitePixel` may be settable on some screens and, in any case, may not actually be black and white. The names are intended to convey the expected relative intensity of the colors.

Creating a Window

Once the connection to the server is successfully opened, the first thing most applications do is create one or more windows.

The `CreateWindow` request is more complicated than most X protocol requests, but all requests have the same structure: a block of data consisting of an opcode, some number of fixed length parameters, and sometimes a variable-length parameter. Every request begins with an 8-bit major opcode, followed by a 16-bit length field expressed in units of 4 bytes. The length field defines the total length of the request, including the opcode and length field, and must equal the minimum length required to contain the request, or an error is generated. Unused bytes in a request are not required to be 0. Major opcodes 128 through 255 are reserved for extensions. Extensions are intended to contain multiple requests; all requests within a particular extension would use the same major opcode. Therefore, extension requests typically have an additional minor opcode encoded in the data byte immediately following the length field.

We'll describe the fixed- and variable-length components of `CreateWindow` after you have seen the data sent in this request. Table 9-4 shows the byte stream sent by client to the server to create a window. (Don't be put off by its complexity; most requests are much simpler than this one.)

TABLE 9-4. The `CreateWindow` request

# of Bytes	Type	Values	Description
1	1		opcode of request
1	unsigned integer		depth
2	8+n		request length
4	WINDOW		client selected ID for window
4	WINDOW		parent's ID
2	signed integer		x (position)
2	signed integer		y
2	unsigned integer		width (size, inside border)
2	unsigned integer		height
2	unsigned integer		border-width
2		0 (CopyFromParent), 1 (InputOutput), 2 (InputOnly)	class
4	VISUALID	(ID), 0 (CopyFromParent)	visual
4	BITMASK		
		#x00000001	background-pixmap
		#x00000002	background-pixel
		#x00000004	border-pixmap
		#x00000008	border-pixel
		#x00000010	bit-gravity
		#x00000020	win-gravity
		#x00000040	backing-store
		#x00000080	backing-planes
		#x00000100	backing-pixel
		#x00000200	override-redirect

# of Bytes	Type	Values	Description
	#x00000400	save-under	
	#x00000800	event-mask	
	#x00001000	do-not-propagate-mask	
	#x00002000	color map	
	#x00004000	cursor	
4n	LISTofVALUE		value-list
VALUES			
4	PIXMAP	(pixmap), 0 (None), 1 (ParentRelative)	background-pixmap
4	unsigned integer		background-pixel
4	PIXMAP	(pixmap), 0 (CopyFromParent)	border-pixmap
4	unsigned integer		border-pixel
1	BITGRAVITY		bit-gravity
1	WINGRAVITY		win-gravity
1		0 (NotUseful), 1 (WhenMapped), 2 (Always)	backing-store
4	unsigned integer		backing-planes
4	unsigned integer		backing-pixel
1	BOOL		override-redirect
1	BOOL		save-under
4	SETofEVENT		event-mask
4	SETofDEVICEEVENT	do-not-propagate-mask	
4	COLORMAP	(color map), 0 (CopyFromParent)	color map
4	CURSOR	(cursor), 0 (None)	cursor

The most interesting aspect of CreateWindow is that it varies in length according to how much information needs to be transferred. The fixed-length components of CreateWindow include the ID of the parent window; the ID the client has chosen for this window; the window size, position, and border width; the window class (InputOutput or InputOnly); and the window's visual (ID of a server-created resource that describes how color should be used in the window). The final component of the fixed-length portion of CreateWindow is a bit mask, that describes which of the optional components are present. Optional components are always bits of information for which the server has a reasonable default for the ones not specified. The bit mask tells the server which items are going to be present in the remainder of the request.

The optional components in CreateWindow are the window attributes. The window attributes control the background and border colors or patterns, whether contents of windows are saved when the window is resized and where the old contents are placed (bit gravity), whether and how subwindows should be automatically moved when the parent is resized (window gravity), whether windows contents should be preserved by the server (backing store), whether the server should save under a temporary window to speed redrawing when this window is unmapped (save under), the events that should be delivered to the client when they occur in this window (event mask), events that should not propogate to higher windows in the hierarchy (do-not-propogate-mask), whether the window should be immune to window manager intervention (override-redirect), which color map should be used to translate pixel values into colors for this window (color map), and what cursor should be used in this window (cursor).

There is also a request that sets the window attributes separately from creating a window (ChangeWindowAttributes), even though it is slightly more efficient to set the desired attributes when creating the window.

The only attribute that every client sets is the event mask.

The server is capable of sending many types of events to the client, each of which contains information about a different user action or side effect of a request. The client is not always interested in every type of event, and it is wasteful of the network to send them over simply to be thrown away. Therefore, each window has an attribute that controls which events are sent over when they occur in that window.

The event mask can be set in CreateWindow or as part of a somewhat simpler request called ChangeWindowAttributes. However, if the correct event mask is known when the window is created, it is more efficient to set the event mask at that window creation time rather than with a separate request. Note that the time delay between window creation and setting of the event mask when done in separate requests is not a problem because events can't occur in this window yet because it isn't yet displayed. Windows do not appear on the screen until they are mapped, which is our next topic.

For this sample session we will select Expose and ButtonPress events. The Expose events are necessary to tell us when our window appears on the screen so we can draw on it, and the ButtonPress event will allow us to escape from the closed event-handling loop.

A Request with Reply

Some requests require an immediate reply from the server because the client cannot continue without the information. Most of these get information about server resources such as windows, fonts, and properties. Another set reports success or failure of a request whose effects must take place before the client can safely continue. Some requests require replies for both these reasons. A particular request either has a reply or it doesn't; there are no requests that sometimes have replies and other times do not.

As an example, we demonstrate here a request that allocates a color. To describe color handling in X completely would take more space than we have here, and it is unnecessary for a conceptual understanding of the protocol. But you can understand the request and the reply if you understand just a little about color. As a minimum, you should know that the X server is capable of maintaining multiple virtual color maps, and it can install one or more of them depending on the hardware. Each of these color maps has an ID and can be read-only or read/write. Read-only color maps contain cells with preset color values, and these cells can be shared because no client can change them, but often clients won't find the exact color they need in the color map. Read/write color maps can have color cells that are private to a single application and others that are shared among applications. X specifies colors in red, green, and blue values that are each 16-bit numbers.

The `AllocColor` request (Table 9-5) allocates a read-only color from a color map. Therefore, it works on any kind of color map. However, the exact color the client asks for might not be available, so the server has to supply the closest color that exists in the map. At one extreme, if the color map happened to be monochrome, the closest color allocated will always be either black or white. The reply to `AllocColor` tells the client the ID of the color cell (X calls this a pixel value) of the closest color available and the red, green, and blue values of the color stored in that cell. The client needs an immediate reply because it must know the ID of the color cell, and it must decide whether the red, green, and blue values of the cell are close enough to the color allocated to be adequate.

TABLE 9-5. The `AllocColor` request

# of Bytes	Type	Values	Description
1		84	opcode
1			unused
2		4	request length
4	COLORMAP		color map ID
2	unsigned integer		red
2	unsigned integer		green
2	unsigned integer		blue
2			unused

The `AllocColor` request specifies which color map the client wants to use and the red, green, and blue values for the desired color. The server replies with the ID of the read-only cell in the color map that comes closest to the color desired and the actual red, green, and blue values in that cell (Table 9-6).

The reply opcode is always 1; this number in errors is 0 and in core events ranges from 2 to 34. The sequence number is a count kept by the server of the last request processed before sending this information. Everything that the server sends to the client (replies, events, and errors) contains a sequence number field.

Notice that replies, like requests, contain a length field even when they are a fixed length. This makes it easier to write client library code to process the requests and replies correctly because there is no need to look up the length in a table based on the opcode. This is a tradeoff that simplifies the client library code in exchange for transferring a few unnecessary bytes over the network.

As in requests, the field length is expressed in units of 4 bytes. Unused bytes within a reply are not guaranteed to be 0.

The unused field right after the blue field is present to align the pixel field, which is a 32-bit value, with a 32-bit boundary for easier handling on architectures that require either 16- or 32-bit alignment.

TABLE 9-6. Server reply to AllocColor

# of Bytes	Type	Values	Description
1		1	reply opcode
1			unused
2	unsigned integer		sequence number
4		0	reply length
2	unsigned integer		red
2	unsigned integer		green
2	unsigned integer		blue
2			unused
4	unsigned integer		pixel
12			unused

Table 9-7 lists all X requests that generate replies. From this table you should get an idea of the types of request that require replies. Each of these requests is briefly described later.

TABLE 9-7. Requests that have replies

QueryKeymap	QueryFont	QueryTextExtents
QueryColors	QueryBestSize	QueryExtension
QueryPointer	QueryTree	GetKeyboardMapping
GetKeyboardControl	GetPointerControl	GetScreenSaver
GetImage	GetPointerMapping	GetModifierMapping
GetWindowAttributes	GetGeometry	GetAtomName
GetProperty	GetSelectionOwner	GetMotionEvents
ListFonts	ListInstalledColormaps	
ListExtensions	ListHosts	ListProperties
LookupColor	AllocColor	TranslateCoordinates
SetPointerMapping	SetModifierMapping	InternAtom
GrabPointer	GrabKeyboard	

Creating a Graphics Context

A graphics context (GC) is a resource that controls the server's interpretation of graphics requests. The GC controls line width, how lines connect, how they end, what colors are used, what planes of the display are affected, how the existing contents of the screen are factored into the calculation, and how areas are filled or patterned.

GCs should be created early and set once (if possible) to speed up the loop that responds to user events. That's why we create the GC here instead of just before the request that draws.

The `CreateGC` request is very similar to the `CreateWindow` request, in that one member of the request is a bitmask, which defines the length and composition of the remainder of the request. Only the members of the GC that are being set to values other than the default take up space in the request (Table 9-8).

Since `CreateGC` shows nothing new, we won't show you the detailed contents of the request here.

TABLE 9-8. The CreateGC request

# of Bytes	Type	Values	Description
1	55		opcode
1			unused
2	4+n		request length
4	GCONTEXT		cid
4	DRAWABLE		drawable
4	BITMASK		value-mask (has n 1-bits)
		#x00000001 function	
		#x00000002 plane-mask	
		#x00000004 foreground	
		#x00000008 background	
		#x00000010 line-width	
		#x00000020 line-style	
		#x00000040 cap-style	
		#x00000080 join-style	
		#x00000100 fill-style	
		#x00000200 fill-rule	
		#x00000400 tile	
		#x00000800 stipple	
		#x00001000 tile-stipple-x-origin	
		#x00002000 tile-stipple-y-origin	
		#x00004000 font	
		#x00008000 subwindow-mode	
		#x00010000 graphics-exposures	
		#x00020000 clip-x-origin	
		#x00040000 clip-y-origin	
		#x00080000 clip-mask	
		#x00100000 dash-offset	
		#x00200000 dashes	
		#x00400000 arc-mode	
4n	LISTofVALUE		value-list

# of Bytes	Type	Values	Description
VALUEs			
1			function
	0	Clear	
	1	And	
	2	AndReverse	
	3	Copy	
	4	AndInverted	
	5	Noop	
	6	Xor	
	7	Or	
	8	Nor	
	9	Equiv	
	10	Invert	
	11	OrReverse	
	12	CopyInverted	
	13	OrInverted	
	14	Nand	
	15	Set	
4	unsigned integer		plane-mask
4	unsigned integer		foreground
4	unsigned integer		background
2	unsigned integer		line-width
1			line-style
	0	Solid	
	1	OnOffDash	
	2	DoubleDash	
1			cap-style
	0	NotLast	
	1	Butt	
	2	Round	
	3	Projecting	
1			join-style
	0	Miter	
	1	Round	
	2	Bevel	
1			fill-style
	0	Solid	
	1	Tiled	
	2	Stippled	
	3	OpaqueStippled	
1			fill-rule
	0	EvenOdd	
	1	Winding	
4	PIXMAP		tile
4	PIXMAP		stipple
2	signed integer		tile-stipple-x-origin
2	signed integer		tile-stipple-y-origin
4	FONT		font

# of Bytes	Type	Values	Description
1			subwindow-mode
	0	ClipByChildren	
	1	IncludeInferiors	
1	BOOL		graphics-exposures
2	signed integer		clip-x-origin
2	signed integer		clip-y-origin
4	PIXMAP		clip-mask
	0	None	
2	unsigned integer		dash-offset
1	unsigned integer		dashes
1			arc-mode
	0	Chord	
	1	PieSlice	

Mapping a Window

Mapping makes a window eligible for display on the screen. In the simplest case, when the application is alone on the screen, mapping does actually display the window. But more generally, whether the window appears depends on the following:

- The window must be mapped with `MapWindow` or related routines.

- All the window's ancestors must be mapped.

- The window must be positioned so that it is not obscured by visible sibling windows or their ancestors. If sibling windows are overlapping, whether or not a window is obscured depends on the stacking order. The stacking order can be manipulated with `ConfigureWindow`.

- The request buffer must be flushed. More information on this topic is provided later.

- The initial mapping of a top-level window is a special case since the window's visibility may be delayed by the window manager. For complicated reasons, a client must wait for the first `Expose` event before assuming that its window is visible and drawing into it.

Table 9-9 shows the request that maps a window, `MapWindow`. It's a refreshing sight after the connection information and `CreateWindow`. The `MapWindow` request simply sends the ID of the window that is to be marked for display, so that it will be visible when these listed conditions above are met.

TABLE 9-9. The MapWindow request

# of Bytes	Type	Values	Description
1		8	opcode of request
1			unused
2		2	request length
4	WINDOW		window

The Expose Event

From the client's point of view, the only true indication that a window is visible is when the server generates an Expose event for it. Only after receiving this Expose event can the client begin drawing into the window. The server generates one or more Expose events for a window when it meets all the criteria previously listed. There may be more than one Expose event because each one describes an exposed rectangle, and it may take several such rectangles to describe the areas of a window not covered by overlapping windows.

Table 9-10 shows what the server sends to the client to represent an Expose event. Note that all events are exactly 32 bytes long.

TABLE 9-10. The Expose event, as sent from server

# of Bytes	Type	Values	Description
1		12	code
1			unused
2	unsigned integer		sequence number
4	WINDOW		window
2	unsigned integer		x
2	unsigned integer		y
2	unsigned integer		width
2	unsigned integer		height
2	unsigned integer		count
14			unused

The code indicates which type of event this is. The sequence number is the number assigned by the server for the most recently processed request; it is used in tracking errors. The window field specifies which window was exposed, and the x, y, width, and height fields specify the area within that window that was exposed. Count specifies how many more Expose events follow that were generated as the result of the same protocol request.

Fig. 9-6 shows a window arrangement in which four Expose events would be generated to report that the four corners of window E have now become visible if window E were raised.

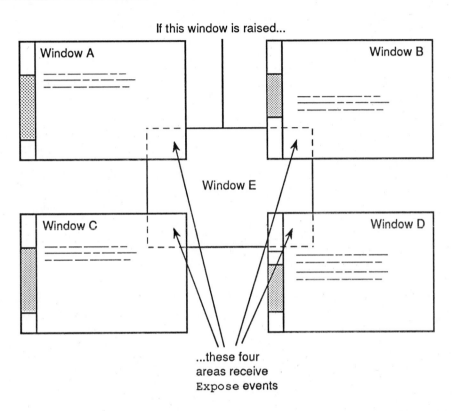

If this window is raised...

Window A

Window B

Window E

Window C

Window D

...these four
areas receive
Expose events

Fig. 9-6. Expose events generated when window E is raised

The X protocol specifies that all the Expose events resulting from a single protocol request must be contiguous.

In client programs, events are gathered and processed one at a time in a closed loop. Expose events will always be processed in these loops (unless the client has no windows). Clients may, but need not, provide any way to exit since a separate client (called xkill in the standard X distribution) is normally available to kill running programs.

Drawing a Graphic

The `Expose` event says to the client, in effect, "go ahead and draw now." This applies not only to the first time the window is displayed on the screen but also to any later time when the window becomes obscured and then exposed. It applies to redrawing as well as to first-time drawing.

Now let's draw some lines. The protocol request to draw connected lines is `PolyLine`, shown in Table 9-11.

TABLE 9-11. The `PolyLine` request

# of Bytes	Type	Values	Description
1		65	opcode
1			coordinate-mode
		0 (Origin)	
		1 (Previous)	
2		3+n	request length
4	DRAWABLE		drawable
4	GCONTEXT		GC
4n	LISTofPOINT (pair of signed integers)		points

The opcode indicates that this is a `PolyLine` request. The coordinate-mode specifies whether points are to be interpreted relative to the origin of the window or relative to the previous point in the list. Then comes the request length, which specifies how many points are in the list. Next are the ID of the drawable (window or pixmap) in which the lines are to be drawn and the ID of the graphics context to be used in interpreting the request. Finally, there is the list of points. A point is a pair of 16-bit signed integers, since 8 bits would not be enough to cover the number of pixels on the screen (usually around 1,000), and an unsigned value would not allow the x and y values to be outside the drawable, which is quite valid.

By now you should be seeing the pattern that all the requests and events that are likely to be issued during the loop that processes events are normally short, while the requests to setup things before this loop are long. Response to user actions is kept fast by spending the time necessary to setup before the event loop.

Closing the Connection

You may have noticed that there seems to be no way to exit this session. Some X clients are actually written this way. They can be killed only by a separate X client (called `xkill`) or by finding the process ID and killing the process from the UNIX shell. Other clients supply a button or command for exiting. Outside termination is acceptable because the client need not do anything to terminate the session properly. There is no request that the client sends to the server that means "I'm about to quit." It is the server's responsibility to be able to clean up after the client dies.

The client library closes the session simply by closing the network connection (with `close` on 4.2 BSD systems). The operating system also does this automatically when the client dies abnormally. The application program itself needs only to free any local structures that may have been created. The server then cleans up after the client by destroying the resources the client created.

The X protocol does, however, provide the `SetCloseDownMode` request to modify this behavior so that resources created by a client are not immediately destroyed when the client exits. This allows a new invocation of the client to attempt to recover from fatal errors such as a broken network connection that caused an earlier invocation to die before valuable information stored in the server could be saved to disk. A companion to this request is `KillClient`, which is used to kill the preserved resources when they are no longer needed.

Errors

We have described how requests, replies, and events operate during a successful client session. But what happens when a parameter does not meet the server's specifications for a given request, or the server cannot allocate enough memory to complete the request? An error packet is generated and sent to the client.

Usually errors indicate a client programming error, but they can also occur in such situations as when the server is unable to allocate enough memory. Therefore, all clients must prepare for receiving errors. The definition of "wrong" depends on the particular request. The server does range checking to make sure that the arguments sent with each request are valid, and it also makes sure that each request sent from the client is the length it says it is. The client library doesn't do range checking because it does not have access to all the information necessary to check ranges (like window depths) and because it makes more sense to have the server do it than to have multiple copies of this code in every client.

Although the error packet looks much like an event, the client handles it differently. Unlike events that are queued by the client library to be read later, errors are dispatched immediately upon arrival to a routine that processes the error. This routine may be a general routine that simply reports the error before exiting, or it may attempt to recover from the error by correcting the mistake in the request. However, recovery is normally difficult because of the delay between when a request is invoked by the application program and when the mistake is detected by the server and the the error packet is sent to the client. Often a number of other requests will have already been made in the intervening time, and the server will continue to act on these requests even after sending the error to the client. There is no way to "take back" the requests that have already been processed since the error. Anyway, the X protocol specifies that the client is not allowed to respond to an error by making requests to the server such as drawing to the screen because this might cause a cycle of errors. For these reasons, the normal response to an error is to print an error message and then exit the client process.

Another form of error occurs when any sort of system call error occurs, (e.g., the connection with a server dying due to a machine crash). These types of errors are detected on the client side, and the client library normally contains a routine for handling them. There is no alternative in this case but to report the error and exit the client process.

Let's continue our client session. This time we'll make an illegal request and see what happens.

- Client queues a illegal request for the server (just so we can see what happens).

- Client sends the illegal request to the server.

- Server processes the queued request and sends an error report back to the client. Client processes the error and recovers somehow if the error is not fatal or exits.

As an example, lets say the client sends a request to draw a line to the server but gets the window and GC arguments reversed. The server will return a `BadWindow` error report as shown in Table 9-12.

TABLE 9-12. The `Error` packet as sent from server

# of Bytes	Type	Values	Description
1		0	Error (always zero for errors)
1		3	code (BadWindow)
2	unsigned integer		sequence number
4	unsigned integer		bad resource ID
2	unsigned integer		minor opcode
1	unsigned integer		major opcode
21			unused

Error reports are sent from the server to the client in a package identical to that used for events. This is because errors are so rare that they do not justify separate handling even though this could save a small amount of network time (21 bytes are sent but not used by every error). They are basically treated just like events all the way to the routine in the client library that receives them. At this point, they are sent to the error-handling routine instead of being queued.

The first field is the one used to identify the various event types and is 0 for all errors. The code field identifies the type of error that occurred. Error codes 128 through 255 are reserved for extensions. The sequence number, as in events, gives the last request that was successfully processed just before the error. The sequence number can be used to determine exactly which protocol request caused the error, which, as we will see after discussing how the client library is actually implemented, becomes quite important. The bad-resource-ID field gives the value that was unacceptable for all the errors that are caused by invalid values and is unused by the other errors. The major and minor opcodes identify the type of request that caused the error. In the core protocol, the major opcode identifies which protocol request contained the error, and the minor opcode is unused. For extensions, typically the entire extension will use a particular major opcode, and the minor opcode will identify each request within that extension.

Unused bytes within an error are not guaranteed to be 0.

◆ Implementing the X Protocol ◆

MIT includes on its distribution tape of the X Window System implementations of the X protocol in a "sample server" for several different machines and in two client-side libraries, one for C and the other for Lisp.

Connection Setup

Byte Order. X servers are required to swap the bytes of data from machines with different native byte, in all cases except in image processing. The first byte in the packet that opens the connection between the client and the server, sent from the client library, tells the server which byte order is native on the host running the client.

Image data is always sent to the server and received from the server using the server's byte order because image data is likely to be voluminous and byte swapping is expensive. The client is told the server's byte order in the information returned after connecting to the server. The client may then be able to store and operate on the image in the correct format for the server, eliminating the need to swap bytes.

Word Alignment. Some architectures require 16-bit quantities to be aligned on 16-bit boundaries and 32-bit quantities to be aligned on 32-bit boundaries. To allow efficient implementation of the protocol across a variety of 16- and 32-bit architectures, the protocol is designed to consist of blocks that are always multiples of 32 bits, and each 16- and 32-bit quantity within a block is aligned on 16- and 32-bit boundaries.

Client Library Implementation

The client programming library that implements the protocol can do several things to improve performance. This section describes how Xlib, the lowest-level C language interface to X, handles the network to improve performance. These techniques have been developed based on a lot of trial, error, and experience, and the current version of Xlib is required by the X Consortium on all systems that support the X Window System and the C language. If you can gain access to the source code for Xlib, you can look at how it handles the network by inspecting the files XConnDis.c and XlibInt.c.

Xlib buffers requests instead of sending them to the server immediately, so that the client program can continue running instead of waiting to gain access to the network. This is possible for several reasons:

- Most requests are drawing requests that do not require immediate action.

- The network stream is reliable; therefore, no confirmation message from the server is necessary to indicate that the request was received.

This grouping of requests by the client before sending them over the network increases the performance of most networks because it makes the network transactions longer and less numerous, reducing the total overhead involved.

Xlib triggers the sending of the buffer full of requests to the server under four conditions. The most common is when an application calls a blocking Xlib routine to get an event, but no matching event is currently available on Xlib's queue. Because the application must wait for an appropriate event anyway, it makes sense to flush the request buffer. This says to the server, "I need some information; act on these requests and then give it to me right away".

Second, some of the client routines get information from the server, requiring an immediate reply. In this case, all the requests in the buffer are sent before waiting for the reply. This says to the server, "I'm waiting for a certain kind of event, so I'll check if you have already sent the event over to me. If not, please act on these requests immediately, and then I'll be waiting for an event from you".

The client would also like to flush the request buffer manually in situations where no user events are expected. Note that flushing the request buffer is not a protocol request because it is a local instruction to Xlib. This third situation says to the server, "I don't need any information from you now, but I need you to act on these requests immediately." Normally, this is not used because there are enough of the first two types of calls in the client to make the flushes frequent enough.

Xlib also flushes the request buffer when it fills up.

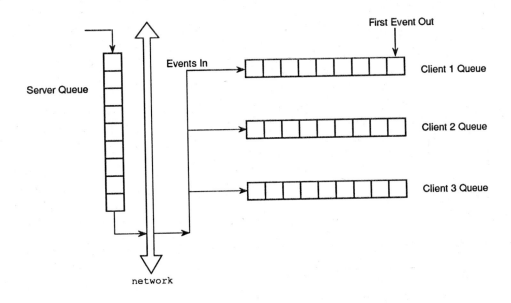

Fig. 9-7. The server's event queue and each client's event queue

Client-side buffering of requests has important implications for errors. A request that contains an error may be queued and sent later after several other client-side library calls are made and their requests queued behind it. Then these requests are sent together to the server when one of the conditions already described is met. The server then detects the error when it attempts to process the bad request, and the server sends an error report to the client. This error report is sent directly to one of the error-handling routines that reports the error to the user.

In other words, the error doesn't come to the user's attention until the request buffer is sent, the server processes the requests up to the one containing the error, the server sends the error report to the client, and the client error-handling routine processes it. This delay makes it more difficult to discover which request actually contained the error. The server goes on processing requests after sending the error, so the screen may reflect actions that take place after the error occurred. That's why error reports contain both the sequence number of the last request processed by the server and the opcode of the protocol request that caused the error.

The client library can also make programming easier by providing convenience functions that perform common tasks while hiding the complications in the actual protocol request to be issued. For example in Xlib, XSetForeground sets the foreground color for drawing in a graphics context. XSetForeground really issues the events that will be sent to the client, issues a ChangeGC request to the server, but allows the client to ignore all the other aspects of the GC.

Convenience routines may seem like an invitation for inefficient programming. What if the client sets three different GC values using three convenience routines? This could lead to three round-trip protocol requests when only one would suffice. The solution to this problem is for the library to take advantage of the fact that requests are queued by combining all these similar requests into a single one before sending them to the server. Xlib actually does this: It provides convenience routines for setting all elements of a GC and combines these calls into a single protocol request that is sent just before it is needed by the next drawing call that uses that GC.

Server Implementation

As described earlier, a true X server is any server that accepts X protocol requests and generates replies, errors, and events according to the specifications in the X protocol document. The servers supplied by MIT are known as "sample servers" because no claim is made that they do everything in the best possible way for all machines and cases. In fact, some of the sample servers suffer from poor performance in color because few optimizations were attempted. Building reliability has been the main goal in the first three releases of X version 11.

The essential tasks of the server are to demultiplex the requests coming in from each client and execute them on the display, and to multiplex keyboard and mouse input back onto the network to the clients. On single-threaded architectures, the server is typically implemented as a single sequential process, using round-robin scheduling among the clients. Although the server might be placed in the kernel of the operating system in an attempt to increase performance, this makes the server much more difficult to maintain and debug. Performance under UNIX does not seem to suffer by having the server run as a process. The number of operating system calls in both the server and client library are minimized to improve performance.

The server is typically made up of a device-independent layer and a device-dependent layer. The device-independent layer includes code that is valid for all machines. Even this portion has not been highly tuned even though it affects all servers based on it. It is primarily designed to be extremely portable between machines. Some improvements can be made by optimizing this code for each machine it is to run on, but the device-dependent layer is where most of the performance improvement can be had. Of course, this code will be different for almost every model by every manufacturer.

The server must be designed so that it never trusts clients to provide correct data. It also must be designed so that if it ever has to wait for a response from a client, it must be possible to continue servicing other clients. Without this property a bad client or a network failure could easily cause the entire display to hang.

The server normally has a buffering mechanism similar to Xlib's for sending data back to clients. When it is processing a request, it queues up all the events that the request generates (e.g., unmapping a window could generate a lot of little exposures) and then tries to send them all. This is the buffered part and is an optimization that clients never find out about.

Any events caused by executing a request from a given client must be sent to the client before any reply or error is sent.

If the client is a little slow at reading data from the network (usually because the application is doing something complicated, such as garbage collection in Common LISP), the server can get an error telling it that the network was unable to transmit all the data. In Release 2 and before, the server would assume that the client was hung and would drop the connection. In Release 3, it keeps track of what needs to be sent and waits for the client to be ready for more data (in BSD UNIX, this is taken care of by the "writable" mask argument to the `select` system call). This is the called *delayed writing*.

Reducing Network Traffic

X uses several techniques to reduce network traffic. One major technique is to have the server maintain resources such as windows, fonts, and graphics contexts and allocate an integer ID number for each one as a nickname to be used by clients. Whenever an operation is to be performed on a resource, the ID of the resource is specified in the request. This means that instead of an entire structure or string being sent over the network with a request, only a single integer is sent. Remember that since the client and the server may be on separate machines, pointers can't be used to refer to structures. Moreover, not all languages allow use of pointers.

The caveat of the resource approach is that the client must query the server when it needs information about resources, which, as mentioned above, leads to network delays. As it turns out, clients normally don't need to query the server very often, and the resource abstraction greatly simplifies programs.

◆ Implementation on Multithreaded Architectures ◆

There is nothing in the definition of the X protocol that prevents either the server or the client programming library to use multithreaded features of the hardware.

For the server, there are obvious opportunities for separating elements of its task among separate processors. As a primitive example; one could handle events, and another could do drawing. Or perhaps each processor could handle different clients. The task of drawing can also be divided up to increase performance, perhaps along the lines of how the GC separates patterning from selecting pixels and planes to be drawn (which we have not described here).

For clients, the opportunities depend more on the particular characteristics of each application. Depending on the tools that are available on a particular system, the compiler may automatically look for parallelisms to exploit, or the application programmer may be able to give the compiler hints.

◆ The Requests ◆

A description of the X protocol would not be complete without a description of the many requests that it includes and the assumptions they encapsulate. The following sections describe all the protocol requests, grouped according to their application.

Window Manipulation by the Client

The following requests are the basic requests to create, display, and destroy windows. Two of these you have already seen used in the sample session.

- **CreateWindow**—Creates a window.

- **DestroyWindow**—Destroys a window.

- **DestroySubwindows**—Destroys an entire hierarchy of windows.

- **MapWindow**—Marks a window as eligible for display.

- **UnmapWindow**—Removes a window and all its subwindows from the screen.

- **UnmapSubwindows**—Removes all subwindows of a window but not the window itself from the screen.

Window Manipulation by the Window Manager

Unlike many window systems, X does not build in the user interface that allows users to move window about on the screen. Instead, it provides the capability so that any client can perform these functions. Practically speaking, however, only one client must have the authority over the layout of windows on the screen and other limited resources of the server. Some of the window manipulation requests are meant to be used only by window manager clients to give them the authority to enforce their window management policy. In addition to the previously described requests, which are used by all applications, several requests are designed primarily to allow the window manager to execute its unique role in the X Window System.

- **ChangeSaveSet**—Allows the window manager to restore applications it has iconified when the window manager dies unexpectedly. The window manager adds each window it iconifies to the save set so that if the window manager dies without deiconifying any application, the server will automatically remap the applications window.

- **ReparentWindow**—Allows the window manager to change the window hierarchy to insert a frame window between each top-level window on the screen and the root window. The window manager then can decorate this frame window with a title for the application, buttons for moving and resizing the window, etc.

- **CirculateWindow**—Lowers the highest window on the screen or raises the lowest one, depending on its parameters.

- **QueryTree**—Allows the window manager to get the window IDs of windows it did not create.

- **ConfigureWindow**—Allows the window manager to move, resize, change the border width, or change the stacking order of a window.

Window Characteristics

These routines set and get the window attributes, which control the appearance and semantics of windows.

- **ChangeWindowAttributes**—Sets any or all of the window attributes. See "Creating a Window" for a brief description of this powerful request.

- **GetWindowAttributes**—Gets the current values of some of the window attributes described for ChangeWindowAttributes and a few additional bits of information, including the characteristics of the window that were set when it was created (InputOnly or InputOutput, and visual), whether its color map is installed, and whether it is mapped or viewable.

- **GetGeometry**—Returns the position, dimensions, and border width of a window plus the depth of the window and the ID of the root window at the top of the window's hierarchy.

The Graphics Context

These routines manipulate a context in which graphics requests are interpreted. There may be any number of graphics contexts, each identified by an ID. This ID is used in graphics requests that are to be interpreted using the specified GC.

- **CreateGC**—Creates a graphics context and optionally sets any or all of its characteristics. If not set, each characteristic has a reasonable default.

- **ChangeGC**—Changes any or all characteristics of an existing GC.

- **CopyGC**—Copies any or all characteristics of one GC into another.

- **SetDashes**—Sets the dash pattern for lines, in a more powerful way than is possible using CreateGC or ChangeGC.

- **SetClipRectangles**—Sets the clip region of a GC to the union of a set of rectangles.

- **FreeGC**—Frees the memory in the server associated with a GC.

Drawing Graphics

- **ClearArea**—Clears an area of a window.

- **CopyArea**—Copies an area of a window to another area in the same or a different window. If the source area is obscured, this request generates a GraphicsExpose event to identify the area of the destination for which the source is not available.

- **CopyPlane**—Copies a single plane of one drawable into any number of planes of another, applying two pixel values to translate the depth of the single plane.

- **PolyPoint**—Draws one or more points.

- **PolyLine**—Draws one or more connected lines.

- **PolySegment**—Draws one or more disconnected lines.

- **PolyRectangle**—Draws one or more rectangles.

- **PolyArc**—Draws one or more arcs, each of which is a partial ellipse aligned with the x- and y-axis.

- **FillPoly**—Fills a polygon, without drawing the complete outline.

- **PolyFillRectangle**—Fills one or more rectangles, without drawing the entire outline.

- **PolyFillArc**—Fills one or more arcs, without drawing the arc itself.

Images

The byte order for images is specified by the server in the image-byte-order field of the connection information and applies to each scanline unit in XYFormat (bit map) format and to each pixel value in ZFormat. All images sent to or from the server must be in this format.

- **PutImage**—Dumps an image into a drawable.

- **GetImage**—Places an image from a drawable into a representation in memory.

Colors and Color Maps

- **AllocColor**— Allocates a read-only color cell specifying the color with RGB values.

- **AllocNamedColor**— Allocates a read-only color cell specifying the color with a color name.

- **AllocColorCells**—Allocates read/write color cells. This request does not set the colors of the allocated cells.

- **AllocColorPlanes**—Allocates read/write color cells for overlays. This request does not set the colors of the allocated cells.

- **FreeColors**—Deallocates color cells.

- **StoreColors**—Stores colors into cells allocated by AllocColor-Cells or AllocColorPlanes.

- **StoreNamedColor**—Stores colors into cells allocated by AllocColor-Cells or **AllocColorPlanes**.

- **QueryColors**—Returns the colors in the specified cells of a color map.

- **LookupColor**—Returns the RGB values associated with a color name and returns the closest RGB values available on the display hardware.

- **CreateColormap**—Creates a virtual color map.

- **FreeColormap**—Frees a virtual color map.

- **CopyColormapAndFree**—Copies the color cells that have been allocated by one client into a new virtual color map and frees these color cells in the old color map.

- **InstallColormap**—Copies a virtual color map into the display hardware so it will actually be used to translate pixel values.

- **UninstallColormap**—Removes a virtual color map from the display hardware so it won't be used to translate pixel values.

- **ListInstalledColormaps**—Lists the IDs of the color maps installed in the hardware.

Fonts and Text

- **OpenFont**—Loads a font so that it can be used for drawing. If the font has already been loaded, this simply returns the ID.

- **CloseFont**—Disclaims interest in a particular font. If this is the last client to be using the specified font, then the font is unloaded.

- **QueryFont**—Gets the table of information describing a font and each character in it.

- **QueryTextExtents**—Calculates the width of string in a certain font.

- **ListFonts**—Lists the fonts available on a server.

- **ListFontsWithInfo**—Lists the fonts available on a server, with information about the specifications of each font.

- **SetFontPath**—Set the path that the server uses to search for fonts.

- **GetFontPath**—Gets the path that the server uses to search for fonts.

- **PolyText8**—Draws text items using 8-bit fonts. Each item can specify a string, font, and horizontal offset.

- **PolyText16**—Draws text items using 16-bit fonts. Each item can specify a string, font, and horizontal offset.

- **ImageText8**—Draws text string in 8-bit font. The bounding rectangle of the string is drawn in the background color from the GC before the text is drawn.

- **ImageText16**—Draws text string in 16-bit font. The bounding rectangle of the string is drawn in the background color from the GC before the text is drawn.

The Pointer and Keyboard

In X, the mouse is more generally called the pointer so that it can be a trackball, joystick, or tablet instead of being limited to a mouse. The pointer may have from one to five buttons.

- **GrabPointer**—Declares that all pointer events (button presses and motion) will be delivered to a particular window regardless of the location on the screen of the pointer.

- **UngrabPointer**—Releases a grab on the pointer.

- **GrabButton**—Declares that all pointer events (button presses and motion) that occur while the specified combination of buttons and modifier keys are pressed will be delivered to a particular window regardless of the location on the screen of the pointer.

- **UngrabButton**—Releases a grab on a button.

- **ChangeActivePointerGrab**—Changes the events that are sent to a window that has grabbed the pointer or keyboard.

- **GrabKeyboard**—Declares that all keyboard events will be delivered to a particular window regardless of the location on the screen of the pointer.

- **UngrabKeyboard**—Releases a grab on the keyboard.

- **GrabKey**—Declares that all keyboard events that occur while the specified combination of buttons and modifier keys are pressed will be delivered to a particular window regardless of the location on the screen of the pointer.

- **UngrabKey**—Releases a grab on a button.

- **AllowEvents**—Releases events queued in the server due to grabs with certain parameters.

- **QueryPointer**—Gets the current pointer position.

- **WarpPointer**—Moves the pointer.

- **QueryKeymap**—Gets the current state of the entire keyboard.

- **SetModifierMapping**—Sets the mapping of physical keys to logical modifiers such as Shift and Control.

- **GetModifierMapping**—Gets the mapping of physical keys to logical modifiers.

- **ChangeKeyboardMapping**—Changes the keyboard mapping seen by all clients.

- **GetKeyboardMapping**—Returns the keyboard mapping seen by all clients.

- **ChangeKeyboardControl**—Changes personal preference features of the keyboard such as click and auto-repeat.

- **GetKeyboardControl**—Gets personal preference features of the keyboard such as click and auto-repeat.

- **Bell**—Rings the keyboard bell.

- **SetPointerMapping**—Sets the mapping of physical buttons to logical buttons.

- **GetPointerMapping**—Gets the mapping of physical buttons to logical buttons.

- **ChangePointerControl**—Changes personal preference features of the pointer such as acceleration (the ratio of amount the physical mouse is moved to the amount the cursor moves on the screen).

- **GetPointerControl**—Returns personal preference features of the pointer.

Events

- **GetMotionEvents**—Some servers are equipped with a buffer that records the position history of the pointer. Returns segments of this history for selected time periods.

- **SetInputFocus**—Identifies a window and its decendents as the recipients of all keyboard input.

- **GetInputFocus**—Returns the current keyboard focus window.

Cursors

- **CreateCursor**—Creates a cursor resource from characters in a special cursor font.

- **CreateGlyphCursor**—Creates a cursor resource from characters in any font.

- **FreeCursor**—Destroys a cursor resource.

- **RecolorCursor**—Changes the foreground and background colors of a cursor.

Security

X provides a minimal security method in the server that identifies the remote hosts from which connections will be accepted. Two protocol requests configure this behavior:

- **ChangeHosts**—Modifies the list of hosts that are allowed access to a server.

- **SetAccessControl**—Turns on or off the mechanism that checks the host access list before allowing a connection.

The X Consortium is developing a authorization mechanism for X servers. As you may have noticed, there is provision for one in the X connection procedure.

X does not provide any protection from unauthorized access to individual windows, pixmaps, or other resources, once a connection has been made. For example, if an application gets (or guesses) the resource ID of a window it did not create, using the `QueryTree` request, it can manipulate or even destroy the window. This property was necessary so that window managers could be written independently of the window system. Applications other than window managers do not attempt this sort of antisocial behavior as a matter of courtesy.

Interclient Communication

The server must provide a means whereby clients operating on the same server can communicate because the clients may not be running on the same machine. Otherwise, clients would not be able to communicate directly except by opening a separate network connection between them. This would introduce a operating system dependency in client programs, which is to be avoided.

X calls the base communication mechanism *properties*. Each property has a name and an ID (atom). The name is used by client programs to determine the ID and implies the meaning of the data by convention. For example, the `XA_WM_COMMAND` atom by convention identifies a property that contains a string describing the command line that invoked an application. The format of the data is not necessarily implied by the property name, but for most of the properties for which conventions currently exist, the type is implied. Colors are an example of a property that might have more than one format. A particular color could be expressed as a string name such as "purple" or as a set of red, green, and blue values. Client applications that wished to set and read this property would have to agree on a code that distinguished the two formats.

Properties are attached to windows. In other words, window A may have the data "blurb" for property USELESS, while window B has data "flub" for the same property. Therefore, a window ID and a property ID uniquely identify a particular piece of data. Protocol requests are defined to set and get the values of this data.

The maximum size of a property is not limited by the maximum protocol request size accepted by the server. The requests that read and write properties provide ways to read and write them in chunks of the maximum request size. Since the field length is a 16-bit value and is in units of 4 bytes, the maximum request size is 262,144 bytes. However, the maximum property size is server dependent and usually depends on the amount of memory available.

- **InternAtom**—Gets the ID of a property given its string name and, optionally, creates the ID if no property with the specified name exists.

- **GetAtomName**—Gets the string name of a property given it ID.

- **ChangeProperty**—Sets the value of a property.

- **DeleteProperty**—Deletes the data associated with a particular property on a particular window.

- **GetProperty**—Gets the value of a property.

- **RotateProperties**—Rotates the values of a list of properties.

- **ListProperties**—Lists the IDs of the current list of properties.

There is also a higher-level communication procedure called *selections* that uses properties but allows the two parties to communicate back and forth about the format of the data in a particular property. As for the color example, selections allow the client that wants to get the property (the requestor) to specify which of the two formats it desires. Then the client that sets the property (the owner) can set it according to the desired format, before indicating to the requestor that the property is ready to be read. There is, of course, also a way to respond when the owner is unable to translate the data into the required format.

- **SetSelectionOwner**—Sets a window as the current owner of a particular selection property.

- **GetSelectionOwner**—Gets the current owner of a particular selection property.

- **ConvertSelection**—Requests that the owner of a particular selection convert it into a particular format and send an event informing the requestor of the success of the conversion and the name of the property containing the result.

Miscellaneous

- **SetCloseDownMode**—Determines whether resources created by a client are preserved after the client exits. Normally, they are not, but if the client has a means for reclaiming its resources in a later encarnation, it can use this request.

- **KillClient**—Kills the resources that remain alive after a client exits, due to the SetCloseDownMode request.

- **NoOperation**—This minimum request contains only the opcode and request length.

- **SetScreenSaver**—Sets the characteristics of the mechanism that blanks the screen after an idle period.

- **GetScreenSaver**—Gets the characteristics of the mechanism that blanks the screen after an idle period.

- **ForceScreenSaver**—Activates or resets the screen saver.

- **QueryExtension**—Determines whether a certain extension is available in the server.

- **ListExtensions**—Lists the extensions available on the server.

- **QueryBestSize**—Queries the server for the fastest size for tiles, stipples, or the largest support size for cursors.

- **SendEvent**—Sends any type of event to a particular window.

- **GrabServer**—Initiates a state where only requests from a single client will be acted upon. Events for other clients and requests made by other clients will be queued by the server until the grab is released.

- **UngrabServer**—Releases the grab on the server, processes all requests outstanding, and sends all queued events.

- **TranslateCoordinates**—Translates coordinates from a window frame of reference to a screen frame of reference.

- **CreatePixmap**—Creates an off-screen drawable.

- **FreePixmap**—Frees the memory associated with an off-screen drawable.

The Events

The X server is capable of sending many types of events to the client, only some of which most clients need. Therefore, X provides a mechanism whereby the client can express an interest in certain events but not others. Not only does this prevent wasting network time on unneeded events, it speeds and simplifies clients by avoiding the testing and throwing away of these events that would be necessary. Events are selected on a per-window basis.

As mentioned in the previous sample session, all events begin with an 8-bit type code. The following is a list of all the event types, what they signify, and any special notes about how they are selected.

- **KeyPress, KeyRelease**—A keyboard key was pressed or released. Even the Shift and Control keys generate these events. There is no way to select just the events on particular keys.

- **ButtonPress, ButtonRelease**—A pointer button was pressed or released. These events include the pointer position and the state of the modifier keys on the keyboard such as Shift.

- **MotionNotify**—The pointer moved. MotionNotify events can be selected such that they are delivered only when certain pointer buttons are pressed, or regardless of the pointer buttons. Also, they can be selected such that only one MotionNotify event is sent between each query of the pointer position or button press. This reduces the number of

`MotionNotify` events sent for clients that don't need a complete pointer position history.

- **`EnterNotify, LeaveNotify`**—The pointer entered or left a window. These events are generated even for each window not visible on the screen that is an ancestor of the origin or destination window.

- **`FocusIn, FocusOut`**—The keyboard focus window has been changed. Like `EnterNotify` and `LeaveNotify`, these events can be generated even for invisible windows.

- **`KeymapNotify`**—Always following `EnterNotify` or `FocusIn`, `KeymapNotify` gives the complete status of all the keys on the keyboard.

- **`Expose`**—Signify that a section of a window has become visible and should be redrawn by the client.

- **`GraphicsExpose, NoExpose`**—Generated only as the result of `CopyArea` and `CopyPlane` requests. If the source area specified in either request is unavailable, one or more `GraphicsExpose` events are generated, and they specify the areas of the destination that could not be drawn. If the source area were available, a single `NoExpose` event would be generated. `GraphicsExpose` and `NoExpose` events are not selected normally, but instead are turned on or off by a member of the graphics context.

- **`VisibilityNotify`**—Generated when a window changes from fully obscured, partially obscured, or unobscured to any other of these states and also when this window becomes viewable (all its ancestors are mapped).

- **`CreateNotify, DestroyNotify, UnmapNotify, MapNotify, ConfigureNotify, CirculateNotify`**—Generated when one of these requests is actually made on a window. These are used to tell a client when some other client has manipulated a window. Usually this other client is the window manager. All these events and `GravityNotify` and `ReparentNotify` can only be selected together.

- **`GravityNotify`**—Notifies a client when a window has been moved in relation to its parent because of its window gravity attribute. This window attribute is designed to allow automatic positioning of subwindows in certain simple cases when the parent is resized.

- **`ReparentNotify`**—Tells the client that a window has been given a new parent. Reparenting is used by the window manager to decorate and provide space around each window for a user interface for window management. One meaning of this event is that the coordinates of this window are no longer in relation to the old parent, which is normally the screen.

- **ResizeRequest,** **MapRequest,** **ConfigureRequest, CirculateRequest**—Selected by the window manager to enforce its window management policy. Once selected, any request to resize, map, reconfigure, or circulate a window by any client other than the window manager will not be acted on by the server but instead will result in one of these events being sent to the window manager. The window manager then can decide whether to allow, modify, or deny the parameters of the request given in the event and then reissue the request to the server.

- **PropertyNotify**—Issued whenever a client changes or deletes a property, even if the change is to replace data with identical data.

- **SelectionClear, SelectionRequest, SelectionNotify**—Used in the selection method of communicating between clients. "See Creating a Window" for a description of selecting events. These events are not selected, but are always generated by the requests involved in the selection procedure.

- **ColormapNotify**—Tells a client when a color map has been modified or when it is installed or uninstalled from the hardware color map.

- **MappingNotify**—As described in "Division of Responsibilities," this event tells the client that a client has changed the keyboard symbol table in the server. This event cannot be selected; it is always sent to the client when any client calls `ChangeKeyboardMapping`.

- **ClientMessage**—These events, or any other type, can be sent from one client to another using the `SendEvent` request. This event type is for client-specific information.

As mentioned in the list, a few of these event types cannot be selected because they are automatically delivered to all clients whenever they occur. This is either because virtually all clients need them or because they only get generated by clients that have an interest in them.

Unused bytes within an event are not guaranteed to be 0. Event codes 64 through 127 are reserved for extensions, although the Core Protocol does not define a mechanism for selecting interest in such events. Every Core event (with the exception of `KeymapNotify`) also contains the least significant 16 bits of the sequence number of the last request issued by the client that was (or is currently being) processed by the server.

The server may retain the recent history of pointer motion and to a finer granularity than is reported by `MotionNotify` events. Such history is available by means of the `GetMotionEvents` request. The approximate size of the history buffer is given by motion-buffer-size.

◆ The Errors ◆

This section lists and describes the various types of errors. In general, when a request terminates with an error, the request has no side effects (e.g., there is no partial execution). The only requests for which this is not true are ChangeWindowAttributes, ChangeGC, PolyText8, PolyText16, FreeColors, StoreColors, and ChangeKeyboardControl. All these requests perform an operation multiple times or set multiple values, and all the operations or values up to the one containing the error will be performed.

The following error codes can be returned by the various requests:

- **BadAccess**—An attempt to grab a key/button combination already grabbed by another client. An attempt to free a colormap entry not allocated by the client. An attempt to store into a read-only or an unallocated colormap entry. An attempt to modify the access control list from other than the local host (or otherwise authorized client). An attempt to select an event type, that at most one client can select at a time, when another client has already selected it.

- **BadAlloc**—The server failed to allocate the requested resource. (Note that the explicit listing of Alloc errors in requests covers only allocation errors at a very coarse level and is not intended to cover all cases of a server running out of allocation space in the middle of service. The semantics when a server runs out of allocation space are left unspecified, but a server may generate an Alloc error on any request for this reason, and clients should be prepared to receive such errors and handle or discard them.

- **BadAtom**—A value for an atom argument does not name a defined atom.

- **BadColormap**—A value for a color map argument does not name a defined color map.

- **BadCursor**—A value for a cursor argument does not name a defined cursor.

- **BadDrawable**—A value for a drawable argument does not name a defined window or pixmap.

- **BadFont**—A value for a font argument does not name a defined font. A value for a fontable argument does not name a defined font or a defined GContex.

- **BadGContext**—A value for a GContext argument does not name a defined GContext.

- **BadIDChoice**—The value chosen for a resource identifier either is not included in the range assigned to the client or is already in use.

- **BadImplementation**—The server does not implement some aspect of the request. A server that generates this error for a core request is deficient. As such, this error is not listed for any of the requests, but clients should be prepared to receive such errors and handle or discard them.

- **BadLength**—The length of a request is shorter or longer than that required to contain the arguments minimally. The length of a request exceeds the maximum length accepted by the server.

- **BadMatch**— An `InputOnly` window is used as a drawable. In a graphics request, the GContext argument does not have the same root and depth as the destination drawable argument. Some argument (or pair of arguments) has the correct type and range, but it fails to "match" in some other way required by the request.

- **BadName**—A font or color of the specified name does not exist.

- **BadPixmap**—A value for a Pixmap argument does not name a defined Pixmap.

- **BadRequest**—The major or minor opcode does not specify a valid request.

- **BadValue**—A numeric value may fall outside the range of values accepted by the request. Unless a specific range is specified for an argument, the full range defined by the argument's type is accepted. Any argument defined as a set of alternatives typically can generate this error (due to the encoding).

- **BadWindow**—A value for a window argument does not name a defined window. The `BadAtom`, `BadColormap`, `BadCursor`, `BadDrawable`, `BadFont`, `BadGContext`, `BadPixmap`, and `BadWindow` errors are also used when the argument type is extended by union with a set of fixed alternatives, for example, <`WINDOW` or `PointerRoot` or `None`>.

♦ Future Directions ♦

X was meticulously designed not to be limiting in the near future. The extension mechanism allows new features that work at the same performance level as the core X protocol to be built into the server. In practice, extensions are being used by system manufacturers to take advantage of the unique features of their hardware and by the X Consortium to implement and standardize features such as 3-D graphics.

Now that X Version 11 has become widely accepted, development work on it has actually accelerated rather than subsided. The X Consortium at MIT is now very well funded and has a long agenda of improvements and additions that will be made to X. Among the work currently in progress is extensions to support multiple and various input devices, X for Japanese use, multibuffering and stereo, and PHIGS (3-D graphics).

The lowest levels of X are stable and unlikely to change in incompatible ways. However, performance improvements can still be made, even though the programming interfaces will remain the same.

10

Networking NeWS

Owen Densmore
Senior Staff Engineer
Sun Microsystems

◆ Introduction ◆

This portion of the book presents the Network Extensible Window System (NeWS). Why, might you ask, does a book on networking discuss window systems? Modern UNIX window systems such as X and NeWS separate the display functionality from the rest of the application. The separation is achieved by having the application process communicate to a second, independent display process that represents the workstation display and input devices. The communication between these two processes may take place over a network and, indeed, uses standard network interprocess communication protocols.

We first present a comprehensive overview of NeWS. Readers needing only a brief introduction to NeWS may find this sufficient for their needs. Because NeWS is based on PostScript, we then offer a survival PostScript section that includes a discussion of NeWS extensions. This is followed by a detailed analysis of NeWS communications and how NeWS uses the network. We end with a miscellany containing references and a summary of the NeWS operators.

Unless otherwise specified, this material is based on the 1.1 release of the NeWS server and the "Lite" toolkit delivered with that release.

◆ NeWS ◆

This section presents a broad overview of NeWS. This is done in terms of questions that are frequently asked by people being introduced to NeWS.

What Is NeWS?

NeWS stands for Network Extensible Window System. Taking each item in turn:

- **Network.** NeWS uses the network environment to separate the display functionality from the rest of the application. This allows the application, and the environment in which it operates, to be on a different machine than the workstation providing the user interface to the application.

- **Extensible.** NeWS replaces static display protocol with an interpreted language that is used as a dynamic extension mechanism. The language is based on PostScript, the language developed by Adobe Systems for use by laser printers.

- **Window System.** NeWS is a UNIX process that manages the input (keyboard and mouse) and output (display) hardware of the workstation. This process, called the *window server process*, acts like a window kernel for display-oriented client applications. Other window systems, such as X11 and Andrew, are similarly server based (Fig. 10-1).

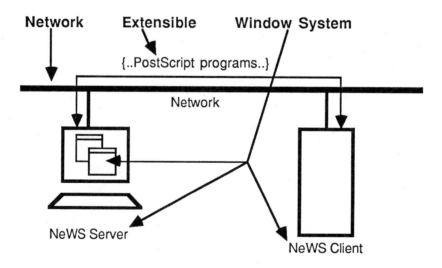

Fig. 10-1. NeWS = Network Extensible Window System

Why Is NeWS?

Why do we want a Network Extensible Window System? Again, taking each item in turn:

- **Network.** To see why we'd like a networked window system, consider the disapointing situation of a Macintosh user dialing into a communications system such as CompuServe. The Mac has a mouse, keyboard, and bit map display capable of using multiple windows and a variety of fonts. Yet, none of these are usable; instead the user, must work with a terminal emulator, which uses very few of these capabilities. A similar situation occurs when UNIX workstation users remotely log into other machines; no longer can they use all the capabilities of their workstations; they are similarly limited to terminal emulation. A networked window system solves this by executing remote client applications that use the local display server, utilizing all the workstation's capability.

- **Extensible.** Workstation display hardware is rapidly evolving. For example, there are many pixel resolutions, color and grayscale schemes, hardware graphics accelerators, and unusual input devices. A single client application is expected to run reasonably on this wide range of devices. By choosing the PostScript graphics model and language, NeWS solved two problems. First, by using the PostScript high-level graphics model rather than the device-dependent raster operation and pixel coordinate imaging model typical of most window systems, NeWS allows client applications to span widely varying workstation hardware. This means the client need not determine, for example, if curve drawing hardware is available; the server will use it automatically. Second, by choosing the PostScript language rather than a static window protocol, NeWS allows the client to extend the server to better match the application. For example, this means that the client can program the server to draw objects unique to the application.

- **Window System.** Server-based window systems have several advantages. By removing the window system from the kernel, greater portability is achieved. Different versions of UNIX can even use the same server binary. Removing the window code from the kernel reduces the size of the kernal itself and promotes snappier user interaction. It allows structuring NeWS as a simple user process containing a PostScript interpreter. A subtle advantage to this is that NeWS can be run like any other UNIX command. As we will see, this lets the user do such things as convert PostScript files into raster files for use by other window systems or by non-PostScript printers.

The importance of both the PostScript graphics model and the PostScript language must be emphasized. The former isolates the client from differences in workstation hardware; the second lets the client easily and naturally extend the window system. This programmability returns UNIX window systems to their UNIX roots: The PostScript interpreter is to the window kernel what the UNIX shell is to the UNIX kernel. In fact, the first NeWS client written was psh, the P-Shell, which simply connects standard input to the NeWS server. This provides a delightful interpreted environment for writing simple window-oriented programs. In fact, most applications start out this way and are converted later to compiled clients, much the same way as many UNIX programs start out as shell scripts and are later rewritten in C.

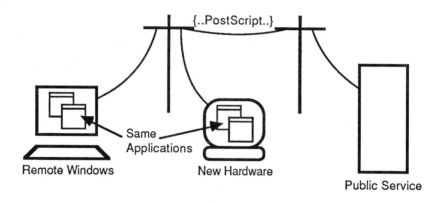

Fig. 10-2. Heterogeneous remote windows

Why PostScript?

Quoting from the NeWS Reference Manual:

NeWS is based on a novel sort of interprocess communication. Interprocess communication is usually accomplished by sending messages from one process to another via some communication medium. Messages are usually streams of commands and parameters. One can view these streams of commands as programs in a very simple language. What happens if this language is extended to be Turing-equivalent? Programs no longer communicate by sending messages, they communicate by sending programs that are elaborated by the receiver. This has interesting effects on data compression, performance, and flexibility.

The PostScript programming language identified by John Warnock and Charles Geschke at Adobe Systems is used in just this way. What Warnock and Geschke were trying to do was communicate with a printer. They transmit programs in the PostScript language to the printer, and this elaboration causes an image to appear on the page. The ability to define a PostScript function allows the extension and alteration of the capabilities of the printer.

Thus, one view of PostScript is that it is the logical evolution of a command protocol into a complete language with loops, conditionals, complex data types, files, and so on (Fig. 10-3). In addition, it has a complete and sophisticated graphics model. PostScript's rich set of capabilities presents creative opportunities to the programmer. For example, the Apple LaserWriter print manager has to convert Macintosh QuickDraw graphics commands into PostScript. The method used is to down-load an emulator for QuickDraw-like commands into the printer rather than doing all of the work on the Macintosh. The first time a print job is submitted to the LaserWriter, a file defining the emulator (the "LaserPrep" file) is sent to the printer. This installs the emulator for subsequent use.

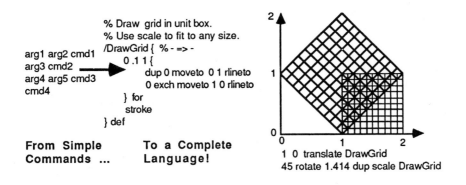

Fig. 10-3. PostScript—from commands to language

How does NeWS Extend PostScript?

NeWS adds three new objects to PostScript to support window systems: lightweight processes, canvases, and events. It also replaces the memory allocation scheme with a reference-counted garbage collector and extends the file notion to include network sockets (Fig. 10-4).

- **Lightweight Processes (LWP).** The NeWS server maintains a set of simultaneously-executing lightweight processes. Each process is an individual thread of control with its own PostScript environment. These processes all exist in the same address space; they may easily share objects. Each new client connection to the server exists in a new process.

- **Canvases.** A canvas is an individual drawing surface, much like separate sheets of paper. It is also a target for input events. Each NeWS process has a current canvas that currently executing PostScript commands draw on. These canvases exist in a hierarchy with child canvases overlapping both parent canvases and younger sibling canvases. Canvases correspond to windows in X11. They may take on any shape.

- **Events.** Processes communicate to one another using events. Input devices like keyboard and mouse are considered to behave like processes that generate events when activated. Indeed, new devices are often added to NeWS by simply launching a process to "listen" to a device "file" (e.g., /dev/foo), responding to activity by sending events.

- **Garbage Collection.** Garbage collection is a scheme for removing an object from virtual memory when it is no longer referenced. When a process exits, all its references are removed, automatically removing any objects referenced only by that process.

- **Networking.** The NeWS primitive, acceptconnection, listens for a connection request from another UNIX process to the NeWS server. It blocks until a request is received, then it returns a file object. Things that the client writes to the server will appear on this file, and things written to this file will be sent to the client.

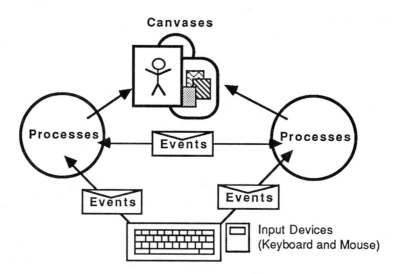

Fig. 10-4. NeWS extensions

How Is NeWS Organized?

NeWS is simply a UNIX command that executes its command line as a PostScript string. If this command string is not present, it defaults to executing the PostScript commands in the file init.ps and invoking the procedure &main that init.ps defines. NeWS relies on three external resources: PostScript files (like init.ps), UNIX environment variables, and font files.

It is important to emphasize that NeWS is just a user process containing a PostScript interpreter augmented for use as a window system. In fact, much of the work of turning NeWS into a window system is done by PostScript code in the external PostScript files (e.g., init.ps) rather than by the NeWS server itself.

A few of the environment variables are worth mentioning here:

- **NEWSHOME**—The root directory for the rest of the NeWS system

- **NEWSSOCKET**—The socket on which NeWS listens for connections.

- **NEWSSERVER**—The socket used by clients to contact NeWS.

- **FONTPATH**—The set of directories used to find font files.

- **FRAMEBUFFER**—The device to use for the display.

Note that having both the client and the server use different environment variables for their ends of the connection allows one workstation to support multiple NeWS servers. This is useful for debugging and supporting multiple users on a single workstation.

Initialization proceeds as follows. The file init.ps is found in $NEWSHOME/lib/NeWS. The PostScript run command executes it. It in turn runs files that install the rest of the system such as the window and menu utilities. The user owns two PostScript files. The file startup.ps is read as early as possible to override very basic operations of the rest of initialization. The file user.ps is read at the end of initialization to customize the system for the user (Fig. 10-5).

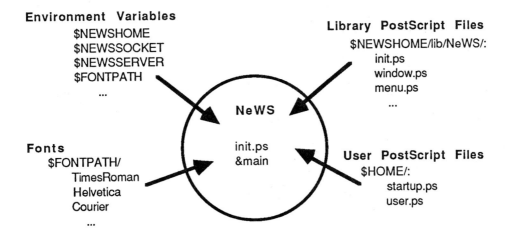

Fig. 10-5. NeWS initialization

How Do the PostScript Libraries Extend NeWS?

NeWS is designed to be a very stable window "kernel" and as such does not address volatile issues such as toolkits and user interface styles. Instead, this is done by the PostScript libraries loaded during initialization. This allows NeWS to approach standardization serenely without the controversy currently raging in the "look and feel" debates. The NeWS toolkit, named Lite, is written entirely in PostScript.

To manage these libraries, NeWS has adopted the object-oriented style of Smalltalk. This means not only is "data abstraction" achieved by use of opaque handles to private data objects, but "inheritance" is also gained by use of a class-based system. The NeWS class system is implemented entirely in PostScript, and in fact is only roughly four pages of code! This includes two primitives, classbegin and classend, that construct classes; the self and super method selectors; and the send primitive for invoking methods within a class.

The Lite toolkit includes classes for windows, menus, and user interface control items (Fig. 10-6). It also has classes for building simple event managers. It has a selection service and a completely programmable input system. It has a thin user interface manager that handles different keyboard focus protocols. And it has a reasonable set of miscellaneous utilities. A new version of Lite is being written to support the Open Look user interface.

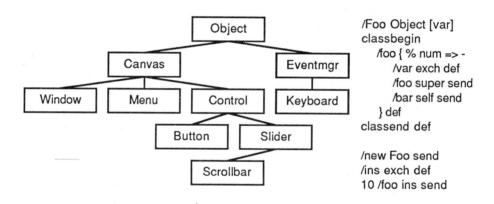

Fig. 10-6. NeWS libraries use classes

How Do Clients Communicate with NeWS?

NeWS establishes communications with client programs by listening for connection requests on the socket specified by $NEWSSOCKET. The client makes the request on $NEWSSERVER. These must agree for a connection to be made.

When communication is established, each new client is given its own lightweight process, which interprets the PostScript commands appearing on the connection. The communications is bidirectional; the server may write back to the client. Although both directions can be strictly textual data, for efficiency reasons there are encodings for integer, real, and token data types as well as both counted and null-terminated strings.

The sequence of events follows. The server, at the end of initialization, forks a lightweight process that listens for connection requests. When one is received, it forks another lightweight process for the client and makes the connection request file the current file for the client process. The client process then simply executes the PostScript appearing on the connection file until the end of file. It then kills all the processes associated with the client, including itself. This causes garbage collection of all objects referenced solely by that client.

The client will down-load code into the server, which will, in turn, talk back to the client. Although this communication may be a simple text stream, it is generally broken into segments identified by tags followed by arguments that represent the data expected when that tag is used. For example, upon receipt of a request for the size of a line, the client may elect to send four floating point numbers back to itself representing the two endpoints of the line. It would do this by defining a unique integer tag for this, `LineTag = 100` say. To send the line, the client would cause the tag to be sent using the PostScript primitive `tagprint` followed by four calls to the NeWS primitive `typedprint` to send the four floating point numbers (Fig. 10-7).

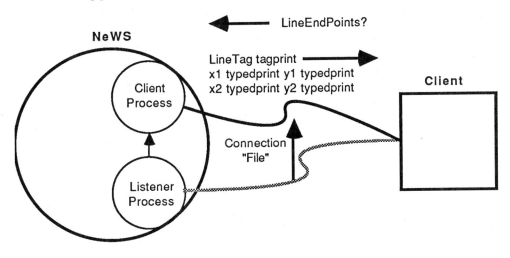

Fig. 10-7. Client server communication

How Are Client Applications Written?

A NeWS application generally starts life as a P-Shell script, a convenient means for testing the various parts of the program. This helps the designer decide which parts of the application should reside in the server as PostScript and which need to reside in the client. Several factors take part in this decision:

- **Performance.** The client programmer must take into account the relative performance of both the client-side programming environment and PostScript, an interpreted environment designed for window and user interface programming. The cost of the communication itself must also be taken into account.

- **Network design.** If the application is targeted for use over low speed communications links, the programmer must carefully analyze the communications overhead of their design. At a minimum, this means programming the user interaction portions in PostScript. It may also mean programming the portion of the application that displays the application's data in PostScript.

- **Preference.** Someone quite familiar with PostScript may actually prefer programming in NeWS. After all, it offers lightweight processes, garbage collection, programmable events, an interpreter, and object-oriented programming; this is a very sophisticated environment indeed! On the other hand, newcomers might prefer their more familiar C environment.

NeWS provides CPS, a simple but elegant client package for binding C to PostScript. CPS performs two tasks: It provides tools for communicating with the server, and it provides a language to bridge the gap between C and PostScript. The programmer creates a .cps file that contains the PostScript portions of the application. This includes C-callable interfaces that convert C data types to PostScript types and vice versa using the tagprint and typedprint operators. This file is then processed by the CPS program, producing a standard C .h header file. This is included in the C application.

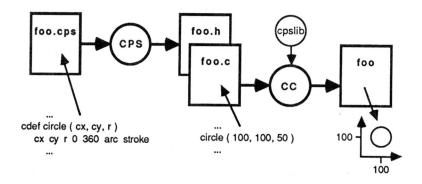

Fig. 10-8. CPS, the C-to-PS translator

The example in Fig. 10-8 shows the steps used to create a circle procedure for the application `foo`. The designer decides that the specification will include the center location and the radius. The interface is C defined using the CPS `cdef` operator. The first line of the definition is the C-callable interface, which is `circle (cx, cy, r)`. The second line is the translation of this interface into PostScript, which puts the parameters on the PostScript operand stack and calls the PostScript `arc` operator. The `foo.h` file will contain the macro definition for circle such that when included in the `foo.c` source file, `circle ( 100, 100, 50 )` will be converted into the proper internal CPS library calls.

Summary

All of the features of NeWS have been introduced. We've seen what NeWS is and why it was developed. We've looked at the use of PostScript as a universal and extensible interface language and seen the extensions NeWS developed for using PostScript in a window system. We then looked at how NeWS fits into the user's environment and how it is organized. We have seen how the NeWS client-server communications is managed. Finally, we looked at the way client applications are written.

◆ Survival PostScript ◆

This section is a tutorial on using PostScript as a systems language. It is an unusual presentation in that it concentrates on the language itself rather than PostScript's powerful graphics capabilities. Serious NeWS programmers will want to read Adobe's excellent books, especially the *PostScript Language Reference Manual*.

First, we present an overview of the language and its components followed by a guided tour through a selection of the PostScript operators. This is followed by a similar summary of the three major NeWS extensions: canvases, processes, and events. The goal of the section is to make you proficient enough with PostScript to understand its use in a network environment.

Basics

PostScript is a Forth-like interpreted language based on an operand stack using postfix notation in which operators are preceded by their operands. The fragment:

```
1 2 add
```

consists of three operations: 1 puts the integer one on the stack, 2 places two on the stack, and add pops off these two integers and puts the result of adding them on the stack (Fig. 10-9).

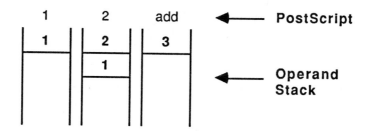

Fig. 10-9. PostScript operand stack

PostScript views each syntactic element of the language as an object having a type. There is little differentiation between procedure and data: 5 is viewed as the object that, when executed, places the integer 5 on the stack while the operator add is an object that, when executed, replaces the top two elements of the stack with their sum.

The PostScript interpreter distinguishes three types of characters:

- **White space.** space, tab, and newline
- **Special.** ( ) < > [ ] { } / %
- **Regular.** All other characters

White space separates other syntactic elements. Any number of consecutive white space characters are treated as a single character. Special characters delimit text and hex strings, arrays, procedure bodies, names, and comments. A comment consists of the characters between a % and the next newline and is treated as a single white space character.

Objects

PostScript *objects* are either simple or composite. Simple objects are atomic and occupy no additional storage. Composite objects (strings, arrays, and dictionaries) are collections of other objects and refer to additional storage in PostScript's virtual memory. When composite objects are replicated by putting them on the operand stack, only the object, not the additional memory, is replicated. Thus, composite objects share virtual memory; they act like pointers to virtual memory data.

The following is an overview of PostScript objects. Each object is shown with one or more examples of how it might appear in a PostScript program. A concise explanation is then given.

Integer `4 +17 -3 8#177 16#FF 2#100`
Integers consist of an optional sign and one or more digits. Integers may be represented by a radix number: base#number, where 2≤base≤36 and number is composed of digits and the characters A through Z (or alternatively a through z).

Real `-1.45 12.7e14`
Reals consist of an optional sign and one or more digits with either an embedded decimal point or a trailing exponent or both.

Boolean `true false`
Boolean objects have the value `true` or `false` and are typically the result of comparisons and logical expressions. They are mainly used to control the `if` and `ifelse` operators.

Mark `mark`
PostScript has a unique object, `mark`, used to mark a location on the stack.

Null `null`
PostScript has a unique object, `null`, used for uninitialized objects.

Name `Foo /Foo 1:30AM $bill b@ /&burn`
Name objects are non-numeric tokens composed entirely of regular characters. Names are used for identifiers. A slash (/) preceding the name tells the interpreter to treat the name as a literal constant, putting the name object on the stack, while the unslashed form tells the interpreter to execute the object associated with the name. The slash is not part of the name.

Array `[1 2 3] [(a) 1 Foo]`
An array is a heterogeneous collection of PostScript objects delimited by [and]. Arrays have an associated length. An array's objects are accessed by an integer index ranging from 0 to 1 less than its length.

String `(Hello, world) <a190ff> (Tab= ) ( (177)`
Strings are special homogeneous arrays consisting of integers in the range 0 to 255. Text strings are delimited by parentheses while hex strings are delimited by < and >. PostScript has no character type; each character is simply a small integer. Text strings support the usual backslash form of escape.

Procedure `{1 2 add}`
Procedures are executable arrays delimited by { and }. A procedure is said to be *deferred* in that the objects within the executable array are not evaluated until later when the name associated with the procedure is referenced.

Dictionary `1 dict dup /a 1 put`
A dictionary is a table associating keys with values. Either the key or value may be any PostScript object (except for null keys), although keys are usually names. There is no simple dictionary constructor analogous to arrays and strings; however, the above code fragment builds a dictionary with one key-value pair whose key is the name a and whose value is 1. Dictionaries are not ordered (indexable).

NeWS differs from PostScript in that NeWS uses a reference-counted, garbage-collected virtual memory while PostScript uses a block style `save/restore` virtual memory.

Dictionaries

Dictionaries are a unique and powerful facility. Although dictionaries are a general table construct, they also play a special role in PostScript programming: they provide the association between variables (names) and their values. This association is managed with a second PostScript stack: the dictionary stack. The dictionaries on this stack define the name context for the executing procedures. Names are evaluated by looking in the topmost dictionary first, then lower dictionaries, until the name is found. A name may be overridden by redefining the name in a dictionary higher in the dictionary stack.

The initial dictionary stack consists of `systemdict`, which contains the names of the PostScript operators and the procedures that implement them. Thus, `add` is simply a procedure defined in `systemdict`. The second dictionary in the stack is `userdict`, a dictionary defining the names private to the current program. `userdict` may override the definitions in `systemdict` by redefining their names. Thus, names like `add` are not reserved words in PostScript, they are simply predefined objects that may be replaced or modified by the current program.

Additional dictionaries may be placed on the dictionary stack. Fig. 10-10 illustrates how individual procedures define local variables.

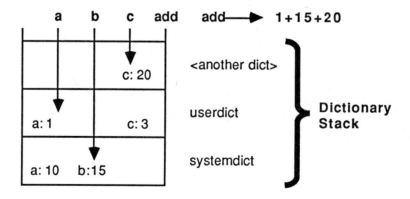

Fig. 10-10. PostScript dictionary stack

Operators, Guided Tour

We give here a guided tour through a condensed set of the PostScript operators. We'll do this by selecting entries of the *PostScript Language Reference Manual*, Chapter 6 Operator Summary, interjecting explanations and examples. The Operator Summary uses a one-line-per-operator format:

$operand_1$ ... $operand_n$ operator $result_1$ ... $result_n$ brief description

The inputs to the operator are given on the left, with $operand_n$ being the top of the stack. The operator leaves resultant objects on the stack, with $result_n$ being the top of the stack. A dash (–) is used to indicate either no operands or no results. A tee (⊢) is used to indicate the bottom of the operator stack.

Operand Stack Operators

any	pop	–	remove topmost element
any_0...any_n	clear	⊢	remove all objects
any	dup	$any\ any$	duplicate top element
any_n...$any_0\ i$	index	any_n...$any_0\ any_i$	duplicate ith prior object
$any_1\ any_2$	exch	$any_2\ any_1$	exchange topmost two elements
any_1...$any_n\ n\ j$	roll	any_{n-j+1}...$any_n any_1$...any_{n-j}	cycle n objects up j positions
⊢ any_1...any_n	count	⊢ any_1...$any_n\ n$	count objects on stack
any_1...$any_n\ n$	copy	any_1...$any_n\ any_1$...any_n	duplicate top n elements

Operand stack operators manipulate the operand stack directly. pop removes the topmost object while clear removes all objects. dup replicates the topmost object on the stack, while n index replicates the nth object (0 relative) back in the stack. exch swaps the top two elements while n j roll moves up the top n elements of the stack j positions. count returns the number of objects currently in the stack. n copy replicates the top n items on the stack.

Fig. 10-11 shows the use of these operators after initializing the stack with three objects: the integer 1, the string (two), and the array [3 4] containing two integers. The stack is shown two ways: a pictorial representation and a standard PostScript commenting convention—use line-end comments for showing the result of the stack after executing the code on the line. The stack grows to the right with the top of stack at the end of the line. (Note: Each example immediately follows the 1 (two) [3 4]; they are not in sequence.)

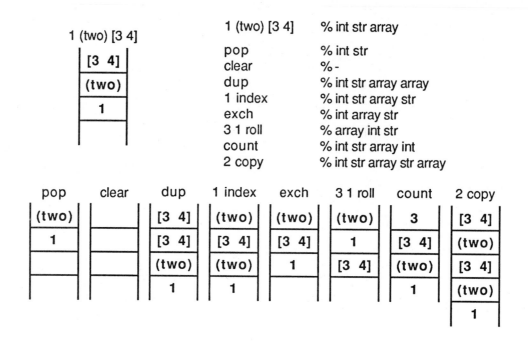

Fig. 10-11. Operand Stack Operators

Arithmetic and Logical Operators

num_1 num_2	add|sub|mul|div	num_3	return the result of num_1 + - * / num_2
any_1 any_2	eq|ne	bool	any_1 == != any_2?
$num\|str_1$ $num\|str_2$	ge|gt|le|lt	bool	$num_1 \geq > \leq < num_2$?
$bool\|int_1$ $bool\|int_2$	and|or	$bool\|int_3$	logical/bitwise and | or
$bool\|int_1$	not	$bool\|int_2$	logical/bitwise not

PostScript has the usual arithmetic and logical operators, plus many not shown here. add, sub, mul, and div perform the indicated operation on the top two numbers on the stack, returning the result. eq and ne compare any two objects, while ge, gt, le, and lt apply to numbers or strings only. In the string case, the elements are compared one by one as integers. and, or, and not may be applied to integer pairs to produce a bitwise operation between each of their bits.

Array and String Operators

int	array	*array*	create empty array of length *int*
int	string	*string*	create empty string of length *int*
either	length	*int*	number of objects in array or string
either index	get	*any*	get array or string element at *index*
either index any	put	–	put element into array or string at *index*

array	`aload`	*any₁...anyₙ array*	puts elements on stack, followed by *array*
any₁...anyₙ array	`astore`	*array*	pops elements from stack into *array*
either proc	`forall`	–	apply *proc* to each array or string element

PostScript array and string operators have much in common. Each has a creation operator, `array` and `string`, that takes the length of the object being created. `length` returns that length. `put` stores an element in the array or string at a given index, while `get` returns the element at a given index. Indices are 0 relative; the first element being at index 0. `aload` is used to put each element of the array on the stack, followed by the array itself, while `astore` puts n elements from the stack into the array, where n is the length of the array.

The `forall` operator is a powerful concept: an enumeration operator for arrays and strings, as well as dictionaries as we shall see later. The operator applies the procedure to each element in the string or array by repeatedly putting another element on the operand stack, then calling the procedure. The procedure may do anything it likes with the object; it need not even consume it. The fragment:

```
0 [1 2 3] {add} forall
```

adds the numbers in the array. It does this by initializing the sum to 0, then adding the array elements to the sum, one at a time. The fragment:

```
(ABC) {} forall
```

puts `65 66 67` on the operand stack by doing nothing at all with each element. Finally:

```
dup {exch} forall
```

implements the `aload` operator. It does this by first duplicating the array, using it in a `forall` that leaves each element on the stack, and finally flipping the original array past the element each time. Using stack style comments and lots of lines, it works like:

```
dup          % array array
{            % array any1
    exch     % any1 array
} forall     % any1..anyN array
```

Strings may be created by the scanner using the `(...)` or `<...>` syntax. Similarly, arrays may be made using the `[...]` notation. There is a difference, however. The `[` and `]` are actually operators: The `[` puts a mark on the operand stack, while the `]` collects all the intervening objects into an array of the correct size. This allows arrays to have dynamically created objects. Thus, `[1 2 add]` creates the array `[3]`; `[ (ABC) {} forall ]` creates the array `[65 66`

67]; and [(ABC) {1 add} forall] creates the array [66 67 68]. Unlike many languages, PostScript allows the elements of the array to be of different type. Thus, [1 (Hi!) [1 2]] is an array containing a number, a string, and another array.

Dictionary Operators

int	`dict`	*dict*	create empty dictionary of capacity *int*
dict	`length|maxlength`	*int*	number|capacity of key-value pairs in *dict*
dict key	`get`	*value*	get value associated with *key* in *dict*
dict key value	`put`	–	associates *key* with value in *dict*
dict proc	`forall`	–	apply *proc* to each *dict* key-value pair
dict key	`known`	*bool*	is *key* in *dict*?
dict	`begin`	–	push *dict* on dictionary stack
key value	`def`	–	associate *key* & *value* in current dictionary
key value	`store`	–	replace topmost definition of *key*
–	`currentdict`	*dict*	put top of dictionary stack on operand stack
–	`end`	–	pop dictionary stack

Many of the dictionary operators are analogous to the string and array operators. Dictionaries are created with the `dict` operator: `10 dict` creates a dictionary with the capacity for ten key-value pairs. Unlike arrays and strings, no constructor is analogous to `[]` and `()` for dictionaries. The size of a dictionary is obtained using `length`, each key-value pair is counted as one entry, not two. The creation size of the dictionary is obtained using `maxlength`. Dictionary values may be accessed by `get` and `put`, using the key rather than an index. The `forall` operator puts both the key and the value on the stack before executing the procedure. An unusual feature of `forall` for dictionaries is that the key-value pairs are put on the stack in arbitrary order! `known` returns whether or not a dictionary contains a particular key.

As mentioned in the discussion of dictionaries, the dictionary stack is another way to access dictionaries. `begin` places a dictionary on this stack; the stack is initialized to have two dictionaries: the `systemdict` and the `userdict`. `def` defines a new key-value pair in the topmost dictionary of the dictionary stack. `store` looks for the topmost instance of the key in the dictionary stack, replacing its value. It is equivalent to `def` if the name is not found. `currentdict` returns the topmost dictionary. `end` pops off the topmost dictionary.

A common use for dictionaries is to store *variables*, values bound to PostScript name objects. Thus:

```
/Foo exch def
```

is a common PostScript fragment defining the value on the top of the operand stack to have the name `Foo` in the current dictionary. Another common form is:

```
/avg { % num num => num; average two numbers
```

```
        add     % num
        2 div   % num
    } def
```

which is used to define procedures. The outer form is `/avg {...} def` which binds the executable array (procedure) to the name `avg`. The procedure consists of three tokens: `add 2 div`, which adds the two topmost operand stack objects and divides by 2. The commenting convention used on the first line denotes the inputs and outputs to `avg`, followed by a brief description. The other two comments describe the state of the stack.

Most PostScript programs perform their operations using the operand stack only. Dictionaries, however, allow for *local variables*. The `avg` procedure could be (poorly!) rewritten to use them:

```
/avg { % a b => c; average two numbers
    3 dict begin                % a b
        /b exch def             % a
        /a exch def             % -
        /c a b add 2 div def    % -
        c                       % c
    end
} def
```

The `3 dict begin` line creates a local dictionary for storing the local variables `a`, `b`, and `c`, which hold the two arguments to `avg` and an intermediate result. The next two lines store the two arguments in `a` and `b`. Note the reverse order of storing: `b` is stored first. The next line performs the average calculation. This line shows another common form: `/foo` *calculation* `def`, wrapping a calculation with the `def`. The last line uses `end` to reset the dictionary stack to its initial state. Because there is no further reference to that dictionary, it will be garbage collected.

Control Operators

bool proc	`if`	–	execute *proc* if *bool* is `true`
bool proc1 proc2	`ifelse`	–	execute *proc1* if *bool* is `true`, *proc2* if *false*
int proc	`repeat`	–	execute *proc int* times
init incr limit proc	`for`	–	execute *proc* with integer on stack
proc	`loop`	–	execute *proc* until `exit` called
–	`exit`	–	exit innermost loop

`if` takes a Boolean and procedure from the stack, executing the procedure if the Boolean is `true`. `ifelse` takes a Boolean and a pair of procedures, executing the first if the Boolean is `true` and the second if it is `false`. Here is a minimum procedure:

```
/min { % num1 num2 => num; min of two numbers
     2 copy gt      % num1 num2 bool
     {exch} if      % smaller-num greater-num
     pop            % smaller-num
} def
```

The first line determines if num1 > num2. Note it cannot just use gt; the 2 copy is needed to avoid removing both numbers from the stack. The second line exchanges the two numbers if the test succeeded. Finally, we pop off the larger number. This may be written using ifelse:

```
/min { % num1 num2 => num; min of two numbers
     2 copy gt {      % num1 num2; num1 larger
        exch pop      % num2
     }{               % num1 num2; num2 larger
        pop           % num1
     } ifelse         % num
} def
```

Here we use a common formatting convention for control constructs:

> *control initialization* {
>   *control body*
> } *control operator*

The *control initialization* is a Boolean with if and ifelse, an integer with repeat, three integers with for, a string, array, or dictionary with forall, and arbitrary setup with loop. This is most common when the *control body* is large.

Note that PostScript allows recursion, as in the time honored factorial function:

```
/fact { % num => num!; factorial of num
     dup 1 ne {      % num; num != 1
        dup 1 sub     % num (num-1)
        fact mul      % num * (num-1)!
     } if             % num
} def
```

repeat executes the procedure a fixed number of times. The following procedure adds the elements of an array:

```
/arrayadd { % array => num; sum array elements
     aload            % a1..an
     length 1 sub {   % a1..an n-1
        add           % a1..ai sum
     } repeat         % sum
} def
```

This would more likely be done using `forall` with one additional `add:` `0` `exch {add} forall`. If this is not clear, try rewriting it using the formatting convention and commenting each line.

The `forall` operator repeatedly executes a procedure, passing it to the next element of an array, string, or dictionary during each iteration. Similarly, the `for` operator passes its procedure a new integer in a sequence specified by three numbers: an initial value, an increment, and a limiting value. The fragment:

```
[0 2 100 {} for]
```

creates an array of even integers: `[0 2 .. 98 100]`. The following is a nonrecursive factorial:

```
/fact { % num => num!; factorial of num
    1                   % num result
    exch -1 1 {         % result i
        mul             % result*i
    } for               % num!
} def
```

`loop` executes its procedure forever. The procedure must use `exit` to terminate the loop. Thus, `loop` is a `repeat` which exits on a condition rather than a count. Typical usage is:

```
SetUpCommands
{
    GetNextCommand
    dup /Quit eq {pop exit} if
    ExecuteCommand
} loop
```

Note that `exit` may be used to terminate any of the iterating operators prematurely; it does not just terminate `loop`. Thus the following checks to see if an array contains a given element:

```
/arraycontains? { % array object => bool
    exch false exch { % object false ai
        2 index eq {  % object false; found it
            not exit  % object true
        } if
    } forall          % object bool
    exch pop          % bool
} def
```

Miscellaneous Operators

–	mark	*mark*	place a mark on the stack
mark any₁...anyₙ	cleartomark	–	clear elements down through mark
mark any₁...anyₙ	counttomark	*mark...n*	count elements down to mark
any	type	*name*	return name of *any*'s type
any	cvx	*any*	make object be executable
any	exec	–	execute the object
any str	cvs	*substring*	convert to string
name access	file	*file*	open *file*
file string	readstring	*substring bool*	read string from *file*, *bool* = true on EOF
file string	writestring	–	write string to *file*
string	run	–	exec contents of named file
–	executive	–	execute commands interactively
string	print	–	print string on standard out
any	=|==	–	print topmost element of stack
–	stack|pstack	–	print all values currently on stack

There are three mark operators: mark leaves a unique mark object on the stack, cleartomark pops objects up through the mark off the stack, and counttomark puts the number of objects to the mark on the stack. The [and] operators may be implemented with marks:

```
/[ {mark} def
/] {counttomark array astore exch pop} def
```

A common use for cleartomark is to clean the stack of intermediate results. Suppose we have a result preceded by six intermediate calculations:

```
...              % c1 c2 c3 c4 c5 c6 result
mark 8 2 roll % result mark c1 c2 c3 c4 c5 c6
cleartomark   % result
```

type returns the name for the type on the top of the stack. This is often used to support *polymorphism*, variable interfaces to a single procedure.

```
/avg { % int int | array
    dup type /arraytype eq {
        0 1 index {add} forall % array sum
        exch length div        % avg
    } {
        add 2 div
    } ifelse
} def
```

cvx converts the topmost object to executable (rather than literal), while exec executes the topmost object. They are often used as a pair: cvx exec. Thus:

```
(3 2 add) cvx exec => 5
```

This allows programs to pass programs to each other as strings, for example. Similarly, a file object (see below) may be executed (execute the instructions contained in the file) by exactly the same code: *file* cvx exec. This prompts the following utility:

```
/execobj { % obj => -; execute the object
    cvx exec
} def
```

Another use is when passing in procedures to other procedures. Sort utilities take a comparison procedure as an argument. It is more effecient to pass /ge than {ge}. Thus:

```
/sort { % array proc => array; sort array
10 dict begin
    /comp exch cvx def
    ...
end
} def
```

Often procedures are constructed in NeWS using cvx. For example, notification procedures, which are called in response to user interaction with toolkit objects, are often constructed so as to contain additional arguments. Suppose the client of the toolkit wanted the notification procedure to put an array on the stack and call the proc foo. This procedure can be constructed using this utility:

```
/makeproc { % arg /name => {arg name}
    cvx [3 1 roll] cvx
} def
```

Calling makeproc with [1 2 3] /foo produces {[1 2 3] foo}.

cvs converts any object into a textual representation. This forms the basis of an sprintf utility in NeWS, for example.

PostScript supports a simple notion of a file as a stream of bytes. file opens the named file with the given access, returning a file object. The access may be either (r) for read or (w) for write. Certain special names are used, such as (%stdin) and (%stdout). The file is accessed using readstring and writestring. run is simply (r) file cvx exec. executive starts an interactive session with the user. It is a simple PostScript procedure that reads a line of user input as a string, converts it to executable, and executes it.

For the LaserWriter, plug in a terminal to use `executive`, while for NeWS, use the P-Shell. `print` writes a string to standard output. Both `=` and `==` print the topmost object on the stack to standard output; `==` prints in greater detail. Similarly, `stack` and `pstack` print the entire stack; `pstack` prints in greater detail. These are generally used to debug programs run interactively using `executive`.

Graphics State Operators

–	`gsave | grestore`	– push/pop graphics state
num	`setgray`	– set color by grayness: 0=black, 1=white
num num num	`setrgbcolor|sethsbcolor`	– set color by RGB or HSB values
$t_x t_y$	`translate`	– translate user space by (t_x, t_y)
$s_x s_y$	`scale`	– scale user space by (s_x, s_y)
angle	`rotate`	– rotate user space by *angle* degrees

The PostScript imaging model is delightfully, and sometimes deceptively, simple. An image is built by defining a *path* composed of a sequence of lines and curves. This path may be stroked (outlined) or filled with the current color. The painting may be limited to an area defined by a clipping path. The painting operations entirely obscure any prior drawing. This is refered to as an opaque painting model. All graphics as well as text follows this simple model.

The painting operations use many implicit arguments, which together comprise the current graphics state. The current pen color, the current path, and the current transform matrix (CTM) are all part of this state. PostScript defines a third graphics stack (in addition to the operand and dictionary stacks) to manage these contexts.

`gsave` and `grestore` push and pop the current graphics context and thus, allow the user's graphics procedure to isolate local graphics state changes from the caller. The current color used by the painting operators is set by `setgray`, `setrgbcolor`, or `sethsbcolor`. The current graphics transform is set by `translate`, `scale`, and `rotate`.

Graphics Path Operators

–	`newpath`	–	initialize current path to empty
x y	`moveto|rmoveto`	–	set/adjust current point
x y	`lineto|rlineto`	–	append line from current pt
$x\ y\ r\ ang_1\ ang_2$	`arc`	–	append arc with center (x, y) to current path
$x_1\ y_1\ x_2\ y_2\ r$	`arcto`	–	append tangent arc to current path
$x_1\ y_1\ x_2\ y_2\ x_3\ y_3$	`curveto`	–	append Bezier cubic section to current path
–	`closepath`	–	connect path to initial point
–	`fill|stroke`	–	fill/outline current path with current color
–	`clip`	–	set clipping path to current path
–	`clippath`	–	set current path to clipping path
–	`pathbbox`	$x_1\ y_1\ x_2\ y_2$	return bounding box for current path

newpath clears the current path. moveto sets the current pen location to be x y, while rmoveto (relative moveto) sets the new pen location to be x y relative to the current pen location. lineto appends a line segment to the current path from the current location to x y, while rlineto treats x y as an increment to the current location. arc, arcto, and curveto add curves to the current path (see the *PostScript Language Reference Manual* for details). closepath adds a line segment from the current point to the initial point of the path. The fill operator fills the area defined by the current path, while stroke outlines the path. Painting operations may be limited (masked) to a given area by using the clip operator. clippath returns the clip path by making it the current path. pathbbox returns four parameters defining the lower left and top right corners of the current path's bounding rectangle.

The following defines a procedure that draws a unit grid:

```
/DrawGrid { % - => -; draw a unit grid
    0 .1 1 {            % i
        dup 0 moveto    % i; on x axis
        0 1 rlineto     % i; vert line
        0 exch moveto % -; on y axis
        1 0 rlineto     % -; horz line
    } for
    stroke
} def
```

We'll now use it to draw two grids; a black one that is 1 inch (72 points) on the x-axis, and a gray one that is at the same location but rotated and scaled so that it touches the y-axis at one inch as shown in Fig. 10-12.

```
gsave                % save context
    72 72 scale      % use inches
    0 setgray        % black ink
    1 0 translate    % 1" on x axis
    DrawGrid         % 1st grid
    45 rotate        % tilt
    1.414 dup scale % scale by sqrt 2
    .5 setgray       % gray ink
    DrawGrid         % 2nd grid
grestore             % restore context
```

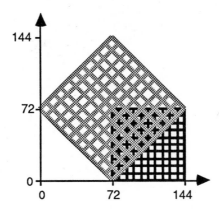

Fig. 10-12. PostScript graphics

Text Operators

name	`findfont`	*font*	return unit font identified by *name*
font num	`scalefont`	*font'*	return font scaled by *num*
font	`setfont`	–	set current font
string	`show`	–	print *string* at current point
string	`stringwidth`	$w_x\,w_y$	return width of *string* in current font

One of the implicit graphics parameters is the current text font. This is a dictionary object that contains the information needed to render text using the standard PostScript path and paint operations. `findfont` returns a font dictionary given the font name. This font is initially at a unit scale; its point size may be set using `scalefont`. `setfont` makes the given font be the current font for this context. `show` paints a text string in the current color at the current location, leaving the pen at the end of the string. The string's width vector is obtained by `stringwidth`. The y component is usually 0 but can be nonzero for certain oriental or rotated fonts.

To paint `Hello World` in black at 1 inch up the y-axis with a 1-inch margin, using the Times Roman font at 12 points, use:

```
gsave
    72 72 moveto            % set x y
    0 setgray               % use black
    /Times-Roman findfont   % dict
    12 scalefont            % dict'
    setfont                 % -
    (Hello World) show      % paint string
grestore
```

NeWS Extensions

NeWS adds three new object types to PostScript: canvases, processes, and events. It also extends the memory allocation scheme to use a reference-counted garbage collector and extends the file notion to include network sockets. This section briefly summarizes these three types. The networking extensions will be discussed in the data communications section. A complete list of NeWS operators appears in the "Miscellany" section.

These three objects are "magic dictionaries," much like the PostScript fonts: They may be accessed exactly like dictionaries but return their own type from the type operator. Thus, they can be used with the standard dictionary operators: `get`, `put`, `begin`, `def`, etc, but their types are `canvastype`, `processtype`, and `eventtype` rather than `dicttype`.

Canvas Operators

canvas	`newcanvas`	*canvas'*	creates a new canvas
canvas	`reshapecanvas`	–	shapes *canvas* to current path
canvas	`setcanvas`	–	set current canvas to *canvas*
x y	`movecanvas`	–	moves canvas to *x y*
–	`currentcanvas`	*canvas*	return current canvas

A canvas is both a drawing surface and an input area, corresponding to an X11 window. The canvas dictionary keys include three Booleans: `/Mapped`, `/Retained`, and `/Transparent`, all of which determine whether the canvas is visible, has backing storage, and obscures canvases under it. The dictionary also has keys for accessing sibling, parent, and child canvases in the display hierarchy.

`newcanvas` creates a new unmapped and unshaped canvas that is a child to the given canvas. There is a special canvas, `framebuffer`, corresponding to the entire display. `reshapecanvas` gives a canvas the shape and coordinate system of the current path. `setcanvas` makes the canvas be the current drawing area and sets the clip to be the canvas' shape. It also sets the transform to be the same as when it was last reshaped. `movecanvas` puts the origin of the current canvas at x,y. `currentcanvas` returns the current canvas.

This procedure creates a circular canvas of radius r centered at x,y in the parent canvas' coordinate system. Note that we use a `translate` in the second line to set 0,0 to be the center of the circle. This causes the new canvas to have its origin there.

```
/circlecanvas { % parent r x y => canvas
    gsave
        3 index setcanvas    % parent r x y
        translate            % parent r
        0 0 3 2 roll         % parent 0 0 r
        0 360 arc closepath  % parent
```

```
        newcanvas                % canvas
        dup reshapecanvas        % canvas
        dup /Mapped true put % canvas
    grestore
} def
```

This procedure fills the given canvas with the given gray value. It does this by filling the clip path established by setting the canvas.

```
/fillcanvas { % gray canvas => -
    gsave
        setcanvas        % gray
        setgray          % -
        clippath fill
    grestore
} def
```

We use these to build a black circle at 100, 100 with radius 50 on the frame buffer:

```
/can framebuffer 50 100 100 circlecanvas def
0 can fillcanvas
```

Process Operators

proc	fork	*process*	create a new process
process	waitprocess	*value*	wait until *process* completes
–	pause	–	let other processes run
–	currentprocess	*process*	return current process object
–	newprocessgroup	–	create a new process group
process	killprocess	–	kill *process*
process	killprocessgroup	–	kill entire process group

NeWS maintains a set of simultaneously executing lightweight processes. We mean lightweight in both the technical sense (shared address space) and in the resource sense (extremely cheap to create and use). A newly created process inherits much of the execution environment of the process that created it. This includes the operand and dictionary stacks of the process that created it, the group the process belongs to, the graphics state of the process, and any open files it may have.

Processes are ubiquitous. Each time a button is pushed or a menu is popped up, a process is forked to track the interaction. Each new connection to the server is given a new process in which to run. Not only are they cheap, they are a very convenient programming aid. For example, a client whose painting can be lengthy often will fork a process to do the painting to return immediately to watching for more user interaction.

A process object contains `/DictionaryStack` and `/OperandStack` keys as arrays of dictionaries and objects, respectively. It also contains a `/State` that can be `/runnable`, `/zombie`, or `/input_wait`. `/Interests` is an array of events (see the discussion of event operators) that will cause the process to be notified when they occur.

`fork` creates a new process that executes the procedure argument. `waitprocess` blocks the current process until the specified process completes, returning the topmost element of its operand stack. (Multiple results may be returned by placing an array on the stack.) `pause` allows other processes to run. `currentprocess` returns the current process object. `newprocess-group` defines a new group of processes and makes the current process the first member. `killprocess` destroys a single process, while `killprocessgroup` kills it and all the processes in the same group.

The following interactive session with a P-Shell illustrates the dynamics of processes. (The notation `=>` indicates printed results.) We first make a procedure that simply adds 2 and 2. We then use it as a forked process, inspecting its progress. Finally, we use `waitprocess` to ask it to "return" its result.

```
    /p {2 2 add} def
    p =
=>  4
    /pp {p} fork def
    pp =
=>  process (7661234, runnable)
    pause pp =
=>  process (7661234, zombie)
    pp waitprocess =
=>  4
```

Event Operators

–	`createevent`	*event*	create an event
event	`expressinterest`	–	queue input events
event	`revokeinterest`	–	revoke interest in *event*
–	`awaitevent`	*event*	block for *event*
event	`sendevent`	–	launch an event

Lightweight processes communicate with each other using events. Input devices are managed by processes that send events when device activity occurs. Events may be used as templates, called `Interests`, for describing which events a process is interested in.

Events have two keys, `/Name` and `/Action`, to specify the event type. For example, the keyboard uses the ASCII character for the `Name`, and either `/UpTransition` or `/DownTransition` for the `Action`. The `/Canvas` key limits events to a given canvas if nonnull, or all canvases if null. Similarly, the `/Process` key may limit event distribution to a given process if nonnull. The location of the event is available using `/XLocation` and `/YLocation` and the event time is in `/TimeStamp`.

`createevent` creates an empty event. By filling out the fields in such an event and using `expressinterest`, a process specifies which events it wants to receive. `revokeinterest` will remove such an interest. `awaitevent` blocks the process until an event is detected satisfying one of the process' interests, returning the event. A process uses `sendevent` to queue an event for another process.

The following expands on the black circle canvas example, making it respond to mouse clicks by switching color between black and white. This is similar to the way the Lite toolkit builds buttons.

```
% create a button; initialize to black.
/can framebuffer 50 100 100 circlecanvas def
/color 0 def
color can fillcanvas
/p {
    % make an interest for left mouse down
    createevent
    dup /Name /LeftMouseButton put
    dup /Action /DownTransition put
    dup /Canvas can put
    expressinterest
    % loop on clicks; flipping the color
    {   awaitevent pop
        /color 1 color sub def
        color can fillcanvas
    } loop
} fork def
```

This can be stopped using:

```
p killprocess
```

Summary

This section has presented an overview of the PostScript language design, its operators and their use, and the NeWS extensions for canvases, processes and events. The next section shows how NeWS uses PostScript as an effective tool in a distributed window system. There we will look at further NeWS extensions that are specific to network usage.

♦ NeWS Communications ♦

Communications is a pervasive theme in NeWS. The PostScript language, for example, was chosen not only for its graphics excellence but also as a powerful systems language in a distributed environment.

The key feature PostScript provides for network users is replacing static protocols with a language. The stream from the client to the server is a PostScript program, while the stream from the server to the client is whatever the client chooses. Both streams are either ASCII text or an equivalent binary compression. This effectively replaces predefined window-oriented protocols with a flexible, client-defined protocol that best suits the application. Applications designed to use low-speed communications lines may decide to implement time-critical portions in the server. A Draw program, for example, may maintain a specialized display-list format in the server, minimizing the time for redisplay.

NeWS adds to PostScript further network capabilities such as the ability to create network connections, the ability to transmit formatted data in both directions over such a connection, and lightweight processes to make such capabilities usable in a multi-user display server process. Even NeWS' decision to use garbage collection was based on network usage: When the client's connection process dies, all data referenced solely by the client is returned to the server's memory pool. Designers must consider the communications implications of these features. The Draw program mentioned previously might decide to use a lightweight process to "fork" the repainting of the display so that control can return to the program immediately without waiting for the repaint to complete.

The following sections examine NeWS communications. We start by looking at the overall client-server communications scenario. We then start at the lowest levels looking at the network communications packages used by NeWS for its client-server data stream and the encodings used on that stream. We then examine the CPS libraries at two levels: the `printf`/`scanf` level and the CPS data-type conversions used by the CPS preprocessor. Finally, we investigate the NeWS networking extensions and how they are used by the server.

The NeWS Communications Scenario

Before getting into communications details, we need to expand the overall model of NeWS communications presented in the Overview section. We do this by examining the workings of the NeWS `server` procedure.

The NeWS display server, as part of its initialization, executes the PostScript procedure server which is written in PostScript and defined in the initialization file `init.ps`. This procedure forks a lightweight listener process that watches for connection requests using the NeWS `acceptconnection` primitive. The server procedure uses the environment variable `$NEWSSOCKET` as the specification of the IP address to use. Similarly, NeWS clients open a connection to the server using the IP address specified by the environment variable `$NEWSSERVER`. The procedure `ps_open_PostScript()` in the NeWS library, `libcps.a`, is provided to perform this task (Fig. 10-13).

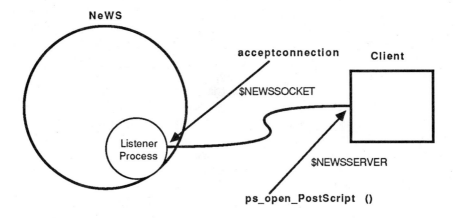

Fig. 10-13. `server`: establishing the connection

When communication is established, the listener process forks another client process, then returns to listening for new connection requests. The connection consists of two files, an input file from the client and an output file to the client (Fig. 10-14).

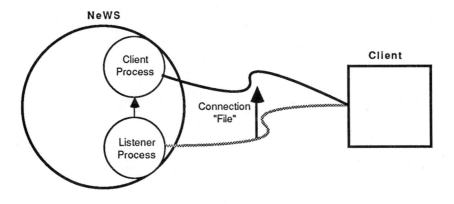

Fig. 10-14. `server`: establishing the client process

The client process does several things: It starts a new process group for the client, it creates the client's PostScript userdict and initializes its graphics context, it executes the PostScript program appearing on the connection's input file, and finally it kills the client process group when the file reports end-of-file. This process group includes the initial client process and any new processes subsequently started by the client. The reader will be amused to note that the way the server procedure executes the PostScript program on the connection input file is by first converting the file to an executable object with the `cvx` primitive, then simply causing it to execute with the `exec` primitive.

The data sent from the client to the server is a PostScript program. As part of its execution, it will communicate back to the client using either standard PostScript file primitives or two additional NeWS primitives that support use of a binary encoding. This is the extent of the definition of network protocol for NeWS: the input to the server is a program; the output to the client is whatever the client wishes (Fig. 10-15).

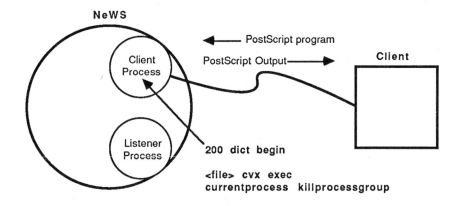

Fig. 10-15. `server`: client management

As an illustration of the power of PostScript as a system tool, we've included a version of the server procedure. Note that it has only 11 lines of code, other than comments and `{/}` lines.

```
/server { % - => -
    % Fork the listener process:
    {   % Clean operand stack, make listener's processgroup.
        clear newprocessgroup                    % -
        % Open socket for listening ($NEWSSOCKET env. var.)
        (NEWSSOCKET) getenv (r) file             % f
        % Loop creating new clients.
        {   % Pause 'till connection:
            mark 1 index acceptconnection        % f [ f'
            % Got client; now fork client process:
            {   % Clean operand stack
                exch pop exch pop                % f'
                % Create userdict and put on dict stack.
                200 dict begin
                % Initialize graphics, client process group.
```

```
            initmatrix newprocessgroup          % f'
            % Execute the connection!
            cvx exec                             % -
            % kill the client and associated processes.
            currentprocess killprocessgroup
        } fork cleartomark
      } loop
    } fork pop % pop off listener process
} def
```

NeWS Data Stream

This section explores the low-level NeWS data stream and TCP/IP communications.

NeWS may be built upon any reliable data stream package. The standard implementation uses a library for the TCP/IP protocol family widely available for UNIX. Two environment variables determine the IP addresses used to establish the connection. NEWSSOCKET is the address used by the NeWS server to listen for connection requests, while NEWSSERVER is the address used by the client to specify which server it desires. These addresses consist of two numbers, the first specifying the host IP address and the second the port number, which defaults to 2000.

The data flow between NeWS and its clients is a byte stream that contains PostScript programs. The data stream uses two encodings. The first is simple ASCII characters, much like the Apple LaserWriter uses. Freely intermixed with this may be a compressed binary encoding. The two encodings are differentiated by the top bit of the 8 bit bytes of the stream. The encoding provides for integers, fixed point fractions, floating point numbers, PostScript language tokens, and user-defined tokens.

Each compressed token is a single byte with the top bit set. There may be a parameter encoded in the bottom bits of the code byte. This use of the bottom bits causes a single encoding to span several adjacent numbers. For example, in the fixed encoding, the span is 16, giving 2 bits for the number of bytes in the fixed number and 2 bits for the decimal place. Following the token may be further parameter bytes and data bytes. These need not have their top bit set.

In the following description, the token encodings are given symbolically. For example, the fixed encoding is denoted by $\text{Fixed}+(d<<2)+w; \text{Num}[w]$: $0<=w<=3$, $0<=d<=3$. This means the encoding byte encodes the fixed token plus two parameters, w and d, in the rest of the byte. The semicolon (;) denotes following bytes. Here Num[w] denotes an array of w bytes, which make up the fixed encoded number. The colon (:) specifies the parameter ranges. Table 10-1 gives the actual values used for these symbols and the span of values used for further parameters.

Fixed `Fixed+(d<<2)+w; Num[w]: 0<=w<=3, 0<=d<=3`

> The next `w+1` bytes form a signed fixed point or integer number, high-order bytes first. The bottom `d` bytes are after the binary point. Note `d=0` for integers.

ShortString `ShortString+w; String[w]: 0<=w<=15`

> The next `w` bytes are a string. The high-order bits of the string may be set. This allows for binary strings used in PostScript images and for characters in non-ASCII encodings.

String `String+w; Num[w]; String [Num]: 0<=w<=3`

> The next `w+1` bytes form a signed integer, high-order bytes first. Following these are that number of bytes in a string. The high-order bits of the string may be set.

SysCommon `SysCommon+k: 0<=k<=31`

> One of 32 PostScript language tokens. NeWS maintains a table of PostScript objects, generally operators. These tokens are an index into the table. This allows the most common PostScript objects to be encoded as one byte.

SysCommon2 `SysCommon2; k: 0<=k<=255`

> One of 256 PostScript language tokens, similar to `SysCommon`. The value `k` addresses the PostScript object at table location `k+32`. This allows the less-common PostScript objects to be encoded as 2 bytes.

UserCommon `UserCommon+k: 0<=k<=31`

> Similar to `SysCommon`, but for user-defined tokens. Each client connection to the server has associated with it a user-token table similar to the system token table. Users define entries in the table with the NeWS `setfileinputtoken` primitive. This allows the most common application-specific tokens to be encoded in 1 byte.

LongUserCommon `LongUserCommon+j; k: 0<=j<=3, 0<=k<=255`

> Similar to `SysCommon2` but, because of the encoding style, provides for 1024 additional user-defined tokens. The index is `(j<<8)+(k+32)`.

IEEEfloat `IEEEfloat; Num[4]`

> The next 4 bytes, high order to low, form an IEEE floating point number.

IEEEdouble `IEEEdouble; Num[8]`

> The next 8 bytes, high order to low, form an IEEE double-precision floating point number.

As an example of encoding, the PostScript fragment:

```
10 300 moveto
(Hello World) show
```

can be encoded simply as the 33-byte long ASCII text string:

```
"10 300 moveto\n(Hello World) show "
```

TABLE 10-1. Encodings

Octal Value	Span	Symbolic Name and Format
0200	16	Fixed+(d<<2)+w; Num[w]
0220	16	ShortString+w; String[w]
0240	4	String+w; Num[w]; String [Num]
0244	1	IEEEfloat; Num[8]
0245	1	IEEEdouble; Num[8]
0246	1	SysCommon2;k
0257	4	LongUserCommon+j;k
0253	5	unused
0260	32	SysCommon+k
0320	32	UserCommon+k
0360	16	unused

Note the last blank is needed as a delimiter. The same string can be encoded as binary tokens in 19 bytes as follows:

```
0200 0012 0201 0001 0054 0261
0233 H e l l o   W o r l d 0262
```

Note the encoded form of the string was used to avoid use of the " (" and ")" required to specify the string in ASCII, thus saving one byte. See Table 10-2 for interpretation.

TABLE 10-2. Encoding example

Byte	Meaning
0200	encoded integer, one byte long, no fractional bytes
0012	the number 10
0201	encoded integer, two bytes, no fractional bytes
0001	the first byte of 300
0054	the second byte of 300
0261	"moveto" ..if it were first in the table, which it isn't!
0233	(0220+11) the start of an 11-character string
0110	"H"
0145	"e"
...	...
0144	"d"
0262	"show" ...if it were second in the table, which it isn't!

Although we've emphasized using binary encoding for writing from the client to the server, NeWS provides for encoding data being written from the server to the client with the primitives `tagprint` and `typedprint`.

`tagprint` takes an integer argument and writes it to the client encoded as a special "tag" used to identify a new set of data being sent to the client. Think of it as a user-defined packet identifier. `typedprint` takes an argument of any of the types—fixed, float, and string—and transmits them to the client using the binary encoding. We shall see later how the CPS preprocessor uses these primitives to provide correspondence between C and PostScript data types.

The CPS Library

The encodings used by NeWS are made transparent to programmers by the CPS library, `libcps.a`, and the CPS preprocessor. These operate at two levels. The first is a standard I/O-like package that aids in encoding and decoding the token stream discussed in the last section. The second is a preprocessor for C clients, which provides automatic conversion between C data types and PostScript data types.

NeWS wraps around the TCP/IP library mentioned in the last section its own standard I/O-like package, `psio`, which resides in `libcps.a`. The procedure `ps_open_PostScript()` is used to establish the connection to NeWS. This function returns a file pointer if a connection is successfully made; otherwise, it is 0. It uses the `NEWSSERVER` environment variable to determine which server to connect to. The function `ps_flush_PostScript()` is called to flush the communication buffer, while `ps_close_PostScript()` is used to close the connection. The package maintains two file pointers: `PostScript`, the file used to write client output to NeWS, and `PostScriptInput`, the file used to read input from NeWS. The function `psio_error()` takes one of these files as an argument and returns 0 if there is no error pending; otherwise, it returns the error number. Similarly, `psio_eof()` returns whether either of these files is at the end of file.

The `libcps` function `pprintf()` is invoked in a manner identical to `fprintf()`, using a format string interpreted in the same way. When values are output with `%s` or `%d` or any of the other formatting specifiers, they are output as compressed binary tokens. The rest of the format is output as is; it may contain compressed tokens or simple ASCII. Similarly, the function `pscanf()` is used to read input from NeWS to the client (Fig. 10-16).

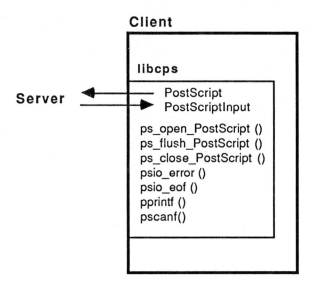

Fig. 10-16. The CPS library

The typical client program uses these procedures in the following fashion:

```
#include "psio.h"
main()
{
    if (!ps_open_PostScript()) {
        fprintf(stderr, "Cannot connect to NeWS server\n")
        exit(1)
    }
    ...
    while (!psio_error(PostScriptInput)) {
        ...
        if (psio_eof(PostScriptInput)) break
        ...
    }
    ps_close_PostScript();
}
```

The CPS Preprocessor

Although programs could be written with just the CPS library, NeWS also provides a CPS preprocessor. The CPS preprocessor uses macros to generate automatically the correct CPS `pprintf()` and `pscanf()` library calls. These calls use the binary encoding to optimize the client-server data stream.

The CPS model is that the client makes declarations in a `.cps` interface definition file, which get preprocessed into a `.h` header file containing macro definitions. This in turn is included in the application's `.c` file. Refer to Fig. 10-8.

There are three types of CPS declarations:

- The `#define` declaration defines a constant for use within the `.cps` file.
- The `c:` declaration places the following text in the `.h` file. This is useful for `#defineing` the same constant in both PostScript code and C code.
- The `cdef` code fragment declaration defines a correspondence between C-callable macros and the resulting PostScript code fragments.

The `.cps` file may contain standard PostScript `%` style comments.

The syntax of a `cdef` macro declaration is:

```
cdef name (argument-list) PostScript => tag (result-list)
```

Everything but the name is optional, and the result specification may preceed the PostScript code fragment. Line breaks may be used whereever blanks are allowed. The arguments are typed, defaulting to integer type. The result-list specifies which of the arguments are return values (thus passed by reference as a pointer). The order of the result-list reflects the order of receipt of the data from the server.

An important feature of the typing of arguments and return values is that it forms the bridge between PostScript types and C types. Argument types are converted into the compressed binary encoding and are decoded in the server into the corresponding PostScript type. Similarly, the NeWS `typedprint` operator converts a PostScript object into the binary encoding, which is converted into the appropriate C data type by the CPS library.

TABLE 10-3. CPS types

CPS Type	C Type
int	int
float	float or double
string	char *
cstring	char * with an accompanying count
fixed	a fixed-point number (int) with 16 bits after the decimal point
token	a user-defined token

Let's look at a `cdef` fragment in detail. This macro causes a string to be imaged in the current PostScript graphics context. It returns the location of the PostScript "pen" to be used for the next drawing operation.

```
C:#define SHOW_XY_TAG 42
#define SHOW_XY_TAG 42
% Image the string, returning new current point.
cdef ps_show_xy(string s,float x,float y) => SHOW_XY_TAG(y,x)
     % image the string
     s show
     % put current point on operand stack
     currentpoint            % x y
     % output the correct tag
     SHOW_XY_TAG tagprint     % x y
     % output the 2 numbers; note reverse order
     typedprint              % x
     typedprint              % -
```

First, we define the SHOW_XY_TAG constant. Note that we use both declaration styles so that both the CPS and C files will contain the constant. Following these is a comment using the PostScript % style. We then declare the cdef interface ps_show_xy() to use three arguments, one null terminated string and two floating point numbers. The right arrow indicates there will be return values, identified by the SHOW_XY_TAG tag in the input stream from the server. The return list indicates that two of the three arguments are to be used for return values. This means they are implicitly declared as pointers to floating point numbers. Following this is the PostScript fragment that is sent to NeWS upon invocation of the ps_show_xy() macro.

The code fragment initially causes the string s to be imaged in the current PostScript graphics context. Then the current point is placed on the operand stack as two numbers. These are sent back to the client as a packet tagged with the SHOW_XY_TAG identifier, followed by the two numbers. Because the numbers on the operand stack are processed from the top of the stack, they will be received in reverse order. This is handled by also reversing the order of the parameters in the return declaration.

The sequence of events after invocation of the ps_show_xy() macro are:

1. A pprintf() that has a format string and one argument—the string s appearing in the argument list—is executed.
2. This causes a data stream consisting of the results of evaluating the format string and argument string to be sent to NeWS. (Note that CPS optimizes the format string by using the binary encoding for system tokens wherever possible. The stream consists of only seven items: the string, five system tokens, and 42 encoded in 2 bytes.)
3. NeWS receives the data stream and execute it.
4. The tagprint and two typedprint operations cause data to be written back to the client. The use of the tag identifies the correct packet in case others are already pending.

5. An invocation of `pscanf()` returns the two typed values to the C program (Fig. 10-17).

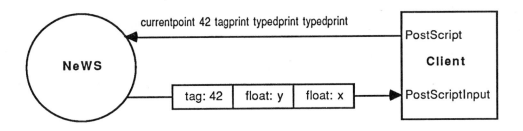

Fig. 10-17. Data stream for `ps_show_xy()`

    The CPS macros are converted into a form usable by the C program by the CPS preprocessor `cps`. The usual naming convention is `foo.cps` for the CPS macro declaration file and `foo.h` for the resulting C include file. Invoking CPS via:

```
cps foo.cps
```

produces the include file `foo.h`. The application must add the CPS library `libcps.a` to its list of libraries used by the linker. Assuming the application file is `foo.c`, the following would be used:

```
cc -I$NEWSHOME/include foo.c $NEWSHOME/lib/libcps.a
```

    The application file would not need to include other standard NeWS header files; they are included in the constructed header file.

    The application using the sample CPS fragment above would contain:

```
#include "foo.h"
main()
{
    char* s;
    float x,y;
    ...
    ps_show_xy(s,&x,&y);
    ...
}
```

It is common practice for applications to define permanently procedures like `ps_show_xy()` in the server during initialization of the application. This reduces even further the amount of data needed to send to NeWS. The following example has added the `cdef` macro `initialize()`, which defines `show_xy()` in the server's memory. This procedure is a PostScript-only version of `ps_show_xy()`, which assumes that string `s` is already on the operand stack. This is then invoked by the new version of `ps_show_xy()`, which now only puts the string `s` on the operand stack and calls `show_xy()`. The `.cps` file would contain:

```
C:#define SHOW_XY_TAG 42
#define SHOW_XY_TAG 42
% Perform initialization:
cdef initialize()
    /show_xy { % s => -; image s, return new pt to client.
        % image the string
        show
        % put current point on operand stack
        currentpoint            % x y
        % output the correct tag
        SHOW_XY_TAG tagprint    % x y
        % output the 2 numbers; note reverse order
        typedprint              % x
        typedprint              % -
    } def
        . . .
% Image the string, returning new current point.
cdef ps_show_xy(string s,float x,float y) => SHOW_XY_TAG(y,x)
    s show_xy
```

The application would now add the initialization call:

```
#include "foo.h"
main()
{
    char* s;
    float x,y;
    initialize();
    . . .
    ps_show_xy(s,&x,&y);
    . . .
}
```

This reduces the data flow to just the two strings:

```
s show_xy
```

Although this reduces the data flow to just the string and the procedure name, the name itself is a string and, thus, costs a byte per character in the name. This can be reduced by using short names, but a further optimization is available: user-defined tokens. These provide the user's data with the same degree of compression as provided for system tokens. Looking at the encoding tables, we see that 32 of the user's tokens will be 1 byte and 1024 tokens will be 2 bytes. This could reduce the example above to 1 byte more than the string itself.

There are two steps required to define the user token. First, the CPS declaration:

```
usertoken show_xy
```

tells CPS you want to transmit the user token show_xy in compressed form. Second, the client application must establish the meaning of the token in the server before the first use of the token. This is done by using one of the following:

- `ps_define_stack_token(UT)` takes the value on the top of the PostScript operand stack in the server and defines it to be the value of the token *UT*.
- `ps_define_value_token(UT)` defines the user token *UT* to be the same as the current value of the PostScript language variable *UT*. This statically binds the token to have this value even though the PostScript variable may change.
- `ps_define_word_token(UT)` defines the user token *UT* to be the name *UT*. This dynamically binds the token to have the value *UT* takes on over time.

Each of these takes on the next available token value in turn, using 1056 values. The first 32 of these will be encoded in one byte, the rest in two.

To install the user token, the CPS file would include the user token declaration, preferably just before its first use in the file. In this case, we'd place it before the cdef for ps_show_xy():

```
% Image the string, returning new current point.
usertoken show_xy
cdef ps_show_xy (string s,float x,float y) => SHOW_XY_TAG (y,x)
    s show_xy
```

The C main program would require an additional initialization step defining the token meaning to the server. This is done just after initialize() with:

```
initialize();
ps_define_word_token(show_xy);
```

This extreme flexibility and client control of the client-server communications is the essence of the NeWS philosophy: extension through language.

NeWS Networking Extensions

This section looks at the extensions NeWS has made for networking. We'll first look at the new and modified operators; then we'll discuss more general adaptations NeWS has made for networking purposes.

The following are the specific operator extensions made by NeWS. The format is:

operator: *arguments* → *results*

The operator name is given along with its input argument and results on the first line. A brief explanation is given on the following lines.

file   *string1 string2* → *socket*
            NeWS has added sockets to the PostScript file operator. Socket files
            are created by invoking file with the special file name (%sock-
            et1*XX*) where *XX* is the IP port number to be used for listening.
            Example: The server default socket is (%socket12000)

acceptconnection   *socket* → *file*
            Blocks listening for a connection from another UNIX process to the
            NeWS server on the socket file (see file). The resulting file connects
            the server with the client. Things the client writes to the server will
            appear on *file*, and things written to *file* will be sent to the client.

localhostname   – → *string*
            Returns the network host name of the host on which the server is run-
            ning. Example: (bigmac).

getsocketlocaladdress   *socket* → *string*
            Returns a string that describes the local address of the socket file. This
            is generally used by servers to generate a name that can be passed to
            client programs to tell them how to contact the server. Example:
            (2173708338.2000;bigmac).

getsocketpeername   *socket* → *string*
            Returns the name of the host that *socket* is connected to. The socket
            may be the result of acceptconnection. This is generally used
            with currentfile to determine where a client program is contact-
            ing the server from. Example: (localhost).

tagprint   *integer* → –
            Prints the integer, where $-2^{15} \leq N < 2^{15}$ is encoded as a tag on the
            current output stream.

typedprint   *object* → –
            Prints *object* in an encoded form on the current output stream.

setfileinputtoken   *object int* → –
            Define *object* to be the user-defined token identified by *int*. This is

used by the CPS preprocessor to define compressed tokens for communication efficiency.

NeWS has other network-oriented features that are not specific operators. These include the garbage collection and dictionary memory model, its lightweight process mechanism, and the programmable event system.

NeWS' lightweight process mechanism, although not usually considered a network facility, is required to support multiple client connections to the server. It is also used to tune the application to its network communication style. For example, suppose the client's screen painting procedure is slow. The client might choose to fork a process to do the painting. This frees the server to continue serving the client and other clients, while the independent paint process completes its task. This is much simpler than it sounds. All the client has to do is wrap the simple painting code with an initial "/PaintProcess {" and a final "} fork def". (The process object is stored as PaintProcess in case the client later needs to inspect or alter its state.)

NeWS' garbage collection, the removing of objects from virtual memory when no longer referenced, is also important to networking. When a process dies, the various PostScript stacks associated with it are dereferenced. The dictionary stack, in particular, will have each dictionary, and each entry in each dictionary, dereferenced. This means each object referenced solely by the client will be reclaimed, while shared objects will have the terminated client's references removed.

NeWS clients all share the same system dictionary. This allows clients to use systemdict for a shared memory area. A common use of this facility is for each application, when first activated, to store its initialization data in systemdict. This is usually done by creating a class for the application. This will not be dereferenced upon termination of that instance of the application. Subsequent activations of this application will create a new instance of this class rather than going through complete reinitialization. This can be a considerable performance win, especially when using a slow-speed communication medium.

The NeWS programmable event mechanism provides interprocess communications within the server. This can be used to establish client-to-client communications and provide a client interface to global resources such as the selection service, the keyboard focus arbitrator, and the window manager. By allowing these negotiations to occur entirely within the server, many client-server round trips can be avoided. For example, the X11 "external" window manager for the X11/NeWS merged server is implemented entirely in PostScript. This eliminates the need for a separate window manager client and cuts typical external window manager communications by half.

Summary

This section looked into NeWS communications in minute detail. We found how PostScript, with the NeWS extensions, acts as a network toolkit to provide the basis for building a window server. We found, in fact, that the server portion of

NeWS can actually be written in 11 lines of PostScript. We see that NeWS designers have to consider three parts to their application: the server portion (written in PostScript), the client portion (written in C), and the link between the two (written in CPS). To better make the design decisions, we've looked in detail at the data formats used for client-server communications. This allowed us to understand exactly the data appearing on the network resulting from our CPS programs that link the server and client.

I believe that NeWS is simply one of the first of a long list of network applications that will be implemented in a similar fashion: build a coherent model by using a network-based, interpreted language with "application" extensions.

◆ Miscellany ◆

This section has miscellaneous items of interest relating to NeWS, along with a complete list of NeWS operators.

Keeping Current

By the time this is published, two major NeWS events will likely have taken place. The first is the publication of *The NeWS Book*, the first commercially available, comprehensive reference for NeWS. The second is the X11/NeWS release of NeWS. This incorporates a "merged" server that supports both the NeWS protocol and the X11 protocol. It also includes a significant upgrade of the Lite toolkit that supports the Open Look user interface.

There are two major network resources for NeWS. The first is the NeWS-Makers mail group. To get on that group, send mail to:

```
NeWS-makers-REQUEST@brillig.umd.edu
```

The `comp.windows.news` USENET netnews group carries the same messages (in a slightly different order). Free NeWS programs and other tidbits are available via anonymous `ftp` from the same source using `tumtum.cs.umd.edu`.

The second is the NeWS archive server maintained by Sun Microsystems:

```
news-archive@sun.com
```

To find out more about the archive service, simply send an email message to the above address, putting `send index` in the subject or body of the mail. You will receive an explanation of the service by return mail. Adobe also maintains an archive server that can be used by sending mail to:

```
adobe-archive@adobe.com
```

Of particular interest will be the Encapsulated PostScript File standard, as well as many interesting font-related topics.

Readers interested in the evolution of server-based window systems in UNIX will also want to find out about the NeXT window system which is server based and uses the Display PostScript system from Adobe Systems.

References

PostScript Language Reference Manual, Adobe Systems, Inc., Addison Wesley, Reading, MA, 1985.

The Display PostScript System, Adobe Systems, 1988.

NeWS 1.1 Manual, Sun Microsystems, Mountain View, CA, 1988.

NeWS Technical Overview, Sun Microsystems, Mountain View, Ca, 1989.

The NeWS Book, J. Gosling, D. Rosenthal, and M. Arden, Springer Verlag, New York, 1989.

◆ NeWS Operator Summary ◆

The following is a complete list of NeWS operators, sorted by type.

Canvas Operators

w h bits xfm proc	buildimage	*canvas*	construct canvas object
canvas	canvastobottom	–	move to bottom of sibling list
canvas	canvastotop	–	move to top of sibling list
–	clipcanvas	–	clip canvas to current path
–	clipcanvaspath	–	set current path to canvas clip
str	createdevice	*canvas*	create new canvas
canvas	createoverlay	*canvas*	create overlay canvas
–	currentcanvas	*canvas*	return current canvas
–	eoclipcanvas	–	even/odd clip to current canvas
canvas	eoreshapecanvas	–	even/odd reshape of canvas
*file	str*	eowritecanvas	–	write canvas to *file*
*file	str*	eowritescreen	–	write screen to *file*
canvas	getcanvaslocation	*x y*	return canvas location
canvas	imagecanvas	–	render *canvas* on current canvas
bool canvas	imagemaskcanvas	–	analogous to imagemask
canvas x y	insertcanvasabove	–	insert above current canvas
canvas x y	insertcanvasbelow	–	insert below current canvas
x y	movecanvas	–	move canvas to *x y*
canvas	newcanvas	*canvas'*	create a new canvas
*file	str*	readcanvas	*canvas*	read raster file canvas
canvas	reshapecanvas	–	shape *canvas* to current path
canvas	setcanvas	–	set current canvas
*file	str*	writecanvas	–	write canvas to *file*
*file	str*	writescreen	–	write screen to *file*

Event Operators

–	awaitevent	*event*	block for event
num	blockinputqueue	–	block input events
–	countinputqueue	*num*	return count of input queue
–	createevent	*event*	create an event
event	expressinterest	–	queue input events
–	geteventlogger	*process*	get event logger process
–	getmousetranslation	*bool*	are events translated?
–	lasteventtime	*num*	return time stamp of last event
event	recallevent	–	remove *event* from queue
event	redistributeevent	–	enter *event* into queue
event	revokeinterest	–	revoke interest in *event*
event	sendevent	–	queue *event*
–	unblockinputqueue	–	release input queue block

Mathematical Operators

num	arccos	*num*	compute arc cosine
num	arcsin	*num*	compute arc sine
num	arctan	*num*	compute arc tangent

a b	max	*c*	compute maximum
a b	min	*c*	compute minimum
–	random	*num*	return random value

Process Operators

–	breakpoint	–	suspend current process
process	continueprocess	–	restart suspended process
–	createmonitor	*monitor*	create monitor object
–	currentprocess	*process*	return current process object
proc	fork	*process*	create a new process
str	forkunix	–	fork a UNIX process
process	killprocess	–	kill process
process	killprocessgroup	–	kill entire process group
monitor proc	monitor	–	exec process with locked monitor
monitor	monitorlocked	*bool*	check state of monitor
–	newprocessgroup	–	create new process group
–	pause	–	suspend current process
process	seteventlogger	–	make *process* event logger
process	suspendprocess	–	suspend *process*
process	waitprocess	*value*	block on completion of *process*

Path Operators

dx dy	copyarea	–	copy path to *dx dy*
–	currentpath	*shape*	return current path
–	damagepath	–	set path to damage path
–	emptypath	*bool*	test current path
dx dy	eocopyarea	–	copy area to *dx dy*
–	eocurrentpath	*shape*	return current path
–	extenddamage	–	extend damaged path
–	eoextenddamage	–	extend damaged path
x y	pointinpath	*bool*	is *x y* in path?
path	setpath	–	set current path

File Operators

file	acceptconnection	*file*	listen for connection on *file*
str1 str2	file	*file*	extended Adobe implementation
file	getsocketlocaladdress	*str*	return address of *file*
file	getsocketpeername	*str*	return name of host connected
num	tagprint	–	put *num* on output stream
object	typedprint	–	put *object* on output stream

Color Operators

color	contrastswithcurrent	*bool*	compare colors
–	currentcolor	*color*	return current color
hsb	hsbcolor	*color*	return color matching *hsb*
rgb	rgbcolor	*color*	return color matching *rgb*
color	setcolor	–	set current color

Keyboard and Mouse Operators

–	currentcursorlocation	*x y*	return mouse coordinates
–	getkeyboardtranslation	*num*	return mode of translation
–	getmousetranslation	*bool*	are events translated?
–	keyboardtype	*num*	return type of keyboard
bool	setkeyboardtranslation	–	is translation on?
bool	setmousetranslation	–	set mouse translation mode
–	startkeyboardandmouse	–	initiate input processing

Cursor Operators

–	currentcursorlocation	*x y*	return mouse coordinates
canvas	getcanvascursor	*font char char*	get cursor for canvas
font char char	setcanvascursor	–	set current canvas cursor
x y	setcursorlocation	–	move cursor to *x y*

Miscellaneous Operators

–	currentautobind	*bool*	autobinding enabled?
–	currentlinequality	*num*	current line quality
–	currentprintermatch	*bool*	return printer match value
–	currentrasteropcode	*num*	return RasterOp function
–	currentstate	*state*	return graphics state object
–	currenttime	*num*	return time in minutes
str1	getenv	*str2*	return environment variable
–	localhostname	*str*	return network host name
array	pathforallvec	–	path for all with conics operator
str1 str2	putenv	–	set environment variable
bool	setautobind	–	set autobinding
num	setlinequality	–	set line quality value
bool	setprintermatch	–	set printer match flag
num	setrasteropcode	–	set RasterOp function
state	setstate	–	set graphics state
dict key	undef	–	remove *key* from *dict*

Index

O